The Rebirth of Europe

ELIZABETH POND

The Rebirth of Europe

Second edition

BROOKINGS INSTITUTION PRESS
Washington, D.C.

Copyright © 2002
THE BROOKINGS INSTITUTION
1775 Massachusetts Avenue, N.W., Washington, D.C. 20036
www.brookings.edu

Library of Congress Cataloging-in-Publication data

Pond, Elizabeth.
    The rebirth of Europe / Elizabeth Pond.—2nd ed.
        p. cm.
Includes bibliographical references and index.
    ISBN 0-8157-7159-2 (pbk. : alk. paper)
    1. European Union. 2. Europe—Politics and government—1945– 3.
Europe—Economic integration. 4. Europe—Foreign relations—1945– 5.
World politics—1945– I. Title.
    JN30 .P66 2002
    327'.094—dc21   2002004573

9 8 7 6 5 4 3 2

The paper used in this publication meets minimum requirements of the
American National Standard for Information Sciences—Permanence of Paper for
Printed Library Materials: ANSI Z39.48-1992.

Typeset in Sabon

Composition by Cynthia Stock
Silver Spring, Maryland

Printed by R. R. Donnelley and Sons
Harrisonburg, Virginia

To Mary Vance Trent

Contents

Preface

Europe matters. It mattered enough for the United States to sacrifice half a million men and women in World Wars I and II. It mattered enough for American forces to stay on the old continent for half a century thereafter to keep the cold war cold.

Now, at this beginning of a new millennium, Europe still matters. Its spreading zone of peace and prosperity is, at the least, a bastion against spillover from turmoil to the east or, at the most, a conveyor of some of its own stability to the lands of the former Soviet super-power and continuing Russian nuclear power.

Its $8 trillion output matches that of the United States.[1] In our glo-balized era, it absorbs more U.S. overseas investment than any other region. Reciprocally, Europe contributes the most foreign investment to the United States as a whole and to virtually every single state. Europe's economic clout will only grow as the European Monetary Union makes the continent's corporate structure more like America's. In all probability the euro will shortly equal the dollar as a reserve currency. For the first time Europe's equity markets will grow to rival America's. As more investment then flows to Europe and less to the United States, the world's biggest debtor will have to find new ways to fund its record trade deficits.

Politically, too, Europe is experimenting in ways that should inter-est us. A congenitally war-prone continent has, with our help, turned into one of the safest and most humane places on earth—and is now reinventing itself. It is pioneering a postnational, postmodern "pool-ing of sovereignty" that is supplanting the nation-state system of the past three centuries. The European Union is not and probably never will be a united federation, but it is already far more than a loose confederation. It is asserting, in Americanesque fashion, that history is not destiny. It is renouncing the hereditary enmity between French and Germans. It is rejecting the repeated crushing of Poles between aggressive Russians and aggressive Germans and is inviting Warsaw—after a thousand years of Polish striving—to join the Western family. In a leap of faith, it has converted the mark, the franc, and the guilder—e pluribus unum—into one euro. It is, after a justly pessimistic twentieth century, importing America's optimistic sense of possibility.

Europe's transformation will challenge us economically and psychologically. The world's sole superpower is not yet prepared for the shock to come.

This book is one attempt to begin the preparation necessary for our new century. Its genesis goes back to a summer day in 1987. I had already lived in Europe for some years. But like every other American reporter, I avoided covering the boring European Community as much as possible. If I visited the European capital of Brussels at all, it was only to look into the hot (and now forgotten) issue of theater nuclear missiles. Then, at the height of a stagnation in the EC that had earned the nickname "Eurosclerosis," I attended an omnibus conference in a Bavarian castle.

One of the first speakers was a University of Virginia professor who described in gripping detail the birth of the American Constitution two centuries earlier. The convention of Benjamin Franklin, James Madison, and their friends and foes audaciously exceeded its mandate. It struck unhappy compromises between small and large states; it wrestled with issues of how to control commerce; in the end it turned a failed confederation into an enduring federation. Many states were suspicious of the resulting document, fearing loss of their powers. In a cliffhanger roll call, the New York legislature approved ratification by one vote. Until the last minute, what Americans now accept as the bedrock of their nation was touch and go.

The next speaker was a pollster for the European Community, who analyzed public opinion about European integration. To the surprise of everyone around the table, his results showed a large majority—ranging up to percentiles in the 60s—in favor of more integration in all EC member countries except Britain and Denmark. Specific issues were still controversial, of course—clashes of interest between the small and large states, the precise control of commerce, and confederal competence. But the basic desire for more joint European governance was constant.

The juxtaposition was electrifying. It was as if a cartoon light bulb went on over the heads of all the participants. The eccentric thought coursed around the room: *Maybe we are not as far away from a united Europe as we all assume.*

From that day on I tracked the European Community. I watched as the goal of forming a real single European market by 1992 took hold. I saw the business community begin to make investment decisions as if this union would actually come to pass. And of course I stared transfixed as the Berlin Wall fell and Chancellor Helmut Kohl vowed that German unification must lead to European unification.

Kohl's correlation was not coincidental. Once it became clear that West and East Germany would merge, "the German question" again reared its head. How could the old, sometimes terrifying Teutonic energies be channeled into constructive rather than destructive uses as Germany became overnight one-third larger than the other big European nations of Britain, France, and Italy? How could this third rise of Germany in a century avoid being as disastrous as the first and second times, with the carnage of World War I and the Holocaust?

Kohl's answer was to embed Germany so thoroughly in a European structure that it could never again dream of national solutions. In the chancellor's words, the integration of Europe must be made "irreversible" before another generation came to power that would not personally remember the horror of World War II and would therefore see less urgency in the pan-European enterprise. The result, he said, borrowing Thomas Mann's phrase, must be a European Germany, and not a German Europe.

This compulsion explained Kohl's drive for European political union and then, as political union foundered, for a monetary union that would itself impel further integration. It also explained Bonn's determination to get Poland into the EU so that Germany would no longer be the frontline to the east, but would be totally surrounded by allies.

This inner dynamic is poorly understood by Americans. European integration has repeatedly been dismissed in the United States; observers have often let the manifest difficulties of each step toward greater union blind them to the fact that the steps were actually being taken. Since a major cause of the American failure of perception seems to have been a disproportionate focus on Britain (which has consistently opposed EC "deepening" to any political or economic integration beyond a simple free-trade zone) and on France (which for years opposed EC "widening" to Germany's backyard in central Europe), this book aims to compensate. It tells the story of the past decade from the point of view of the main movers of "deepening" and "widening," Germany and Poland.

Here, then, is the thesis of this book: on the eve of the twenty-first century, a miracle occurred. Europe was reborn.

For the first time since 1648, nation-states became convinced that they had more to gain than to lose by surrendering fundamental attributes of sovereignty to a supranational body. For the longest period since the Middle Ages, Europeans suddenly realized, they have enjoyed continuous peace. For the first time since the Age of Exploration (or at least since the nineteenth-century belief in inevitable progress), they have recovered a sense of purpose.

On a bloody continent, in which every other generation has gone to war as far back as folk memory extends, every one of these impulses was astonishing. For three centuries the idealists, the ambitious, and the defeated of Europe had fled to the New World to escape the old, to outwit pogroms and poverty, habit and hierarchy. America, not Europe, was where one could get a second chance, could begin anew, could homestead land, worship according to conscience, invent telephones and mail-order houses and a new identity. Europeans loved the cowboy and, later, the on-the-road biker. They might find Americans naive or shallow, but they envied American exuberance. America was the land of promise.

Europe, by contrast, was the land of the Thirty Years' War, the Napoleonic wars, the potato famine, inherited social status, slaughter in the trenches of World War I, genocide in World War II, the despair of Nietzsche and of Kafka.

There was no sudden inversion of this dismal self-image. There were, rather, a tectonic shift as the cold war ended and, in parallel, a series of incremental pragmatic advances that accrued to metamorphosis.

In this context the tale is less a whodunit than a howdunit. Kohl, with the assistance of European Commission president Jacques Delors and French president François Mitterrand, was the obvious protagonist. But just how did the German chancellor get a population that was two-thirds opposed to European monetary union to give up its cherished deutsche mark? How did the EMU project survive the worst recession since the 1930s? How did Kohl get reelected in 1994 on the heels of that recession before being dumped by voters in 1998 and turned into a virtual nonperson after revelations of his illegal party slush funds at the turn of the millennium? How did deepening and widening come to be seen by others, as well as by the Germans, as not only compatible, but even complementary? How did happy-go-lucky Italy manage to meet the strict "convergence criteria" of top economic performance and qualify for EMU? How did the Poles manage to produce 5 or 6 percent growth for five years running, without overheating?

How was the lowest common denominator that one might expect from fifteen very different European Union states turned into "benchmarking," in which the best achievement becomes the standard for the rest? How did the allies, including those honorary Europeans in North America, hang together long enough to force the retreat of Serb strongman Slobodan Milosevic in Kosovo?

How, in sum, was Europe reborn? And will this new Europe prove strong enough to survive future storms?

Acknowledgments

This book has benefited greatly from suggestions by J. D. Bindenagel, Robert Cooper, Hans-Joachim Falenski, Catherine Kelleher, Michael Mertes, Virginia Nordin, Hans-Friedrich von Ploetz, Wilhelm Schönfelder, Peggy Simpson, Elisabeth Wendt, Cynthia Whitehead, Robert Zoellick, and Brookings reviewers, as well as from a seminar at the Brookings Institution in March 1998 on my initial concept. Any failure to meet the high standards set by these readers is my own. Financial support came from the John D. and Catherine T. MacArthur Foundation in a research and writing grant (1991–93); from the Woodrow Wilson International Center for Scholars, where I was a fellow in 1994–95; and from the German Marshall Fund of the United States (1998).

Permission to use substantial portions of my essays in the following magazines is gratefully acknowledged: "Letter from Bonn: Visions of the European Dream," *Washington Quarterly*, vol. 20, no. 3 (Summer 1997), pp. 53–72, ©1997 by the Center for Strategic and International Studies (CSIS) and the Massachusetts Institute of Technology; "Kosovo: Catalyst for Europe," *Washington Quarterly*, vol. 22, no. 4 (Autumn 1999), pp. 77–92, ©1999 by the Center for Strategic and International Studies (CSIS) and the Massachusetts Institute of Technology; "Letter from Kiev: Crisis, 1997 Style," *Washington Quarterly*, vol. 20, no. 4 (Autumn 1997), pp. 79–87, ©1997 by the Center for Strategic and International Studies (CSIS) and the Massachusetts Institute of Technology; "Miracle on the Vistula," *Washington Quarterly*, vol. 21, no. 3 (Summer 1998), pp. 209–30, ©1998 by the Center for Strategic and International Studies (CSIS) and the Massachusetts Institute of Technology; "The Escape from History," *World Link*,

January/February 1998, pp. 64–68 (*World Link* is the magazine of the World Economic Forum); and "A New Constitution for the Old Continent?" *Washington Quarterly,* vol. 24, no. 4 (Autumn 2001), pp. 29–40, ©2001 by Elizabeth Pond.

I am also most appreciative of the editorial guidance I received from Nancy Davidson and Deborah Styles.

Glossary of Abbreviations and Terms

acquis communautaire—the 90,000 pages of laws and regulations already adopted by the EU that every new entrant must endorse

Amsterdam Treaty of 1997—follow-on agreement to the Maastricht Treaty of the European Union

Baltic Sea Region Accord—agreement signed in 1998 for cooperation between Poland, Denmark, Sweden, Kaliningrad, Latvia, and Lithuania

Benelux—Belgium, Netherlands, and Luxembourg

Bundesbank—the powerful German central bank that the ECB is modeled on

CAP—EU's common agricultural policy

CEFTA—Central European Free Trade Agreement; grouping of Poland, Hungary, Czech Republic, Romania, Bulgaria, Slovakia, and Slovenia that aims to remove all tariffs in trade between them as a step toward EU membership

CEI—Central European Initiative, an informal group of 16 countries, including Italy, Austria, Ukraine, Belarus, Moldova, and all the central European and Balkan countries except Serbia

CESDP—Common European Security and Defense Policy; same as ESDP

CFE—treaty limiting conventional forces in Europe, signed in 1990 and subsequently modified

CFSP—EU common foreign and security policy

CIS—Commonwealth of Independent States, the Russian-led grouping of former Soviet states, excluding the Baltics

CJTF—Combined Joint Task Force, or European forces that would borrow NATO assets for operations to be run without direct American participation

CNAD—Conference of National Armaments Directors of NATO countries

Council of Europe—organization to promote and certify observation of democratic norms and human rights in Europe (not to be confused with the EU's European Council)

Council of Ministers, often, just Council—see European Council

COREPER—Committee of Permanent Representatives of EU heads of government (and state, in the case of France) that make the bulk of the European Council's decisions between summits

COREU—Correspondant Européen (communications system linking EU foreign ministries and cordinating EU policies at the civil service level)

CSCE—Conference on Security and Cooperation in Europe based on the 1975 Helsinki Agreement (after 1995, OSCE)

DG—Directorate General, division in the European Commission corresponding to a national cabinet ministry

EAPC—Euro-Atlantic Partnership Council that brings together ambassadors from NATO members and from the Partnership for Peace countries

EBRD—European Bank for Reconstruction and Development to help Central and East European economies

EC—European Communities (or European Community); after 1993, European Union

ECB—European Central Bank

ECJ—European Court of Justice

Ecofin—Council of Economic and Finance Ministers

EEA—European Economic Area, establishing the same rules for, initially, the EC and EFTA countries

EEC—European Economic Community (later just EC)

EFTA—European Free Trade Association between Western European nations not in the EEC; merged (except for Switzerland) with the EC to form the European Economic Area in 1992; after Sweden, Finland, and Austria left to join the EU in 1995, EFTA consisted of Iceland, Liechtenstein, Norway, and Switzerland

EIB—European Investment Bank, set up in 1958 to provide long-term development financing in Europe

EMI—European Monetary Institute (forerunner of the ECB)

EMU—European Economic and Monetary Union

EPC—European Political Cooperation, the more modest forerunner of CFSP agreed on in 1969

ESDP—European Security and Defense Policy (formerly ESDI, for "identity")—the hardest part of the CFSP goal to achieve; to be realized in cooperation with NATO

EU—European Union, the 1993 successor to the EC

EURATOM—European Atomic Energy Community

Eurocorps—multilateral European force (with troops from France, Germany, Belgium, Spain, and Luxembourg)

Euro Group—the informal consultative, but not decisionmaking, group of eurozone finance ministers

euroland/eurozone/euro-12—the twelve EU members that are members of EMU (Austria, Benelux, Finland, France, Germany, Greece, Ireland, Italy, Portugal, Spain)

European Agreements—agreements between the EU and candidates that are promised eventual membership

European Commission—the EU's supranational executive and legislation-initiating institution, consisting of a president, a collegium of commissioners, and the administrative bureaucracy under them

European Council—the EU's intergovernmental institution, which meets at least twice a year in summits of EU heads of government (and state, in the case of France); summits are supplemented by Council of Ministers' meetings of EU ministers in a single competence, such as foreign or interior ministers

European Parliament—Strasbourg-based parliament of directly elected deputies from all EU member countries

E-15—all EU members before eastern enlargement (as distinct from the twelve members of EMU)

G-3—the informal inner grouping of the United States, Germany, and Japan on financial and economic policy

G-7—Group of seven leading industrial democracies—the United States, Canada, Germany, France, Britain, Italy, and Japan (plus the European Commission president)—that meet in annual summits

G-8—see P-8

G-10—(actually 11) G-7 plus Belgium, the Netherlands, Sweden, and Switzerland; these finance ministers meet informally at the fringes of IMF or World Bank meetings

G-20—established in 1999, after Asian financial crashes, to avert future crises; convenes finance ministers and central bankers from the G-7 and key emerging economies in Asia, Africa, and Latin America, along with EU, IMF, and World Bank representatives

G-24—Group of twenty-four states that joined forces in 1989 to support economic and democratic reforms in Eastern Europe; the fifteen EU members plus Iceland, Norway, Switzerland, Turkey, Australia, New Zealand, Japan, the United States, and Canada

GATT—General Agreement on Tariffs and Trade (succeeded in 1995 by the WTO)

GDP—gross domestic product

IEPG—Independent European Program Group of all European NATO members except Iceland; aims at cooperation in arms procurement

IFOR—Implementation Force (UN–mandated, NATO–led peacekeepers in Bosnia from December 1995)

IMF—International Monetary Fund

NAC—North Atlantic Council of ambassadors permanently stationed at NATO headquarters in Brussels

NACC—North Atlantic Cooperation Council

NATO—North Atlantic Treaty Organization

NGO—nongovernmental organization

OCCAR—the joint arms cooperation structure for defense procurement, set up by Britain, France, Germany, and Italy in 1996

OECD—Organization for Economic Cooperation and Development; grew out of the cooperative administration of the Marshall Plan; grouping of thirty leading industrialized nations

OSCE—Organization for Security and Cooperation in Europe (before 1995, CSCE)

P-8—"political 8," the G-7 nations plus Russia

PfP —NATO's Partnership for Peace with nonmembers of the alliance

PHARE—Poland and Hungary: Aid for the Restructuring of Economies (later extended to aid other central European states too)

QUAD—group of United States, EU, Canada, and Japan in GATT and WTO

Rome Treaty—the 1957 founding treaty of the EEC

Schengen Agreements—1985 and subsequent agreements between the inner EU core to scrap border controls; implemented so far (partially) by Germany, France, Benelux, Spain, Portugal, Austria, Italy, Greece, Denmark, Sweden, Finland, and non-EU members Norway and Iceland

SFOR—Stabilization Force in Bosnia (succeeded IFOR at the end of 1996)

SHAPE—NATO's Supreme Headquarters Allied Powers Europe in Mons, Belgium

Single European Act—the amendment to the Rome Treaty adopted in 1986 that led to the single market of 1992

TACIS—EU technical assistance for Soviet successor states

TEU—(Maastricht) Treaty on European Union, 1992

TREVI—EU police cooperation on terrorism, radicalism, extremism, and internal violence

Troika—Until 1999, the steering team of the states holding the previous, current, and next European Council presidency; now the state holding the current presidency (and, by invitation, its successor) plus the European Commission and the High Representative of the European Council for common foreign and security policy

UNMIK—UN administration mission in Kosovo

UNPROFOR—UN Protection Force in Croatia and Bosnia, 1992–95

Visegrad states—Poland, Hungary, and Czechoslovakia (later the two states of the Czech Republic and Slovakia)

WEU—Western European Union, the European-only security alliance that predated NATO in the Brussels Treaty of 1948 but has no troops or military structure; now being folded into the EU

World Bank—bank to "reduce poverty and improve living standards by promoting sustainable growth and investments in people," in its self-description; cooperates closely with European Commission, EBRD, and the EIB in supporting accession to the EU by central European countries

WTO—World Trade Organization (succeeded GATT in 1995)

CHAPTER ONE

Images of Europe

Heartland Europe is finally escaping from its past slaughter and division. Francis Fukuyama's thesis that liberalism's victory over absolutism means the end of history is demonstrably true for this part of the globe.[1] To be sure, optimism is tempered by all the contrary scenarios of the disaster that looms if the European enterprise does not go forward. No Frenchman struggling to adapt to the post–cold war primacy of a united Germany—and to the Bundesbank's no-inflation credo—would interpret his lot as rosy. And every upstanding German, horrified by the accusation that he or she might actually be a closet optimist, would recoil from the very suspicion of such weakness of character.

Yet Europe's postnational change of consciousness and activism at this start of a millennium would be unthinkable if Europeans were not braced by a new self-confidence. Most fundamentally, members of the European Union trust each other in a way they never have before. No matter how often they have fought in the past, they have no doubt today that they have banished war among themselves. More and more they are surrendering, or "pooling," once sacrosanct sovereignty and now allow a full 50 percent of their domestic legislation and 80 percent of their economic legislation to be written in Brussels. And they are leaping into the unknowns of monetary union and of enlarging the European Union to absorb the fledgling, unproven central European democracies.

There are, of course, rational motivations for all of these innovations in an era of globalization and interdependence; ozone holes and instantaneous worldwide transfers of billions of dollars make every European state too small to cope alone.[2] But such motivations at any previous point in history would have been swamped by all the opposing impulses of nationalism, habit, and fear. Today they are not.

Probably never before in history has a transformation of such magnitude been so little remarked as it occurred. The assumption of the divine right of kings fell in battle. The transatlantic slave trade ended only after a titanic struggle. Today, by contrast, the maturing beyond nineteenth-century nationalism that is occurring in central as well as western Europe has been undramatic—and obscured by countervailing wars in the Balkans and the Caucasus. It flouts conventional wisdom to note that what is most striking about the savagery in these fringes of Europe in the 1990s is that it was in fact the exception, a phenomenon occurring at Europe's periphery but not its core. The heartland— and today this heartland already goes well beyond Carolingian Europe to include the whole space of the old Holy Roman Empire and more— is already postnational and no longer inclined to solve its problems through war. Against all the probabilities of history, the core Europe of prosperity and peace has already spread hundreds of miles to the east in just the decade following the fall of the Berlin Wall.

Europe's postnational change of consciousness is most pronounced, of course, among Germans, who recoiled from Hitler's atrocities initially by seeking to submerge their dishonored German identity in a larger European identity. The long-time parliamentary leader of the Christian Democratic party, Wolfgang Schäuble, speaks for many when he says, "What is our national interest? Our overriding interest is stability in Europe, political, economic, and social stability. And this can be achieved only through the Atlantic Community and the EU. . . . It is not an act of altruism, but perhaps the result of a certain process of maturing or learning from earlier experience."[3]

The new cooperative mind-set powerfully attracts non-Germans as well, as a way not only to avoid old-style German national domination, but also to maintain economic competitiveness in an age based on knowledge and loosed from geopolitics. Italy and Spain strove mightily to meet the criteria to become founding members of monetary union in 1999. Spain has joined the integrated military command of the North Atlantic Treaty Organization without waiting for France to do so. Sweden, Finland, and Austria, following the collapse of communism, have formally joined the commonwealth of the European Community/European Union that for decades was in fact determining their economic environment. Even Switzerland, while still eschewing membership in the United Nations as well as in the EU, is participating in NATO Partnership for Peace exercises. Farther east, the central Europeans are clamoring to be admitted to both blue-ribbon western clubs, the EU and NATO.

Because they have generated neither telegenic bloodshed nor eight-second sound bites, these startling departures from centuries of more confrontational intercourse in international relations have gone largely unnoticed in the United States—but historically they are far more novel and significant than the resort to archaic chauvinism that is going on at Europe's margins. Voters in Poland deliberately rejected irredentism and right-wing anti-Europeanism in the 1990s—and, despite financial evidence to the contrary, rate themselves in opinion polls to be as much middle class as did Americans in the 1950s. Similarly, voters in Hungary, the country that was left with the largest number of compatriots outside its borders after the murders and dislocations of World Wars I and II, have rejected notions of the kind of greater Hungary their forebears claimed. And even the apparatchik Romanian government that ruled with anything but liberal leanings in the early 1990s agreed with Budapest on rights for the Hungarian minority in Transylvania. Repeatedly, these conciliatory choices resulted from the yearning by governments and citizens to qualify for admission to the magic circle of the EU and NATO.

In Berlin and Warsaw, then, the vision of the twenty-first century is one in which the western European nations progressively cede sovereignty to the EU and European Monetary Union, then look east to integrate central European states into their commonwealth. As it did for western Europe in the second half of the twentieth century, NATO, the European Union's military analog, provides the assurance of security—partly against any possible resurgence of Russian imperialism, partly against petty Balkan or other tyrants. And this assurance fosters in an ever widening circle the kind of trust and cooperation that developed in western Europe during the cold-war threat and has now become routine.

From this point of view the main task of European politics today is to institutionalize the expanding cooperation so that it will endure. Just as post–World War II statesmen like Dean Acheson and Jean Monnet seized the opportunity to force the hitherto warring western European states to work together in the European Community and NATO, so today's leaders need to seize the opportunity to intensify west European collaboration and bring those willing and able central European states into the privileged community. This requires a new kind of self-confidence and a willingness to take political and economic risks.

Thus, in the case of European monetary union, no philosopher, historian, or economist could say whether or not the experiment would really work. But it was launched anyway in 1999. A critical mass of politicians, whose very livelihood depends on healthy caution, dared this leap and brought to the gamble the kind of political will that is usually associated with gung-ho Americans. EMU must work, the logic went, or else we incur catastrophe. Therefore we will make it work. End of discussion.

Moreover, although monetary union was an elite project carried out despite popular disapproval, various ordinary Europeans came to share the spirit. Well before the 1999 inauguration, shopkeepers in Finland, Spain, and Italy were proudly advertising their countries' inclusion as founder-members of EMU by posting prices of goods in euros as well as in markka, pesetas, and lira. Even those conservative German voters who reelected Chancellor Helmut Kohl twice in the 1990s on the strength of his Adenauer-like promise of no experiments— and did not notice that he was plunging them into the biggest experiment of all—took the surrender of their beloved deutsche mark in stride.[4] And certainly the Social Democrat who ousted Kohl in a landslide vote in 1998, Gerhard Schröder, dropped his misgivings about the euro when he became chancellor.

Much the same could be said about Europe's second grand project, enlargement of the EU and the North Atlantic Treaty Organization in the ambitious reuniting of a continent that was split at Yalta in 1945. In its own way this enterprise is just as bold, and just as unprecedented, as monetary union. No central European country, with the exception of the Czech lands, was a practicing democracy or had reached western European economic levels before World War II.[5] And all suffered from dysfunctional economies and politics in the half century of Soviet hegemony. Yet the optimism of Poland especially, the largest of the central European nations, is striking. Their tragic history has inclined Poles to fatalism. But today an upbeat mood is prevalent as they lead the reforms and economic recovery in the region. Their centuries-old inferiority complex toward the Germans is gone—in part, because they have compared themselves with the east German recipients of Bonn's largesse and have realized proudly that although they are poor, their steady 5-plus percent growth in the late 1990s was the result of their own efforts, with no charity from others. This self-assurance enabled them at last to feel at ease with the surrounding Germans, Ukrainians, and even Russians.

Escape from History

In 1990 neither the western nor the central European success was foreordained. Serious commentators warned that the post–World War II era of EC (and transatlantic) cooperation was an aberration, no more than an emergency response to the existential and ahistorical Soviet threat. With that Soviet threat gone, defense would now be "renationalized"—that is, revert from routine NATO-alliance coop-eration to fierce nineteenth-century-style national clashes. Transat-lantic trade wars would have nothing to constrain them. In the turbulence following the certainties of the cold war, the Europeans would revert to nasty balance-of-power free-for-alls. France and Ger-many would no longer be held to their marriage of convenience. The United States might well bring the GIs home and fall back into tradi-tional isolationism. The United States's abdication of its role as me-diator would aggravate old intra-European antagonisms—between Britain and Germany, between the rich north and the poor Mediterra-nean, certainly between Greece and Turkey.

Predictions about nations to the east were even more dire as the new would-be democracies underwent impossible instant economic, political, social, and institutional revolutions, at a dizzying speed that no Western nation ever had to match during the slow evolution of complex democratic and free-market practices. These nations of cen-tral and eastern Europe had to build capitalist economies from scratch, with suspicious peasantries but no stable middle class, at a time when western Europe itself had sunk into recession and could offer no sav-ing markets for central European exports. Given the wrenching change, skyrocketing prices, ruined savings, and loss of meager but steady so-cial benefits in the early transition, there was a high risk that disori-ented voters would equate democracy with misery rather than with plenty and would turn to populists for salvation. Many observers feared the spread of Yugoslav-style xenophobia as the Soviet lid was removed, releasing passions from the pressure cooker of central Europe's old rival nationalisms.

In the case of Poland, the largest central European country, there was also grave doubt that the heroic streak that was so magnificent during the century of Polish partition could assimilate the contrary art of democratic compromise. Indeed, Solidarity saint Lech Walesa became president by inciting a baleful "war at the top" and running against Solidarity prime minister Tadeusz Mazowiecki. The resultant clash within Solidarity temporarily threatened to vault Stanislaw Tyminski, an unknown populist émigré interloper, into the presidency; and the first fully free parliamentary elections seated twenty-nine squabbling mini-parties in the Polish parliament, the Sejm.

Nevertheless, western Europe discovered that its European Community was in fact more than just an anomaly. Even after the Soviet Union collapsed in 1991, the West did not revert to Hobbesian anarchy; the greatly feared renationalization of trade and security issues never took place. The benefits of European Community cooperation and of NATO's shared defense proved far too attractive to discard. Both organizations turned out to be hardy enough to survive even the loss of the enemy.

France had forfeited the most influence of any country as a result of German unification and the subsequent devaluation of nuclear weapons, revaluation of the deutsche mark, and extension of Europe proper to the east. Nonetheless, France concluded that the only way to beat the rising Germans was to stay joined to them. The quaint French notion of the 1960s and 1970s that the French political rider would steer the German economic workhorse dissipated. At the same time, the small countries that have had such a disproportionately large say in the EC and the EU became resigned to lowering their voices so as to preserve the EU's ability to act.

United Germany, alone for a long time in the conviction that deepening and widening of the EU are not only compatible but complementary processes, drove both by sheer political will. Chancellor Kohl, with his first dream of German unification fulfilled, single-mindedly pursued his second dream of making European integration irreversible.[6] This was, he preached melodramatically, "a question of war and peace."[7] To be sure, he had to give up his goal of European political union. But with time he expected EMU to create its own pressures for more political integration—and he also expected the threat of gridlock as the EU doubles in size to create its own pressures for more veto-proof majority voting. In this context, timing did not matter so much, despite the artificial debate in the United States about whether NATO or the EU would admit new members first. What was important was to get EMU and EU expansion started and let all the central Europeans know they could count on eventually gaining EU membership.

Moreover, the transatlantic alliance has endured. In the early 1990s President Bill Clinton and a bipartisan congressional leadership bridged the period when the United States might have withdrawn into itself after the cold war was won; Congress finally approved the rescue of NATO even at the cost of stationing GIs in Bosnia. The United States shares its burden as a superpower and magnifies its influence by steady engagement in Europe, Clinton argued successfully. So firmly did he commit a new generation of politicians to the alliance that the Senate's big debate about NATO enlargement hardly raised the fundamental question of whether, half a century after World War II, GIs should be in Europe at all.

In the twenty-first century, Clinton's successor did look as if he wished to extract the world's sole remaining superpower altogether from European, and global, entanglements. During his election campaign, George W. Bush called for pulling U.S. forces out of the far-away Balkans and sought to dump the scorned project of "nation building" there onto the Europeans. And once he was in office, he pulled out from negotiations on the Kyoto Protocol for cutting greenhouse gas emissions; treated China as a strategic adversary; announced that the United States would scrap the three-decades-old Anti-Ballistic Missile Treaty, no matter what the Russians or anyone else said; reduced U.S. funding for Russian destruction of nuclear weapons; and rejected the biodiversity treaty, a ban on antipersonnel land mines, international inspections to implement the old Biological Weapons Control Treaty, a nonbinding treaty limiting the export of small arms, an international war-crimes court that might one day indict the United States, and international cooperation on money laundering on anything other than U.S.-decreed terms.

This unilateralist instinct did not die on September 11, 2001, as two hijacked airliners slammed into the World Trade Center in New York City, killing 3,000 and shattering Americans' sense of invulnerability—but it was modulated. Even war on terrorists by the most powerful nation on earth required some help abroad in a coalition of the willing, especially in air rights over Russia and Pakistan, air and basing rights in Central Asia, shared intelligence, and indigenous ground troops to fight against the Taliban in Afghanistan. In this operation Europe and NATO were less essential. In an irony of history, European allies instantly pledged total solidarity with Washington, invoked the NATO treaty's Article 5 for the first time in half a century, and volunteered forces for just the kind of "out-of-area" operations they had been resisting, and the United States had been demanding, for a decade. But this time Washington, unwilling to be encumbered by target selection by committee, turned down all but some token British and other allied assets. After its stunning defeat of the Taliban in Afghanistan, the United States returned to its earlier agenda, discarded the ABM Treaty, and brusquely left the germ-warfare negotiations.

The United States did welcome United Nations support for its cause—and paid up on its dues—though still stressing that it required no UN approval for its actions. Washington further joined others in restarting world trade talks at Doha—a move it might not have contemplated before September 11. It sought a better atmosphere with a newly supportive Russia and a still suspicious China. It reengaged in the attempt to bring money laundering under control. For their part, the West Europeans, once more in awe of raw American military might and relieved by how much coalition building Washington did resort to—but unsure as to how the United States now values its European allies—decided yet again that there was no alternative to U.S. leadership.

Contemplating the new world disorder, senior British diplomat Robert Cooper concludes that we are witnessing the end, not only of the cold war, but of the whole continental system that has prevailed since the Peace of Westphalia in 1648. In our "postmodern" world European nation-states no longer pursue exclusive national interests with a heedless zero-sum reckoning. In an electronic age in which territory hardly matters, nations have little desire—except in the Balkans and the Caucasus—to acquire each other's terrain. As a consequence, the stunning new fact is, as Cooper says, that "Western European countries no longer want to fight each other." This approach goes well beyond the "crude" hope of earlier decades "that states which merge their industries cannot fight each other." It rests on the realization that war and conquest in Europe are no longer useful.[8] It sanctions unprecedented outside interference in members' domestic affairs. It presumes a new relationship mixing both cooperation and competition in what the business world is already calling "coopetition." And it is simultaneously bringing the central Europeans into the family and enabling them to catch up with the West's prosperity and newfound peace for the first time in a millennium.

Oddly, the bipolar cold war—which Cooper regards not as an exception, but rather as an extreme form of the nineteenth-century balance of power—froze political Europe long enough for the new realization about the virtues of the West's transnational cooperation to sink in. The EC's four decades of teamwork proved to have been habit forming.[9] And the Community's sister organization, NATO—though it first seemed to be no more than a traditional defense alliance against a powerful adversary—also transformed relations among the allies themselves. In the 1950s it introduced a permanent integrated multinational command. In the 1960s it supplemented this with a mutual review of each member's medium-term defense planning that let every nation see clearly its allies' military capabilities and intentions. The resulting transparency strongly inhibited aggression or any slide into hostilities, while promoting progressive transnational collaboration, even in the sensitive realm of weapons manufacture. By now, no NATO member could possibly launch a surprise attack even on an outside country—as Britain and France did in 1956 in trying to recapture the nationalized Suez Canal from Egypt—without the previous knowledge of its partners.

If the rhetoric of current leaders does not reflect this extraordinary transformation and evoke a United States of Europe as Winston Churchill did after World War II, the reason may be found in the twentieth century's disillusionment with all utopias. Post–cold war Europe is wary of grand designs. Modesty, not charisma, is the hallmark of this new beginning. Contemporary statesmen see themselves as carpenters, not as architects. And there is virtue in such diffidence, argues Michael Mertes, domestic adviser to Chancellor Kohl in the 1990s. It demonstrates the loss of a Hegelian trust in a dialectic of progress of the nineteenth-century variety. It shows a healthy skepticism and sobriety after the failure of utopian visions, which are in any case superfluous in the presence of vigorous pragmatic action. "We are in a phase in which we are implementing the great projects conceived at the end of the 1980s and the beginning of the 1990s," asserts Mertes. European monetary union, the first project, will itself compel further needed changes in EU institutions. And "widening to the east, the second grand task," will not only bring added security to Germany and central Europe, but will increasingly spread stability from Poland to its east. "It's a kind of reverse domino theory," he concludes. "You might say that the lack of great visions is a good sign, because at the moment there is so much to do."[10]

The perspective of Mertes—as of the bulk of the German political and bureaucratic elite—offers hope for the future. But a century ago Europe also exhibited optimism in expecting constant progress, only to have this faith shattered by the carnage of World Wars I and II. Were the twentieth century's five decades of peace, then, just as much a false dawn as the four decades of peace before the guns of August 1914?

No, because of the A-bomb, above all, thinks Dominique Moïsi, deputy director of the French Institute for International Relations, savoring the irony of this blackest of reasons for hope. "The big difference today is that, to a large extent because of nuclear weapons, the return of war in a classical sense, if not excluded, is at least very far-fetched. It's a totally new phenomenon in world history."[11]

Besides, adds Wladyslaw Bartoszewski, Polish foreign minister in the mid-1990s and again in the early twenty-first century, people have learned caution precisely because twentieth-century history was so terrible. He declares, "I am a practicing Christian, and I have faith in the capacity of people to change." He speaks as both a historian of the twentieth century and a participant in that history, a veteran of Nazi and Communist jails, and the only central European member of the commission that tracked Nazi gold in Swiss banks.[12]

Europe's Miracles

Bronislaw Geremek, Polish foreign minister in between Bartoszewski's two terms and a distinguished medieval historian, is less shy than Western counterparts about using romantic language. He seizes every opportunity to hark back to the eleventh-century east-west summit on the northern European plains between Otto III of the Holy Roman Empire and Boleslaw the Brave of Poland. The wish of these two rulers to unite their empires was not realized, Geremek notes, until a thousand years later, as part of the miracle of the present chain reaction of reconciliation in Europe.

In this chain, the first miracle was the French-German rapprochement after almost two centuries of bitter enmity. So successful was the personal reconciliation that today's young French and Germans take it for granted and find incomprehensible their great-grandparents' assumption that contests between these two neighbors would periodically erupt into war. So solid is the political fraternity that it now prevails, time and again, even over major bilateral differences over the European Central Bank, nuclear power, and the very goals of European Union.

The second miracle, perhaps, was the rejuvenation of the European Community in the mid-1980s, as it roused itself from Eurosclerosis to aim for that real single market by 1992. This new momentum ensured that subsequent German unification could be embedded in a larger European framework rather than bursting the existing framework. Unlike 1871, 1914, or 1939, this latest rise of German power has been peaceful. Today we are finally getting Thomas Mann's European Germany, and not a German Europe. Or rather, it is a German Europe as forged by a very European Germany.

The third miracle was the annus mirabilis itself, 1989, and its aftermath. Against all the odds of history, the world's last great empire, the Soviet Union, collapsed without bloodshed, except in Romania. There were many to thank for this: the stubborn Polish Solidarity free trade union, American deterrence, Soviet president Mikhail Gorbachev, the 70,000 Leipzigers who expected to get shot but still turned out to demonstrate for freedom on October 9 and foreshadowed the opening of the Berlin Wall a month later. The Czechs—concluding that in Gorbachev's world if enough demonstrators gathered, the police would not shoot—came next. The Bulgarians and Romanians—and then the Lithuanians and Muscovites—followed with their own street protests that toppled communist governments. Russia's internal as well as external empire disintegrated. And the central Europeans, with the democratic Germans as their new tribunes for admission into the Western organizations, began modernizing and escaped their perennial suspension between a big, predatory Russia and a big, predatory Germany.

The cornerstone of the benign central European evolution was the reconciliation that had long been pending between Germany and Poland, the country that had suffered the highest per capita death rate of any large nation under Nazi occupation. The two countries signed treaties pledging friendship and recognizing as permanent the post-

World War II border realignment that awarded German Silesia and parts of East Prussia to Poland. Kohl gambled on opening the Polish-German frontier, despite all the fears about a flood of migrant labor from a region with wages only a tenth of those in western Europe.[13] And Germany, determined not to be western Europe's border on the East any longer, joined the United States in prodding their allies to help the Poles and other central Europeans join the West by providing them with financial aid, technology, managerial know-how, and institutional models.

Most of all, of course, in the new climate the central Europeans helped themselves by emulating the golden West. They craved membership in the EU and NATO, and they altered their behavior significantly in order to qualify. In varying degree they instituted rule of law, with protection of human rights, minorities, and commercial contracts. They set up independent judiciaries and allowed robust media to emerge. They privatized business. They accepted World Bank and International Monetary Fund conditions of austerity and did not make the IMF the scapegoat for the agony of modernization. They passed legislation to align themselves with EU requirements. They nurtured an incipient civil society. And the central European governments were not even deterred by the prospect of subordinating much of their newly acquired full sovereignty to the EU and a European Court of Justice empowered to sit in judgment over national laws.

To show their readiness for NATO membership, the governments raced to establish civilian control of their militaries and to open their defense planning to outside scrutiny. Poland began exporting stability, in part by donating weapons to the infant Lithuanian army, in part by forming joint peacekeeping units with its Ukrainian and Baltic neighbors, and generally blurring the new line between East and West as much as possible. Even noncandidate Ukraine, eager to have the alliance's nimbus radiate beyond the designated candidates for NATO membership, set aside disputed claims to Serpent Island to sign a friendship treaty with Romania and made the most of its opportunities under NATO's Partnership for Peace program.

Central Europeans are already reaping the rewards for their strenuous efforts. They have begun the march toward EU prosperity. They regard NATO membership as insurance against any imperial recidivism on the part of Russia and against any military contagion from the Balkans. Most fundamentally, they regard their admission to the

West's premier clubs as certification, at last, of their Western identity. For them, this signifies deliverance from centuries of being the passive victims of history to becoming codeterminants of their own destiny.

Europe's final contemporary miracle might be identified as the new energy on the continent. To be sure, Europeans agonize about ruthless globalization, their stubbornly high unemployment, their loss of competitiveness to American rivals, and the crippling costs of their social welfare programs. But the dynamism is real. So is the intuition that one must use to the full the rare historical gift of choice in an era when old institutions have dissolved but new ones have not yet solidified. The propitious moment must now be seized to build a European Union that can save Germans from themselves and Europeans from themselves. "Such a historic opportunity doesn't come often," warns one senior German diplomat. "And if we give it up frivolously for a return to nationalism and protectionism, coming generations will never forgive us."[14]

And so European monetary union has been realized, with an unanticipated normative and disciplining power to force down inflation rates and budget deficits across the continent. After prodigious efforts, even Italy, Spain, and Greece are participating. At the same time, central Europe is beginning to get the payoff from austerity during its painful first transition years. Northern central Europe, at least, has finally rebuilt the quantitative gross domestic product it had when the communist systems collapsed, on a much sounder qualitative base. Poland should essentially catch up with the western European standard of living in a generation or two—for the first time in a thousand years.

That is the European self-image.

American Skepticism

American observers have a more jaundiced view of Europe. In capsule, elite conventional wisdom reads like this: Henry Kissinger's famous taunt—What telephone number do I call for Europe?—is as justified as ever. Without the Soviet threat to compel unity, Europe is relapsing into nationalism and war and the natural anarchy of international relations. Yugoslavia is a harbinger. The Europeans had their chance to deal with Bosnia, and fumbled it; in Kosovo, too, the United

States had to pull their chestnuts out of the fire. Deepening and widening are irreconcilable, and the Europeans are acting either hypocritically or irresponsibly in trying to do both.

Internally, Europeans squabble over mad cows and agricultural handouts. While the United States recently enjoyed the lowest unemployment in memory, Europe has 12 million unemployed and has forgotten how to create new jobs or venture capital. The exorbitant welfare entitlements of European countries smother initiative. The old continent is in crisis and will not admit it. There is a public backlash against the 1992 Maastricht Treaty establishing the European Union; Helmut Kohl had to give up his chimera of European political union.[15] Europe plunged ahead in an upbeat mood as it pulled out of recession in the mid-1990s, but with the next downturn, true to form, European integration will again stagnate or regress. The consensus system of fifteen very different members produces only stasis. Europe is a museum of the past. This is a simplification, but not a falsification, of much mainstream writing about Europe in the United States.[16]

The rebuttal from Bonn and Warsaw, equally compressed, would read something like this: You Americans have been misled by the neorealist school into expecting only Hobbesian contests among European nations in the wake of cold-war bipolarity. Conversely, you are setting up a straw man when you measure European integration against some imagined United States of Europe and conclude that it is failing. The new hybrid we are developing pragmatically does not fit on any hypothetical charts. It falls well short of your federation, but it also goes well beyond what you understand as a confederation, in which commonalities have to be thrashed out anew with each transaction. It lets national identity and idiosyncrasies flourish, but it also authorizes a growing area of pre-agreed united action in trade negotiations and in the whole *acquis communautaire,* the 90,000 pages of laws and regulations already adopted. However ungainly it may appear, the EU continues to function because it brings tangible benefit to its members. The old Westphalian nation-state is no longer an option in Europe; it is simply too small to be viable. The megadeaths of World Wars I and II, the existential nuclear threat, the Chernobyl nuclear meltdown of the 1980s, and today's digital globalization have all impressed this truth on central Europeans and even on the French, if not yet fully on the British. We are already pooling our sovereignty to a remarkable degree. And in synergy with you in NATO, we are performing the historic task of drawing central Europe into the West's circumference of peace and prosperity.

Yes, Europe (like America) did initially fail the test of Yugoslav breakup. But in the end the Balkan atrocities and humiliations finally compelled the West to do the right thing there, and in the process to reorient NATO for twenty-first-century crisis management.

Yes, European unemployment is a blight, and it will not be easy for us to regain the competitiveness lost in the past decade, especially since the Amerian motor that drove world growth in the 1990s is now sputtering. But our business cycles differ. While we applaud your recent record in job creation and will try to emulate you, we regard the 1990s more as your turn to surge than as evidence of our permanent inferiority. Europe has already begun its own round of boosting productivity. And in the interim, before we liberalize our labor markets and reduce long-term unemployment, our compassionate social safety net will enable the jobless to lead decent lives even in the midst of wrenching change; we have no explosive underclass. Currency union is focusing minds on fiscal discipline throughout Europe and will make our bottlenecks obvious, so we can correct them.

Europe is indeed in a structural crisis, the Europeans continue—but this very crisis is impelling unprecedented cooperation. It is a high-risk venture. But not acting together would pose even greater risk. And the present course promises high rewards, if competitiveness can be restored and if this war-prone continent can banish mass bloodshed in an ever-widening arc. Central Europe, with its low wages, well-educated workers, and pent-up consumer demand, will help the whole European continent. Already Poland produces half as much output as the much larger Russian Federation.[17]

Birth Pangs and Birth

What accounts, then, for the stark difference in the view of Europe on the two sides of the Atlantic? Why do Americans see only the birth pangs, while the Europeans experience the birth?

Again, from the point of view of Berlin and Warsaw, Americans would seem to be prisoners of previous patterns in their stereotypes, even as the old patterns are dissolving. They seek to squeeze the emerging Europe into a nineteenth-century mold of nationalism, into old cold war definitions of power, or perhaps into Gaullist expectations. They have been strongly influenced—especially before Prime Minister Tony Blair brought a friendlier view of the continent to 10 Downing Street—by British Tory fears about being sucked into some homogenized, bureaucratic Europe. And, it must be added, they have been reinforced in their dismissal of the EU by the absence in Brussels of staff reporters for any major American periodical other than the *Wall Street Journal*. No journalist for a general quality newspaper or news magazine in the United States scrutinizes the increasingly central institution of the EU the way, say, the *Financial Times* does. The American political class therefore lacks the osmosis of the European system that it might acquire from daily exposure.

Judged by traditional categories, of course, Europe is ineffectual. It lacks the glue of any single nationalism or any other overarching purpose beyond the dry rationality of cooperation in an era of interdependence. Ever since Hitler's terrible abuse of patriotic loyalty, Europe's more responsible politicians have eschewed emotional appeals. In consequence, Europe as a whole has a "myth deficit," as Munich historian Wolfgang Schmale points out.[18] It has never articulated the goals of integration in a way that would stir the hearts of its citizens, let alone convince outsiders of its dynamism.

Besides, a superpower with the fierce national pride of the United States can hardly credit the willing surrender of sovereignty by smaller nation-states that is now occurring in Europe. Many American commentators argue, on the contrary, that resurgent nationalism is the key to everything since the dissolution of Soviet hegemony in eastern Europe. As proof, they point to the war in Chechnya, the war of the Yugoslav succession, and Abkhazian (and Flemish and Walloonian) separatism. Nationalism is patently growing, not shrinking, they assert. So why, they asked—until a scant few months before EMU became a reality—should a reunited, newly sovereign Germany, with the third-largest economy in the world, voluntarily denationalize the Bundesbank and cede its might to a less predictable and more diffuse European Central Bank? Or, obversely, why should countries surrounding Germany rush to melt their identities into a greater Europe that the economic giant of Germany must necessarily dominate?

Furthermore, superpower America knows that Europe cannot make its military weight felt without the support of American airlift and intelligence and the U.S. nuclear umbrella. Even if it could, Europe has no single political authority to apply that capability. Oddly enough, for the country that invented the "soft power" of persuasion and example, the United States does not seem to recognize the potency of agenda setting or the habit-forming nature of daily consultation and compromise across Europe on everything from drug running to passports.[19] These matters are low politics, Americans argue; when push comes to shove in high politics, only the British and French, acting as nations, are capable of dispatching troops and pilots to restore peace and order.

An additional reason for U.S. dismissal of confederation-plus consensus politics within the EU follows from American incomprehension of the consensual style of national politics in the Germanic and Low Countries. For all their similarities, each democracy has its own peculiar mixture of cooperation and confrontation. The United States favors a robust clash of opposing interests until one side wins or compromise is finally hammered out. Many Europeans, by contrast, practice a consensual or even corporatist style of politics that translates easily into the backroom give-and-take of EU trade-offs.[20]

The U.S. sense of European impotence was only enhanced in the first decade after the cold war by a widespread continued fixation on its one-time superpower adversary, even though Russia's army was in disarray and Russia's GDP below that of the Netherlands. The preoccupation was understandable. The central Europeans did not and do not have nuclear weapons to claim Western attention, and all Soviet successor states, other than Russia, that inherited Soviet nuclear missiles renounced them. Besides, in Russia itself nuclear weapons were in some ways more dangerous than during the cold war, because controls on them slackened and Moscow compensated for its weakness in conventional military forces with a new military doctrine of first nuclear use.[21] These circumstances—plus the need to avoid stoking resentment and humiliating a weak Russia as Germany was humiliated after World War I—required extra solicitude of Moscow, the argument ran, even at the expense of central European concerns. The overriding priority was to ensure Russian adherence to START II arms control, and this required sublimation of central European interests.

One final explanation for the downbeat American reading of European integration was—and perhaps still is—psychological. Intellectually, it is less risky to be pessimistic than to be optimistic. It is always easier to reconstruct old shapes than to decipher new ones, in any case—and the old European configurations of hegemonic totalitarianism in the twentieth century and balance of power in the nineteenth century certainly invited pessimism. Then, too, predictions of failure take a long time to be proven wrong (rather than simply delayed in impact), whereas predictions of success, which presume that all key elements will succeed together, can be confounded momentarily by any single spoiler. Finally—since the German movers and shakers of European integration unconsciously use pessimism the way Americans use optimism, to galvanize corrective action—periodic German alarums can be overinterpreted by onlookers.

In the aggregate, these instincts colored U.S. commentary on Europe until the very eve of the launch of monetary union, the most concrete of Europe's integrative projects. In late 1997 Martin Feldstein, president of the National Bureau of Economic Research, went so far as to ask whether Europe's quest for a common currency might not unleash a new war.[22] Veteran diplomatic analyst John Newhouse still expected Germany to lurch in an anti-EU direction, saw EMU as a "massive distraction" that would very likely produce "economic chaos," believed that eastern enlargement was "unlikely in the foreseeable future," and called the whole sorry mess "a collective nervous breakdown."[23] Noting these and other "funereal" warnings, a *Financial Times* columnist rued the "intellectual gulf" between European perceptions and the American obsession with the "famine, pestilence, and war" that European monetary union would supposedly set off.[24] In February 1998 Irving Kristol, the dean of American neoconservatives, still expected the combination of a common European currency and statist continental economies to generate crisis and perpetuate high unemployment, thus "subverting the political institutions of the nations in the [European] union," leading to "ultimate impoverishment," and reinforcing the "hedonistic" refusal of young Europeans to procreate in adequate numbers.[25] *New York Times* columnist William Safire added his disapproval of "Alice in Euroland" as EU heads of government gathered to found the European Central Bank in May of 1998.[26]

By then straight news coverage, as distinct from commentary, in the United States turned at least neutral or even positive.[27] The shift came far too late, however, to prepare the general American reader intelligently for the realities of monetary union.

Despite the widespread "funereal" U.S. perception of Europe, the real surprise at the turn of the millennium is not the atavistic wars at the margins of Europe, but rather the absence of war in all those other places where blind, repetitive history might have decreed it. Today the magnetic attraction of the voluntary Western system of peace and prosperity for those states in the cursed space between the Germans and the Russians has a benign effect, subduing chauvinism and reinforcing moderation. Europe's blessed zone of peace and prosperity is expanding—and thereby enhancing American security as well. The new paradigm is not, after all, the atrocities of the former Yugoslavia, or even the old nineteenth-century balance-of-power jostling. It is an unaccustomed reconciliation in the heart of Europe, between France and Germany, Germany and Poland, Poland and Ukraine, Romania and Hungary, Germany and the Netherlands. In Bartoszewski's simile, Europe is indeed experiencing, after a millennium, its second birth.

CHAPTER TWO

Prologue I:
The Fall of the Wall

In the beginning was the cold war. Or so it must have seemed to the generation of leaders who governed in the 1980s. U.S. president George H. W. Bush had come of age as the youngest combat pilot in the U.S. Navy in World War II and become a congressman in 1967, at the height of the Vietnam War. Chancellor Helmut Kohl had lost a brother in Hitler's war, had pulled corpses out of bombed buildings as a teenager, and never forgot the chocolate distributed by GIs in occupied Germany. Soviet president Mikhail Gorbachev had attended university after Stalin's death, but rose through the nomenklatura communist elite that took Leninist struggle with the West as a given. Polish president Wojciech Jaruzelski, despite the repressions his own parents had endured at the hands of the Soviet regime, was still a janissary in the Warsaw Pact machine as a general of the Polish army.

In retrospect, the cold war years were good ones for Western Europe. To be sure, they began with some of the coldest winters and one of the worst droughts in memory, with near famine, cramped living space, shortages of everything, cities in ruins. There were millions of displaced persons. Manufacturing, trade, and societies themselves had broken down. The black market rewarded the criminal and punished the honest. Italy and France looked vulnerable to communist pied pipers. Even Britain, spared the worst ravages of World War II, had to ration bread after the war in order to send wheat to hungry Germans— and had to ration tea, its national drink, until 1951. Grain acreage in France was 25 percent below prewar levels, and the balance-of-guarantee of the Federal Republic would, moreover, give France the security behind which it could occasionally flirt with the Soviet Union and tweak Uncle Sam's nose.

The Federal Republic of Germany, too, for all the existential angst of living on the nuclear front line, led a comfortable life in the cold war. NATO, as Lord Ismay noted pithily, was designed to keep the Soviets out, the Americans in, and the Germans down. Yet that "down"—after fierce domestic controversy Germany rearmed and joined the alliance in 1955—was as much blessing as curse. Often enough it allowed the Germans the luxury of abdicating from messy security situations in their environs. And above all, it neatly solved the dilemma of European leadership in which no Belgian would defer to France, no Irishman to the United Kingdom, and certainly no other European to Germany. The Europeans found that they liked having the outsider United States lead them (as long, of course, as it was in the direction they wanted to go). On occasion, they found they also liked the very fact that the United States was big enough to cut through prolonged debate and force a decision—even if they did not always agree with specific policies. And relief from excess burdens of defense freed the Germans to concentrate on their new economic miracle and social market contract, according entrepreneurs low profits but promising them as compensation labor stability and generous pensions when they finally retired.

Behind the NATO shield, then, France, Germany, and the rest of Western Europe could begin their unprecedented integration. The United States pushed them in this direction by requiring recipients of Marshall Plan aid to administer the funds jointly. Visionaries like French foreign minister Robert Schuman and planning commissar Jean Monnet went further in proposing the European Coal and Steel Community (ECSC)—and France endorsed this as a way to ensure that Germany would never again be able to build a war machine on the basis of its mining and heavy industry in the Saar and Ruhr valleys. France, Germany, Italy, and the Benelux countries duly formed the ECSC in 1951, and two years later instituted a common market for coal, iron ore, scrap, and steel. In the mid-1950s they added nuclear collaboration in EURATOM. In 1957 they signed the Treaty of Rome, establishing the European Economic Community, which would aim for a common market with the "four freedoms" of unhindered movement of goods, services, capital, and people.

At the heart of this new experiment was an explicit attempt to solve the recurring problem of a Germany that was bigger and, repeatedly, more aggressive and efficient than its neighbors. The memory of the wars of 1870, 1914, and 1939 hung in the air as Belgian foreign minister Paul-Henri Spaak praised Germany's "passionately pro-European" founding father, Konrad Adenauer, and urged European institutions to embrace Germany as "the most effective, and perhaps the only means to defend Germany from itself. . . . European integration gives Germany a framework to limit its expansion, and creates a community of interests that gives it security, while securing us against certain probes and adventures."[3]

Specifically, the Treaty of Rome resulted in a French-German deal and a small-big deal. In the former, France got subsidies for its farmers, while Germany got an open market in Europe for its industrial goods (and also profited, especially in Bavaria, from agricultural support). In the latter bargain Belgium, Luxembourg, and the Netherlands got augmented votes in EEC decisions out of proportion to their tiny populations and were also ensured one commissioner each (as against two each for France, Germany, and Italy) in the quasi cabinet and secretariat that was to write agendas, run daily operations, and generally represent common rather than national interests. With time, the small states would come to regard the European Commission as their special shield against any directorate by the large states.

The other new EEC institutions were the European Council, the European Court of Justice, and the European Parliament. Of these, the European Parliament started out as—and has continued to be— the weakest. The European Council, consisting of the roving summits of the leaders of the still sovereign member states, was and is the dominant body. It shares executive powers with the Commission and legislative powers with both the Commission and the parliament, but always from a commanding position.[4] The Council had no permanent structure but constituted itself in ad hoc meetings among all six finance or agricultural ministers or, at summit level, of all six heads of government or state. It was and is "a more or less permanent negotiating forum and recurrent international conference, yet its primary members are ministers drawn from the member states," according to the pioneering study of the institution. It is "unashamedly national," directly accountable not to the Commission but "to national parliaments and national electorates."[5] With time, the Council would come to substance."[7] After this contretemps the vaunted French-German relationship remained in limbo until Social Democratic chancellor Helmut Schmidt and conservative French president Valéry Giscard d'Estaing reactivated the partnership a decade and a half later.

In the meantime de Gaulle displayed French grandeur by boycotting EEC summits in 1965 and by withdrawing France from NATO's integrated military command in 1966. With his "policy of the empty chair" in the EEC, he forced his five partners to accept the "Luxembourg compromise," in which members could veto any item touching on what they deemed vital national interests. With the French departure from the NATO military command, Paris asserted its independence from the United States, but also lost the touchstone of constant rehearsal and comparison with other armies and the boost this gave to readiness.

By 1970 the six members of the EEC gave up national competence for trade negotiations, ceding this authority to the European Community (EC), as the organization was called after 1967. In 1972 free trade was introduced among all EC and EFTA countries. In 1973 (after de Gaulle's departure from the political scene) the United Kingdom was finally admitted to the EC, along with Ireland and Denmark. In 1974 the European Council of nine members began meeting regularly. In 1975 the European Commission got its own budget and set up regional funds—and the Tindemans Report argued that the EC would need to develop "two-speed" possibilities for further integration, to prevent holding back those wishing to proceed more quickly. In 1977 all tariffs were removed among the nine members. In 1978 Schmidt and Giscard, as a defense against any new oil shocks and the now floating and fluctuating dollar, pushed through the European Monetary System, with exchange rates held within narrow bands. In 1979 the first direct elections to the European Parliament were held. In 1981 Greece entered the EC, and six years later Spain and Portugal joined, making an even dozen members.

The EC and the Single Market

After its inception, the EC settled into useful but low-key economic tasks. High politics remained the province of national capitals. Beginning in the 1970s an attempt was made to expand the domain of coordination to include foreign policy, in what was called European Political

Cooperation, but this was only moderately successful. It failed the first test of forging a united approach to the oil crisis of the early 1970s, worked better as a motor for the Helsinki Conference on Security and Cooperation in Europe, and in 1976 gave birth to the TREVI cooperation among national police and antiterrorist agencies.[8] In that period it also backed West Germany's new "Ostpolitik" of détente with the Soviet bloc—and it regularized contacts among foreign ministry political directors and working groups in phone calls, meetings, and thousands of annual "COREU" ("European correspondence") telegrams over a secure communications network. In the sharp judgment of Anthony Forster and William Wallace, however, the talking shop of European Political Cooperation, lacking resources and any commitment to common action, produced only "procedures without policy [and] activity without output."[9] That left the European Community, many complained, as little more than a forum for arguing about groceries and apportionment of subsidies for the mountains of wheat and lakes of wine that were devouring two-thirds of the entire EC budget.

Through the early 1980s Eurosclerosis reigned, with one little-noticed exception—the European Court of Justice. Unobtrusively, the very activist court asserted more and more power, curbing national sovereignty to a far greater extent than did any other European organ in the EC's first quarter century. The court did not confine itself to interpreting existing treaties or legislation, but set out general principles of European law, including "proportionality, equality, legal certainty, fundamental rights," and the "mutual recognition" that has underpinned harmonization and market liberalization. It "endorsed a set of values to underpin European governance" and strengthened the autonomous role of the European Commission as against the European Council.[10] Even without a pan-European enforcement agency behind it, it assumed that the national courts and police of EC member states would enforce its "preliminary rulings"—and they did so with remarkably few exceptions, even in the case of such sensitive issues as the Irish prohibition of divorce; German bans on radicals in the civil service and import of beer that did not meet German "purity" laws; a proscription on registry of Spanish fishing boats in the United Kingdom; the French government's liability for French farmers' destruction of imported produce; and EU quotas on banana imports.[11] It established that European law takes precedence over national law. It required governments to pay retroactive damages to individuals for violation of European law. And it arrogated to itself the authority to decide which appeals it may adjudicate, including cases brought by individuals as well as those brought by states.[12] So critical has the role of the European Court of Justice been in expanding the EC/EU writ that it is often compared with the role of the U.S. Supreme Court in interpreting the U.S. Constitution's interstate commerce clause to expand Washington's federal powers over the states.[13]

By the early 1980s European judicial activism had run its course and was encountering the first backlash, as national governments (and courts) noticed what was happening and objected. By the early 1990s the objections led to formal delimitation of the court's powers in the Maastricht Treaty. And the German Constitutional Court felt constrained to declare, in its 1993 ruling on the constitutionality of the Maastricht Treaty, that the German high court and not the European Court of Justice would decide whether EU institutions were staying within their proper bounds.[14] But at this point, for a variety of reasons, the politicians roused themselves from their slumbers to take over from the court the initiative in European integration.

The new political movement was first manifest in the Schengen Agreement, in the decision to turn the spotty common market into a real single market, and in the European Commission's competition and environment policy. The 1985 Schengen Agreement on open borders actually started as a bilateral initiative by France and Germany to relax controls on their common frontier. Out of fear that exclusive agreements among a few EC members might destroy the commonality of the European Community, however, the Benelux countries pressed France and Germany to open the inner club to them, too. The Schengen Agreement among these five states was the result—as was pressure on the respective national police forces to coordinate their activities more, lest open borders give a free hand to terrorists, drug-runners, smugglers of illegal immigrants, and other transnational criminals.

The goal of tearing down the many remaining trade barriers to establish a real European single market was revived in the mid-1980s—and changed the entire character of the community. The primary aims were to stimulate the slumped European economy, reverse high trade deficits, combat Eurosclerosis, and recover the competitiveness that was being lost to American and Japanese firms. The Federal Republic, exporting a third of its GDP, was eager to improve its markets. And since most of these exports went to European partners, Bonn was especially keen on countering, in this time of recession, the new trend of protectionism and erection of nontariff barriers among other EC states. The cause was also perfect for the liberal United Kingdom, which was only too happy to steer the EC away from grand political designs and toward a free trade zone pure and simple. And it suited the incoming French president of the European Commission, Jacques Delors, an activist who from his first day in office in January 1985 deployed the issue to make the presidency, for the first time, a major player on the European scene.

By December 1985 the Single European Act was agreed on by the European Council and given the target date of 1992 for its completion. It committed EC members to pass 282 pieces of detailed harmonized legislation to produce at last the proclaimed four freedoms of capital, goods, services, and people. It incarnated a broad European swing away from the Social Democratic–conservative consensus of the 1960s and 1970s on the social responsibility of business and governments and toward a conservative–Social Democratic consensus on neoliberalism. It blurred the distinction between government and the private sector, as the EC's use of consultants mushroomed to meet new demands and various think tanks, which were in part advocacy groups, received contracts to help the EC work out the modalities of adjustment. It revolutionized business strategy, as executives began to think not of segmented Swedish or Spanish markets but of a huge transnational market of 320 million consumers. And it would generate momentum toward what would soon be called "deepening" of the community, or a strengthening of its common political governance.

Delors's first initiative was to issue two documents on budget reform that became known as the Delors Package, then simply, Delors-1. As adopted in 1987, the package consisted of a classic trade-off. The poor Mediterranean states and Ireland approved the single market that would end their protectionism. In return, they got their financial aid doubled between 1988 and 1993, as the EC's earmarked "structural" fund rose to strengthen "economic and social cohesion" between northern and southern members. Simultaneously, a ceiling was put on farm support. Predictably, national finance ministers welcomed the limits on agricultural subsidies, while farm ministers, including Bonn's, protested. The European Parliament—which had rejected the commission's 1980 and 1985 draft budgets as too miserly for the parliament's desired social and other projects—accepted the Delors bargain. Paymaster Kohl then brokered a deal that gave rebates to British prime minister Margaret Thatcher in 1988, and budgetary peace reigned for the next decade. The Commission, it calculated, got 90 percent of what it had first laid out; Delors became a man to be reckoned with.[15]

In another way the Commission also turned into a force to be reckoned with through the maneuvering of a person who was very different from Delors—Sir Leon Brittan, the commissioner for competition from the late 1980s to the early 1990s. Sir Leon was as much a believer in the British liberal hands-off tradition as Jacques Delors was in the French dirigiste tradition of active government intervention, and Sir Leon was said to be the one commissioner who could stand up to Delors. Certainly the Englishman did not blanch at taking on both Delors and various EC governments to establish the Commission's authority in trust-busting and in setting limits on just how much aid governments could give their national industrial champions.

The latter issue had already come before the European Court of Justice in 1981; the court had ruled that the European Commission was justified in outlawing Dutch special benefits for the Philip Morris company, and even egged the Commission on to take a tougher line. Sir Leon did so, going so far as to insist that such stars as Renault and Rover pay back excessive national subsidies they had already received. His successor in the 1990s, Karel van Miert, would later carry on the same row with east German state premier Kurt Biedenkopf over Saxon subsidies to Volkswagen, block an all-German Bertelsmann–Kirch Group media merger, win concessions in the all-American Boeing–McDonnell Douglas aerospace merger, and dun Swedish-Swiss engineering giant ABB for its role in a market-rigging cartel.

In the case of mergers, there was nothing in the Treaty of Rome that gave explicit oversight to the European Commission. The treaty did forbid *abuse* of a dominant position, but not monopolies per se. If anything, this implied possible ex post facto, not prior, restraint. But Sir Leon leapfrogged the EEC Treaty and based his claims on the original European Coal and Steel Community, which allowed the High Authority to declare a merger in that specific branch illegal. The unspoken intent in the ECSC was in fact not to prevent monopolies as such, but to prevent any reassertion of German dominance—but Sir Leon interpreted the provision in the broadest possible sense. He deliberately sought out a large merger that he could prohibit and found it in the French-Italian ATR firm's proposal to acquire the Canadian de Havilland aircraft producer. Against the objections of the French and Italians—and the abstention of Delors, who did not want to be on the losing side—Sir Leon successfully pushed through a ban on the merger with a 9-to-7 vote in the commission. The precedent of premerger approval by the commission was established, and Sir Leon moved on to take on even the "natural monopolies" in energy and related sectors. Later, as commissioner for external economic relations in the seven-year-long Uruguay negotiations to lower tariff and nontariff barriers, he would similarly arrogate powers to speak for all of the EC/EU, even in the highly sensitive area of agriculture.[16]

In the 1980s EC environmental policy also gathered momentum. German ecologists, sensitized by dying forests and frustrated by the domestic resistance to thorough clean-up by large chemical and other firms, hoped they could circumvent national industrial lobbies by taking their case up to the European level. And as Germany's own antipollution laws were in fact made tougher, German business, too, joined in the European environmental campaign, partly because it feared loss of competitiveness if rival firms did not have to incur the same purification costs. The whole issue was a tricky area at first, since the Treaty of Rome did not assign environmental affairs to the Community, but the proactive European Court of Justice ruled in 1985 that "environmental protection was one of the Community's essential objectives." With support from Denmark and the Netherlands, Germany led the successful fight for EC legislation limiting sulfur dioxide emissions from large combustion plants in 1982—and for a general European tilt toward preventive rather than remedial action thereafter. Once the Single European Act explicitly gave the Community authority in environmental affairs, a burst of European antipollution legislation followed.[17]

Simultaneously, the French-German "alliance within the alliance" also shook itself out of its lethargy. The agents were the odd couple of new German chancellor Helmut Kohl and new French president François Mitterrand. The two men were utterly different. Mitterrand was short, elegant, intellectual, sphinx-like, with a personal history of working for the Vichy regime before settling on socialism as his philosophy and then, as president, moving France away from its time-honored exceptionalism to become "more like the others" in a shrinking Europe. Kohl, by contrast, was huge, bluff, folksy, and suspicious of intellectuals' lack of common sense. His personal history was a straight, less spectacular, middle-of-the-road line from student days in the Christian Democratic youth wing to party leader to chancellor of received conservative verities.

The one thing the two shared, however, they shared deeply: they were contemporaries in the tragic history of their age. When they stood at Verdun and clasped hands in memory of the dead, the gesture may have seemed embarrassing in its contrivance—but it was real. Whatever their stylistic differences, whatever their many policy quarrels, both were determined above all to prevent another Verdun from ever arising, even in the subconscious of their respective nations. Their generation, they felt in their bones, was bound in a *Schicksalsgemeinschaft*—a community of shared fate. The British, by their own choice, were not part of that community.[18] Nor would Kohl ever develop the same bond with Mitterrand's successor, Jacques Chirac, despite their shared position on the conservative side of the political spectrum.

This kinship explained much in the Kohl-Mitterrand relationship. It gave the French-German tie a stability that outlasted day-to-day lurches of interest. It would allow Kohl to excuse even Mitterrand's attempted conspiracy in 1989 with Soviet president Mikhail Gorbachev and East German leader Egon Krenz to block German unity.[19]

In the heightened East-West tension in the early 1980s after the Soviet invasion of Afghanistan, the first arena for the odd couple's joint action was security. For Mitterrand, the primary motivation was concern about a possible German drift toward accommodation with the Soviet Union. In particular, he feared that the hundreds of thousands of German nuclear pacifists who were marching in the streets against deployment of new NATO nuclear missiles might succeed in blocking that deployment. For Kohl's defense ministry, by contrast, a primary motivation was the wish to nudge Paris away from funding expensive and useless nuclear forces at the expense of the French infantry that alone could give Germany the ground reserves it would need to feel confident that it could repel any Soviet surprise attack.

In an anomalous role for the Socialist leader of a nation that was still refusing to rejoin NATO's integrated command, Mitterrand traveled to Bonn to tell parliamentarians in a special session that they must stand firm and deploy the alliance's Pershing and Cruise missiles. Kohl's center-right German government indeed did so. Shortly thereafter, the French and Germans formed a joint brigade that would later be supplemented by troops from Belgium, Spain, and Luxembourg to become the "Eurocorps." They also held bilateral maneuvers in Bavaria, in which French units conspicuously operated east of the restrictive mid-German line that de Gaulle had earlier drawn as the outer limit for French deployment. At the time, the French veto on official NATO observers at the exercise grabbed the headlines. The real news, however, was the publicity Mitterrand was now willing to grant to his generals, who chafed at the French aloofness from NATO and from the alliance's advances, and had long used discreet French-German defense collaboration as a conduit for catching up on NATO experience.[20]

Less dramatic but even more significant for bilateral relations was the quiet abandonment by Mitterrand and the French Socialist party in the early 1980s of Keynesian pump-priming. With this shift Paris implemented a "franc fort"—strong franc—policy that pegged the franc to the deutsche mark and adopted, at least cerebrally, the Bundesbank's anti-inflation target as its own highest goal. Now economic convergence could really begin. Paris and Bonn would become the motor of Europe; thereafter, what the two proposed jointly would set Europe's agenda.[21]

The timing was auspicious. Throughout Europe the consensus was growing—even during the kind of snail-like economic growth that in the past traditionally induced backsliding from European integration—that nation-states are simply too small today to cope with the challenges of globalized production, electronic currency flows, crime, and pollution. In the new jargon, the only hope for coping with the problems at the end of the millennium was pooled sovereignty.

CHAPTER THREE

Prologue II: Maastricht

Pooled sovereignty was not the first thought of those who witnessed the extraordinary night of November 9, 1989, in Berlin. Maybe bananas were, if you were one of the tropical fruit–starved East Berliners streaming through the accidentally opened Berlin Wall into the West's cornucopia.[1] Perhaps alarm was your primary reaction, if you were the commandant in the British sector and had no idea what provocations a desperate Stasi secret police might resort to, or what flare-up of tempers might spark an incident. Or perhaps it all seemed like "insanity," if you shared the unanimous slang judgment of events of those thousands of tear-streaked, ecstatic East Berliners interviewed by journalists as they crossed to the other side of the city for the first time in twenty-eight years and mixed and danced and sang and scaled the wall together all night with their West Berlin cousins.

Pooled sovereignty was not even the second thought of Margaret Thatcher, whose nightmare was German unification. But it quickly became the preoccupation of Chancellor Kohl, precisely because his very different nightmare was that of his famous nineteenth-century predecessor, Otto von Bismarck: a Germany surrounded by a hostile coalition of neighbors. His method of warding off this danger was to bind his countrymen irrevocably to a pan-European structure and preclude "renationalization" of defense and foreign policy on the continent. Kohl was above all a master politician, a doer and not a thinker, a man who deliberately avoided detailed knowledge of the work of the ministries under him, sat out decisions whenever he could, and was reassuring to German voters in this time of dizzying change precisely because he seemed to embody the folk wisdom of the *Stammtisch*, or table of regulars in the local pub.[2] But he held two strong policy convictions: at some point Germany must be unified and Europe must be integrated. The one was the obverse of the other. His monologues explaining the need for the continent to come together were laced with personal reminiscences about having pulled down toll barriers on the French-German border in his youth—and with detailed allusions to the successive tragedies as Spanish, Bavarian, Swedish, and French troops swept across his native Palatinate in the seventeenth, eighteenth, and nineteenth centuries.

Younger Germans, who had not personally experienced war and holocaust, might not share his European drive, Kohl feared; therefore he had to lock the Federal Republic as soon as he could into European institutions that could not easily be dismantled. Again and again he preached that German unification must not be a barrier to, but a catalyst for European integration. Characteristically, the last sentence in his quasi autobiography closes with the chancellor's musings on the heady day of German unification in 1990: "I was also aware, of course, that we had realized only half of our vision after the war. Before us lay—and still lies—the realization of the other half: the unification of Europe."[3]

In this aspiration he had the general backing of Germans, whose nationalism had been totally discredited by Hitler's atrocities—and whose formidable economic success in the previous three decades had been achieved in the benign framework of the European Community. Yet in what would soon shape up as the crucial policy issue of the decade, he would encounter strong popular opposition to yielding the deutsche mark to an unknown European currency, since the deutsche mark was itself the denationalized badge of German success, prosperity, and even good behavior in a way that the German flag or national anthem never again could be.

French president François Mitterrand initally did not share Kohl's vision of the future. After the wall fell, Mitterrand's first instinct, like Thatcher's, was to revert to nineteenth-century balance-of-power national games, to try to make common cause with Soviet president Mikhail Gorbachev to block German unification, and to slip into East Germany to court the new premier, Hans Modrow, before Kohl could get there. Within two months Mitterrand and Thatcher called a four-power meeting—including the Soviets—in Berlin to discuss the future of the absent Germans, and they would have continued to exclude the Germans from deciding their own fate had not Washington vetoed the idea and forced Paris and London to accept swift German union.

Yet Mitterrand's hand was greatly weakened by the end of the cold war. Unification might not greatly increase German territory; the Federal Republic would grow only from the size of Oregon to the size of Montana. But German union, along with the regrafting of central Europe onto western Europe, would move the heart of the continent from the thousand-year-old "French hexagon" and from Adenauer's chosen capital of Bonn to Berlin. It would multiply Germans from the 61 million inhabiting the old Federal Republic—roughly equal to the French, British, or Italian populations—to a dominant 81 million. It would enhance Germany's already preeminent economic power, once the obsolescent eastern German plants had been replaced. Germany's forthcoming full sovereignty would rob France of the prestige of being an occupying power in Berlin. And it would eradicate Germany's reliance on cooperation with France for legitimacy in foreign policy.

Psychologically, too, the central Europeans' rebellion against state-run socialism in 1989 was calling into question the first glorious French revolution just in the midst of its gala 200th anniversary.[4] And with Gorbachev's promised withdrawal of Soviet army divisions from east Germany and central Europe by 1994, Paris's vaunted nuclear weapons were suddenly worthless politically. The old Gaullist dream of France as the brain to Germany's economic brawn in Europe died. And, if it chose go-it-alone nationalism, France could not hope to win against this more powerful Germany.[5]

As the two Germanys raced toward unification in 1990, other Europeans faced the same dilemma as Mitterrand. Once again, the memory of all the destabilizing ascents of German power in the past century haunted them. Would the Germans again become assertive? And now that the Soviet threat was gone, what could hold the West Europeans together? Had their ahistorical suspension of national quarrels and cooperation in the EC during the half century of cold war been no more than an emergency response to existential nuclear jeopardy? Did this not foreordain a return to history and to Hobbesian anarchy?[6] How could the dynamic Germans be tamed this time?

Jacques Delors, as president of the European Commission, was among the first Europeans to say that the only possible answer to

these questions was to embrace the post–World War II German democrats and not to demonize them by expecting the worst. He interpreted the Federal Republic's membership in the EC as instantly
including its new eastern German citizens, without requiring any de-
meaning process of accession that would set the other Europeans in
judgment over the Germans. Mitterrand eventually followed his
compatriot's example, revisiting his own realization of the early 1980s
that if you can't lick 'em, you might as well join 'em. But in the coming
decade the French would repeatedly face the same agonizing choice.
The ultimate answer would always be that the one thing worse than
domination by the Germans within the EC would be domination by
them outside the EC.

If the project for a single market by 1992 had not already broken
the EC's two-decade-long stagnation, it is doubtful whether embedding a united Germany in European institutions could have worked.[7]
The structure of the old EC before the single market was far too weak
to have contained German energies, and the political deals and coalition building (and misjudgments) that went into the single-market
enterprise would probably have been impossible to strike in the postwall
atmosphere of disorientation and latent suspicion. A Europe that was
in fact well on its way to "1992," however, would prove capable—
just—of turning the fourth rise of Germany in 120 years to creative
rather than destructive uses.

The means first seemed to be combined monetary and political union,
but soon this would be narrowed to monetary union alone. The goal of
currency union, which had been around for decades, had been revived
with the Single European Act of 1986. The intent was to get beyond
mere lowered trade barriers to establish a fully open single market.
Capital was to move freely by 1990 and would subsequently evolve into
a common EC currency as the final step in achieving a genuine common
market. The concept of monetary union was promoted especially by
German foreign minister Hans-Dietrich Genscher at various Council
meetings in the two years following adoption of the 1986 act, though it
was initially regarded with indifference by Kohl.

As it became clear in 1989 and 1990 that Germany was going to
unify rapidly, however, it was President Mitterrand who seized on the
project as a way to tame the Germans. It was, of course, a two-edged
sword. Since they had linked their money to the deutsche mark seven
years earlier as a way to beat inflation, the French had had to abide by

terms dictated by the Bundesbank, and they now welcomed a chance to secure at least some shared decision with the German central bank by getting a seat of their own on a new European Central Bank.[8] Obversely, though, a powerful new ECB might magnify the power of Germany as the leading economy in Europe and the third largest in the world. Mitterrand weighed the pros and cons and chose monetary union as the lesser evil.

Despite conventional wisdom to the contrary both inside and outside Germany, Kohl was not opposed to the scheme at this point. To be sure, he did not yet regard it politically as the key development that would make European integration irrevocable. Tactically, he wanted to avoid monetary union becoming a major issue before the 1990 election among German voters wedded to the deutsche mark. Strategically, he would not make a final commitment to EMU until he was assured of his one absolute condition: independence of the European Central Bank from politicians. But already he favored monetary union as an additional tie binding Europe together.[9]

Kohl, of course, did not mind letting France think that Paris would have to pay a price to get German assent to monetary union. As Kohl met with Mitterrand in April of 1990 to prepare bilateral initiatives for the next council summit, the price that he asked for was concomitant political union. The two asserted, "It is necessary to accelerate the political construction of the Europe of the Twelve" and effect political union, "which is close to citizens and corresponds with its federal vocation."[10] As Kohl elaborated on October 3, 1990, on the occasion of German unification,

> The coming years will show that unified Germany means a victory for all of Europe. . . . Even in the future France and Germany will remain the motor of European unification. [The EC] should remain a firm foundation for the growing together of all Europe and form its core. . . . But there must be no doubt: We want political union; we do not want a glorified free-trade zone, but the political unification of Europe in the sense of the Treaties of Rome.[11]

The new Rome summit in December (after Kohl's reelection) duly endorsed both currency and political union, even if few apart from the Germans were enthusiastic about the political goal. With greater zeal (or perhaps desperation, given resistance by a strong faction within the bank to a common European currency), Bundesbank president Hans Tietmeyer took to promoting political union as a guarantee that monetary union would work and would be backed by governance with compatible fiscal policies.

The Conference

By the end of 1991, EC members were ready to open the conference at Maastricht in the Netherlands that would conduct the first major overhaul of the 1957 Treaty of Rome and chart the future course. The most controversial issue on the agenda was Germany's pressure on its allies to recognize Croatian and Slovenian independence from Yugoslavia. Bonn argued that such recognition would escape the taboo against interfering in a sovereign nation's internal affairs and allow the newly recognized states to call for outside assistance. Paris and London saw the issue very differently, especially since Bonn would still labor under its own domestic taboo against sending German armed forces abroad, and any intervention would in practice have to be carried out by the French and British. Under the circumstances, they interpreted Bonn's pressure as the reassertion of a heavyweight Germany that wanted to recreate Hitler's old sphere of influence in the Balkans. They further regarded premature acceptance of Croatian independence as the trigger that would extend the terrible bloodshed to Bosnia, and they blamed Bonn for heartless indifference to this certain consequence of recognition. Yet they went along with recognition, in part for the sake of promoting agreement on other issues at Maastricht.

In the end no agreement was reached on the hot issue of deepening—intensifying the formal and informal practices that served the six well but were already strained in a community of twelve. The Germans could not win their hoped-for reforms of more majority voting in the council, pruning of the burgeoning number of commissioners, more democratic powers for the European Parliament, and greater continuity in the EC presidency, which rotated every six months. Nor was the issue of widening the EC to take in fledgling central European democracies seriously addressed. In the early 1990s the Germans were still alone in Europe in believing that deepening and widening were, in fact, compatible.[12]

Yet even if its political aims remained vague, Maastricht was a watershed. The summit dared to give the European Community the ambitious new name of the European Union. And it meddled in the formerly forbidden areas of currency, defense, and foreign policy.

The Treaty of European Union itself, hammered out in thirty exhausting hours of final summit negotiations at Maastricht, was a potpourri. It established the Court of Auditors—court in the sense of a watchdog office, not a judicial court—which, astonishingly, had never before existed. It instituted the new Committee of the Regions in recognition of the growing sense of subnational and local identity that cut across existing political boundaries. It envisioned establishment of an effective Europol police agency by 1994.[13] It set up three "pillars"— the first, a Community pillar of economic powers delegated to Brussels by member-states; the second and third, "intergovernmental" pillars for foreign policy and home and justice matters that would be coordinated among the several national ministers in meetings of the Council of Ministers.

It set up, in addition to the structural aid to Greece, Spain, Portugal, and Ireland, the new Cohesion Fund to promote environmental cleanup and transportation lines in these poorer member-states. It wrote a "social charter"—with an opt-out for Britain that for the first time officially endorsed differentiation within the EC. At the paradoxical insistence of the British, who ran a highly centralized domestic polity, it also endorsed "subsidiarity," or devolving all powers to the lowest possible level. It bravely called for a European "common foreign and security policy," even though there was little sign of any common response to the barbarity in Yugoslavia or even the dramatic contemporary collapse of the Soviet Union. The treaty modestly accorded the European Parliament more rights of "codecision" with the Commission and confirmed a future increase by eighteen seats of the united Germans' representation in the European Parliament. And it deferred issues of political union by setting up yet another intergovernmental conference to look at the question, beginning in 1996.

Kohl considered the results a resounding success. In his euphoric report to the Bundestag he declared, "The way to European Union is irreversible. . . . The German-French partnership and friendship was, is, and remains decisive for Europe. Above all, we are united with France in the vision that Europe grow together not only economically, but also politically."[14] Given his own regret that the summit achieved little in the way of political union—and the German public's opposition to exchanging the deutsche mark for an invented currency—Kohl did not brag about the centerpiece of the conference, monetary union. But at Maastricht he secured agreement on his two nonnegotiable conditions for surrendering the deutsche mark. The future European Central Bank, the treaty stipulated, would be independent of national governments, and the Bank's commandment would be stability approaching zero inflation. Moreover, the central banks of every founding member of the European Monetary Union—including the Banque de France—would also have to be freed from government interference by the time they became part of the ECB system, at the beginning of monetary union. With this foundation, the Germans were convinced, the ECB would be just as strict as the Bundesbank—even if a German were not its chief—since any good central banker, whether French, Dutch, or Italian, would obviously think exactly like the Bundesbank.

The Maastricht Treaty thus represented "an absolute novum," said Jürgen Stark, the state secretary in the German Finance Ministry responsible for preparing G-7 summits and monetary union in the 1990s and subsequently vice president of the Bundesbank. "We [Germans] have something to lose. For the first time in history a good currency is being given up," and there must be firm measures to ensure that its replacement will have the same credibility and value. For this reason, again for the first time in history, the independence of a central bank "is now anchored in international law" and can be changed only unanimously by the signatories of Maastricht. Euroland will henceforth have "a centralized monetary policy, but decentralized fiscal and economic policy." The system would require closer cooperation among participating governments and more flexibility in capital and especially labor markets. But "if everything works well, out of it will come a policy mix that does not need fine tuning." And already the "convergence process has established a stable, healthy basis on which we can build this project."[15]

Concretely, the Maastricht summit agreed on a tough measure to define which states would qualify for monetary union, composed of five convergence criteria corresponding to Germany's "stability culture": inflation no higher than 1.5 percent above the average of the EC's three best performers; long-term interest rates no higher than 2 percent above the average of the three best performers; budget deficits no higher than 3 percent of GDP (with some wiggle room); public debt no higher than 60 percent of GDP (with some wiggle room); and exchange-rate adherence to the European Monetary System's bandwidths for two years. There would be no collective bailout of any EMU member's debts. Britain, and later Denmark, at their request, were granted opt-outs. What turned out to be the most innovative aspect of these guidelines was the concept of "benchmarking," by which the achievements of the stars would not be dragged down to a medio-cre average, but would instead set the standard for others to reach.

While Kohl was still cheering, the backlash hit. The chancellor had been right in his premonition that Germans would protest the loss of their deutsche mark—but even he was not prepared for the shock, as the *Bild* boulevard newspaper trumpeted, "Our lovely money/The mark is being abolished."[16] Bavarian premier Edmund Stoiber called the planned currency "esperanto money." *Der Spiegel* agreed. Various German economists joined in to savage the whole idea of currency union; some of them filed a challenge to the constitutionality of EMU with the German Constitutional Court.[17]

Elsewhere in the obligatory process of unanimous ratification, the Danes rejected the treaty in a referendum, threatening to reopen all the intricate 2 a.m. deals that had been reached, as usual, only under pressure of the Maastricht deadline. This setback was bad enough, but it was at least understandable in a nation that resembled Britain in its suspicion of European "federalism"—and had grave doubts about splitting off from Scandinavian nonmembers of the EC. The barely favorable majority in the French referendum was almost more dis-heartening for occurring in a country that was one of the motors of integration.

Moreover, France's closest ally, Germany, was the negative target of much of the plebiscite campaign in France, on both sides. Oppo-nents charged that the EU Treaty's "ever closer union" gave Germany a vehicle to magnify its preeminence. Recent defense minister Jean-Pierre Chevènement objected that the agreement would bind France more than Germany. Jacques Chirac, the head of the neo-Gaullist Rassemblement pour la République and soon to be the president of France, accused fellow conservatives allied with Valéry Giscard d'Estaing of being too sympathetic to foreigners. Philippe Séguin, his party colleague, went further and wrote a bestseller castigating Maastricht and branding its negotiators worthy successors to Hitler. "Almost fifty years after the collapse of the Third Reich, will Hitler's dream be resurrected in another form, and will Germany dominate Europe?" asked the newspaper *Le Point* in the same vein.[18]

Nor were the arguments of the French proponents of Maastricht any more flattering to Germany. Basically, their position was that it would be much safer to have the regional giant constrained by having to work within pan-European institutions than to allow the dynamic Germans once again to become a dangerous loose cannon.

In exasperation, writer Alain Finkielkraut reproached his fellow French for a two-faced policy that he deemed far more dangerous than the old "German question." "Everybody in France fears Germany," he wrote in *Liberation*. "Some allege that the Europe of Maastricht is the German Europe; the others say that if we really want to keep an eye on, anchor, and westernize German power, we must vote for the Treaty of European Union. And it does not occur to anyone that there are good reasons today to watch out for France itself. In the eyes of the French, only Germany is disturbing, only Germany has evil demons."[19]

To add to the strife, at this point a bitter quarrel over interest rates arose between the German and French (and other European) elites. It compounded resentment of the German pressure to recognize Croatia and called into question some of the fundamental assumptions of monetary union. Bonn, rather than taxing its own citizens to pay for the resuscitation of eastern Germany, borrowed the money for much of its $100 billion annual transfers to the east, vacuuming investment away from its neighbors. To neutralize the inflationary pressures thus generated, the Bundesbank raised interest rates by 6 points in five years, even as the continent's economy sagged; other EU countries could not then cut their own interest rates to stimulate growth. European partners complained that Germany was prolonging recession and thus taxing them without their consent, just as the monetary super-power, the United States, had exported its deficit financing of the Vietnam War in the 1960s. The French implored the Bundesbank to lower interest rates and threatened, if it did not do so, to abandon the "franc fort" and their own earlier abandonment of Kenyesian inflation. To those chafing under the Bundesbank yoke, European monetary union looked more necessary—and more unattainable—than ever.

Yet to the German population EMU looked all too attainable and threatening. The folk memory of hauling wheelbarrows full of Reichsmarks to the local bakery in the 1920s—and losing savings again in the 1948 currency reform—had given Germans a fear of inflation second to none in the industrialized world. And the phobia was only reinforced by the groundswell of "deutsche mark patriotism"—pride in the strong currency that had been so good to Germans for four decades—as the politically correct substitute for nationalism.

Kohl's response to the popular malaise was not at all the public relations blitz that one might expect in a similar situation in the United States. Instead, the chancellor adopted tactics designed for a society that operates by elite consensus. Scorning populism, he deliberately imitated Konrad Adenauer's earlier defiance of overwhelmingly negative public opinion (and fierce Social Democratic opposition) to bind the Federal Republic to the West, form an army, join the EC—and win the gratitude of later generations. To this list Kohl added his own successful defiance in the 1980s of the hundreds of thousands of demonstrators arrayed against stationing medium-range missiles in Germany.[20] It is the job of the statesman, Kohl asserted repeatedly, not to cater to voters when they are wrong, but to lead them in the right direction even if they do not want to go that way. Afterward they will appreciate this tutelage.

Kohl's main target audience was thus not the public as such, but the Bundesbank. This revered keeper of the deutsche mark grail enjoyed the kind of political prestige and popular trust that less revered and more technical central banks in other countries could only marvel at. If the Bundesbank could be persuaded that the new pan-European currency would be almost as hard as the deutsche mark, Kohl reasoned—not a foregone conclusion, by any means—then the Bundesbank would reassure the little savings banks in every town and village, and they, in turn, would reassure their depositors. As a corollary, the Kohl team determined to blame the unavoidable belt tightening in the next few years only on the challenge of globalization—and never on EMU— in order not to brand monetary union a job killer. In this it would be astonishingly successful, especially in contrast to France.

Kohl's secondary audience was the German political class. Here— remarkably, given the bitter past feuds over European and foreign policy—the conservatives, the Social Democrats, the Liberals, and the Greens' parliamentary caucus all united behind the chancellor's leap of faith. Later, when planning for the EMU was back on course and sniping at it was cost free, the premiers of Bavaria, Saxony, and Lower Saxony would all air doubts about EMU or its tempo. But in the trough of Europessimism in the early 1990s, it was only outsiders like Manfred Brunner who did so. And Brunner's anti-EMU League of Free Citizens, like all new single-purpose parties in the Federal Republic with the exception of the Greens, would sink without a trace.

The Hangover, 1992–93

In the early 1990s Europe slumped into its worst recession since the 1930s. The European Monetary System, even though it was far less demanding than full monetary union would be, succumbed to speculative market attack in September of 1992, forcing the British pound and the Italian lira to devalue by one-quarter and obliging Spain, Portugal, Ireland, and Denmark to devalue their currencies to a lesser degree inside the system. The French franc, too, would have plunged out of the agreed exchange bands but for massive intervention by the Bundesbank—and stretching of the bandwidths so far that by August 1993 the new elasticity was initially regarded as collapse of the system.[21]

Then, as recession continued in 1993—the long-awaited inaugural year of the single European market—the economy, far from quickening as advocates had prophesied, fell into an absolute decline of 1.1 percent for Germany and 0.3 percent for the continent, with 10.5 percent unemployment. The ground was laid for the widespread social unrest that would later break out in France. And even after growth eventually resumed, structural unemployment would continue to rise inexorably.

Under the circumstances, plans for monetary union looked ludicrous. A few short years before the hoped-for launch of a single currency, only the tiny bankers' paradise of Luxembourg met the stiff Maastricht criteria. Outstanding central bankers were notably reluctant to take on the job of president of the European Central Bank's forerunner, the European Monetary Institute, apparently out of doubts that the project would ever get off the ground. Only Kohl, it seemed, maintained the confidence that the ambitious plans would proceed as scheduled, if not in 1997, then in the fallback year of 1999.

As had happened so often before in the history of the EC, when recession hit, momentum ground to a halt. The institutional and budgetary reforms that were essential if the EU was to double its members were postponed. There was no movement to increase majority voting, to rectify the cumbersome distribution of Commission posts, or to change the erratic leadership of half-year presidencies rotating among all members of the EU. No initiatives were forthcoming to readjust the bias favoring small members, who could outvote the largest countries if their numbers were extended by a dozen tiny new entrants. Yet without change, doubling the dozen members would clearly freeze up institutions designed for the cozy interaction of the original six signatories of the Treaty of Rome. Talk of Eurosclerosis was revived, not least in the American media. The demoralization was profound. Everything conspired to confound the disciples of Jean Monnet and Robert Schuman.

In pocketbook issues, France (and Germany) continued to resist any more meddling with the farm subsidies that even after the increase in other EU spending still ate up half of EU budgets. Spain, Portugal, Greece, and Ireland accepted their fresh cohesion funds and prepared to defend these new entitlements against any future sharing out with the east. Yet calculations indicated that extending existing EU programs to the four Visegrad states alone would increase EU spending by an untenable half or more.[22] And milk cow Germany, staggering under the huge transfers to its new eastern *Länder* (states), began declaring that it would not continue indefinitely to pay a disproportionate share of net EU outlays. The first step in Bonn's campaign to ease its financial burden was to leak to the German public the scale of its contributions, which had previously been kept quiet, and to publicize the country's drop in ranking, after absorbing east Germany, to only the fifth-richest EU country per capita.[23]

Domestically, all the large EU nations were in trouble. Italy was wracked by a systemic breakdown, as scandals revealed pervasive official corruption and collusion with the mafia, and had little spare time to contemplate Europe at large. France, with a new conservative prime minister at odds with its Socialist president, was distracted by the vicissitudes of "cohabitation." Nor was it certain how well the more Europe-minded prime minister, Edouard Balladur, might cohabit with his more nationalist neo-Gaullist leader, Jacques Chirac. And the specter of the xenophobic right was not banished either; Jean-Marie Le Pen's National Front claimed an influential and rising 14 percent in the general election. In Britain, Prime Minister John Major was reaping the whirlwind after Margaret Thatcher, and, despite his promise to bring the United Kingdom into "the heart of Europe," was failing to unite a Tory party in which Euroskeptics were in full cry.

For their part, the Germans were discovering just how many economic and psychological barriers still hindered them from becoming the "one people" that the Leipzig demonstrators had dreamed of in the heady fall days of 1989. True unification, it turned out, would take much longer and would be far more painful than anyone had imagined. Many an (eastern) "Ossi" accused (western) "Wessis" of arrogance. Many a Wessi resented being compelled to pay a surtax for charity to the east. A hangover of cynicism and disgust with politics and parties settled in, palpable enough for the zeitgeist to win the unmistakably Germanic nickname of *Politikverdrossenheit,* or "political sulkiness."[24]

Most alarming of all, right-wing extremists were lethally tormenting third world foreigners who sought refuge under the constitution's generous promise of asylum. In 1992 some 700,000 new foreigners entered Germany—and the death toll of outsiders from arson and beatings rose to seventeen. Improved police work, stiff jail sentences, and popular outrage at such behavior stopped the wave of murders in 1993. But politically, antiforeign resentment brought the xenophobic right into three state legislatures in 1993, with an alarmingly high vote of 11 percent in Baden-Württemberg. Surveys suggested that the far right might even win enough in the next general election to put extremists into the Bundestag for the first time since adoption of the 5 percent minimum requirement.

Nor did prospects look better in the "widening" half of the European enterprise, righting the historic wrongs of the division of Europe sealed at Yalta by welcoming the new central European democracies into the EC/EU. In both its own programs and those of the G-24 group of states aiding reform in central and eastern Europe, the European Union was providing substantial financial and technical assistance for development of new institutions and markets, along with ready commercial, administrative, and other models to help smooth transformation. And with prodding from Bonn and the European Commission (with the help, surprisingly, of Italy and Spain), the EC summit in Copenhagen in June 1993 did offer binding promises of future membership to those central Europeans in "Europe Agreements," while defining the criteria that would qualify candidates for membership. For the first time, this promised a political framework that advocates could cite in trying to make the single market more hospitable to central European imports.[25]

Yet in this most crucial area of opening its markets to the east, the EC was dragging its feet. It did offer progressive lowering of tariffs, aiming at free trade in industrial goods from 1995, steel from 1996, and textiles in 1997—but its own weak demand hardly sucked in central European imports. And in response to west European lobbyists, who were much more adept at playing the fragmented Brussels bureaucracy than were the central European neophytes, the EC kept imposing ad hoc quotas on Polish cherries or Ukrainian tablecloths or Slovak steel in precisely those sectors in which the central and east Europeans had a comparative advantage.[26] Even the central Europeans' champion, Germany, with a crisis in its own downsizing steel industry, showed no eagerness to expand imports in this branch.

The Poles, profiting from their open border with Germany, initially made huge unrecorded sales of gasoline, ceramic garden dwarfs, and prostitutes' services to consumers across the Oder River, and thus kept their real trade balance in the black. But overall, the EC/EU registered an official trade surplus of 5.6 billion European currency units (ecus) in 1993 ($6.1 billion), with 8 percent of this arising from food exports that logically should have been flowing in the other direction. And France, which never had been keen on magnifying German influence by extending the EU into Berlin's backyard, now proposed as a precondition for candidates a minimum GDP that would long bar entry to central Europeans living at a third of EU levels. Moreover, while Rome, Paris, and Bonn fiddled, the former Yugoslavia continued to burn.

In the face of these multiple tribulations, the European allies displayed only grudging solidarity. Even the hallowed French-German alliance within the alliance suffered. The two partners were still jockeying for position in the post–cold war world; Germany still continued to honor France, but Kohl was becoming less malleable, even as he continued to regard the bilateral relationship as the sine qua non for Europe. And divergent perceived interests split the two on trade issues, in residual French dirigiste instincts, and in shaping the new European Central Bank. After it was outvoted on the issue in the EU, Bonn had to yield to the French desire to protect the insatiable German banana market against Chiquita and Dole and ensure large sales for the blander fruit from former French colonies.[27] It went along with Paris, too, in setting bureaucratic rather than market standards for European color TV—though it did not agree to let the European Commission guide the invisible hand more broadly by picking and promoting industrial winners.

Kohl also deferred to his friend Mitterrand in rejecting American urgings to press Paris to reduce EU subsidies for agricultural exports and to lower barriers against audiovisual imports in the GATT Uruguay round negotiations that were then in their seventh interminable year of bargaining. In the end the French did accept a complex intra-EU formula that managed to trim EU outlays largely because of the high world price for cereals; another bruising trade war was averted with the United States before the American president's fast-track authorization lapsed; and Kohl maintained his balancing act between Paris and Washington.

Even for the sake of French and European harmony, however, there was one central issue on which Kohl would not and could not compromise. In April 1990 his acceptance of the ultimate sacrifice of the deutsche mark in agreeing with Mitterrand to enact monetary union was premised on the condition that the European Central Bank must be totally independent of political influence. Again and again, up to the very last moment of instituting EMU, Kohl would return to this standard; again and again Paris would challenge it. He therefore insisted not only that the institutional autonomy of the European Central Bank must be guaranteed, but also that the ECB and its forerunner European Monetary Institute must be located in the same city as the Bundesbank—and that the common currency must not carry the name of the old ecu.

These were no mere whims. Kohl believed that EMI officials must have their backbone strengthened by daily contact with Bundesbank officials as they drafted all the ECB's detailed regulations and procedures in the brief half decade of preparation for launch. And the new coin of the realm must not be tarnished in the public mind by association with the bureaucratic basket currency, ecu, which had devalued against the deutsche mark in its two decades of notional existence.

Ironically, for all of Kohl's ardor, Germany was the last state in the European Community to ratify the Maastricht Treaty. On October 11, 1993, the German Constitutional Court finally approved German acceptance of the Maastricht Treaty and entry into monetary union, contingent on the Bundestag's democratic approval. The Bundestag promptly voted for ratification. On November 1, 1993, the European Union staggered into existence. No one could have accused it of excessive euphoria.

CHAPTER FOUR

Post–Cold War NATO

The North Atlantic Treaty Organization emerged from the cold war with glory and perplexity. Its deterrence had produced the longest peace on the European continent in history, and it had never fired a shot in anger.[1] Yet it appeared to many to have put itself out of business, now that Moscow's troops had retreated a thousand miles to the east and the democratic Germans had regained unity and full sovereignty. Especially after the Warsaw Pact dissolved in 1990, the Soviet Union dissolved in 1991, and the Russian successor to the Soviet army completed its withdrawal from Germany in 1994, NATO no longer seemed necessary to keep the Russians out or the Germans down.

The U.S. Engagement

Its strongest remaining rationale, then, was to keep the Americans in Europe—and various European and American voices argued that to prolong Pax Americana would be no more than bureaucratic self-perpetuation.[2] Other organizations that did not embody outdated U.S. hegemony, like the Conference on Security and Cooperation in Europe, were proposed for the continent's security architecture in the dawning era of peace. So strong was this sentiment that President George H. W. Bush testily warned the Europeans in 1991, "If your ultimate aim is to provide independently for your own defense, the time to tell us is today." If so, he implied, the United States would happily go home and leave the Europeans to be hoist by their own petard.[3]

As they took a second look at the uncertain world about them, however, NATO governments and the new central European democracies saw an urgent need for the United States to stay engaged in Europe—and saw NATO as the only possible instrument of this engagement. In its desire to reap a peace dividend so that it could focus on neglected domestic needs, the U.S. Congress was hardly in a mood to approve some new defense commitment to foreign allies. But after four successful decades, Americans felt comfortable with NATO; they might be willing to preserve its existence and even, the central Europeans devoutly hoped, extend its reach.

Essentially there were three reasons for the wish to keep the United States as a major player in Europe. The most important was reinsurance against any imperial recidivism by a Russia still armed with nuclear weapons. Three episodes contributed to European nervousness.

The initial scare came with the attempted hard-line putsch against President Mikhail Gorbachev in mid-1991. The second scare, after Soviet collapse, came when the Russian 14th Army intervened in Moldova on behalf of separatist ethnic Russians to secure the breakaway of the newly invented Trans-Dniestr Republic. Subsequently, all thirteen blocs in parliament and the Russian government itself affirmed the Russian Federation's "great power" interests in the "near abroad"—the Baltic and other newly independent states that had emerged out of Soviet collapse—and implicitly sanctioned Russian military action there.

The third fright came in the fall of 1993, as President Boris Yeltsin and his former vice president, Alexander Rutskoi, engaged in a proxy shootout, with Yeltsin ordering troops to fire on parliament while CNN cameras covered the events live. Within months voters protested against price rises and the new chaos by giving the most seats in the Duma to the party of Vladimir Zhirinovsky, an out-and-out chauvinist who wanted to reconstitute the Soviet Union, irradiate Lithuania, and even reclaim Alaska. Shortly thereafter Yeltsin, who had initially condoned the concept of a more civic and less ethnic Russian state, turned more nationalist in viewing the 25 million Russian speakers in the near abroad as an integral part of the Russian nation.[4] By April 1994 the Russian government indeed announced establishment of thirty military bases in the "CIS and Latvia." The CIS, or Commonwealth of Independent States, was the organization of Soviet successor states that nominally resembled the voluntary European Union, but which Moscow increasingly saw as a vehicle for reconsolidating Russia's hegemony over the near abroad.[5] Moscow also pointedly refused to recognize the borders of the second-largest Slav scion of the Soviet Union, Ukraine. And at the turn of 1994–95, the Russian army started what it thought would be a brief campaign to suppress Chechen secessionists by brutally razing civilian districts in Grozny, the capital of Chechnya.[6] A new Time of Troubles loomed.

None of this posed any direct threat to western Europe, of course, especially after the Russian army failed disastrously in Chechnya and deteriorated to only two combat-ready divisions, according to Western intelligence. And the West, however much it might deplore Russian deviations from the common understanding of democracy, essentially refrained from criticizing Yeltsin out of fear of weakening him against more hard-line rivals. Yet every new reminder of the old Soviet imperial policy made the NATO security blanket look more comforting to the western Europeans, and doubly so to the central Europeans and Balts, who were much more exposed to the erratic Russian army. Only the United States, with its airlift, intelligence, and real-time state-of-the-art battlefield technology—and ultimately, nuclear guarantee—was in a position to counterbalance every possible military risk, should things lurch out of control in Moscow.

The second reason for embracing NATO was the conspicuous preference (on the part of Germans as well as other Europeans) for American security leadership over the alternatives of German leadership or no leadership. Even two generations after World War II, the British, French, and Danes still balked more at deferring to a big Germany than at deferring to an even bigger United States. And some kind of strong leadership was often needed to force inconclusive allied debates into decision and action.

The third reason, which became clear as the atrocities mounted in the former Yugoslavia, was the need for credible force—which only the Americans could provide—to constrain local bullies on the peripheries of Europe. As television brought the bloodletting on Europe's southern doorstep to living rooms every night, a remarkably broad consensus about the need to defend the weak overcame the European left's residual suspicion of the United States. The antinuclear (and anti-American) demonstrations by hundreds of thousands during the

1980s were forgotten. And even the French, however much they might bridle as American officials called the United States a European power, concurred in these broad judgments.

On the U.S. side, President George Bush continued the transatlantic connection in the early post–cold war years and helped steer the adaptation to the new environment that was essential if NATO was to remain viable. Even before the Soviet Union fell apart, the alliance modified NATO doctrine, downgraded nuclear missiles to "truly weapons of last resort," sharply cut forces and especially "forward deployment" on the eastern border of NATO, offered cooperation instead of confrontation to Moscow, and began thinning out American troops in Europe to a politically sustainable 100,000 or less.[7] Washington, its allies, and Moscow concluded the long-drawn-out negotiations on major reductions in Conventional Forces in Europe (CFE) with the agreement in late 1990 to melt down 33,000 tanks, artillery, and other heavy weapons, and thus bring the Soviet bloc forces down to NATO levels.

In 1991 President Bush, relying on NATO infrastructure in Europe while not engaging the alliance itself in such an operation outside alliance territory, led a coalition of the willing to deny Saddam Hussein's takeover of Kuwait. At the time Washington regarded the action as a likely model for the "new world order" that would now prevail, with the United States as the only superpower and NATO Europe as the solid logistical base for Western operations in the Middle East. Within NATO territory the alliance maintained collective defense, at reduced military level; but it also upgraded its political tasks, establishing the North Atlantic Cooperation Council for dialogue with the Soviet Union and the new central European democracies—only weeks before the Soviet Union fell apart, as it happened. Then in 1992 Washington steered NATO to revise its basic "strategic concept." NATO still saw itself as the continent's primary defense organization, but it now welcomed the "European defense identity" the western Europeans desired.

More fundamental questions about U.S. interest in Europe arose once Bill Clinton became president in 1993, deliberately subordinated foreign policy to domestic concerns, and largely ignored Europe in his first year in favor of the more fashionable Pacific Rim. The Europeans waited and would take his measure in three tests: trade negotiations, NATO enlargement, and war in the former Yugoslavia.

Trade negotiations came to a head at the end of 1993. The president's fast-track authority was about to expire, and before it did Clinton had to win ratification of the North American Free Trade Agreement, as well as settle on the final bargain of the long-running Uruguay Round of GATT negotiations to cut nontariff barriers. In both cases, to the cheers of the Europeans, Clinton won against strong protectionist sentiment in Congress. He then took his first, triumphal tour of Europe. Once he finally noticed the old continent, his instincts paralleled Bush's. He arrived in Brussels for the NATO summit at the beginning of 1994 and told the western Europeans what they wanted to hear in committing his administration to continued alliance and European engagement. He traveled on to central Europe to tell the Poles, Czechs, and Hungarians what they wanted to hear by promising them admission to NATO. Illustrating the sort of thing the United States could do that Europeans could not, he also cajoled Ukraine into making the continent a safer place by giving up the nuclear arsenal it had inherited from the Soviet Union and its sudden status as the world's third-largest nuclear power. Within NATO, too, even the long rift between France and the United States looked as if it might be resolved, as Paris joined contingency planning for Bosnia and returned for the first time since 1966 to participate in NATO's Military Committee (if not the Defense Planning Committee).

Bosnia

On the fighting in the former Yugoslavia, however, Clinton remained silent, and quarrels on this issue would risk the very breakup of the transatlantic alliance. The new president had come into office criticizing the Bush administration for its passivity as the Serbs swept beyond conquering ethnic Serb parts of Croatia to dismembering (in collusion with the Croats) the long-time Bosnian model of multicultural tolerance. Yet in his first two years as president, Clinton himself took no more action than his predecessor. Within the alliance, American aloofness was initially welcomed; Luxembourg's foreign minister, Jacques Poos, famously announced, "The hour of Europe has dawned."[8] Even the British told Washington that Yugoslavia was Europe's business. Secretary of State Warren Christopher made one half-hearted attempt to promote the American idea of "lift and strike"—lifting the arms embargo on the outgunned (Muslim) Bosniaks and striking their Serb besiegers from the air, without putting any GIs in harm's way on the ground—in allied capitals, but when he met a lukewarm response, he retreated.

As the United States approached midterm elections in 1994, the Bosniaks had been pushed back into vulnerable enclaves. The Bosnian capital of Sarajevo, best known to the outside world as the site of the winter Olympics a decade earlier, had been besieged and shelled by Bosnian Serbs for two years, with one bombardment killing sixty-eight civilians in a single hit. Both the Serbs and the Croats were practicing "ethnic cleansing," brutally driving other nationalities out of their conquered villages, murdering old people and children, setting up prison camps reminiscent of Nazi concentration camps, and, in the case of the Serbs in particular, raping captive Bosniak women serially for months on end to produce Serb babies and defile the women for Bosniak husbands.

Anguished by the brutality, the United Nations for the first time provided food and medicine to civilians in the midst of a war, and some 10,000 to 25,000 French, British, Dutch, and other United Nations Protection Force (UNPROFOR) troops were deployed to guard these relief operations, then later to guarantee Bosnian "safe areas." The UNPROFOR troops had strict orders to be "neutral." In practice, this euphemism meant they never intervened to protect defenseless civilians. On the contrary, they abetted ethnic cleansing by transporting women and children out of Bosniak towns and leaving the men to be massacred, or else they themselves became de facto hostages. When Bosniaks pleaded for allied air strikes against Bosnian Serb warlords who were shelling them, UN commanders and civilian officials repeatedly refused, partly in order to avoid favoring one side, but also to avoid retaliation against exposed UNPROFOR troops.[9]

In early 1994 the United States had at least managed to get the Croats and Bosniaks to stop fighting each other and to establish a federation in the 30 percent of Bosnia not controlled by the Serbs. And a "Contact Group" of the four largest European nations plus the United States and Russia had been established to make both Washington and Moscow accept some responsibility for a settlement and not let Serbs play the Russian card or Bosniaks play the American card in rejecting European peace proposals. But NATO, the world's most powerful security alliance, was a minor actor, doing no more than monitoring sanctions together with the Western European Union, conducting overflights on invitation in Hungarian airspace (and thus stopping

Yugoslav bombing of Hungarian border towns), enforcing a no-fly zone in Bosnia mandated by the United Nations, and conducting pinprick retaliatory strikes against Bosnian Serb besiegers of Sarajevo and other Bosniak enclaves.

To be sure, everyone had a reason for not acting or for acting timidly. As war broke out in the Balkans, the Germans were preoccupied with unification, and the conviction that had characterized discourse on the German left ever since the Vietnam War—that peace constituted the highest morality—had not yet been challenged as sometimes condoning evil. European coordination of foreign policy was still in its infancy, and before the breakup of Yugoslavia the taboo, under the nuclear balance of terror, against intervening within the borders of a sovereign country remained absolute. Britain—besides having great awe of the Serb partisans' legendary resistance to Hitler's legions and holding a certain romantic view of the Serbs derived from the bible of Rebecca West's *Black Lamb and Gray Falcon*—calculated cynically that since Serbia was the regional strongman, the sooner it finished conquering the Croats and the Bosniaks, the sooner stability would return.

Across the Atlantic, Washington viewed the former Yugoslavia as a far-off land and a distraction from more pressing issues. Bush's secretary of state, James Baker, noted pungently in 1992 that the United States had no "dog in this fight."[10] Clinton still saw himself as a domestic, not a foreign policy, president, and he recalled this priority ever more vividly as the 1994 and 1996 elections drew closer. For its part, the U.S. military hierarchy, recalling Vietnam and, later, the TV shots of a GI's naked corpse being dragged through the streets of Mogadishu, shrank from any assignment that might produce "mission creep" and did not entail a sure "exit strategy." Various northern democrats in both the United States and Europe, seeing the barbarity that was practiced by all sides in the south Slav lands, simply washed their hands of the affair. Indeed, many dismissed the Balkan tribes as incorrigibly bellicose and—despite the fact that it took Serbian president Slobodan Milosevic a full two years to stoke nationalist hatreds up to the passions of war—viewed such a reversion to chauvinism as the natural recycling of history after the removal of the artificial constraints of the cold war.[11]

As the horror mounted in 1995, so did recriminations among NATO allies. The Americans castigated the French and especially the British for their studied neutrality between the heavily armed Serbs (and increasingly, Croats) and the poorly armed Bosniaks and for blocking air strikes against those Serbs who were bombarding civilians in the Bosniak enclaves. The French and especially the British castigated the United States for threatening to break unilaterally the UN arms embargo on Bosnia and for preaching morality to others when it would not risk a single GI on the ground. As they feuded, up to 8,000 Bosniak men were executed in Srebrenica, the largest single mass murder in Europe since World War II. Despite American satellite photography of the atrocity at the time, neither American planes nor European infantry intervened. The word *genocide* again made the rounds in a Europe that thought it had banished that demon.

The Bosnian Serbs, emboldened by the lack of opposition to their savagery, this time took UNPROFOR soldiers as literal hostages against NATO air strikes, chaining them to lampposts in front of the international corps of photographers. The French, who for some time had wanted to suppress the heavy Serb weapons, now insisted on forming rapid reaction forces with real combat capability. The Europeans as a whole now regarded their UNPROFOR mission to date as having only delayed final Serb victory, thereby increasing the total death and destruction.

As the lightly armed UNPROFOR troops appeared to be increasingly at risk, Clinton reluctantly pledged that American ground troops would help extricate them if it became necessary—without realizing the potential scope of casualties to which the NATO contingency process committed the United States.[12] And this time, unlike the aftermath of Suez, there was no overarching Soviet threat to force the Western allies back together again after their split. On the one hand, if Clinton delivered on his promise and dozens or hundreds of American lives were lost in nothing more than ignominious retreat, Congress might order all the troops home, from Germany as well as from Bosnia. On the other hand, if Clinton left allied forces to fight their own way out against both Serbs and the deserted Bosniaks—and the president seemed to think he still had a choice—the whole American security guarantee and process of NATO consultation would be exposed as a sham. Either way, in the view of Assistant Secretary of State Richard Holbrooke, "It was not an overstatement to say that America's post–World War II security role in Europe was at stake."[13] Stanley R. Sloan, the Congressional Research Service's specialist on NATO, worried,

"Neither the United States nor the Europeans have been willing to risk the sacrifices that could have been required to impose and enforce a peace in Bosnia. Now there is a growing tendency on both sides of the Atlantic to blame each other and NATO for the consequent policy failure."[14]

The only way, then, to avoid an inglorious withdrawal, unacceptable loss of American soldiers' lives, or the death of NATO was to up the ante. The Croats suddenly helped by applying the weapons they had been quietly accumulating with tacit American approval. In a mini-blitzkrieg they won back not only the Serb-conquered parts of Croatia, but also 20 percent of Bosnian territory, effecting a more even 51-49 percent division of terrain between the Bosnian Serbs and the Croat-Bosniak "federation." NATO aircraft for the first time responded disproportionately to Serb bombardments of Bosniak enclaves, flying 3,400 sorties in two weeks and destroying Serb heavy weapons ringing the enclaves.

Holbrooke seized the opportunity. He all but imprisoned the three Yugoslav parties (and Washington's European allies) in "proximity talks" at a Dayton airbase and bored in on Milosevic, who by now had abandoned his Bosnian Serb protégés in order to end Western economic sanctions on Belgrade.[15] An uneasy deal was cut; the hypnotism of war was broken long enough for participants to realize their own war exhaustion. The four years of battles and massacres had claimed some 200,000 lives, made refugees of half of the Bosnian population of 4.3 million, and displaced the largest number of children since World War II.

As part of the settlement, some 60,000 Implementation Forces (IFOR), a third of them now American, were sent into Bosnia with supporting firepower and robust rules of engagement to impound (primarily Serb) heavy weapons and police the peace. IFOR functioned for a year, to be succeeded by the smaller Stabilization Force (SFOR). NATO suddenly became the core of a multinational operation, with Russian, Ukrainian, central European, and other military units from twenty-one non–NATO countries cooperating under the alliance's new Partnership for Peace program.[16] And a new International Criminal Tribunal for Former Yugoslavia was established at The Hague to try the few low- and medium-level Yugoslav thugs delivered to it as defendants.

The jury is still out as to whether the NATO-led truce enforcers can produce a peace sturdy enough to outlast their armed presence, in

Bosnia or in Kosovo. But they did at least stop the bloodshed, and they did provide the space for more moderate politicians to surface in Montenegro, in the Srpska Republic in Bosnia, in Croatia, and finally, even in Serbia.

Poland and Enlargement

The enlargement of NATO to take in new members to the east followed a less stormy course than did Western policy on the former Yugoslavia. Initially the West cheered on the new democracies without promising them membership in NATO or offering any timetable for joining the EC. It was not until early 1993 that the first senior Western politician, German defense minister Volker Rühe, proposed that central European countries be welcomed into the defense alliance. Concern was rising in the West at that point about the more belligerent voices in Moscow, who were starting to call for a Russian sphere of influence not only over the whole territory of the former Soviet Union, but also in the entire former Soviet bloc. And the central Europeans again felt as if they were falling into a power vacuum of the sort that throughout history had pulled belligerent neighbors in to war over them.[17]

Into this breach leaped Rühe, declaring, "Eastern Europe must not become a conceptual 'no-man's land.' . . . I cannot see one good reason for denying future members of the European Union membership in NATO." And since qualifying for membership in the fiercely competitive and complex EU would be far more difficult for fledgling market economies and polities than would qualifying for NATO, the defense minister further floated the notion that NATO membership might even precede EU membership.[18]

He spoke of central Europe generically, but he was thinking of Poland specifically; the Polish question was the problem that animated the widening of both the EU and NATO, as fully as the German question animated the deepening of the EU. With a population of 39 million, Poland was by far the largest of the central European countries—and over three centuries it had repeatedly been buffeted between assertive Germans and assertive Russians. Eighteenth-century partition among Russia, Prussia, and Austria set the pattern; Hitler's attack on Poland, triggering World War II, and what Poles viewed as a half century of occupation by the Soviet Union, were only the latest examples. In the early 1990s, Poles still recited the number of times they felt abandoned by the West—in their doomed periodic revolts against Russian rule under the partition, in the German attack in 1939, and in the Warsaw uprising in 1944, then in 1945 as the East-West lines drawn at the Yalta conference of the great powers once again delivered them to Moscow. With bitterness some Poles anticipated a new betrayal by the West in relegating Poland to a post–cold war limbo and subjection to pressure from the Russians.

Making the same point more positively about Poland's thousand-year yearning to be accepted as part of the West, Janusz Onyszkiewicz asserted in an interview, "Our aspirations to join the European Union and NATO are two sides of the same coin." Speaking with the authority he acquired as Solidarity spokesman in 1980–81 and as defense minister twice in the 1990s, he continued, "We simply want to join the community of democratic countries of the northern hemisphere."[19]

Foreign Minister Bronislaw Geremek, accepting the 1998 Charlemagne Prize, expressed the same sentiment. Europe and Poland have a common "Judeo-Christian and humanist tradition," he proclaimed, that is finally asserting itself in a twenty-first-century Europe that is both whole and free. Geremek welcomed the belated coming together as expressing a "geocultural" commonweal that should now replace the geopolitics, chauvinism, and national and class "egoism" of the past. He praised in particular Germany's rapprochement with Poland in 1990 and Germany's contemporary role in helping Poles and other central Europeans enter the Western clubs. This "surprising and wonderful change" in bilateral relations, he declared, is "one of the greatest events of our century. . . . Thanks to the reunification of Germany, Poland could become free, and thanks to the freedom of Poland wrested in the great epic of Solidarity, Germany could achieve reunification."[20]

Despite this new bilateral warmth, Rühe remained a lone prophet for almost a year in calling for NATO expansion. Kohl displayed little interest in the subject. And unlike Rühe and Geremek, Washington saw many compelling reasons for not enlarging NATO. The most important consideration was to avoid provoking Moscow and strengthening all the Russian Zhirinovskys who resented their abrupt loss of empire.

Two incidents in 1993 changed America's view, however. The first occurred during Russian president Boris Yeltsin's visit to Poland at the invitation of Polish president Lech Walesa. In Warsaw the old Solidarity electrician-hero, using a time-honored ploy of diplomacy, got his guest drunk and let him say publicly, No, it would not bother Russia if Poland joined NATO. Back home, Russian officials quickly corrected their chief, and eventually Yeltsin himself changed his position. But by then it was too late; what previously had been the universal assumption that NATO expansion would be utterly unacceptable to Moscow had been cast into doubt.

The second incident occurred in Washington, where Walesa and Czech president Vaclav Havel used their participation in the opening of the Holocaust Museum to press their case personally with Clinton. Against the somber memory of Auschwitz, their pleas that history should be rectified—and central Europeans given the chance to create the prosperity and security that their more fortunate west European cousins had been granted half a century earlier—sounded persuasive to the American president. The central Europeans had paid the penalty of being on the wrong side of the Iron Curtain for two generations. The courage of the Poles in particular—who had gone on mass strike against their communist government and its Russian masters in the 1980s and in the end brought down Moscow's whole internal as well as external empire—deserved reward. The prospect of the very rich reward of NATO and EU membership would buttress the still shaky central European democracies and market economies, give citizens the patience to endure painful short-term adjustments in order to attain the larger goal, and refute extremist demagogues. By September 1993, National Security Adviser Anthony Lake, in his first major foreign policy speech, was urging replacement of the old strategy of containment with a "strategy of enlargement—enlargement of the world's free community of market democracies." This would offer the Poles, Czechs, and others "an essential collective security."[21]

The Pentagon balked. It feared that expansion would dilute NATO, spreading the alliance too thin—especially in a period of sharp defense budget cuts—and bringing in new members whose militaries would be far below alliance standards in equipment and training. In part to deflect enlargement, in late 1993 the Defense Department and its allies in the civilian bureaucracies launched a far weaker substitute, the Partnership for Peace program, under which any eastern partner who wished to do so could join NATO officers and troops in individually tailored exercises and exchanges.

For the next two-and-a-half years a tug of war raged within the Washington bureaucracies and on the op-ed pages of U.S. newspapers. Those who opposed NATO enlargement argued that it was unnecessary in the more benign post–cold war environment, that it would be self-fulfilling in presuming Russia to be the adversary, and that it catered only to ethnic politics in the United States and to American arms manufacturers who wanted to sell their jets and electronics in new central European markets.[22]

Those who favored expansion contended that the reinsurance of NATO membership would enlarge the west European zone of peace and stability, deter threats from any quarter at an early stage (including disputes between candidate countries themselves, on the Greek-Turkish model), and thus make it less likely that NATO would ever have to use force ex post facto to restore peace in the region. They argued further that expansion could be sold politically in the United States as an appeal to ethnic voters. Moreover, they asserted, the central Europeans should no longer be regarded as pawns of the superpowers but as sovereign countries with a right to choose their own alliances. The carrot of NATO membership would help the young democracies meet the membership preconditions of military transparency and civilian control of the military, and defense would cost them less cooperatively than it would individually.[23]

The bureaucratic victory for enlargement in Washington was signaled by the appearance of an essay on its behalf by no less than Strobe Talbott, the Russo-centric deputy secretary of state.[24] After William Perry became secretary of defense, the Defense Department also shifted to favor this policy. And when Madeleine Albright became secretary of state, she was especially vigorous in promoting admission of Poland, Hungary, and her native Czech Republic into NATO.[25]

Once the United States had decided its course, the Europeans followed. The Germans were delighted to have the United States take the lead in a policy that so clearly served their desire to have NATO allies to their east as well as to their west. Other Europeans did not have strong opinions on the question; the only real disagreement pitted France against the United States over the tactical issue of whether to include Romania in the first tranche of new admissions. Given the urgent need to secure two-thirds' U.S. Senate approval for every new member, Washington won that fight; only Poland, Hungary, and the Czech Republic would be admitted in the first cut.

Once the political debate was closed, the main diplomatic task became damage control in Moscow. With Polish membership, the alliance would border Russia for the first time, along the Baltic exclave of Kaliningrad (Königsberg) that the Soviet Union had wrested from Germany in 1945.[26] And even though NATO, in the wake of the cold war, had sharply reduced its total troops, deployed the troops in a defensive pattern, and promised not to place any outside units or nuclear weapons in Poland under the contemporary lack of threat, the psychological stress on the former superpower would be great.

Nor could the West expect a smooth transition for alliance expansion just because the Soviet Union had tolerated East Germany's leaving the Warsaw Pact and immediately becoming a member of NATO as a result of the GDR's merger with the Federal Republic. In one sense, East Germany had been Moscow's biggest prize from World War II and was the hardest for it to give up. Yet ever since the time of Catherine the Great, the Russians had been in awe of the Germans' technological and military prowess. The one thing they did not want to have happen was for a dynamic reunited Germany to "renationalize" its defense and foreign policy, go it alone without the constraints of its allies, and possibly become more assertive. On balance, binding the Germans into the Western alliance seemed the lesser of two evils.

No such considerations applied to Poland in the late 1990s. The Russians had no comparable awe of Poland, which Moscow regarded not as a major player like Germany, but only as a subordinate buffer zone insulating Russia from the West. Nor could Moscow hope to receive any financial compensation for the "loss" of Poland equal to the largesse Bonn bestowed as recompense for the "loss" of the German Democratic Republic.

Nonetheless, the West still proceeded from the assumption that with enough diplomatic effort it could expand NATO in cooperation rather than confrontation with Moscow—and calculated in any case that its foreign policy would have little political impact on a Russia absorbed in its own economic troubles. The oligarchs who held both economic and political power in Russia would want to preserve their profitable deals with the West rather than force a clash, Washington concluded, while the disillusioned and struggling Ivan Ivanovich would not easily be mobilized against the West on abstract questions of superpower status.

Out of deference to Moscow as well as out of internal policy disagreement, then, the West moved only slowly to take in new NATO members; it avoided surprises and signaled each step to Russia well in advance. While helping to train the tiny new armies in Estonia, Latvia, and Lithuania and signing a charter anticipating future NATO membership for the Baltic states, the West postponed this especially sensitive question to the twenty-first century and left its implied security engagement in this militarily indefensible region to discreet joint Scandinavian or Partnership for Peace exercises. It made the unilateral pledge to refrain from nuclear or NATO troop deployments on the territory of Poland and other new alliance members under the existing low threat.[27] And it established the NATO-Russian Permanent Joint Council to give Moscow, as the shorthand had it, "a voice but not a veto" in alliance policy debates. In addition, the Group of Seven leading industrial powers conferred prestige on Russia by taking it in as the eighth member at its annual summits. And this package helped secure a mild Russian reaction when NATO did make the formal decision in the summer of 1997 to admit the first new central European members. Noting the Russian equanimity, Western proponents of NATO expansion said I told you so, while opponents who had predicted more dire consequences observed tartly that history sometimes forgives mistakes.

The West, with some arm twisting of Ukraine and Turkey by the United States, further offered Moscow the adjustments Russia sought in easing CFE conventional weapons restrictions on its flanks. NATO secretary-general Javier Solana argued forcefully in Moscow that NATO enlargement should actually help Russia by consolidating democracy, stability, and peaceful behavior to its west. A country that had its hands full with unrest in the Caucasus and central Asia, he suggested, should welcome having a peaceful border it did not need to worry about.

As the key new NATO candidate, Poland added that the promise of membership would actually give it the confidence to improve relations with Russia, since with NATO backing it need not fear that its overtures might be misunderstood as subservience. In 1997, shortly before he became defense minister for the second time—and shortly before Poland went on NATO's short list—Onyszkiewicz explained the paradox:

Because we were more or less accepted as viable applicants to NATO, we could try to intensify cooperation with Russia. In 1989, or 1991 even, we would have run a certain risk that if we did try to make some opening to Russia, this could have sent the wrong signal to the Russians—that Poland is hesitating or has still not decided where our place is. So before we were able to embark on this policy, to develop our "Ostpolitik" [détente with the east], we had not only to define our position but also to get acceptance from the West.

He ticked off the areas of rapid improvement already appearing in bilateral relations, including contracts for delivery of Russian gas and Poland's rise to become Russia's fourth-largest trading partner, after the United States, Japan, and China. "In that context, if new Zhirinovskys came up, [with NATO membership] we could afford to give them the benefit of the doubt" and not react with countermoves that might increase tension, he continued. "If not, we would be too jumpy to do so. Look who has the worst relations with Russia—Estonia, just because it is so vulnerable."[28]

Assessing the situation in mid-1998, a year after NATO's firm promise of admission and a year before formal induction, Bartolomiej Sienkiewicz, director of the Polish Eastern Studies Center, echoed Onyszkiewicz's observation. The Russian foreign policy elite has now begun treating Poland with new "normality" and "equality of rights," he found, and has dropped the old "imperial superpower" arrogance toward an inferior. President Yeltsin, far from regarding Polish activism in the region as trespassing on Russia's sphere of influence, marveled Sienkiewicz, even complimented visiting Polish president Alexander Kwasniewski about Poland's policy toward Ukraine, the Baltic states, and Belarus.[29] The Balts also sensed a new respect in Russia's treatment of them, despite the continuing Russian feuds with Latvia and Estonia about ethnic Russians in those countries.[30]

The Poles are thus convinced that the three new central European members that were admitted into the alliance in 1999 have neither soured relations between Russia and the West nor—in the contrary fear of some prominent U.S. opponents of enlargement—weakened the alliance. Hungary contributes positively to NATO by providing important bases for its operations in the former Yugoslavia. (The Czech Republic does not figure in the criticism, since it is a small country located south of the historic arena of East-West confrontation and therefore does not cost the alliance anything in its defense commitment.) Poland, the main actor, contributes above all the traditional esprit that distinguished its pilots in the Battle of Britain and its foot soldiers at Monte Cassino, suggests Nicholas Rey, U.S. ambassador to Poland in the mid-1990s.[31] Poland would also, in the unlikely event of any return to East-West military confrontation, provide the depth for maneuver that NATO lacked throughout the cold war—and in peacetime it certainly provides shooting ranges where live ammunition can be used without provoking citizen petitions against the practice. Nor is there any doubt that Polish home territory would be defended by forces that are no longer massed for attack on the west as in the old Warsaw Pact days, but are now deployed more evenly throughout the country.

In equipment, the Poles have better tanks than the Greeks and the Turks, and even the Italians and the French, says Onyszkiewicz. Under its $2.3 billion upgrading plan, Poland will essentially be wired into NATO's air defense by 2003; its fighter planes will mostly be equipped with alliance IFF (identification friend or foe) electronics; its communications will be essentially compatible with NATO's; and military maps will have been redrawn according to alliance specifications. While they will long remain as far behind the west Europeans as the west Europeans are behind the United States in advanced battlefield technology, with the prod of Target Force Goals assigned by NATO, they are at least heading toward the compatibility, or in NATO jargon, "interoperability," of their and NATO's main weapons by about 2010.

Ukraine and Other Neighbors

Poland's accession to NATO poses the question of how to deal with Ukraine as well as with Russia, of course. Ukraine, with territory and population matching those of France, has never had any lasting sovereignty of its own, and for the past three centuries it has been essentially a province of Russia. Its new independence of 1991 was widely considered illegitimate and temporary by Russians, even those of a liberal persuasion; the common expectation was that Ukraine would prove to be too immature to govern itself and would therefore fall back into Russia's lap fairly soon.

Yet any attempt by Russians to reclaim Ukraine—in the 1990s Moscow mayor Yuri Luzhkov ostentatiously claimed the Crimean port of Sevastopol, 800 miles away, as a Moscow municipal district—would be the first step to restoring the Russian empire and would probably be accompanied by an antidemocratic backlash in Russia. A stable independent Ukraine, by contrast, would be not only a buffer for Poland, but also a brake on reversion to an imperial mentality in Russia. As Volodymyr Vernadsky, the first president of the Ukrainian Academy of Sciences, warned almost a century ago, "Russian democracy ends where the Ukrainian question begins."[32] More positively, a senior Polish diplomat puts it this way today: "If Ukraine stays independent, Russia has a chance to become a normal nation-state."[33]

Kyiv was acutely aware of the dangers, and various foreign policy strategists in the entourage of Ukrainian president Leonid Kuchma campaigned hard for a NATO guarantee of Ukrainian independence— or, as second best, a "special relationship" with NATO that might exhibit as much alliance interest in Ukraine's continuing independence as in the independence of the Baltic states. In nonprovocative tandem with the NATO-Russian relationship, in the spring of 1997 the Ukrainians finally attained what NATO cautiously called a "distinctive" partnership—and the Ukrainians translated as their greatly desired "special" partnership. The showcase of the agreement was a joint NATO-Ukrainian commission that would parallel the new NATO-Russian council.

The impact of this symbol of NATO-Ukraine rapprochement on bilateral Russian-Ukrainian relations was immediate. Within a week of Moscow's acceptance of the NATO-Russian Permanent Joint Council and tacit acquiescence in Polish entry into NATO—and concurrent signing of the NATO-Ukraine partnership—Yeltsin reversed his six-year-long refusal to regularize relations between the two largest Slav states. He suddenly flew to Kyiv in May 1997, signed a comprehensive treaty of friendship, and agreed on the final Ukrainian and Russian shares of the former Soviet Black Sea fleet. Moreover, he acknowledged Ukrainian sovereignty over the previously contested Crimean Peninsula by paying Kyiv rent for berthing the Russian ships that would continue to be based in Sevastopol. In the eyes of the Ukrainians, this more benign Russian policy was the direct result of NATO's willingness to guarantee the security of neighboring Poland and to embrace Ukraine, even if not to guarantee its borders.[34] Linkage was sealed with the first multilateral Partnership for Peace maneuvers in western Ukraine and with a bilateral Ukrainian-American naval exercise off the Crimean coast. For the cash-strapped Ukrainian navy, it was a godsend to have Washington foot the bill every now and then for joint exercises that got the Ukrainian ships out of their docks.

A further accomplishment of NATO enlargement, long before the first accession of new members, came from the prophylactic effect of the very hope of admission to NATO. The alliance categorically bars entry to any candidates with unsettled territorial or other disputes with neighbors. And this precondition for EU as well as NATO membership—plus the compelling contrast between French-German reconciliation and shared prosperity on the one hand, and the Yugoslav vortex of self-perpetuating war and impoverishment on the other— combines to form a powerful incentive to peaceful resolution of conflicts. Between 1996 and 1998, points out NATO secretary-general and subsequent high representative for EU foreign policy Javier Solana, in a series of "bilateral agreements the central and east Europeans have solved problems that have been with them since [before] World War II: Romania-Hungary, Romania-Moldova, Ukraine-Russia—all the century-old issues have been solved. Why?" he asks. "Because we said very clearly, you have no chance of being in this club [unless you make a real effort to solve] minority problems."[35]

The most arresting examples of NATO's preventive peacemaking are to be found in Hungarian-Romanian and in Polish-Ukrainian rapprochement. Hungary is the one country that ended up after the terrible genocide, forced migrations, and border changes of World Wars I and II with many of its countrymen—3 million, or close to 30 percent of the state's present population—still outside its national borders. The largest portion of these live in Transylvania, which was awarded to Romania by the Trianon Treaty of 1920. In any earlier period in the region such a condition would have justified irredentism and belligerence toward neighbors; and some nationalist demagogues in Hungary indeed sought to exploit this grievance in the early 1990s, as did some Romanian nationalists. Yet in both cases the chauvinists lost to moderates in elections—primarily because both countries craved NATO membership and did not want to spoil their chances of admission by bad behavior. There are still strains over Hungarian provision of benefits to ethnic Hungarians abroad and the ethnic Hungarian demand for a Hungarian-language university in Cluj, but Budapest is now seeking joint solutions with both Bucharest and local Transylvanian communities rather than inflaming disputes.

The second major example of NATO's prophylactic effect—rapprochement between the two largest nations in the region—is even more striking. For centuries Ukrainian peasants rebelled periodically against Polish landlords in the region they cohabited between the Vistula and the Dnepr rivers. The two were still butchering each other throughout World War II, and hostility continued after the postwar settlement awarded this territory to Soviet Ukraine (and awarded compensatory German lands in the west to Poland). At the end of the war, Poles avenged themselves by brutally expelling millions of Germans from the area around Breslau (Wroclaw), a city that had been German for centuries; in mirror image, Ukrainians brutally expelled Poles from Lviv (Lvov), a city that for centuries had been essentially Polish and Jewish. Additionally, Polish authorities scattered the Ukrainian minority in Poland throughout the country and broke up its social networks. There was, in sum, far more historical tinder to kindle conflict between Poles and Ukrainians than between the Serbs and Bosniaks, who for generations had lived together in mutual tolerance and intermarriage.

Yet in the post–cold war world both Warsaw and Kyiv decided that traditional enmity is dysfunctional and that they could only gain by adopting Western norms of peaceful cooperation. And although the phenomenon is largely ignored by journalists with a professional bias toward strife and violence, the record suggests that the really startling news on this once bloodthirsty continent is not the atavistic chain reaction of savagery and war in the former Yugoslavia. It is instead the unprecedented chain reaction of reconciliation among old enemies in central Europe. In an arc spreading east from western Europe, war is becoming as obsolete as feather boas or ruling monarchs. "Poland and Ukraine have a window of historic opportunity to repeat what has been achieved by France and Germany after the Second World War," commented Ambassador Ihor Kharchenko of the Ukrainian Foreign Ministry during the run-up to Polish acceptance into NATO. And a senior Polish diplomat echoed his words:

> We are the window to the West for Ukraine, as Germany is the window to the West for us. We would not like to become part of NATO if the price for that would be giving Ukraine back to

Russia. Basically, they [the Ukrainians] say that bordering the Western system would be beneficial and would enhance their independence and security too—provided that NATO expansion would not be a deal with Russia that Poland gets in, but the dividing line is the Bug River, and Ukraine is on the wrong side.[36]

In this spirit Poland is conspicuously sponsoring Ukrainian entry into various central European regional groupings and the two defense ministries are forming a joint peacekeeping battalion, with English as the common language of command.

Perhaps most important in the long run, some Poles are even revisiting Polish-Ukrainian history to explain to their compatriots that Poles were also perpetrators—and not just victims, as the enduring myths would have it—in past Polish-Ukrainian clashes. "History in this part of the world plays an enormous role. As we learned in Yugoslavia so [disastrously], so here too, clearing up the historical problems is very important," observes one of the new breed of historians.[37]

In a similar spirit Ukraine and Romania have set aside their quarrel over Serpent Island. Poland and Lithuania have resolved feuds over the language and other rights of minority Poles in villages around Vilnius, and these two countries are also forming a joint peacekeeping battalion. Among themselves the Baltic states—besides joining Norway, Denmark, Sweden, and Poland in the Nordpol Brigade in Bosnian peacekeeping—are also fielding a joint "Baltbat" battalion, and are setting up "Baltnet" to monitor their airspace. Bulgaria, Romania, Greece, and Turkey have established a multinational Balkan force, with headquarters located in southern Bulgaria during the first four years. Other joint peacekeeping units are proliferating in the region as well, on the models of the Eurocorps, the German-Dutch Corps, the Spanish-Italian Amphibious Force, and NATO's multinational AWACS surveillance-plane crews.[38] Germany, Denmark, and Poland have set up the Multinational Corps Northeast, with staff headquarters in Szczecin (but no German or Danish troops are stationed there, in accord with NATO promises to Russia). The Baltic states, and even Kyrgyzstan, Kazakhstan, and Uzbekistan, have all created joint army units for peacekeeping, and Estonia, Latvia, and Lithuania have also formed a common Baltic squadron. Poland, Hungary, and the Czech Republic, obliged to share their medium-term defense plans with NATO, even started showing them to each other before their induction.

In varying degree the new democracies are being socialized to the West's culture of voluntary cooperation and the talking out of disputes.

NATO-EU Synergy

At the beginning of the new millennium NATO, in part by methodical bureaucratic planning, in part by desperate improvisation under threat of self-destruction during successive Balkan crises, has in fact established itself as the center of Europe's post–cold war security system. The British vetoed French efforts in the mid-1990s to subsume the languishing Western European Union under the EU to produce an independent European security and defense identity (ESDI) that might rival the American-led NATO. The Europeans and Americans finally agreed in 1996 on a formula for developing ESDI within the NATO framework.[39] Under guidelines for "Combined Joint Task Forces," the WEU would borrow "separable but not separate" NATO assets for humanitarian, peacekeeping, or even peace making operations that the WEU might wish to conduct but the United States would not wish to participate in directly.[40]

NATO secretary-general Solana argued passionately that this should produce an ESDI that would give Europe more muscle and at the same time strengthen transatlantic security links by letting the Europeans share more of the burden of common defense. To the European and American defense elites he preached, "Clearly, Europe is not yet the strategic actor it wants to be, nor the global partner the United States seeks. But these shortcomings do not result from 'too much United States,' as some still claim, but from 'too little Europe.' That is why the European integration process is not only relevant for Europe's own identity, but for a new transatlantic relationship as well."[41] What Europe needs now, he continued in an interview, is a wider "architecture based on different institutions acting toward shared strategic objectives," with each component open to taking in new members. He lauded as exemplary the cooperation in Bosnia among NATO, the UN, the EU, and the Organization for Security and Cooperation in Europe (the successor to the CSCE). And he anticipated that these overlapping organizations, along with the Contact Group and the WEU, would increasingly coordinate their crisis prevention, crisis management, and, if need be, peacekeeping and peace making in Europe.

Certainly in peacekeeping, as the former Yugoslavia demonstrates, NATO is at the hub of Western responses because of its political cohesion, clear defense mission, integrated command, and ready forces. "Again NATO is the pole. It has the procedures, capabilities, philosophy that make all the difference," Solana declared. "Without the Article 5 command structure it would be impossible to do peacekeeping or peace enforcing. We have the [central organization], structure, and readiness. In thirty days we put 60,000 people into Bosnia. . . . Without [that] spine, it would be very difficult to be effective."[42] U.S. defense secretary William Cohen concurred, stating, "NATO-led Partnership for Peace operations will be the operational coalitions of the future."[43]

Internally, what initially seemed to be NATO's most difficult tasks— deemphasizing nuclear deterrence, downsizing and reorganizing main forces that had been trained to repel a massed frontal attack, and cutting the number of headquarters from sixty-five to twenty—went fairly smoothly.[44] The alliance's decades-old innovation of an integrated peacetime command with constant multinational rehearsals proved its value in readiness for unprecedented multinational operations at short notice under widely varied conditions. The byproduct of military transparency and trust in allies' intentions and capabilities resulting from shared medium-term planning provided reassurance to members. And NATO's core function of collective security and stability has been maintained in successive "strategic concepts" and extended to fill the old vacuum of Poland.

In addition, Spanish forces have now been fully integrated into the NATO command, ironically under the Spanish Socialist secretary-general of NATO (Solana) who once opposed Madrid's entry into the alliance. The old Spanish-British quarrels over the Rock of Gibraltar, though they have not been resolved, are being finessed without detriment to NATO operations. And if the alliance is no closer to curing Greek-Turkish enmity, it has at least averted the worst danger by establishing rules to keep the two countries' navies and air forces apart in the Aegean Sea and coaxing them into joint maneuvers with NATO in 1998 for the first time in thirteen years.

By contrast, the thirty-year-old anomaly of Paris's withholding of French forces from NATO's integrated command remains. The initial gestures of rapprochement by President Jacques Chirac in the mid-1990s led nowhere, as he demanded too much in insisting that a French general get the alliance's southern command, which includes the U.S. Mediterranean Sixth Fleet. The Germans, who hoped they might be able to mediate, started with some sympathy for Chirac, but lost it as his position hardened.[45]

NATO's various internal adaptations to the post–cold war world were perhaps commendable in their execution, but they were essentially predictable. What has been much more surprising, by contrast, has been the Cinderella Partnership for Peace. It began as an evasion of enlargement, at a time when the Clinton administration had not yet made up its mind on the issue, but it has now turned into both a preparatory school for that enlargement and an effective framework for organizing pan-European security space and softening the line between NATO and non-NATO Europe. An ongoing "Mediterranean Dialogue" is being conducted in this program, and partners discuss common ways to fight terrorism and illicit arms trade. Increasingly, partners, including Russia, not only take part in ad hoc exercises, but also station "Staff Elements" at the NATO military headquarters (SHAPE) in Mons, Belgium, and at regional commands; in the future they are expected to do so at subregional commands as well.

The military Partnership for Peace and its political companion, the Euro-Atlantic Partnership Council, which meets monthly at NATO headquarters in Brussels, are both immensely popular among the more than three dozen participants.[46] The alliance is a "magnetic pole," in Solana's words, and enables NATO "to shape the nature of security" in Europe.[47] "The Partnership can act as a catalyst for a common 'culture' of security cooperation which has never before existed in Europe," he declares.[48] Already it is expanding the stable western European peace, which is far more than a balance-of-power interregnum between wars; it approaches the Kantian concept of an international community.[49] In the same way that today's young French and Germans find it absurd that their great-grandparents took war between their two countries for granted, so should tomorrow's young Germans and Poles find war unthinkable—and the day-after-tomorrow's Serbs and Bosniaks, too. Far from drawing new east-west dividing lines in Europe, then, Solana contends, the developing system of an enlarged NATO and an extended Partnership for Peace is "erasing" these lines. "Dividing lines meant you were totally in or totally out. Nobody is totally out today."[50] Any division today is due to different standards of living, he suggests, not to politics.

One further unexpected byproduct of the Partnership for Peace has been the increasing role played by the traditionally neutral countries. In the post–cold war world it is not obvious what neutrality might mean, but many citizens in these countries still remain attached to it. The Partnership program lets them cooperate with the Western alliance without committing to a domestically controversial goal of membership. In varying degree Austria, Finland, Sweden, and even Switzerland thus feel comfortable in joining Partnership exercises, while their armies get the benefit of working directly with their first-rate foreign counterparts. Eventually Austria, Finland, and Sweden might join NATO as full members, but in the interim all the neutrals find Partnership exercises a useful way to cooperate with NATO without compromising their neutrality. "Only the Alliance has force structures and decision-making mechanisms that are capable not only of providing for deterrence and collective defence but are also adaptable for robust crisis management and peace support operations," explains Finnish defense minister Anneli Taina.[51]

For all the improvisation, the fact remains that NATO today, as in the past, is generally appreciated for providing the security shield behind which the Europeans (and, by extension, the Americans in their transatlantic links) can pursue their happiness in tranquility. The cold war gap between the military-political NATO and the economic-political European Union has not yet disappeared, and there is still little institutional coordination between the two Brussels-based organizations. Yet both are aware, as the Poles keep stressing, that they are the obverse sides of the same coin of keeping Europe as peaceful and united as possible. The enlargement of both to admit central European members is proceeding in parallel and is increasingly being coordinated to avoid the disappointment and political backlash that might otherwise follow a hard and fast division between a smaller core of "ins" ready to join both organizations and a large number of "outs" pushed off into the distant future. In the period before their accession to the EU, the Estonians and Latvians could be rewarded with a faster track toward NATO membership when they heeded Western calls to ease restrictions on citizenship for ethnic Russians. Both NATO and the EU could be effective in blackballing Slovakia under Vladimir Mečiar's autocratic rule until the Slovaks themselves, as in 1998, voted Mečiar out of office to resume democratic development. Bulgaria and Romania could become prime candidates for the alliance's second enlargement precisely because the NATO prize could curb their disappointment at not yet qualifying for the EU prize.

The upshot is that the alliance's attraction (and discipline) of potential members, its ability to build coalitions on its own military core—and, of course, its assurance of U.S. engagement—make western and central European governments regard NATO as the continent's indispensable policeman. By the end of the 1990s concerns remained, admitted Paul Cornish, lecturer in Defense Studies at King's College, London—about the tricky "institutionalization of ad hoc cooperation," organizational details once the Combined Joint Task Force is actually called on to act, and, as usual, the cohesion of what is no longer an "alliance of necessity" but an "alliance of choice." Yet to his own surprise, he concluded that "[t]he U.S.-European security relationship is, remarkably enough, not too unhealthy. The prognosis is therefore good, although full recovery from the end of the Cold War will be delayed for as long as the patient chooses not to believe the diagnosis."[52]

Belief in this diagnosis would indeed be put to the test in 1999 as NATO entered its first hot war, in the Connecticut-sized corner of Yugoslavia called Kosovo.

CHAPTER FIVE

Present at the Second Creation: European Monetary Union

If NATO lurched into strategic evolution as it was confronted by the Bosnia and Kosovo crises, the European Union marched into strategic evolution by provoking crisis—then extricating itself. At this game the Germans excelled. It was an unusual method of agenda management, especially for risk-averse Teutons. It was, however, the only approach possible for EU activists if they were to steer, and not just be buffeted by, the whirlwind of post–cold war change.[1]

Crisis, 1994

Certainly, in the two years after Maastricht Europe exuded crisis. "Europe is failing to prosper," sadly concluded an editorial in the *Financial Times*.[2] "Euro-gloom" was the topic of a six-page *Newsweek* special, and "The Europe Question: Ill or Dead?" a headline in the *International Herald Tribune*.[3] "This is not just an ordinary Euro-cycle," warned the *Economist*," but an "identity crisis of a scale that is only beginning to become clear to its members." The Maastricht Treaty, it continued, is "an almost insulting irrelevance."[4] "Are all our creative energies exhausted?" asked George Steiner plaintively in the *Frankfurter Allgemeine Zeitung*.[5] And even true believer Peter Ludlow, at the Centre for European Policy Studies in Brussels, felt obliged to boost morale by asserting, "The post-Maastricht crisis is far from being terminal in character."[6]

In the face of this adversity, Kohl's approach, as usual, was to dismiss naysayers, continue on course, and wait. Once again he displayed his patience (as his staff preferred to call it), or his formidable capacity to do nothing for long periods (as adversaries saw it). He kept repeating that the German question could be laid to rest only by binding Germans "irreversibly" to Europe.[7] He doggedly pursued his defense against Bismarck's nightmare by encircling Germany with peaceful, friendly, and increasingly prosperous neighbors. And no matter how much the European enterprise might seem to pall, no matter how daunting the polls showing that two-thirds of Germans opposed giving up their lovely deutsche mark, he persisted. He continued to preach the need for strengthening the European institutions and building toward political unity, for enlarging the EU to admit central European members and remedying the "democratic deficit."[8] He continued to insist that deepening and widening were compatible, that widening would compel the deepening needed to escape paralysis, to keep the EU "*handlungsfähig*," or able to act.[9] It was a German vision of progress by crisis that would soon apply also to monetary and economic union.

Kohl's constant reiteration of his old positions was met with cynicism by those immersed in the contemporary malaise. But he never expected his words to inspire the public and mobilize it for European action. That kind of oratory he reserved for campaign exhortations to the faithful of the Christian Democratic Union (CDU). In between elections his rhetoric was much more of a holding action, keeping issues alive in a contrary climate while waiting for outside pressures to compel emergency solutions and create consensus for the policies he advocated. Now he waited for highly centralized France and Britain to discover the virtues of decentralization and devolve some of Paris's and London's concentrated powers to local or regional communities (like Germany's own practice of "federalism," with considerable powers reserved for the *Länder*, the constituent states). He waited for "cohabitation" to sort itself out, as he would soon wait for France's newly elected neo-Gaullist president to decide, like the Socialists before him, that the only thing worse than being in lockstep with the Germans is not being in lockstep with them. He waited for France's new industrial lobbies to confront the old French peasant lobbies and trim anachronistic agricultural subsidies (and for a long enough break between Bavarian elections to do the same in Germany). He waited for Tony Blair to move into 10 Downing Street and cooperate with the City to marginalize the Tory euroskeptics. He waited for Germans, if not to love the euro, then at least to resign themselves to its inevitability. And above all, he waited for the logic of events to persuade others that his course of action, if not brilliant, was probably less bad than any conceivable alternative.

Within Germany, then, there was no visible movement in European integration as Bonn took over the EU presidency in July of 1994. The one client Kohl wished to convince of the wisdom of monetary union was the Bundesbank. The main EMU drama was being played out behind the scenes in Frankfurt—until the "Lamers paper" hit the fan.

Multispeed Europe

On September 1, 1994, politicians were jolted out of their vacation reveries by a paper called "Reflections on European Policy," written by Wolfgang Schäuble, chairman of Kohl's conservative parliamentary caucus, and the caucus foreign policy spokesman, Karl Lamers.[10] Germans had waved goodbye the day before to their last Russian occupation troops. A court in Berlin was about to try the octogenarian East German secret police chief, Erich Mielke, for his role in the killing of hundreds of would-be escapees on the strip separating the German Democratic Republic from the Federal Republic of Germany. The German general election campaign was in its last weeks; the constitutional amendment on asylum had halved the influx of foreigners and, it seemed, the appeal of the far right.

Economically, German growth was in the process of rebounding to 2.9 percent a year, but overall the EU share of world exports in manufacture had dropped by a fifth since 1980, with a particularly wide gap in high technology exports. EU unemployment was again up to mid-1980s levels of over 17 million, or some 11 percent, after having dipped to just 8 percent in 1990. The EU single market now applied, in the "European Economic Area" instituted at the beginning of 1994, to the EFTA countries of Austria, Finland, Iceland, Norway, Sweden, Switzerland, and Liechtenstein, covering a population of 380 million and accounting for 43 percent of world trade. This made the European single market more populous than the U.S. single market—and persuaded most of the EFTA governments that if they were going to live under EU economic rules anyway, they should at least enfranchise themselves to help write those regulations by becoming formal members of the Union.

Surprisingly, at this point only half of the necessary national legislation for the single market had been passed by all twelve EU states; Germany was one notable sluggard, largely because of turf claims by the *Länder*. Nonetheless, the foreign ministry machinery was already humming with daily "COREU" memos requiring answers within twenty-four hours on a growing array of EU issues delegated for bureaucratic decision. Secondment of young diplomats for tours in each other's ministries was also leading to novel pan-European meetings in which a German foreign service officer might well speak for the French delegation (though never would a Briton, however adroit at debating the other side, represent the Germans).[11]

In Frankfurt the European Monetary Institute was beginning its ninth month of operation under its Belgian chief, Alexandre Lamfalussy, and was starting to write detailed provisions for everything from the interconnection of large-value payments to the calculation of the sacred M3 money supply, for all the world as if it really expected a common currency to come into being.[12] The Banque de France, as required by the Maastricht Treaty as a precondition for handing over powers to the forthcoming European Central Bank, had been granted unprecedented independence a few months earlier. The French were still smarting from Sir Leon Brittan's steamrollering over their protectionism in the GATT negotiations. And Chancellor Kohl had cautiously joined his voice to those calling for more equitable sharing of EU costs.[13]

In part, the Lamers paper, as it was immediately dubbed, represented yet another prod to get things moving after two-and-a-half years of conspicuous stagnation. Such an effort was familiar enough from the past, and relatively uncontroversial. What set off a flurry of protest, however, was the paper's attempt to think through some basic conundrums. How, as new opportunity beckoned after the end of the cold war, could the deadlock be broken between those who wished to press forward toward "ever closer union" and those who adamantly opposed such deepening? And how could the fragile—and, apart from Poland, tiny—new democracies in central Europe be incorporated into the EU without bringing the Union machinery to a complete halt under ever more vetoes from its increasingly diverse members? As German foreign minister Klaus Kinkel again asked rhetorically, echoing his chancellor, "Should the convoy in future be held back by its slowest ship?"[14]

The German conservatives' answer to Kohl's and Kinkel's question was an unambiguous no. Those EU members who wished to do so should indeed proceed with greater integration among themselves in economic and monetary union, the Lamers paper proclaimed, as well as in fiscal, social, and foreign policy. A "strong center" should "counteract the centrifugal forces generated by constant enlargement and, thereby, . . . prevent a South-West grouping, more inclined to protectionism and headed in a certain sense by France, drifting apart from a North-East grouping, more in favor of free world trade and headed in a certain sense by Germany."[15] And the "strong center" must not let itself be held back by waiting for the laggards to join in.

The concept was hardly new; such differentiation had been explicitly written into the provisions for British opt-out from monetary union and the social charter in the Maastricht Treaty, as well as in the Schengen Agreement on open borders between consenting members. British prime minister John Major, eager not to be painted as the bad boy of Europe, had once again in the summer called for a "multi-speed, multi-track" Europe.[16]

Yet the Lamers paper immediately set off two firestorms. The first arose from the paper's indelicate identification by name of the presumed inner core of countries that should accelerate integration without regard for the hesitant. Only Germany, France, and the Benelux countries qualified. Italy—cofounder of the EC along with the other five and host to the original Treaty of Rome—was not among them. Nor was newcomer Spain. Fearing that they might forever be excluded, Rome, Madrid, and the other "outs" reacted angrily.

The second protest was an objection to the whole notion of "concentric circles," "two- (or three-) speed Europe," "multitrack," "variable geometry," "core Europe," "flexibility," "differentiation," or "avant garde," as the various code words had it. The very purpose of the European Union was solidarity, ran this critique; inner cores would divide rather than unite Europe.[17] Lamers had made another suggestion a year earlier, in August 1993: that decisions in the EU (except in the shrinking areas in which a veto could be applied) be made by a "super-qualified" or "double majority" of both member nations and the populations they represented. While this plan reassured the large states that they would not be forced into action, or payment, by the growing crowd of little partners, it aroused resistance among those small states whose disproportionate weight would be reduced.[18]

Moreover, behind the terse wording of the 1994 Lamers paper lay implicit German exasperation with the French; some French even suspected this was actually the main message of the exercise. Formally, of course, the alliance within the alliance was operating smoothly. Joint French-German initiatives routinely set the agenda for Council summits. The two had solemnly celebrated the thirtieth anniversary of Charles de Gaulle and Konrad Adenauer's Elysée Treaty in January 1993 and reaffirmed that their destinies were inextricably linked. Paris had finally agreed that the eighteen east German observers at the European Parliament could acquire full membership status with the next Europe-wide elections. To the relief of the Germans, the French were, for the first time in twenty-eight years, even taking part in a meeting of NATO defense ministers and looking as if they might finesse a face-saving formula for rejoining the unified military command.

Bilateral strains were growing, however. French officials were charging that the imminent accession of Austria and Scandinavia to the EU and the future accession of central European states would improperly augment German power. They were musing aloud about how much more they had in common with Britain than with Germany, both in defense issues and in the desire to avert a federal European polity of the sort Kohl seemed to want. Paris was advancing claims to EU financial aid for the French backyard of North Africa to match the claims of central Europe in Germany's backyard—with Bonn, as usual, tacitly understood as the designated paymaster. There were squabbles over defense procurement and the EU budget, which would require much higher contributions from Paris if Bonn paid less.[19] French fears that the EU was now shifting from its previous French domination (and constraint on Bonn) to a future German domination (and constraint on Paris) were fed by the increasing use of English, and not just French, inside the bureaucracy, by the imminent departure of Frenchman Jacques Delors from the Commission presidency, and by the promotion of Germany's top diplomat, Jürgen Trumpf, to become secretary-general of the European Council, a post second in power only to the presidency of the Commission itself. This trend was only reinforced by the use of English as the primary and German as the secondary language in the European Monetary Institute (EMI) and by German provision of a third of the EMI's professional personnel.

To be sure, the personalized French cabinet system rather than the more open German corporate culture still prevailed inside the Brussels bureaucracy and frustrated German newcomers. Moreover, Trumpf's job change could just as well have been interpreted as a weakening of the German drive for political union—with decisions increasingly delegated upward to Brussels—and acceptance of the French "Europe of fatherlands," in which Brussels would remain weak and every common European policy would have to be decided anew by agreement between sovereign EU member nations. That was certainly not the French reading, however. As differences mounted, even the unflappable German foreign minister, Klaus Kinkel, was moved to note, "The time has come . . . when our interests and those of the French do not necessarily coincide."[20]

In this context the Lamers message to Paris was unmistakable. France should recall its own interest in "deepening the Union prior to enlargement" and the need "to integrate a powerful Germany into European structures," it lectured. All EU members should avoid "regressive nationalism" as a response to "the internal crisis of modern society and by external threats, such as migration." If this were not done, there would be less responsible nationalists waiting in the wings, the paper implied, Germany not excluded. Paris and Bonn, in particular, should make strenuous efforts to keep separate interests from pulling them apart. But there would have to be an open debate about the excessive French-inspired trade protectionism and farm subsidies in the EU. The European Parliament (despite French opposition) should get more powers, to redress the democratic deficit. EU members must get beyond "intergovernmental cooperation, which might well encourage a trend towards a 'Europe à la carte.'" And Paris, like Bonn, would have to surrender more of its sovereignty to the common good.

Most pointedly, if France did not stop playing its balance-of-power games against the Germans and end its ambivalence about political union, the paper implied, Bonn could yet respond in kind. For all of its European instincts, Germany, if provoked, might itself revert to the very go-it-alone policy that other Europeans feared. Therefore, France "must rectify the impression" that, despite its flowery words about European integration, "it often hesitates in taking concrete steps towards this objective—the notion of the unsurrenderable sovereignty of the 'Etat nation' still carries weight, although this sovereignty has long since become an empty shell." The study then warned laconically about the unfortunate "tendency, gaining ground once again especially among intellectuals, to seek a 'German special path.'"[21]

The *Frankfurter Allgemeine Zeitung* posed the challenge even more bluntly. Will France give up more sovereignty for the sake of Europe or not? it asked.[22]

Since the threat of a copycat German reversion to a policy of competitive national interest issued from Kohl's parliamentary party rather than the government, the chancellor could and did deny that it carried any official sanction. Yet this was a fiction that was meant to be seen through. Sometimes, noted one staff member dryly, the caucus needs to say things the government cannot.[23]

The French-German tension was of course not resolved by Lamers's démarche. But far more trenchantly than the media sensation of German recognition of Croatia and Slovenia had done, it put down a marker that unified, sovereign Germany was not to be merely the French horse.

For an answer to its challenge, Germany would have to wait at least until Mitterrand's successor was elected in the spring of 1995.[24] In the meantime, Germany and the EU proceeded with other, incremental business. Luxembourg's self-effacing Jacques Santer was selected to succeed the activist Delors as the new president of the European Commission. Germany, as EU president, quietly—to avoid offending small states' sensitivities—institutionalized close coordination on agendas with its immediate successor (France) and with France's next two successors (Spain and Italy) in order to make mid-term planning more coherent and enhance the capacity to generate consensus. This advance coordination indeed paved the way for subsequent decisions on expanding the EU to the east, on financial adjustments, and the new opening toward Mediterranean neighbors that Paris was seeking. Not coincidentally, it also instituted a new intensity of consultation among the larger EU countries.

In October Kohl's reelection ensured the chancellor a tenure of sixteen years, longer even than the term of founding father Konrad Adenauer. Kohl's election campaign was fought on internal economic issues—increasing Germany's competitiveness was the main element of his platform—but his aura as the last European giant certainly helped reassure voters that he was the best guarantor of stability and predictability both in Germany and on the continent as a whole.

In December Germany steered the EU summit in Essen to avoid a transatlantic rift over Bosnia, to approve negotiation of European Agreements with the three Baltic states, to invite central European leaders to audit selected sessions of Council meetings, and to replace the previous ad hoc approach toward central European applicants for membership with a somewhat more coherent policy. Building on Commission studies and on a previous French-German bargain promising aid for Mediterranean states beyond the existing cohesion funds, the Essen summit further asked the Commission to write a white paper on widening. This would give the central European applicants a "structured relationship" (rather than just bilateral accords) and would provide more recourse against piecemeal EU protectionist lobbying. At the same time, it would divide the *acquis communautaire* into unprecedented pre- and postaccession categories, with the latter class much more extensive than it was when Greece, Spain, and Portugal were admitted. This labeling was controversial, since it conceded implicitly that some parts of the *acquis* were more sacrosanct than others, by identifying some legislation as a precondition for membership and leaving other categories to a multiyear transition period after accession.

In the first half of 1995 the French assumed the delicate task of chairing the EU even as they staged their own presidential elections. The EU's easiest enlargement went ahead as planned, enrolling those rich EFTA members who wished to become codeciders inside the EU. In referendums the Swiss and Norwegians had rejected their governments' advocacy of membership. Austrians, however, now felt settled enough in their identity to join the Union without being submerged by Germany (and to begin, finally, to face their willing collaboration with the Nazis in the past). The Swedes too, however strong their misgivings about letting Brussels regulate their snuff and Arctic farms, had narrowly approved membership, and the Finns gratefully seized the opportunity to slip further away from the compulsory deference to Moscow that they had endured for half a century.

In the spring the French finally, more or less, let the ten-year-old Schengen Agreement go into effect, abolishing frontier controls and authorizing mutual cross-border hot pursuit by police among seven of the nine signatories: France, Germany, the Benelux countries, Spain, and Portugal.[25] At the same time, the intrepid EU commissioner for agriculture, Austrian Franz Fischler, fired his first shot toward scaling down the expensive Common Agriculture Policy. Fischler now prepared the way for more radical cuts—even though the General Agreement on Tariffs and Trade (GATT) had just come into force, lowering EU external tariffs with cuts of more than a third in the value of subsidized EU farm exports.

At the same time, the German Bundesrat, or upper house, also fired its first shot aimed at European budget reform, approving Bonn's current contribution to the EU, but insisting that in the future Brussels must take less out of German wallets. Also in the spring, the European Commission issued its White Paper on Central European Accession, stressing the importance of establishing a robust legal and administrative infrastructure in the new democracies and depoliticizing many issues by snatching them away from politicians (and lobbies) and turning them over to technocrats for implementation. The white paper also relaxed social and environmental standards for the central Europeans by assigning them definitively to gradual postaccession transitions.

By far the greatest frisson of the season, however, was provided by the French election itself. The winner turned out to be neo-Gaullist Jacques Chirac, no friend of Europe in the past. His partners soon found him to be considerably more erratic than his predecessor. He reduced French troops in the Federal Republic to token numbers, abolished military conscription with only minimal prior consultation with his close ally Kohl, and sought anachronistic grandeur by resuming unilateral nuclear tests. The new Scandinavian members of the EU berated Paris for the substance of the nuclear tests as well as for Chirac's conspicuous failure to confer with his friends on an existential nuclear issue; Kohl withheld any public criticism.[26]

Nonetheless, the French-German alliance recovered. After some shakedown months, President Chirac made the same Cartesian decision as President Mitterrand had made before him—that the only way to contain Germany was to embrace both Kohl and Kohl's policies of fiscal discipline and European integration. And he drew even more far-reaching conclusions from this premise than had Mitterrand, especially on security issues.[27] Paris did not abandon—but neither did it stress—its vision of "a Europe of fatherlands." And Kohl, for his part, drew back somewhat from both impossible goals of political union and institutional redress of the democratic deficit.

Kohl never retracted these goals publicly, but at some point they ceased to be a staple of his speeches. Gradually—the precise metamorphosis will no doubt occupy doctoral candidates for decades to come—Kohl reversed his priorities. No longer did he cite Winston Churchill's summons for a United States of Europe and portray political union as the necessary prerequisite for monetary union. No longer did he champion enhanced powers for the European parliament. The first was unreachable, the second perhaps less desirable as his political antennae assessed a debating club comprising, for the most part, neophytes and political pensioners who never strove to form a government or even to write a real budget.[28]

In their place, Kohl came to regard monetary and economic union as the centerpiece. Inexorably, the exigencies of EMU itself would advance political union in Europe, he contended. In previewing the work of the 1996–97 Intergovernmental Conference that would prepare proposals on institutional reform for the next set of EU treaty amendments, Foreign Minister Klaus Kinkel echoed Kohl's new modesty.[29] And by the summer of 1998, Kohl would even be singing Britain's refrain about the need for more "subsidiarity" and convening a special summit on the subject.[30]

In the absence of clear signals of this shift in Kohl's own speeches, a few surrogates must be used to suggest the evolution of German policy. As early as the fall of 1993, one independent panel of German specialists on Europe concluded that a federal European state was no longer a realistic objective.[31] The Lamers paper of September 1994 did not address political union, but spoke only of the need "to deepen the Union in institutional and political terms before further enlargement."[32] Subsequently, Kohl's national security adviser, Joachim Bitterlich, was still hoping that Maastricht 2 would write a constitution spelling out federal and national competencies in the EU and increasing the powers of the European Parliament. A year later, however, a senior member of the foreign ministry policy planning staff set forth a German wish list for Europe that elevated "step-by-step evolution" with trial and error over any grander visions of political union.[33]

"At some point Helmut Kohl had to give up the traditional approach that he had believed in for many years, namely, that he would pursue both projects simultaneously, political and economic and monetary union," recalls a senior German official. "I believe that the negotiations on the common currency made it clear that our main coplayer, France, was not going to buy a currency union if we insisted that some sort of political union be created in parallel, and that is why we shifted our own argument from that traditional argument to the argument where we said once we have currency union, the rest will follow."[34]

By 1995, EMU was the name of the game.

EMU *as an Engine*

In no decision was Europe's new activism more manifest than in the plunge into monetary union. It required surrender of some of the most cherished attributes of sovereignty—and even if a shrinking world had already made such surrender a fait accompli, it was remarkable that European leaders willingly ratified that fact in a new supranational institution. Monetary union presumed the instant conjuring up of a potent new European central bank, whereas founding members' own central banks had evolved through trial and error over decades. It demonstrated faith that mutual commitments could be made and honored in a period of severe recession—and faith that when the inevitable crises arose, European leaders would muster the wit and the unanimity to resolve them. It presupposed enough enlightened self-interest for the Germans to give up their most precious asset and symbol, the deutsche mark, and waive any claim to the first presidency of the European Central Bank, in the sheer confidence that the economic approach of whatever central banker took the post would reflect the German philosophy anyway. It trusted that the EU could juggle the overloaded agenda of monetary union on top of historic enlargement and administrative reform and reapportionment of EU finances.

Certainly, no one knew whether EMU would actually work. No previous monetary union on such a scale had ever endured without a political union to enforce it. And if EMU failed after half a dozen or a dozen countries had already abolished their centuries-old national currencies, there would be no simple return to the status quo ante. Far from unifying Europe, critics argued, a single currency could bring down the whole edifice of the EU. The enterprise entailed extraordinarily high risk, in market probes, in the inevitable turf contests among institutions, and in strains over policy preferences among its disparate founding members.

Yet in a world of liberalized capital movement, the enterprise made sense. Daily flows of $1.6 trillion—equal to the total foreign exchange holdings of the world's major central banks—overwhelmed the capacities of central banks to stop any volatile run in inherently unstable financial markets.[35] And in a European market that was being knit together more and more closely, constant transaction costs between currencies were a drag on competitiveness and blocked continentwide financial economies of scale. Merging a dozen different currencies into one could help cope with both hazards. Logic and politics conjoined.

Under the Spanish EU presidency in the second half of 1995, then, bargaining about this most revolutionary of all the changes in the chaotic 1990s gathered pace. The issues now took shape that would frame the debate for the next three years, until the final decision to proceed with EMU in mid-1998. On a theoretical level, the main question was whether monetary union would really unify Europe—or would instead shatter the incremental integration already achieved.[36] On a policy level, the main point of contention was the strictness with which the criteria agreed on in Maastricht would be applied. The trick would be to devise some way to preserve both discipline and solidarity when the southerners, as it was thought, stood no chance of meeting the convergence criteria. The Maastricht Treaty had attempted to solve this riddle with enhanced transfers in the Cohesion Fund,[37] but four years later this no longer sufficed.

Moreover, even if EMU succeeded economically, it would divide Europe politically, opponents charged. If the specified majority of eight EU members defied expectations and met the criteria for monetary union by 1997, they would erect huge barriers between themselves and the others. And if a majority did not make the grade and a fallback minority proceeded in 1999, this would be even more divisive. It would set in cement the barriers between the elite nations of Germany, Austria, and the Benelux countries that already formed a deutsche mark zone—along with France, a guaranteed founding member in any case—and all those who were left out.[38]

In addition to these overarching issues, there were specific economic disputes. The broadest one focused on economist Robert Mundell's 1961 theory about what might constitute an optimum currency area. In size alone, the EU certainly qualified. Its population and economic output roughly matched those of the successful U.S. single-currency zone, and a case could be made that it was little more heterogeneous than a country in which per capita income in Rhode Island was twice that in Mississippi. Moreover, in terms of the foreign trade that would be crucial for exchange rates, the EU (excluding intra-EU trade) slightly surpassed the United States's tenth-plus of gross domestic product.[39]

The hitch would come when countries suffering asymmetrical shocks would not be able to respond to their problems with differential exchange or interest rates, since monetary policy would be the province of ECB technocrats—and fiscal policy, too, would be constrained, both formally and informally. A one-size-fits-all approach from Portugal to Finland would leave only two modes of adjustment to asymmetries (as in the United States): labor flexibility and substantial financial transfers to regions in recession.[40] Yet Europe's labor market was notoriously rigid, not only because its dozen languages and cultures made it hard for a laid-off east German riveter to seek work in a Spanish shipyard, say, but also because sheer stay-at-home habits—and high wages and related social insurance—discouraged people from moving.

The second tool of adjustment was similarly curtailed by the unwillingness of national governments, and especially the German paymaster, to fund EU budgets beyond the present modest ceiling of 1.27 percent of GDP—as well as by the limited legitimacy of the EU in redistributing wealth across countries. A large increase in the EU budget was considered in the 1970s and then rejected, and the huge U.S. equalizers, fluctuating tax revenues and welfare and disaster payments, simply do not exist across national boundaries in the EU framework.

To be sure, there are steady regional transfers from richer to poorer in the EU's structural and cohesion funds, but these are intended to serve long-term development rather than short-term adjustment; they do not begin to approach the scale of redistribution within the national borders of EU member states.[41] Moreover, the EU revenue system and common agricultural policy are regressive, favoring the richer countries (other than Germany and prerebate Britain, because of their lower receipts of CAP subsidies).[42] In any case, contends Deutsche Bank economist Norbert Walter, given today's networks of company branches, price shocks are more apt to affect all of Euroland than to hit different regions asymmetrically.

These economic risks featured prominently in the common American dismissal of EMU, even as monetary union took on new life in 1995. Yet they played only a subordinate role in European calculations about what was far more a political than an economic undertaking. Even in Germany, the key country that had to be convinced to surrender its currency, the pro-EMU consensus of the political elite derived more from notions of good European citizenship than from calculations of economic feasibility. The German government expected economists to devise ways to make EMU work, not write treatises about why it could not. The economics-driven Bundesbank in a sense did both, but its main arguments were oriented more toward the narrow goal of maintaining a hard currency than toward broader economic efficacy. The Bundesbank realized full well that in the end it would be used by the government to justify monetary union, but it accepted this instrumentalization to maximize its own bargaining power in writing the rules of the system.

In mid-1995 the first cracks in the German consensus did begin to appear, but they remained no more than cracks. The premiers of Bavaria, Saxony, and Lower Saxony—Edmund Stoiber, Kurt Biedenkopf, and Gerhard Schröder—might express doubts about the risks or suggest that EMU be postponed to a more propitious time, but they did not oppose monetary union as such. That way, they could appeal to voters' continuing fear of EMU without actually blocking the union. Stoiber and the Bavarian Christian Social Union could play the usual game of running against the federal government (even though CSU finance minister Theo Waigel in the Bonn coalition was one of the major shapers of EMU). Equally, Biedenkopf could appeal to the local patriotism of Saxons in his east German redoubt, display his superior economic knowledge, and tweak the nose of the chancellor who had long ago fired him as Christian Democratic Union party chief in North Rhine–Westphalia. Premier Schröder—the chancellor in waiting and a Volkswagen board member because of Lower Saxony's large bloc of shares in the firm—could show that he was staving off any Italian exploitation of non-EMU exchange rates to undercut German car sales, while still not derailing the enterprise of the century. In the end, only Biedenkopf would actually cast a sole vote against EMU in the Bundesrat.[43]

Under the circumstances, the fundamental controversy about unifying or splitting Europe quickly merged into the concrete issue of the rigidity or flexibility of the Maastricht criteria.[44] Here the knights of strict interpretation were led by the Bundesbank; for good measure Bundesbank president Hans Tietmeyer kept reiterating as well that monetary union could hardly work without political union. As corollaries, the Bundesbank insisted that a "critical mass" of transactions—

the figure of 90 percent was floated—must be conducted in the new European currency once it was introduced; that (in contrast to the position of the Bonn government) introduction of the new currency must be swift rather than gradual; that exchange rates must be fixed before adoption of EMU, to minimize market turbulence;[45] and that data used to measure compliance with the convergence criteria must be based on actual performance rather than forecasts.[46] Finance Minister Waigel, a close second to Tietmeyer in proclaiming that any budget deficit even a whisper over 3.0 percent would disqualify a candidate for EMU, happily exploited the Bundesbank's obduracy to strengthen his own hand in skirmishing with French, Italian, and Spanish colleagues—and with fellow German ministers, whose budgets he was slashing to meet the Maastricht criteria.

So obstinate was Waigel, in fact, that various foreign observers read into Germany's position a desire not only to exclude Italy, but also to wreck monetary union altogether by setting goals that not even Germany would be able to reach.[47] Some of these observers interpreted German declarations that Bonn would not pay more for EU enlargement—and that it needed more equity in EU dues in the next budget negotiation in 1999—to ask if Germany was not also abandoning enlargement and even tiring of the European project altogether.[48]

Not surprisingly, Germany and France were again the main gladiators as EU finance and economics ministers debated strict versus lax convergence at the first Ecofin meeting under the Spanish presidency in September. Bonn was striving to tighten the Maastricht criteria even more, and watching with some concern as the deutsche mark dropped to a nine-year low against the Swiss franc.[49] Paris, by contrast, had both domestic and pan-European reasons to press for a looser interpretation of the criteria. In Paris the jobless were mounting noisy demonstrations, blaming the austerity and unemployment on EMU. And if France could set the hurdles low enough to nudge its Mediterranean allies Spain and especially Italy over the top, it could expect its patronage to produce confederates against German might inside the club and avert competitive devaluations by Madrid and Rome.

Paris and Bonn did, of course, patch up their quarrels enough to issue a joint wish list for the forthcoming meeting of experts on institutional reform. Their list included nomination of a high-ranking "Monsieur X" to guide efforts at formulating a common EU foreign and security policy; more transnational cooperation in fighting organized crime; more majority decisionmaking; and a year-long EU presidency rotating among the four largest members, representing two-thirds of the EU population—Germany, the United Kingdom, France, and Italy.[50]

In this period the one strong constituency that the German government could rely on to back monetary union was Europe's transnational industry and finance. The myriad small banks that characterized Germany's unique financial landscape were less persuaded of the benefits from a revolution that would entail high relative costs for them in a total change of currency. The famous family niche exporters to the world of everything from shoes to specialized machine tools in Baden-Württemberg were equally skeptical. But the large firms that accounted for a hefty share of the third of German GDP that goes into exports expected substantial savings in transaction costs and exchange-rate risks. The large banks also welcomed the long-term chance to become global players by creating Europe-wide financial markets that might eventually compete with the U.S. market in variety and liquidity. The same sentiment prevailed among the Swedish and other transnational European concerns that saw themselves as the pioneers, well ahead of the politicians, in adapting to fast-moving globalization and the challenge of the Asian tigers that had outrun Europe in the 1980s. Already these companies were adopting pan-European strategies. Big business considered the days of national champions—and of national currencies—to be numbered.[51]

The German government thus had the full support of the Bundesbank and the large German industrial associations when it raised the ante in late 1995 and proposed a controversial "stability pact" to plug a major loophole in the Maastricht criteria. That loophole was the failure to specify what discipline would apply *after* monetary union came into existence. If wily candidate members manipulated their statistics for a few years to gain entrance, only to lapse back into inflationary habits once they were in the club, the Germans insisted they should be forced to pay automatic fines, especially on excessive budget deficits. To some this smelled like yet another German plot to scuttle EMU altogether.[52]

The French were appalled.[53] Kohl, undeterred, spoke optimistically in the Bundestag before flying to the last European Council of the year. Again he warned of the "real fears about the size and strength of united Germany," but once more he celebrated "the great success story of our continent" in European integration. He hoped for progress in the near future in common European foreign policy and home affairs, in EU institutions, in reducing the democratic deficit, and, of course, in agreeing on a stability pact and making the unification process "irreversible."[54] But soon he too would scale down his expectations, saying that this conference was only Maastricht 2, and after that would come Maastricht 3, and 4, and 5.

In Madrid the Council tossed the hot potato of a stability pact back to the Ecofin, sensibly dropped the EMU target date of 1997 in favor of the fallback 1999—and agreed to the name Germany favored for the new currency, the "euro." In addition, it acceded to the Bundesbank's demand in specifying that irreversible exchange-rate decisions for founding members would be made by early 1998 on the basis of actual 1997 performance, rather than more manipulable forecasts.

In the background, the Dayton Agreement had just been signed and the first IFOR troops were in Bosnia. Other signatories of the Schengen Agreement were reluctantly accepting Paris's retreat from some of the agreed open-border provisions after a series of bomb explosions in France heightened security concerns there. Traditionally undisciplined Italy, by heroic effort, had ratcheted its budget deficit down 1.5 points from the previous year—but that still left it at 7.7 percent, or two-and-a-half times the Maastricht standard, and its inflation was still at an unacceptable 5.4 percent. The EU feud over bananas was flaring up again.[55] Everybody was waiting for Tony Blair to get elected and move Britain out of its paralysis.

With some *Schadenfreude*, those who assumed the worst of Germany felt their judgments confirmed when Germany indeed failed to meet Waigel's own exacting standards for EMU in 1995—as it would again in 1996.[56] And they saw further confirmation of their suspicion that Bonn itself was turning anti-European as Germans began objecting more loudly to their disproportionate bankrolling of the EU budget and as some joined other Europeans in complaining that the European Court of Justice had arrogated too much power to itself.[57] Precisely because it did not want to fan voter resentment of the EU, the Kohl government gave out no official figures (nor did Brussels) analyzing Bonn's huge net contribution. But as the summit that was supposed to tidy up the Maastricht Treaty and set the EU's course for the future approached, Bonn did let its partners know that when the next apportionment fell due in 1999 it could not continue to pay three times as much as any other member (except for tiny Luxembourg) in terms of percentage of GNP.[58] Under the circumstances, seasoned Anglo-Saxon observers Edward Mortimer, William Pfaff, and Brian Beedham thought, respectively, that monetary union was fading away, that the conflict of national interests in western Europe was the sharpest since World War II, and that Germany was pushing Europe too far too fast.[59]

Yet the European actors held their course. When the intergovernmental conference on EU institutional reform finally opened in March of 1996 it was sheer anticlimax. It had no competence in the most sensitive issues—EMU, agricultural reform, and renegotiation of EU financial assessments. And where it did have formal competence, it had been granted no real authority by heads of government, who thought European policy was far too important to be left to diplomats. The conference beavered on for months to prepare for the Amsterdam summit, but it made no real progress in providing a framework for enlargement to the east or for writing the new EU "constitution" that it had originally been asked to produce.

In what may have been his last try before giving up on the drive for political union, Chancellor Kohl again declared a few weeks before the intergovernmental conference opened (and before another round of *Länder* elections took place in Germany), "European unification is in reality a question of war and peace in the twenty-first century."[60] In the spring of 1996, German voters, heeding his sentiment, rebuffed those Social Democrats who flirted with opposition to the euro—and confirmed Kohl's hunch that he could outlast popular reluctance to give up the deutsche mark. Indeed, Kohl's favorite polling firm, Allensbach, said as much in pointing to the low salience of the issue despite its high negative rating.[61]

Kohl's apocalyptic words about war and peace found a less positive resonance in England. As usual, some chose to interpret them as a German threat.[62]

The French were not similarly upset by Kohl's abstract hyperbole. But they continued to be disturbed by the chancellor's persistent lobbying for a very down-to-earth stability pact. They cherished a vision that was just the reverse of Kohl's. In the ideal world of the Elysée—despite France's signature on the original Maastricht agreement that the European Central Bank would be as independent as the Bundesbank, and despite the Banque de France's own new-found liberation from the politicians—the central bank tail should not wag the government dog. The technocrats—and the Germans' grail of low inflation—should not be allowed to override political judgment and accountability, especially when 17 million Europeans remained out of work. Other critics also asked sardonically if the intent was to push struggling economies under by draining even more money from them when they were in recession—and, now that monetary policy was being taken from governments, to snatch away the one remaining instrument of fiscal policy. For a year Paris and Bonn sparred with each other over these questions, even as they continued to issue pious joint proposals before every Council and ministers' meeting.[63]

And then a funny thing happened. Those who were paying close attention observed that potential candidates for monetary union were in fact growing together. The fierce arguments of the 1970s about convergence were suddenly passé. Everyone had internalized Bundesbank rectitude and the neoliberal orthodoxy (even maverick Greece was in the process of dropping its left economics). The new Scandinavian EU members, it turned out, were trimming their famed social welfare to the new financial realities and were even urging other EU members to aim for budget surpluses. So strong was the drive to get into the exclusive start-up club of EMU that the Maastricht convergence criteria had a preemptive halo effect, much as NATO's criteria for entry to the defense alliance modified central Europeans' behavior even before their countries became serious candidates.

Talking to visitors in Frankfurt's Eurotower in mid-1996, EMI president Alexandre Lamfalussy made no effort to hide his glee. France had achieved lower inflation than Germany for five years running, he pointed out; Spanish inflation was the lowest in forty years. Average EU inflation had been below 3 percent for two years. High debt was still a problem, but national long-term interest rates were also getting closer to one other. Exhibiting a skeptical *Wall Street Journal* editorial about EMU, Lamfalussy commented that all the newspaper's economic analysis was right on the mark—except that the paper had utterly failed to notice the most important development of all: the convergence that was happening before its eyes.[64]

As it turned out, there was even some hope in the air that the EU budget might be held in bounds despite all the new demands on it. The recipients of regional funds had prudently not drawn all the aid they were entitled to, precisely because they were trying to slim down to qualify for EMU—and EU grants required matching appropriations by the beneficiary. The EU therefore had some 20 billion Ecu of unspent credits, or almost as much as its yearly allocations for the purpose.[65]

For the public, however, all of the experts' gathering optimism was upstaged by the spectacle unfolding during the summer, as Finance Minister Waigel—despairing of getting his desired DM50 billion ($34 billion) cuts in the budget deficit through parliament—tried to count Bundesbank gold profits against the deficit. The Bundesbank, flexing its independence, vetoed Waigel on a practice that is routine in many countries, but not in Germany. The humiliated Waigel bounced back to block, along with Britain, an expensive plan for constructing Europe-wide transportation networks.[66] Italy announced, while northerners smirked, that it would return the lira to the European Monetary System.[67] The French floated a new idea, anathema to the Germans, of a G-7 type political club to steer EMU.[68] The European Commission started a major row in Germany by declaring illegal some subsidies that Saxony's premier, Biedenkopf, had granted Volkswagen.[69] John Major threatened to veto everything else until the continent lifted its embargo on diseased British beef.[70] The French engaged in yet another wrestling match about the "franc fort," which the politicians lost to the newly independent Banque de France under its strong-minded governor, Jean-Claude Trichet. The solid German burghers, who always invested in predictable bonds, suddenly made a rush for privatized Telekom shares and found they might like this sort of adventure after all. The *Economist* noted with satisfaction that the European Commission under Jacques Santer was making far fewer legislative proposals than it had under Delors.[71]

None of this persuaded American media or mainstream economists that EMU was anything but a pipe dream. In August 1996 a long article in the *New York Times* focusing on demonstrations against austerity in France and Italy noted that only Luxembourg, Denmark, and Ireland currently met the Maastricht criteria and concluded that nervousness about the project was growing.[72] In the fall, MIT economics professor Rudi Dornbusch debunked the "bad idea" of a "desperate bid for a common money" for readers of *Foreign Affairs*. "Experimenting with a new money is a bad idea at a time when Europe must face the tough realities of abolishing the welfare state, reintegrating millions of unemployed into a normal working life, deregulating statist-corporatist economies, cultivating the supply side of its economy, and integrating Central Europe," he lectured, and warned further that the euro might trigger a severe recession. Harvard economist Martin Feldstein, too, feared that monetary union would remove competitive pressure on Europe and distract it from what should be its top priority of structural liberalization—and might even lead to war. James Tobin, Nobel Prize winner and adviser to Presidents Kennedy and Clinton, argued that removing Keynesian stimuli could only increase unemployment.[73] Lawrence H. Summers, Harvard economics professor turned deputy treasury secretary and treasury secretary in waiting, was still dismissing the euro as a chimera.[74] Other U.S. commentators scolded the Europeans for giving priority to EMU while neglecting widening the EU to bring in the central Europeans.[75] Among big-name American economists, the guru of optimal currency areas himself, Robert Mundell, was one of the few in the countdown to launch who thought the euro could work reasonably well and would be the most important monetary innovation since the dollar displaced the pound during World War I—or even since the rise of the gold standard in the 1870s.[76]

The answer to critics by mainstream European analysts—including some who began as scoffers—was to reverse the cause-and-effect relationship and to expect that EMU, far from diverting attention from the pressing need for more efficiency and competitiveness, would expose deficiencies and force their remedy. The code word for this was that monetary union would be a "catalyst." Its transparency would accelerate in Europe a decade later the kind of reform that globalization forced on the more responsive U.S. economy in the 1980s.[77] It would compel politicians and businessmen to find ways to enable a shrinking work force to support a growing percentage of retirees and to augment funds to meet pension commitments that in Europe were running close to double GDP.[78] Presumably it would at some point even supplant broad social entitlements with means testing and shift income support toward investment.

By the end of 1996, after a year of working over its allies, Bonn at last won its stability pact, albeit with changes, at the stormy Dublin summit.[79] At the behest of the French—and after a screaming match between Kohl and Chirac—it was called a "stability and growth pact." Fines for budget deficits over 3 percent would not be automatic but would be subject to decisions by the Council of Ministers. Some rules were further established for links between "ins" and "outs," to guard against competitive devaluations by outs. German finance minister Theo Waigel came away still championing a "culture of stability"; French finance minister Jean Arthuis came away still promoting "national sovereignty." And the French still urged creation of a political club to oversee the European Central Bank, plus enough leeway for euro devaluation to challenge the dollar in exports.[80] Sample euro coins and bills were unveiled, with their deracinated, generic bridges and windows that would not favor one country's architecture over others'. Germany itself still did not meet the Maastricht criteria, and its growth had slowed to 1.4 percent.

In the homestretch from Dublin to the final decision to proceed with EMU in May 1998, the German approach of counting on crisis to force decisions truly came into its own. The underlying crisis was one of facts, as Kohl kept repeating; everyone knew that the global gun was at Europe's head to improve its competitiveness. Added to this was the manipulated crisis of deadlines as the tempo accelerated at each successive European Council summit, and compromises were wrestled out at 2 or 3 or 5 a.m., before releasing exhausted negotiators—and letting a sovereign Kohl debrief exhausted journalists. To the casual observer it sometimes seemed that no question was ever really resolved and no settlement ever final. The French kept raising anew what the Germans considered obsolete dirigiste or Keynesian demands; the Germans kept tightening the screws on the French, as on the Italians and Belgians, to let the central bankers administer the neoliberal orthodoxy as a technical task, without interference from the politicians. And through it all French and German officials kept issuing their periodic attestations of common European purpose—and the business world kept making its own adaptation, regardless of the political theater.

Thus, in early 1997, Bonn and Paris jointly proposed an EU-wide tax code to eliminate unfair competition. The first euro-denominated bonds went on the market. The Germans reluctantly acceded to French insistence that a political "stability council" must parallel the European Central Bank to coordinate economic management—but blocked giving it real authority. The French kept pressing for more powers for the large states within the EU; the Germans kept arguing that it would be counterproductive to set up a directorate that would alarm the small states. Tony Blair won his election, pledged British adherence to the EU social charter, let the Schengen Agreement on border controls be included in the 1997 Amsterdam Treaty—and gave parliaments to Scotland and Wales, in an intriguing example of the kind of political subsidiarity that London had long championed in the EU but rejected in its centralized government at home. Jacques Chirac called snap elections, which he lost to Socialist premier Lionel Jospin, who promptly told other heads of government that he wanted job growth above all and was not bound by any previous EMU deals. His colleagues hastily wrote an "employment chapter" for the looming Amsterdam summit (while stipulating that it must not cost anything). Mr. Political Union himself, Kohl, under pressure from his *Länder*, vetoed majority voting on immigration issues at the summit.[81] The truncated Amsterdam Treaty promised to bring the third pillar's asylum and immigration policies under the first, or Community, pillar and also to "communitize" justice and home affairs in five years, though it left common foreign policy in the second, intergovernmental, pillar. Although it no longer had any claim to being the anticipated EU constitution, the treaty went out to the fifteen legislatures for ratification. Paris called for EMU to be postponed; Bavarian premier Edmund Stoiber seconded the motion. The *Economist* devoted a special section to Europe's mid-life crisis, speculated that monetary union was dead, and wondered if EU enlargement to the east might not now be pushed far into the twenty-first century. *Die Zeit* asked, "Can EMU still be saved?"[82]

In late 1997 the war of nerves continued—though the *Economist* revised its obituary of EMU to note that while it took Mitterrand two years to drop the old French litany, it took Chirac only six months and Jospin only one month to follow suit.[83] The deutsche mark hit an eight-year low of 1.88 to the dollar. The dispute over subsidies for Volkswagen dragged on, as did haggling over the EU banana regime. Like a deus ex machina, the EU statistical agency suddenly told Bonn that, by the way, hospital debt should not be counted against the public sector deficit—and Germany's 3.2 percent deficit magically shrank to Maastricht's requisite 3.0 percent. Deputy treasury secretary Summers began taking EMU seriously enough to testify to the Senate Budget Committee that the euro should be viewed positively.[84] European investors began showing a new, American-like interest in equities, especially as the EU forced national telecom monopolies to accept competition in January 1998 and power suppliers to do the same in

February 1999. The phrase "shareholder value" joined "happy end" and other Anglicisms in the German vocabulary.

The sluggish European economy began picking up. The Asian crisis hit, and the four European members of the G-7 for the first time took an initiative in managing the world financial system by offering a second line of defense for South Korea. Chirac suddenly (without talking to his friend Kohl beforehand) nominated Banque de France governor Trichet as the first head of the ECB rather than Dutchman Willem F. Duisenberg, the candidate of the central banks and all other governments—and then floated the story that this deal had been quietly arranged with the Germans long before. The European Council met, wrestled its way through to a modified Dublin compromise all over again, and agreed to begin intensive accession negotiations in the spring of 1998 with Cyprus, Poland, Hungary, the Czech Republic, Estonia, and Slovenia.[85] The Council, none too tactfully, also told perennial candidate Turkey that it could join some day, but currently was not eligible even for the further waiting list of five central European states. Turkish officials, in fluent German, uttered rude remarks about Germans and said they would boycott the gala conference designed to make them feel better about their second-class status.

French-German quarrels continued to characterize Council meetings, nowhere more spectacularly than at the European summit to launch the euro in May 1998. There, European central bankers, through the intermediary of German chancellor Helmut Kohl, confronted French president Jacques Chirac for a tense twelve hours. In this round "le Bulldozer" won a Pyrrhic victory, establishing the principle that government leaders rather than central bankers select the president of the European Central Bank—but failing to budge ECB policy, and losing the French monopoly on the presidency of the European Bank for Reconstruction and Development to German Horst Köhler in the process.[86] Conversely, the central bankers won what they suspected was also a Pyrrhic victory as their ECB nominee, Dutchman Willem F. Duisenberg, was in effect appointed for only the first half of the inaugural eight-year term. Duisenberg wiggled out of being held to a fixed date for resigning, however, and in fact his designated French successor, Jean-Claude Trichet, also subscribes to a tough antidirigiste, unFrench approach. Bundesbank president Hans Tietmeyer demonstrated why his post pulls a higher salary than the federal chancellor's when he compelled this compromise, it was said, by threatening to resign otherwise (and thereby to scuttle monetary union altogether by withdrawing the Bundesbank's imprimatur). German commentary about the "lazy compromise" in naming the ECB chief was so negative that Kohl felt obliged to haul German president Roman Herzog before the cameras as stock markets opened the day after the Brussels summit to assure voters and investors that the euro was indeed a felicitous invention.[87]

Yet this tiff too blew over. The conclave decided that a full eleven EU members, including Italy and Spain, met the Maastricht criteria. The biggest surprise of all was just how small a role creative accounting played in this judgment. None of the founding members-to-be had a budget deficit of over 3 percent, at least officially, and five EU members even had a surplus. Their inflation was so low, at 1.4 percent, that most analysts ignored it. Growth ranged from 2.4 percent in Italy to 8.2 percent in Ireland. Italy and Belgium had accumulated debts double the Maastricht 60 percent, but they were working assiduously, as Maastricht made allowance for, to bring them down.[88] Divergent short-term interest rates did pose a problem, but the average EU fiscal deficit had dropped from 6.1 percent in 1993 to 2.4 percent in 1997.[89]

What accounted for this astonishing convergence was the inspired improvisation of "benchmarking" or "best practice" that politics adopted from the business world in the 1990s. In politics it had hitherto been axiomatic that bargaining among heterogeneous equals must degenerate to the lowest common denominator—and the more participants, the lower the commonality. In business, by contrast, investors watched to see who was getting the best returns, and that performance became the "benchmark" that all others tried to emulate. As converted to the novel politics of the euro, the *highest* denominator became the benchmark or norm for inferior performers to strive for and reach. The Maastricht hurdles had been designed to exclude the unworthy—but now they became instead those "benchmarks" for ratcheting up the poor performers. The Italian central bankers and finance ministers, who had imbibed the Bundesbank's anti-inflation gospel, exploited the requirements to force change on their crisis-ridden and almost bankrupt country—under penalty of Italian exclusion from the prestigious EMU founders' club if reform were rejected. So successful were they that when center-left prime minister Romano Prodi clashed with parliament over his 1997 budget cuts, the tables were turned. In any previous year in the past half century, an austerity that offended so many interlocking interests would have toppled the government in Rome. Yet this time, after gnashing of teeth, the tight budget was approved precisely because not doing so would have unseated the government and debarred Italy from the euro club. Remarkably, all this coincided with exposure of the "Tangentopoli," or "Bribesville," scandals, the conviction of one previous prime minister for fraud, the indictment of another for conspiracy with the mafia, and the flight of a third to North Africa to escape arrest.

Italian cabinet minister Beniamino Andreatta traces the metamorphosis back to the 1992 crisis that expelled the lira from the European Monetary System. Successively minister of the treasury, foreign affairs, and defense, Andreatta was intimately involved in the transformation. He, along with Finance Minister Carlo Ciampi and like-minded colleagues, insisted that the country's crony system of politics and economics had to end. They deemed modernization essential, in any case, for Italian exports to stay competitive in today's world, but the shame of ejection from the European Monetary System and the hope of qualifying for European Monetary Union gave them a tool of coercion. France might press for a slackening of the criteria to bring Italy and Spain into the EMU as a counterweight to German stringency; the Italians themselves would instead use the luster of "Europe" and the threat of rejection to compel their compatriots' conformity to the economic mores of that Europe.

With this resolve, in the summer of 1993 they concluded a social contract for moderate wage increases that fully deindexed pay for the first time since World War II (even if the price was a thirty-five-hour week in the name of job creation). They shaved the budget deficit from 9.6 percent in 1992 to 2.7 percent in 1997 and cut inflation from 5.4 percent to 1.7 percent, matching German performance; and they introduced a stability that let bond yields drop 6 points between 1995 and 1998, almost reaching German levels. The Banca d'Italia got full independence in 1992 in setting discount and Lombard rates and, with the zeal of a convert, controlled the money in circulation even more strictly than the Bundesbank.[90] A pension reform was introduced in 1997 that narrowed provisions for early retirement; comprehensive tax reform followed in 1998. Privatization and liberalization put state companies and stocks worth some $38 billion onto the market within four years; allowed more part-time work, so it cost less to create new jobs; pried open somewhat the closed shops of professional guilds; and let stores stay open longer. Segmentation of banks was broken down and transparency increased. Despite its continuing high debt-to-GDP ratio of almost 122 percent, Italy is now a net creditor.[91]

There is a long way still to go, says Andreatta. Italy must also implement microeconomic reforms, liberalize and decentralize more, debureaucratize, cut the number of required licenses, continue tax reform, and fully fund pensions for the 16 percent of the population now older than sixty-five. Ambitiously, Prodi—whose cobbled-together Olive Tree government of Socialists, former Communists, and former Christian Democrats was among the longest serving since World War II—planned, before he was unseated in 1998, to cut debt to 100 percent of GDP by 2003 and to the 60 percent required by Maastricht by 2016.[92]

As it turned out, the mid-1998 summit gave final approval to EMU in what was probably the only available window of opportunity. Russia had not yet collapsed economically, frightening Europeans away from any new experiments. And the rising European growth just before the Asian and Russian crises hit the continent's stock markets was producing economic cycles that were more synchronous for the eleven founders than they had been for decades. On the one hand, the solid rise in production, a current account surplus of 1 percent of GDP, and continental European bourses advancing 28 percent to Wall Street's 14 percent were gifts that no one had expected even a year earlier.[93] On the other hand, the convergence in low inflation, budget deficits, and long-term interest rates was the result of sheer political will and showed the normative power of the whole Maastricht project and its criteria. Member countries did remain far apart in unemployment levels, with Spain having double the high EU average. But the general correspondence gave the euro a favorable sendoff.

As a broad swath of Europe prepared for its first common currency since the time of the Roman Empire, Germany's "stability culture" had triumphed.

CHAPTER SIX

Present at the Rebirth: Poland and Central Europe

To the east, the central European states that suddenly escaped Moscow's domination in the 1990s were playing catch-up, reclaiming a (western) European heritage and pursuing their impossible simultaneous political, economic, and social revolutions.[1] Their goal in every case was to win admission to both NATO and the European Union. And in order to qualify for one of the most complex and sophisticated polities in the world, that of the EU, they had to cram into a few years the kind of institution-building and formation of social trust that western Europeans had taken a leisurely two centuries to develop.

To be sure, the central Europeans had Western models and advice they could follow, and Western financial assistance to help them do so. But the democracies and market economies they now strove to emulate were still alien. Their own mentalities and whole life experience (except for those Czech octogenarians who might still remember President Thomas G. Masaryk) came from an authoritarian environment, both communist and precommunist. There was no foundation of a stable middle class or civil society in any conventional sense.

The strongest popular motivation for the palpable yearning to become Western was probably the desire to attain the West's prosperity rather than the West's freedom and demand for individual initiative. Yet for those with incomes only a third of the EU average, expectations of reaching a Western standard of living fast were bound to be disappointed. First would come social pain, as the once unitary communist structure disaggregated into separate political, economic, and social components; the state no longer took responsibility for jobs; low but reliable welfare subsidies were cut; and men and especially women were laid off from bankrupt industries. Social unrest and perhaps angry, frustrated nationalism were likely responses to the jolts of systemic change, to widespread impoverishment, and simultaneous exposure to the sudden riches of the unscrupulous or even simply those with a superior commercial instinct.

Until 1989 democracy and prosperity had been synonymous—and an unattainable abstract—for central Europeans. By the early 1990s, however, the concrete risk was that democracy might become equated instead with hardship and disorientation. The largest test case was Poland, with a population of 39 million settled on the historical crossroads of Europe's armies.

Extraordinary Politics

In the autumn of 1989, Leszek Balcerowicz, the unknown finance minister in the sudden Solidarity government, looked at the calendar and at the Polish industrial shambles. He had, he calculated, ten weeks in which to destroy the entire existing system so that firms would not simply fall into the habitual cycle and on January 1 grind out their mindless central plans for yet another year.

"I remember every day, every night, every hour since September 1989," says one of his associates. Balcerowicz's team worked up to twenty hours a day, including Sundays. They had to fight not only the deadweight of old communists who still held the "power ministries," but also their own allies, most of whom urged caution and gradualness. "All the advisers and economists even were warning us: you are not prepared," the hardships would be too great, and "people would revolt. [But] sometimes it is much better to make a decision in time even if it is not a perfect one. It is better than a perfect decision made too late."[2]

So Balcerowicz allied himself with the radical course advocated most famously by Jeffrey Sachs, a Harvard fixture by that time. By December 29 his office had rammed twenty major laws and constitutional amendments through the Council of Ministers, the Sejm, and the Senate. By New Year's Day 1990, shock therapy was born.

It was the opening of what Balcerowicz christened a period of "extraordinary politics."[3] For a decade virtually the entire Polish population had been on patriotic strike against the communist government, which had outlawed the Solidarity trade union. When union hero Lech Walesa boldly converted a brokered Solidarity share in parliament into the communist world's first noncommunist government, voters were ready—for a time—to make sacrifices.[4] They would, in any case, not be consulted in parliamentary elections for several years.

Under these circumstances Balcerowicz determined to maximize the initial pain to get it over with as fast as possible, thus minimizing the total pain. He used the window of opportunity to free prices, slash government spending, privatize retail shops and services, make the zloty internally convertible—and kill the 640 percent hyperinflation of 1989.[5] Within weeks shortages and lines vanished. Red-cube kiosks sprouted on Warsaw's broad sidewalks to supplement the bazaars on the grounds of the Warsaw sports stadium and the Palace of Culture; there consumers could buy everything from Vietnamese fast food to shoes and jeans. But real prices rose from their subsidized level—by 40 percent for bread and 400 percent for electricity. Production plummeted. Unemployment grew. The standard of living dropped. Many union activists felt cheated as the very shipyards and factories that had been Solidarity strongholds proved to be uncompetitive in the harsh new market and lost their government handouts.

Nobody knew if this savage experiment with Schumpeterian destruction would really work.[6] Such a "leap into the abyss," as the Poles called it, had never before been attempted. Hungary was making the change more gently, having begun reforms twenty years earlier. Eastern Germany might be conducting the most massive privatization in history—but it was being absorbed into an existing and hugely successful free economy, that of western Germany. The Soviet Union would not collapse and start its reforms for another two years. That left it to the Poles to invent their own instant metamorphosis from central planning to chaotic market.[7]

Transformation was made all the harder by the simultaneous disintegration of political and ecclesiastical authority. Walesa started his disastrous "war at the top," splitting Solidarity. As a result of this fracture, in the 1990 presidential elections the unknown émigré demagogue Stanislaw Tyminski managed to defeat Solidarity prime minister Tadeusz Mazowiecki before losing to Walesa in the run-off. Even Walesa himself sometimes conceived of noncommunist politics in the mold of Poland's 1920s autocrat Jozef Pilsudski and believed that the way to introduce tough reform was for the president or the government to assert special powers, bypassing parliament.

Right-wing, anti-European nationalist groups also sprang up. Tiny "couch parties"—all the members, it was said, could fit on one sofa—won seats in 1991 under proportional representation, splintering the Sejm into twenty-nine bickering factions. Even the venerable and rather medieval Roman Catholic Church—for centuries the surrogate for the nonexistent nation and then for the not fully sovereign nation under Soviet hegemony—plunged in prestige from 90 percent approval in 1989 to 50 percent by the early 1990s. The once-reviled police and army were left as the most respected institutions.[8] Cynicism about all politicians was rife.

Socially and psychologically, too, disorientation threatened disaster. Opinion polls revealed Polish pessimism to be among the blackest in central Europe. Only 20 percent thought things were going in the right direction, while 58 percent were sure they were going in the wrong direction.[9]

"I wonder what would have been the fate of other countries," muses the associate of Balcerowicz, if Poland had not succeeded. "Now it is very easy to say what works—liberalization, stabilization, structural reforms. Then no one knew. We could have collapsed at least five to seven times." He cited three perceived national traits that many were sure would disqualify the Poles from building a competitive market system. The first propensity was summed up in the pejorative phrase "Polish economy," slang for any mess. Second was the short attention span of the Poles, their enthusiasm for rushing on to a new "straw fire"—and their subsequent rush away a moment later. Third was their admirable penchant for heroic martyrdom—but their obverse distaste for compromise and the mundane work ethic. Fourth, he might have added from countless jokes, was a peasant envy that predisposed Poles to claw down anyone who begins to succeed rather than admiring and emulating him.[10]

Besides, after four decades of communist centralism, Poland had no experienced managers, economists, or civil servants to implement a new system. The country's bureaucratized enterprises were immune to market incentives, worried Solidarity's own newspaper, *Gazeta Wyborcza*.[11] "I remember in 1989 many [ordinary] people and intellectuals said, 'Come on, you can't do it [carry out sensible economic reform] with Poles,'" relates the member of Balcerowicz's team.

Was shock therapy, then, a triumph of nurture over nature, the economists over the historians? Did it prove that if you can just change the economic system, even contrary human nature will respond rationally? Yes, says the Balcerowicz ally in retrospect, though he was not altogether convinced at the time. Then, in the frenzy of constant crisis, he really considered the issue only twice: once when Soviet president Mikhail Gorbachev invited Balcerowicz to Moscow in September 1991, then again when Yegor Gaidar, the architect of Russia's post-Soviet economic reforms, solicited Balcerowicz's views in January 1992.

> We wanted to encourage them, [to persuade them] that the cultural and psychological aspects are secondary to the institutions and rules of the game. We made a quick review of various successful economic and political reforms, in South Korea, Hong Kong, Singapore, Chile, western Europe, and Germany, in so many diversified nations and cultures. When you introduced a consistently tough economic program, it worked, in three different cultures. It was clear for me after our two years [that the old mind-set stereotypes] would not apply any more to Poles. At that time we were trying to strengthen ourselves morally, like soldiers on the battlefield. But now with hindsight I am sure it [really] is the case.[12]

Certainly success was not guaranteed. In the early 1990s polemicists still pointed to the Polish example as much to bury the whole notion of shock therapy as to praise it. In the first two years of the Balcerowicz plan, real wages declined 20 percent, unemployment climbed to 12 percent, GDP fell 35 percent, exports to the imploded Soviet Union dropped 90 percent.[13] Farmers' income halved as local factories closed and part-time workers returned to the inefficient tiny plots their parents had stubbornly clung to as they thwarted communist collectivization. Official figures categorized more than a third of Poles as living in poverty.[14] Nine million out of the 39 million population drew a normal, early, or disability pension—and devoured 15 percent of GDP. The budget deficit soared so far above guidelines that the World Bank suspended its $2.5 billion loan to Poland at the end of 1991.[15]

By mid-1992 the growing number of strikes had risen to 6,000 and threatened widespread social unrest. The newest of the shifting coalition governments threatened to substitute witch-hunts for policy. Early foreign investors encountered suspicious work forces that regarded them as exploiters out to destroy Polish jobs and competition. Surveys found that by now almost half of all Poles thought themselves worse off than before the changes; only 10 percent found their situation better; and less than a third approved the economic austerity.[16] The 3 million official jobless triggered memories of the pre–World War II gulf between urban, educated, and relatively well-off "Poland A" and the quarter of the population still stuck in rural, unskilled, deprived "Poland B."

The Turnaround

In retrospect observers identify 1993 as the turnaround year in which the Polish economy, the first in the region to recover from the systemic earthquake, grew by almost 4 percent, recording the fastest increase in Europe outside tiny, underdeveloped Albania.[17] Since the devil is in the details—and since the experience of Poland over the last dozen years has differed so radically from that of its postcommunist neighbor Russia—it is worth pursuing the most significant details since that watershed year.

On the ground the mood was still glum. In the early general election of 1993, popular discontent with economic hardship punished the Democratic Union, Balcerowicz's party of old Solidarity intellectuals; it could not muster more than 11 percent of the vote. Two parties of the center right (in their nationalist Catholic politics though not in their statist, often anticapitalist economics) won another 11 percent in an election in which only 42 percent of those eligible participated. In the tradition of the "liberum veto" (by which seventeenth-century Polish nobles deadlocked their assemblies, allowing any representative to veto any legislation), the rest of the center and right split their 34 percent of the votes so badly that all failed to reach the new 5 percent threshold required to enter the Sejm. By default, with a combined 36 percent of the minority that actually went to the polls, the formerly communist Democratic Left Alliance (SLD) and the Polish Peasant party, a former communist clone, took two-thirds of parliamentary seats and formed the new government.

The victory of the former communists was widely treated in the United States as a resurgence of the old cadres, but this was a gross misreading. From the beginning Jozef Oleksy, who would be the "postcommunist" prime minister in the government, and Alexander Kwasniewski, the young mastermind of the SLD coalition, had cooperated quietly with the reforms. Unlike the Russian communists, the new Russian plutocrats, the Ukrainian socialists, or Vladimir Mečiar's Movement for a Democratic Slovakia, the SLD's leaders, at least, were already genuine social democrats. Under the top layer, various "stoneheads" remained—but the leaders ran the party. And it made perfect sense for them to support a system in which their advantages in education and experience in the ancien régime would predispose the old communist cadres to learn fast how to read markets and prosper as the heads of newly privatized or "commercialized" firms.

In fact, in one of those twists of history, it was the nationalist Catholic right, along with the noncommunist left—including numerous Solidarity chapters—that protested most vociferously against disciplining the budget to affordable, noninflationary size by trimming subsidies and social welfare. And it was the SLD's coalition partner, the Peasant party, not the SLD itself, that insisted on protectionism for farmers and blocked the sale of Polish soil to foreigners.

The outcome of the constant tug of war between the SLD and the Peasant party was that the government—although its campaign platform had demanded higher wages, pensions, and agricultural handouts—basically carried on the Balcerowicz plan. Technocrat finance minister Grzegorz W. Kolodko did some fine-tuning and repackaged the policy as his "Strategy for Poland."[18] The SLD-dominated government wielded its majority in a far more coherent Sejm of seven parties to get inflation down even further, to 38 percent, to decelerate the increase in pension payments, to halve the budget deficit to less than 3 percent, and to cut taxes sufficiently to begin hauling black-market operations back into the legal economy. It fudged on mass privatization by choosing an intermediate road, "commercializing" enterprises still held by the state—that is, leaving ownership unchanged while cutting subsidies and subjecting the firms to market constraints. But it kept its hands off the new small and medium-sized private firms that were becoming the engine of the economy. Already the private sector accounted for more than 92 percent of trade, 80 percent of construction, and 46 percent of industry. Overall, 1.8 million private firms employed 30 percent of the work force and produced 48 percent of output.[19] The fledgling market economy, various Western observers ventured, had already broken loose from dependence on politics and would now forge ahead, no matter what governments did or did not do.

Consumption took off, belying the official 16 percent unemployment and confirming those who said the important point in the exhaustive opinion polls was not the negative reaction to abstract policy but the increasingly positive estimates of their own personal status by those interviewed. Auto and computer purchases soared. The subterranean kiosks in the passageways under Jerozolimskie Street in Warsaw got glassed in and gentrified (and began paying taxes). Upscale Polish traders now left the sports stadium exclusively to Russian and Ukrainian peddlers, whose annual $350 million in sales made this single bazaar the fifth-largest exporter in Poland.[20] Thirty-five-year-olds put to work the trading skills they had acquired in a decade of dodging communist customs inspectors with cars full of sausages and shoes. Twenty-five-year-olds began snaring well-paid junior management jobs in Western companies. One mathematics professor, a fifth-generation Blikle, suddenly became manager of the renowned eponymous conditorei on Nowy Swiat—and to his surprise became fascinated by the game of matching pastry flows with customers. The Szczecin and Gdynia shipyards, turned over to private hands, actually began making profits and finally bought out the famous but bankrupt (and still state-owned) Gdansk shipyard.[21] Poles began thinking, in a sea change, that individual talents and drive were more important for success than personal connections. Sociologist Henryk Domanski discovered that every third Pole considered himself to be middle class, about on a par with findings in the United States in the 1950s.[22] Some 50,000 "third sector" volunteer groups began lobbying for everything from environmental cleanups to education for the handicapped. Imperceptibly, the psychology of relative deprivation yielded to the psychology of rising boats.

By 1995 both the new pain and the new hope had helped the forty-one-year-old Kwasniewski to achieve the unthinkable and defeat the legendary Walesa in the next presidential election.[23] Warsaw still felt grateful enough to Walesa to appreciate his feistiness, overlook his proletarian manners and grammar, and approve him by a 2-1 margin. Rural and small-town dwellers, however, were anxious about the future and less touched by the promise of urban prosperity. They voted overwhelmingly for Kwasniewski, who had barnstormed in their villages, talked to them as if they really mattered, and represented a vanished tranquility. At the other end of the spectrum, 53 percent of all voters under thirty made the same choice. They identified not at all with the old-fashioned anticommunist electrician, but rather with the smooth-spoken yuppie who had willed away thirty-three pounds to fit into his Italian suits and now proclaimed an end to the polarization that Walesa still preached. The Polish "romantic-lyric approach to politics," suggested *Polityka* commentator Adam Krzeminski, succumbed to a new "Americanoid professional election machine."[24]

By now industrial production, and not just overall GDP, had recovered its 1989 levels. The zloty was holding its value so well that Warsaw never had to call on the Western-financed zloty protection fund and the fund was rededicated to helping banks restructure and deal with bad debts and then recapitalize them. Poland had just graduated from IMF stand-by conditionality. Official purchasing power may have been only 75 percent of 1989 levels, but new car sales had reached an annual 275,000 and were increasing. Inflation, though still high at 28 percent, was falling. Some 62 percent of the work force was employed in the private sector. Infant mortality was down from 19.1 per thousand in 1989 to 13.4 in 1995. Trade, following Soviet disintegration, was already reoriented to the West, with 53 percent of Polish exports going to the EU and 66 percent of imports coming from there.[25] Private Western banks, approving the trends, had followed the lead of creditor governments and forgiven half of the debt burden of $40-plus billion that the Republic of Poland had inherited from the People's Republic of Poland.

Kwasniewski's victory was a shock. Walesa could not even bring himself to attend his successor's inauguration. But the very normality of voting an icon out of office also suggested that the 68 percent of the electorate that voted this time was beginning to trust the new democracy and expected to influence it. The era of "extraordinary politics" was over.

Ordinary Politics

In the democratic dialectic, the new generation of leaders in the labor union wing of Solidarity mobilized for the next general election. They themselves had brought down the last Solidarity coalition government and handed the 1993 election to the former communists by refusing to work together. They were determined not to repeat that mistake. Marian Krzaklewski, Solidarity chairman and vehement Catholic critic of the new constitution for failing to accord God due deference, now pulled the fractious right together as Kwasniewski had pulled the somewhat less fractious left together. The stage was set for Poland's third fully free election in 1997.

The SLD, too—without Kwasniewski, who resigned from the party before taking his oath of office in order to be "president of all Poles"—began planning to expand its 20 percent share of votes in 1993 to 30 percent in 1997. It mediated compromises on abortion and on a new constitution that would be approved in referendum. It reaped the benefit of a continuing economic boom, as output growth averaged more than 6 percent from 1994 through 1997. It had negotiated the private debt relief. It had shepherded Warsaw into membership in the Organization for Economic Cooperation and Development, along with Prague and Budapest, and had seen Poland get a high enough maiden credit rating from Standard & Poor's and Moody's to borrow on capital markets at only 0.65 percent above the Bundesbank rate. Fast-growing labor productivity had brought average monthly wages up to $329.[26] Automobile sales were rising to an annual 478,000. By 1997 foreign direct investment stock was up to $16 billion, unemployment down to 12 percent, inflation down to 14 percent, public debt down to 53 percent of GDP, and the private sector's share 70 percent of the economy. As exports picked up, net international reserves doubled in two years, reaching $22 billion. Deficit and debt figures met even the tough Maastricht criteria for the European Monetary Union.[27]

Poland looked especially good in contrast to the Czech Republic, whose initially much-heralded economy fell into crisis in the spring of 1997 over stock manipulation, shortage of enterprise capital, and a soaring trade deficit. The more cautious Polish transparency and regulation of the stock exchange, and even the delay in privatizing large firms, turned out to be an advantage. Prague's early voucher privatization might have produced a nation of nominal shareholders overnight, but it neither restructured obsolescent industries nor gave them the necessary capital to start anew more rationally.[28] Nor did it give the atomized new "owners" any more say in running the companies, which continued to be controlled by the state-owned banks that managed the major investment funds. Instead, the distribution of shares allowed greater concentration of wealth in the hands of a few fund managers—Caribbean tax havens quickly gained new Czech residents—than did the sluggish Polish shift. It did not encourage the start-up of vibrant private small and medium-sized companies as, ironically, the Polish deadlock on large-scale privatization did. Nor—this was taken for granted—did Poland have the bandit capitalism of Russia, in which insiders bought privatized industries in sweetheart deals, stripped assets, and exported mineral wealth as millionaire rentiers, mixed inextricably with mafias, and reconverted their new wealth to become the political power brokers.

Warsaw's foreign policy also looked admirable to Polish citizens. Most important, their country was joining Hungary and the Czech Republic as the first eastern entrants to both NATO in 1999 and the EU in the early 2000s.

Under these circumstances Poles became much more optimistic. EU Eurobarometer surveys in fall of 1997 showed approval rates (positive minus negative responses) of 42 percent for the market economy,[29] equal to popular enthusiasm when "extraordinary politics" began in 1990 and sharply improved from the trough of 26 percent in 1994. Satisfaction with "country direction" in general, while a much lower 19 percent (49 percent approval, as against 30 percent disapproval), still registered a notable improvement over the rank dissatisfaction from 1991 (–41 percent) to 1994 (–29 percent). Domestic Polish surveys also showed 57 percent of families rating their financial position better than the previous year.[30] Correspondingly, 25 percent of households expected their financial situation to improve in the next year, while only 17 percent expected it to worsen; the gloomier figures in 1992 were 21 percent (better) and 34 percent (worse). The upbeat mood, suggested various analysts, indicated not only material improvement, but also an important psychological break from the old instinct to hide good fortune so as not to draw unwelcome attention to oneself.[31]

In the 1997 election the new Solidarity Election Action (AWS) triumphed, attracting all of the 34 percent of center-right voters who had squandered their votes in 1993 to win the largest single bloc of seats in the Sejm. Balcerowicz also triumphed, bringing the Freedom Union's share up to 13 percent and personally outpolling the more populist Krzaklewski in their common rust-belt Katowice constituency. Economic success, at long last, vindicated the author of shock therapy in the eyes of the electorate. "I am voting for Freedom Union because I care about my wallet," commented a Katowice voter, one of Balcerowicz's many eighteen- to twenty-nine-year-old yuppie supporters.

After seven turbulent years, it seemed, parliament had finally reached an equilibrium, with five relatively coherent parties reflecting real voter preferences. The AWS—though tempted ideologically to make common cause to the right with the reduced Peasant party and with the nationalist Catholic Movement for the Reconstruction of Poland, which also entered the Sejm with 6 percent—quickly chose a more centrist coalition with the Freedom Union. Two of the Freedom Union's grand old Solidarity fighters, Bronislaw Geremek and Janusz Onyszkiewicz, took the posts of foreign and defense ministers. And despite the rivalry between Krzaklewski and Balcerowicz, Balcerowicz again became deputy prime minister and finance minister, under moderate AWS prime minister Jerzy Buzek, and was given a relatively free hand in economic policy. Krzaklewski, who chose not to take office himself, secured a virtual ban on abortion, swift ratification of the languishing four-year-old Concordat with the Vatican, and a purge from the security services of anyone associated with the previous government.

The dozen AWS parliamentary deputies associated with the fundamentalist Catholic Radio Marija and the fifty-odd deputies at the right end of the broad AWS spectrum gritted their teeth, voted to cut the budget deficit to 1.5 percent, and accepted a Protestant as prime minister and a man of Jewish descent as foreign minister. The old Solidarity workers at the Ursus tractor factory burned EU flags to protest their loss of subsidies in the new era—but they were the exception that proved just how seldom Poles scapegoated the EU and the West for the hardships of transition.

True to democratic theory, voting out the incumbents broke up some of the patronage networks that had started to regroup under the previous government. The SLD had been restrained in making personnel changes in the foreign ministry, but—imitating Walesa—it had packed the television commission and boards of commercialized enterprises with its own cronies. For its part, the Peasant party had taken over many of the fiefs of voevod governors. And together, the two had passed laws to depoliticize the civil service, but had set experience requirements so high as to penalize democratic newcomers and lock in the old nomenklatura. Now the AWS built up its patronage networks—and within a few years would itself have to answer corruption charges with ministerial resignations.

The center-right coalition began energetically. It stepped up privatization somewhat and presided over a half decade of average 5.5 percent economic growth, the taming of inflation to a single digit, and productivity growth of 10 percent per year. It boldly initiated several major reforms simultaneously, restructuring the politically sensitive coal and steel industries and introducing pay-as-you-go pensions, more patient-paid health care, an overhaul of education, and local self-government. And, in the analysis of Warsaw sociologist Andrzej Rychard, by absorbing society's splits in government at a critical period in the transformation rather than polarizing views between winners inside and losers outside, it performed a useful service. The ideal of social harmony was disrupted periodically by tame Solidarity marches for better pay and by rowdy street protests of militant farmers led by Andrzej Lepper and his Self-Defense movement. But overall, strikes decreased, there was a good deal of pragmatic cooperation on the shop floor, and average wages that were shooting up by 7 percent a year created their own constituencies for further liberalization.

By mid-2000, however, the centrifugal pressures had grown too great for the coalition. With an eye to the approaching elections and under the pressure of a sharp downturn in worldwide and Polish growth that brought unemployment of 16-going-on-20 percent and would slow economic expansion to an annual 1 percent, the AWS rebelled against Balcerowicz's fiscal discipline. Budget outlays and deficits ballooned. The Freedom Union quit the government. By the general election in 2001, dogged by corruption scandals, the AWS reatomized; its quarreling constituent parts all failed to win the minimum number of ballots to get into parliament. Its more populist voters defected to elect nationalist, anti-European parties—Lepper's Self-Defense won 10 percent; the new League of Catholic Families, 8 percent, Euroskeptics together, a fifth of total seats—into the Sejm. The Freedom Union, too, vanished as its voters gravitated to make the new yuppie Citizens' Platform the second-largest bloc, with 13 percent. In a low turnout, the "postcommunist" SLD triumphed with almost half the parliamentary seats, to renew its old coalition with the Peasant party. It briskly resumed fiscal probity and made concessions in negotiations about EU membership. Firebrand Lepper became, briefly, vice marshal of the parliament and vociferously protested the concessions on land sales to foreigners. Centrist observers hoped the traditional Polish reverence for the Sejm would eventually domesticate him.

Catholics, Europe, and Jews

Nowhere is the ongoing assimilation of the nationalist right into the mainstream better illustrated than in the gradual evolution of the Catholic church. As recently as the 1980s Pope John Paul II had still hoped that devout Polish Catholics would save the secular West.[32] There were ample reasons for his hope. During the 123 years when Poland was partitioned, it was the church that kept the nation alive in the hearts of parishioners. Under Hitler's yoke, the church inspired resistance. In the communist era, the church was the only moral authority in the country. For decades Poland exported its surplus of priests to less faithful lands. In 1978 it gave Rome its first non-Italian pope in 456 years, and John Paul's pastoral visit to his native soil in 1979 altered politics by spawning the Solidarity trade union that would shelter under the church and in just ten years shatter the Russian empire.

The church that had thrived under repression, however, seemed far less endearing to many when it returned to power in the early 1990s, reinstated virtually compulsory religious instruction in public schools, got abortion severely curtailed, laid claim to property taken from it as far back as the nineteenth century, tolerated antisemitic slurs by Lech Walesa's Gdansk priest and other prelates—and, often enough, instructed its flock to vote for right-wing nationalists. The church fell in prestige, and by the 1993 and 1995 elections it found that even village voters ignored the injunctions of parish priests to vote against the pagan former communists.

Wounded, the Catholic Church withdrew from politics. In 1997 the hierarchy—apart from ten bishops acting on their own—did not tell Catholics how to vote in the May referendum on the new constitution, despite right-wing protests against the draft. Nor did the church back Krzaklewski in opposing the surrender of some sovereignty to multinational organizations, as sanctioned in article 90 of the new constitution. Nor did it issue any recommendations from the pulpit for the parliamentary vote in the fall. This new modesty signaled retreat from the triumphalism that old-style Catholics had hoped would dominate Polish politics and even vanquish the West's atheism and hedonism.

Yet in one last policy area—the European Union—the church still broadcast its old, rigid views. In an especially memorable sermon in August 1995, Primate Jozef Glemp portrayed the EU as an anti-Polish conspiracy that would bring pornography, divorce, and unbridled sex to the land. EU president Jacques Santer, from impeccably Catholic Luxembourg, immediately flew to Warsaw to invite the primate to visit Brussels—and, perhaps, to note that in the 1950s many western European Protestants had opposed the fledgling European Community as a conspiracy of Catholic Europe.

It took two years and two months before the primate actually accepted the invitation. But in the meantime, some rethinking had begun within the hierarchy. A small colloquium on European integration was conducted for a year at the Catholic theological academy in Warsaw, with contributions by pro-European Catholic politicians. There was one discreet briefing on the EU by bishops from the much more liberal German Catholic Church. And in November 1997 a small group of Polish prelates was finally ready to visit Brussels to meet Santer and other EU officials.

As the delegation departed from Warsaw, Cardinal Glemp declared, significantly, that the church was "not afraid of a united Europe. On the contrary, it is looking to the process with hope."[33] And on the group's return to Poland, Tadeusz Pieronek, the modernizing secretary-general of the bishops' conference, assured reporters that the church understood the pluralistic character of the EU—and, for its part, the EU respected the right of different faiths to make moral judgments on political and economic issues.[34] The church's change of heart was "the most important event of this past year," contended a west European diplomat in Warsaw. Radio Marija, shocked into silence, blacked out all news of the bishops' trip for its 4 million listeners.

Socially, Catholic attitudes toward Jews are also mellowing somewhat as Poland matures in self-government and responsibility. There may be no rush back to the open welcome that Prince Boleslaw extended in the remarkable thirteenth-century Statute of Kalisz, forbidding discrimination against Jews in court, letting them swear their oaths on the Torah, and protecting their life and property. Never again will three-quarters of world Jewry live, as in the eighteenth century, in the land of Oswiecim/Auschwitz. Nor, should the occasion again arise, will the primate ever be enthusiastic in his requests that provocative crucifixes be removed from the environs of the Auschwitz extermination camp.[35]

Within the Polish Catholic Church, however, there developed at least a grudging willingness to discipline prelates like Henryk

Jankowski, Walesa's parish priest in Gdansk, for disparaging Jews from the pulpit.[36] By January of 1998, the church for the first time even joined celebrations for Judaism Day. Among the intellectual elite there is a growing awareness that the everyday folk antisemitism that has survived even the disappearance of most of Poland's Jews is not acceptable. Certainly, in the government and presidency there is a desire to proceed with what may be the Poles' hardest reconciliation of all, more difficult even than Polish-German or Polish-Ukrainian rapprochement. Synagogues and cemeteries—though not private property—are being given back to the few Jews left in Poland. And in the capital a museum has been established to show the prewar life of the third of Warsaw's population that was Jewish.

Any new chapter in relations will have to confront the terrifying memory of a genocide in which 3 million Polish Jews died, along with 3 million other Jews and 3 million other Poles. Twenty percent of the country's population died, including a third of its city dwellers, more than half its lawyers, 40 percent of its doctors, a third of its university professors and clergy, and all but a tiny remnant of its Jews. In the aftermath of such loss the deep animosity between Poles and Jews has periodically erupted into polemics, as in the 1980s, over the movie *Shoah* and the novel *The Painted Bird*, in the 1990s over commemoration of the dead in Auschwitz and restitution of Jewish property, and in the early twenty-first century over the Jedwabne massacre of 1941.

Both Claude Lanzmann's film *Shoah* and Jerzy Kosinski's novel *The Painted Bird* portrayed the Poles as willing abettors of the Nazi genocide. The movie unfairly blamed Poles more than Germans for the Holocaust, many Poles thought; it took no account of the Polish record of unparalleled resistance to the Nazis and of Poles' saving some Jewish lives despite the especially draconian penalty of the death sentence for such acts in Poland.[37] The novel, sold initially as the semiautobiographical account of Kosinski's own childhood persecution, presented the haunting metaphor of the villager who snared drab birds, dipped them in garish colors, then released them to be rejected and pecked to death by their own species. That the novel turned out to be "inauthentic," as Kosinski's oeuvre came to be described—the author's family had in fact been protected during the war by the Polish villagers he portrayed in the novel as antisemitic—did little to lessen its strong impact, especially on American readers.

Nor did disputes about Auschwitz in the 1990s help to lessen mutual hostility. President Walesa long refused to let a rabbi commemorate the fiftieth anniversary in 1995 of the liberation of Auschwitz and to lead prayers for the dead there, and the Polish Catholic hierarchy insisted on maintaining a cloister at the site of the extermination camp long after Jews first complained about it. Walesa then compounded the insult by stalling for weeks before disavowing even halfheartedly the derision of Jews in a sermon by Fr. Jankowski that he himself had attended.

The first impulse for a new Polish-Jewish dialogue came in the mid-1990s, from then–foreign minister Wladyslaw Bartoszewski. Bartoszewski, whose tree grows in Yad Vashem for the Jewish lives he saved as a member of the Polish underground, appointed a special ambassador to the Jewish diaspora (as distinct from the state of Israel), Krzysztof Sliwinski. The new ambassador had been a biology professor at Warsaw University during the communist antisemitic and anti-intellectual crackdown of 1968. He had defended students who were ostracized as Jews and barred from continuing their education, then organized lectures on Jewish culture and rallied a few dozen volunteers to defy secret police harassment and clean up the desecrated Jewish cemetery in Warsaw. His new writ included advising the Sejm about legislation restoring communal property to Jewish communities, assisting in the revision of teaching about Jews in Roman Catholic seminaries, and serving as the channel for the efforts of the very active "Landsmannschaft" associations of American Jews to locate and restore Jewish cemeteries in their ancestral Polish towns. As he described his task, "Poland is trying to reach the level of mature Western democracies. It wants also to achieve international standards as far as minorities or different religions are concerned."[38]

Both Bartoszewski and Sliwinski defend the Poles against the more extreme accusations of antisemitism. "If there was an especially antisemitic mood in Poland, then why did 3 million Jews gather here?" asks Bartoszewski rhetorically. He points out that there were no state-fomented pogroms in Poland, as there were in Russia. And during the brutal German occupation, even though Poles were subject to house searches and summary death in a way Germans were not, an honorable few still did shelter Jews, as thirty trees in Yad Vashem confirm. There should have been more, but in times of stress "few people think of anything other than their own survival. When the house is burning, you think about your own dwelling. Anyone who doesn't do so is exceptional."[39]

After his upset election in 1995 and also after his easy reelection in 2000, President Kwasniewski, too, endorsed the endeavor to improve Polish treatment of Jewish issues. He intervened to stop construction of a shopping center opposite the entry gate to Auschwitz. He was a key mover in the year-and-a-half-long legislative, judicial, and negotiating process that finally evicted Kasimierz Switon and his hundreds of provocatively displayed crosses from the plot next to the Auschwitz concentration camp site. He also supported the first official investigation of the 1946 pogrom in Kielce, which admitted for the first time that Polish persecution of Jews in the 1940s was not just forced on Poles by their German occupiers.

Contrition will not be easy. The return of Jewish cemeteries to the Jewish community is agreed in principle, but many of the burial grounds were destroyed in the past half century without a precise record of where they were located. Others have been covered over by buildings or roads, and fewer than half of the 1,020 Jewish cemeteries in existence before the war are still identifiable. Typically, in the very locality where the Statute of Kalisz was promulgated, a fight raged for years between the World Council of Orthodox Jewish Communities and local officials over a site that was once a cemetery but for three decades had been a sports field for a school for handicapped children.

Disputes about restitution of Jewish private property seized by Germans and Poles in the early 1940s or by the communist government in the late 1940s will be even harder to resolve. Individual descendants have claimed some 10 percent to 20 percent of these properties; various Jewish organizations contend further that the remaining 80 to 90 percent of once Jewish property for which there are no identifiable heirs should be awarded to Jewish groups collectively. The Polish government maintains that it cannot restore these buildings and lands without opening a Pandora's box, since whatever provision it makes for Jews it will also have to make for Germans expelled from the western third of present-day Poland as the Soviet and Polish borders shifted west after German defeat in World War II.

Already this standoff has poisoned other intended areas of Polish-Jewish cooperation. Some potential American donors to the new Jewish museum in Warsaw have refused to give money unless property is restored. Artur Hajnicz, a Polish Jew who was instrumental in postwar Polish-German reconciliation—and who as a Senate adviser opposed restitution because of potential German claims—was so offended at being branded an antisemite by fellow Jews over his tolerance for Germans that he subsequently refused to have anything to do with a Polish-Jewish dialogue.

Beyond this concrete issue—and even harder to deal with—is the psychological confrontation. Is Polish goodwill going to solve the problem? asks a Western ambassador in Warsaw. "I doubt it seriously, because there is a deep, abiding anti-the-other-guy sense on both sides here. The world Jewish community cannot stand the Poles, and no doubt the level of antisemitism in this country is deep and pervasive, the taxi-driver approach. There is a generation, probably two generations of Jews, in the U.S. who think of Poland as the place where all evil was done. It rubs off on the Poles."

In this climate the shift of the dialogue from recriminations about the past to present cooperation that the Polish government seeks is far more easily said than done. It may even seem undesirable to many of the 40 percent or so of world Jewry descended from families that lived in Poland before they were driven out or killed. Their collective memory of the country is harsh. They do not want to forget the whiplash of both communist and anticommunist discrimination against Jews in Poland, the first clearly demonstrated in that antisemitic purge of 1968, the second in popular blame for hated communist rule on the many secularized Jews in the party and secret police. Above all, they do not want to dilute remembrance of the Holocaust. Since the 1980s this memory has been at the heart of a renewed sense of Jewish identity in the United States. For many—in Polish experience this is more true of American than of Israeli Jews, and more true of Jews who have never lived in Poland than those, say, who were expelled from Poland in 1968—a fixed part of Holocaust memory is antisemitism in the land of Auschwitz. They suspect that efforts to turn dialogue toward the future, or even to enshrine an extinct tradition in the planned Warsaw museum, could belittle the horror.

On the Polish side Sliwinski senses a healthy new interest in Jewish life and culture that goes far beyond a "superficial political" interest. Polish-born Yiddish writer Isaac Bashevis Singer, who was ignored by Poles when he won the Nobel Prize in the 1970s, is now a best seller. Krakow sponsors popular Days of Jewish Culture every year and has had an influx of Jewish visitors since the release of the movie *Schindler's*

List. Eighty master's theses and ten doctoral dissertations were written on Jewish themes in Poland in 1994, some 500 books in 1995. And in the mid-1990s the Polish-Israeli Friendship Society, which Sliwinski had helped found when it was still illegal, received 4,000 entries about local Jewish history from high school students hoping to win a trip to Israel. Moreover, Sliwinski points out, the Polish media have become much more critical of antisemitic manifestations. Solidarity underground publications broke the taboo and wrote about the Kielce pogrom in the 1980s; the weekly *Wprost* dug out more information about the pogrom in the 1990s; *Gazeta Wyborcza* even unearthed antisemitism in the sacrosanct Home Army during World War II.

And in 2000 Polish filmmaker Agnieszka Arnold broadcast her grim documentary *Where Is My Older Brother Cain?*, *Rzeczpospolita* reporter Andrzej Kaczynski wrote companion front-page articles on the obscure eastern Polish village of Jedwabne, and Polish-American sociologist Jan T. Gross published his book *Neighbors*.[40] All recounted what happened on July 10, 1941, as the divide between Nazi-occupied and Soviet-occupied Poland shifted, and Polish villagers brutally herded up to 1,600 of their Jewish neighbors—men, women, and children— into a barn, to be burned alive. Gross did not accuse the Poles of ingrained "eliminationist" antisemitism, as Daniel Goldhagen accused the Germans of.[41] He argued that such a terrifying loss of normal human inhibitions could occur only in a time of terror, of Nazi and Soviet sadism and the devastation of war. Yet no extenuating circumstances could excuse the brutality of this day, the defensive lies about it that persisted for half a century, or the generations-long ostracism by Jedwabne villagers of those few Poles in their midst who furtively hid, fed, and saved seven of the town's Jews.

The reaction in the Polish media and in Polish kitchens was very different from reactions to previous revelations of pogroms. In the year 2000 the primary reflex was not defensiveness, but unprecedented soul-searching. Surprisingly few seized on subsequent information that there may have been fewer Jews murdered on that day—or that there may have been more than just a few Germans in the area—to put Polish guilt in a more favorable light. Poles, more self-confident and more accustomed to exercising national responsibility after ten years of democracy, could finally afford to be more self-critical. The political class of the nation that had suffered the most casualties per capita of any large country in World War II symbolically buried its long, bitter feud about whether Poles or Jews had been the more victimized. Many Poles, especially younger ones, felt the same nausea and remorse that so many young Germans had felt in 1945. Many who had grown up proud of the Poles' unparalleled resistance to Nazi occupation and their country's historical role as the suffering Christ among nations, took their first real reckoning of Polish antisemitism. "If you say Poles are heroes and that is part of me, then you have to say these acts [at Jedwabne] are also part of me," mused Martyna Laszewska, a twenty-eight-year-old tax lawyer. Poland's heroic exceptionalism, like the German *Sonderweg* half a century earlier, began to die. Poland's "two memories" and "two cataclysms" were no longer mutually exclusive.[42]

NATO *and the European Union*

Poland, like Germany before it, has now turned its back on the hoary concept that its destiny must be a special path that was morally superior to the West's present-day pragmatism. Poland's journey to accept as its model the antithesis of martyrdom in the West's inglorious tolerance, mundane legal process, and sometimes egotistical individuality began with its fraught reconciliation with (West) Germany—and ended psychologically with membership in western Europe's organizing institutions, NATO and the European Union.

The new Polish-German friendship—the bedrock of peace and stability in central Europe—began when Roman Catholic bishops from both countries, against bitter opposition, issued a joint statement in the 1960s forgiving and asking to be forgiven for past cruelties. Those cruelties were understood to be the deaths of 6 million Poles under Nazi German occupation and up to 2 million ethnic Germans after 1945, as more than 10 million ethnic Germans were expelled from what became Polish territory. Reconciliation continued with Chancellor Willy Brandt's kneeling in grief at the Warsaw Ghetto in the 1970s. It spread to the grass roots as millions of ordinary Germans sent packages of food and clothing to ordinary Poles after Solidarity was banned in the 1980s, and Poles began to distinguish between democratic West Germans and East German "Prussians." Rapprochement was formally sealed by bilateral treaties of friendship and recognition of borders between Poland and the newly united Germany in 1990 and 1991. Its crowning symbol was Poland's award of the Order of the White Eagle to a German—Helmut Kohl—for the first time after World War II. In the past decade Germany has been Poland's special champion in the EU and (along with the United States) in NATO—and has drawn France into regular consultations, in the Weimar triangle.[43]

For Poles, their westward orientation, and its acceptance by the West, was confirmed by membership in NATO. The alliance freed them from being squeezed between Germans and Russians and reassured them that they could entrust their very new friendship with Germany to a postnational European and transatlantic framework. "For over two hundred years, when foreign leaders put their signatures under documents concerning Poland, disasters were sure to follow," Foreign Minister Bronislaw Geremek reminded suddenly teary NATO ambassadors in late 1997, as they united on the simple protocol anticipating Polish, Czech, and Hungarian accession to the alliance. "History has been an unforgiving teacher to us," the fragile-looking, iron-willed medieval historian continued. But "eight years ago we undertook to unlive the past, to restore Poland as a free, democratic, and truly sovereign nation. We have since spared no efforts to return to the roots of our culture and statehood, to join the Euro-Atlantic family of democratic nations. We will not rest until Poland is safely anchored in Western economic, political, and military structures." On this occasion, he concluded, by contrast with the past, "Poland's friends" were signing "a document which is a source of joy, pride and hope for me and my compatriots."[44]

As part of its duty in the "Euro-Atlantic family of democratic nations," Poland accepted the obligation to continue Europe's post–World War II chain of reconciliation to its east. The Polish and Ukrainian publics might still be far from any resolve to "forgive and ask to be forgiven" for past slaughter and forced migration, in the Polish and German bishops' trenchant formulation. But from the top down, the Polish government has cultivated its own special relationship with the Ukrainian government. New Polish foreign ministers tend to make Kyiv their first port of call. A Polish-Ukrainian peacekeeping battalion is operational. And Warsaw has joined Western donor nations in contributing $10 million to help build a new sarcophagus around the Chernobyl nuclear power reactor.

With Lithuania, too—here the psychological gulf is not so great—Poland has sought rapprochement and mutual respect for each other's minority. These two nations are also forming a joint military battalion, and Warsaw is providing helicopters, radar, and patrol boats to the start-up Lithuanian army.

President Kwasniewski, mindful of others' sensitivities, has rejected in an interview the notion of Polish "leadership" in the region. He approves, however, the formulation that Poland is "exporting stability." And he characterizes this key role of Polish foreign policy as ensuring that as Warsaw rejoins the West, no new East-West line of tension will arise on Poland's eastern border. To this end Warsaw is promoting entry of all central European states, including the Baltics, into the EU and NATO. Here, too, Poland is following German precedents; Kwasniewski willingly accepts the analogy with current German promotion of Polish, Hungarian, and Czech membership in the West's two clubs.[45]

Militarily, to qualify for entry into NATO, Poland quickly redeployed its troops away from the massed preparation for attack to the west characteristic of the Soviet era to more even distribution throughout the country. In compliance with NATO transparency, Warsaw provided the alliance with its first five-year defense plan even before it was admitted to the alliance. It established civilian control of the military, depoliticizing both old generals who bonded with Russian counterparts in the Warsaw Pact and those who played partisan politics with Walesa. Without complaint, it accepted an assessment of dues under which it pays 2.48 percent of common NATO costs—more than Turkey, Greece, or Spain. (As the Poles calculate it, this will still be a bargain, since they will save money by pooling defense they would otherwise have to finance from national funds.)[46] It is putting officers through crash courses in English to meet the most rudimentary requirement for "interoperability" of forces. By now it already has division commanders who have graduated from the German Bundeswehr Leadership Academy. Poland, along with Hungary and the Czech Republic, has participated actively in NATO's Partnership for Peace program with non-NATO members; before their own entry into the alliance, the three nations accounted together for 75 percent of the program's activity. It is further offering the alliance large, unpopulated training grounds for the kinds of noisy exercises—including even the firing of live missiles, should NATO wish—that are by now taboo in Bavarian villages.[47]

More broadly, Poles also maintain that their gallant military history—from repelling the Turks in Vienna in the seventeenth century to

Monte Cassino in the twentieth century—shows that they take their army very seriously. They contribute the largest contingent of troops to UN peacekeeping forces. And as defense minister, Janusz Onyszkiewicz highlighted the 65 percent popular approval—in contrast to the inhibitions of voters in the United States, Germany, and every other NATO member state—for sending national troops abroad on any alliance missions. Warsaw's zeal for the alliance, Western diplomats in Poland note, make it a staunch confederate of the United States in NATO's inner councils, by conspicuous contrast to the French allergy to American leadership.

For a country with purchasing power higher than Turkey's, but still only about half the level of that of Spain, Portugal, or Greece, preparing to join the EU will be far more difficult than preparing to join NATO.[48] Agriculture will have to be modernized and farm plots increased from the present eight-hectare average, as economic growth absorbs more and more of the fifth of the work force that remains rural and produces only 5 percent of GDP.[49] Compliance with the EU's clean water regulations alone will cost an estimated $20 billion.[50] Moreover, since the EU is now in dynamic change, the central Europeans will have to aim for a moving target in the *acquis communautaire* in a way that no previous entrants to the EU had to do. The Schengen Agreement on open internal borders will require far better policing of Poland's now relatively porous external borders to the east. At some point, Warsaw must also meet the demanding criteria of the European Monetary Union.

Yet Poles seem convinced that with long-term transition regimes to the EU's single market, they can survive and even thrive. With $50 billion foreign direct investment by 2000, they are already pulling in more new foreign capital than Russia is; and at $157 billion, Poland's gross national income is already half as big as the Russian giant's $329 billion.[51]

Fundamentally, Poland is on track to join the EU by 2004–05. The 2001 European Commission report card on candidates again praised Warsaw's achievements on general democratic and market criteria. Poland is already a stable democracy, according to the EU evaluators, with institutions guaranteeing the rule of law, human rights, and respect for minorities. More reservedly, the Commission also judged that Polish enterprises were generally sturdy enough to stand up to EU competition. However, it prodded Warsaw to speed up privatization, show more discipline in fiscal policy, toughen law enforcement on corruption and organized crime, upgrade public administration, and at long last devise a "coherent strategy" for modernizing agriculture and fisheries. The report also noted discreetly the difficulties arising from the economic slowdown that dragged Poland to only 4.1 percent growth in 2000 and an estimated 1-plus percent in 2001 and 2002.[52]

Informally, EU officials are finding the center-left Polish government elected in late 2001 much easier to deal with than its more prickly predecessor, despite the inclusion of minority anti-European parties in the Sejm. Immediately after its inauguration, the government cut the budget deficit and offered compromises on transition periods for free movement of Polish labor in western European countries and for the purchase of Polish land by EU member nationals—and otherwise heeded earlier EU warnings that Poland was, after all, negotiating to join the EU, not vice versa. In this accommodation the government reflected public opinion; the expected deflation of EU euphoria as voters learned more about the obligations in addition to the monetary benefits of membership never pushed support below a majority.[53]

Within just a dozen years, then, the Poles have already begun to master the new terrain of democracy and a market economy. They are evolving Western institutions with consumer safeguards. They have invented instant governments, parties, civil society, watchdog media, parliaments with the wit and integrity to pass responsible budgets and legislate for an unfamiliar world, fledgling judiciaries independent of politics, subordination of security services to elected officials, ombudsmen, a functioning civil service, a framework for local self-government, civilian control of the military, and the habits of individual initiative and risk.[54] They did not, as Russia and Ukraine did, incur wage arrears of billions of dollars or surrender their economy to robber barons. They did not confine wealth creation to the glittering capital and a few favored regional cities, but spread prosperity and began creating a stable middle class. Their initial faith that democracy brings affluence has been rewarded, after several years of interim doubt—and has fostered the further intuition that there is more to be gained by pooling sovereignty than by nationalist assertion. Their traditional fatalism has mutated even beyond a Germanic pessimism as a tool for action and now approaches an optimism that their cousins in Chicago would readily recognize.

Overall, Poland might well be judged the most successful of the new democracies and market economies in central Europe—but it is not thereby unrepresentative. Indeed, as the largest and arguably the most dynamic country in the region, Poland is the trailblazer, setting standards not only for its fellow western Slavs, the Czechs and Slovaks, but also for the Balts and other central Europeans.

Economically, its rapid resumption of sustained high growth after the shocks of 1990–92—based, perforce, initially on the motor of domestic investment by small and medium-sized firms (and on debt forgiveness)—has convinced both the market and mainstream economists that radical reforms really are the swiftest and least painful route to prosperity. Poland now attracts the highest amount of foreign direct investment in the area (though it still lags behind Hungary, Estonia, and the Czech Republic per capita). Its exports are growing fast, even without being promoted by artificial devaluations, and are maturing out of the garden-gnome and cherries stage to include far more sophisticated semifinished and finished goods, especially in light industry.[55]

In the particulars, Poland is at least beginning the cleanup—in part by imposing high polluters' fees—of the appallingly dirty air, water, and soil it inherited.[56] It has established a workable system of bankruptcy to provide a second chance.[57] It has shown that the incentives of legal protection and access to new investment can draw much of the black and gray sectors into the taxpaying economy. Its infant courts are quickly gaining experience in adjudicating commercial law. Its corruption is episodic rather than a systemic part of intertwined governmental and criminal networks. The country has enormous problems—but they are the ordinary problems of an ordinary, working democracy.

Details would differ, but approximately the same case could be made for all the other first-tranche central European candidates for EU membership—Hungary, the Czech Republic, Slovenia, Slovakia, and the three Baltic states that are now expected to join the EU together in a "big bang" in 2004–05, along with Cyprus and Malta.[58] In a sense EU tutelage of these new democracies continues earlier EC tutelage of the fledgling Spanish, Portuguese, and Greek democracies. But the assimilation of former Soviet-bloc countries is much more complex than was the incorporation of former dictatorships that already had capitalist economies.[59]

Never before has the EC/EU taken in countries that were so much poorer than the Community average, and sensible environmental, trade, and other transitional regimes will have to be arranged to allow fair catch-up time for peasant farming and still-fragile industries. Obversely, the candidates for membership must prove that they are substantially meeting the moving target of 90,000 intricate pages of *acquis communautaire*—and they will be expected sooner rather than later to meet the Maastricht preconditions for monetary union as well. It is therefore exponentially harder even for the most Westernized central European nations of Poland, Hungary, and the Czech Republic to meet EU standards than to fulfill the simpler NATO requirements.

Beyond the specific accommodations negotiated by the two quite different sides, the near-term accession of ten new members from the vacuum between western Europe and the eastern Slavs—and the commitment to take in additional states in the medium term—will alter the self-image of the EU. Some observers even articulate the hope that the central Europeans will energize the European Union and give it a new sense of purpose in progressively unifying the continent.[60] They have certainly avoided the worst excesses of crony capitalism, of either the Russian or the Asian varieties. They have been leapfrogging installed west European plants in telecommunications and computers and might just end up in a few years with information technology superior to much of western Europe's. Their revised funded pension systems could turn into models for welfare reform in western Europe. And after the crash reorientation of trade away from the old Soviet bloc, the combined trade of all of central Europe with its leading west European trade partner, Germany, exceeded German-U.S. trade as early as 1994.[61]

Convergence with the super-rich western European economies will still be, the OECD warns, "a matter of generations rather than of years."[62] But after a lag of centuries, the prospect of reaching rough equivalence even in four decades is a happy one. Those born today should, in their wanderlust years, enjoy the same opportunities for travel as their western colleagues. And they can expect that when their own children reach maturity, they can essentially match their western neighbors in becoming what today's Poles already feel like—middle-class citizens.

Politically, too, Poland, Hungary, the Czech Republic, Slovenia, and probably the Baltic states can already be counted as having achieved liberal democracy. Given the far shakier examples of new Latin American democracies—and illiberal central European history—this must be recognized as a major accomplishment. It owes much—as did the democratic transformation of Spain and Portugal after their dictatorships ended in the 1970s—to the example, encouragement, and financial aid of the EC/EU and to the carrot of membership in this elite club as a reward for good behavior.[63] Rule of law, separation of powers, checks and balances, tolerance, freedom of speech, assembly, religion, and property, and respect for minorities are the norm—whatever the individual challenges to these concepts—in the first-tranche candidates for EU membership and the declared goal in the remaining candidate countries. Free elections have already led to the peaceful voting out of communist incumbents in the region—and their return as their successors, in turn, have been voted out. Armies, bureaucrats, and business magnates have respected these judgments, and often enough political newcomers have offered both coherent alternative policies and officials able to implement them. Parties that articulate and aggregate interests are forming. Independent judiciaries, media, and civil societies are being built, with varying degrees of robustness. Presidents do not rule as tsars, with powers of ukase and arbitrary manipulation of favors for courtiers and clans.[64]

In foreign policy, the central European states have also established a good record. Giving the lie to the many prognoses of widespread nationalist strife in the region that were bruited in the early 1990s, they have not reverted to pre–cold war patterns of armed conflict.[65] The Czech-Slovak divorce was a velvet one. The Slovenes fought their way to independence from Serb-dominated Yugoslavia, to be sure, but that war was brief and only a sideshow to the bloodletting in Croatia and Bosnia. As already noted, Hungary has forgone irredentism.[66] Various populist Hungarian politicians have sought to exploit ethnic ties to Hungarian minorities in neighboring states, but their calls have failed to stir the masses, and moderates have generally prevailed in elections.

There are, of course, exceptions to the good overall picture in central Europe. Slovakia was long a laggard both in the practice of domestic democracy and in respect for its own Hungarian minority. To the south, Bulgaria and Romania are still struggling to catch up with the economic, political, and social reforms they failed to implement as governments run by the old nomenklatura persisted until the mid-

1990s. Albania erupted into anarchy and tribal violence after half a decade of an elected illiberal leader—and a pyramid scam that sucked away the meager savings of thousands. Former Yugoslavia erupted into violence in the 1990s.

Yet the incentives to good behavior to win admission to the EU and NATO are taking hold, and their effect can be seen even in recalcitrant former Yugoslavia. Croatia, having elected moderates to parliament and the presidency after the death of ultranationalist Franjo Tudjman, is striving to prove itself tolerant enough of ethnic minorities and dissidents to qualify for a fast track to EU membership. Serbia finally voted Slobodan Milosevic out of office, and the new government even extradited him to the UN war-crimes tribunal at The Hague to qualify for EU aid and eventual membership. The local Serb Council members in Srebrenica, the site of the worst massacre in Europe since World War II, after stonewalling for three years, finally agreed in mid-1999 to meet with their majority Bosniak counterparts to work for a "new Srebrenica" and receive international assistance.[67] Voters elected more moderate Serbs in Srpska in early 1998 and reaped an immediate reward of $11 million in EU and U.S. aid; in 2001 the virulently chauvinist Serb Democratic Party in Srpska, however cynically, even expelled its notorious founding members, Radovan Karadzic and General Ratko Mladic, from the party.[68] The EU's inducements, so ineffectual against the stoked passions of Balkan war in the early 1990s, proved more effective once the NATO-led coalition denied any prize for aggression and stopped the spiral of hate and bloodshed.[69]

In post–cold war Europe, then, the remarkable thing is not that old enmities flared into fighting on the Balkan and Caucasian fringes of the continent. Nor is it that the Balkan central European states of Romania and Bulgaria find it vastly more difficult to adopt democracy than do their northern neighbors; or that the new market economies keep stumbling as they prepare themselves for world competition.

The astounding development is rather the dog that did not bark. Old enmities between Poles and Ukrainians, or between Romanians and Hungarians, have not flared into armed confrontations. Populist Stanislaw Tyminski did not get elected president of Poland. Vladimir Mečiar, despite his control of the media and the security services, could not prevent Slovak voters from kicking him out. The old party command hierarchies have not disintegrated into rival marauding gangs of shakedown artists. Contracts are not enforced by murder. New robber barons have not hijacked politics. Vested interests have not blocked the breakup of their cozy monopolies as economies prepare for the onslaught of full, open competition with west European transnational giants. Western investments are growing in the region. Populations, whatever their initial hardships, have not lapsed into anarchy (outside of the Balkans). Poland did not collapse at any of the five to seven times that even Balcerowicz reformers thought it might. Western Europe and central Europe are being knitted together. The central Europeans are escaping from history.

Otto III and Boleslaw the Brave would surely be pleased.

CHAPTER SEVEN

Absent at the Rebirth: The Eastern Slavs

J ust how far east does "Europe" go? Next door to the western Slavs in Poland, are the eastern Slavs also escaping from
history in a westward direction? After the Russian financial crash of
August 1998 the answer to that question was an easy no, as a matter
of self-selection.[1] As of 2002, after economic recovery and the tenta-
tive choice by President Vladimir Putin to throw his lot in with the
West in fighting terrorism, the answer has to be a confused maybe.
This chapter examines, first, the initial no, and then, the turnaround
in economic reforms under President Putin.

Time of Troubles

At the time, the crash of the ruble looked like conclusive evidence
of the rejection by the eastern Slav political and economic culture of
the alien graft of democracy and the market. The plunge of the ruble
and of Russian securities gave the lie to the pious hope of economic
liberals in the early 1990s that in Russia, as well as in Poland, these
imported institutions might shape, more than be shaped by, the traditions they encountered. On the day of reckoning, August 17, 1998,
the mounting conflicts between institutions and tradition brought default, devaluation, and a Russia recoiling from the macroeconomic
stability, austerity, and restructuring that Moscow's "young reformers" had attempted. Political crisis followed. Even the country's trea-
sure trove of mineral wealth could not ward off the debacle of the

Russian pyramid scheme as ever more short-term bonds were issued to cover long-term debt and interest payments. Finally, mathematical logic, the Asian economic crisis, and falling oil prices struck.

Previously, the West had been willing to profess belief in the Potemkin village of prettified facades, to pretend that the ballot box would turn Boris Yeltsin into a democratic president, no matter how much he ruled like a tsar, or tried to. Now, in the naked power struggles for the succession to the ill president, such pretense was no longer possible. It died, perhaps, when parliamentarian Galina Starovoitova, one of Russia's most beloved and fearless democrats, was assassinated on her doorstep in St. Petersburg at the end of 1998. What she herself called Russia's "democratic house of cards" collapsed. "The murder of Galina Starovoitova is . . . the start of a mass attack on what remains of the incomplete process of democratization," wrote Marina Salye in *Nezavisimaya gazeta*.[2]

West Europeans concurred in this verdict. They were ready to live with whatever mix of political and economic authoritarianism and individual initiative the eastern Slavs came up with and to hope that the resulting regimes would be as humane and stable as possible. They donated food and medicine to eastern Slav towns and villages to relieve shortages over several winters. They remained ready to give grants and low-interest credits whenever Russia, Ukraine, or Belarus pursued anti-inflationary and growth policies and demonstrated the ability to channel outside money away from private pockets into economic development.

What the West was not prepared to do, however, was to call the interim eastern Slav economies and polities "European"—or to honor the importunate request of an unreformed Kyiv to be admitted to the EU club of market democracies. To be sure, one could argue that the eastern Slavs did move in a fundamentally Western and more open direction when the Soviet Union collapsed and broke up the old Communist party monopoly on power, wealth, and truth. But this seemed to leave the field open for the most ruthless of the second-tier nomenklatura to steal state property in sweetheart privatization deals, strip assets, and become billionaires in the worst Soviet caricature of capitalism—then buy back political power by funding the presidential campaigns of Russia's Boris Yeltsin and Ukraine's Leonid Kuchma. The IMF and Harvard theory—that if only you can create property owners fast, without being too fastidious, the new robber barons will soon behave like economic rationalists and want to protect their riches by rule of law—looked like a chimera. So did the notion that competing clans might turn into protoparties and generate rudimentary pluralism; instead, the ravaging gangs produced a new Time of Troubles.

In Russia the "virtual economy," under a malevolent invisible hand, was actually subtracting rather than adding value, and the demonetarized system was three-quarters dependent on barter.[3] What this economists' language meant in practice was that enterprises "borrowed" money by not paying their workers, their debts, or their taxes. They continued to provide some housing and social services—barely—and a base where employees could socialize when they were not off tending their crucial vegetable plots. It was a new, even more negative variation of the old communist social contract ("They pretend to pay us, and we pretend to work") that might have been rendered as "They don't pretend to pay us, and we don't pretend to work."[4] Official figures showed Russian GDP dropping by half in the 1990s, Ukrainian GDP by two-thirds.[5] Russian output was no larger than that of the city of Houston; and Russia's 1998 grain harvest matched the country's record lows of the previous three decades.[6]

Even worse, contagious diseases that had vanished returned in Russia and Ukraine. The elementary infrastructure of heat, running water, and food distribution, wretched as it was in Soviet times, decayed further; in one example, 80 percent of cement casings for hot water pipes fell away in Russia, leaving lethal steamy mud pits for the burgeoning numbers of drunks to stumble into. Average real incomes fell 58 percent in the 1990s; arrears in wages mounted to $11 billion, and income levels were among the most unequal in the world, with the top decile 13.3 times richer than the bottom decile.[7] Some 31 million, or more than a fifth of the population, were living below the official poverty line.[8] Life expectancy for adult men was not only worse than in Soviet times, but even below the level a century earlier. Births in Russia almost halved in the 1990s, from 2.2 million to 1.4 million a year, while deaths shot up almost 40 percent, from 1.6 to 2.2 million, for a net decrease (discounting immigrants) of 3.5 million and a projected loss of another 10 million by 2010.[9]

Moreover, with the decomposition of the old order, a new arbitrary disorder came to prevail. Bribes no longer guaranteed protection, as various ethnically based mafias gunned each other down for control of the different sectors of the economy. Crime turned out to be less a parasite on the system than the system itself.[10] Contract murders were cheap, at a reported $2,000.[11] Former deputy premier Boris Nemtsov declared that the KGB and other security services were "privatized by the Communists, Nazis, and oligarchic structures."[12] The West's $58 billion of aid and credits (some reports put the outside world's total debt and equity exposure to Russia at $200 billion) had little visible impact on the economy, but joined mineral-export profits for a capital flight of $66 billion into Swiss, American, Cypriot, and Israeli banks.[13] Russia had two successive years in which its stock exchange share prices doubled, but in 1998 its credit rating plunged to below that of Indonesia. And up to 80 percent of the country's wealth continued to be concentrated in Moscow.[14]

Everyone had a different list of culprits. Some IMF officials blamed George Soros and speculators and a West that was too stingy to top off its 1998 Russian bailout of $19 billion with another several-billion-dollar dollop just before the cataclysm.[15] Others blamed the IMF and its "sadomonetarist" policies. Susan Eisenhower scolded an insensitive West for giving Russia enough money to coerce it into a heartless neoliberal straitjacket, but not enough to make a new system function.[16] More melodramatically, Walter Russell Mead condemned the West's policy of "discriminating" against Russia by "shut[ting] it out of both NATO and the European Union" as "a textbook case in how to drive a people to fascism."[17] Conversely, Clifford Gaddy and Barry Ickes censured the West for its credulity in pouring money down the black hole of the virtual economy.[18] Martin Malia argued that liberal reform never went far enough.[19] Russian émigré Dmitri K. Simes, president of the Nixon Center, identified the faults of the old Yeltsin house of cards as "capitalism without investment, the market without regulation or property rights and democracy without respect for the law and separation of powers."[20] Historian Richard Pipes blamed Russian history and the absence of a Renaissance, individualism, and private property.[21]

The Chasm between the Poles and the Eastern Slavs

Whatever the proper apportionment of guilt, the lightning bolt of August 17, 1998, made it clear just how far away Russia was from fulfilling Gorbachev's old aspiration to be part of the European house.

The answer to the question—how far east does Europe extend?—seemed obvious: Poland's Bug River. In the 1990s Warsaw created a virtuous circle, in which democracy and the market reinforced each other in a synergy that qualified Poland, with continued hard work, for admission to the EU. In the same decade Moscow, trying half-heartedly to follow the same recipe, recreated a vicious circle in which political disintegration led to economic impasse, which increased political deadlock. Characteristically, by 2000 Poland and Hungary had already generated one legally registered company for every ten persons, on a par with the industrialized West; Russia had generated only one for every fifty-five persons, and Ukraine, one for every eighty.[22]

In sum, in the categories of Ernest Gellner and Francis Fukuyama, Poland was successfully establishing the civil society and social trust that are essential for democracy and an effective market economy. Russia, with no historical experience in the genre, was discovering just how hard it was "to create a Civil Society from above, by design *and in a hurry.*"[23]

Under the circumstances, the Russian and Ukrainian publics, unlike the Poles, came to equate the West's democracy and market with misery; politicians were applauded when they demonized the IMF and made it the scapegoat for the agonies of modernization.[24] Belarus, under its president and former collective farm chairman, Alexander Lukashenko, never tried to become more Western in any case, but reinstated central planning and authoritarian politics (and would have recreated the Soviet Union, had Moscow's reformers not recoiled from the cost).[25] In Poland, by contrast, the government welcomed tough IMF (and EU) conditions as an additional pressure to do what it must anyway do for its own benefit.

Why the difference between Poland and Russia? What did Russia lack that Poland possessed? Asked this question two months before the Russian economic meltdown, Russian parliamentarian and would-be reformer Grigory Yavlinsky barked out a one-word reply: "Everything!"[26]

Wojciech Kostrzewa, the young chief executive officer of the Polish BRE bank, might have shared Yavlinsky's despair about Russia, but he expressed himself circumspectly. "There is no one-dimensional answer. But I would prefer to explain it in terms of economics rather than history." His own formative years as an economist in the late 1980s were spent, not like Yavlinsky in a tuberculosis ward to which he was forcibly committed by the KGB, but at the Kiel Institute of World Economics in Germany.

First, Kostrzewa explained, Poland came later to the smothering centrally planned economy than did Russia and left it earlier. In Poland "destruction of communism" began in the 1970s and 1980s, when Poles were allowed to travel abroad freely—and came back from Singapore and Taiwan with hard disks and chips they cobbled together to start the computer firms that are now listed on the Warsaw Stock Exchange. The corollary was that "the brightest" of the party nomenklatura understood from the imposition of martial law in 1982 "that a system that needs tanks and soldiers to keep people under control is close to its end." When 1989 came, they did not try to hang on to centralized planning and politics.

"Second, West Berlin was eighty kilometers from the Polish border, so with the removal of tariffs and nontariff barriers and introduction of internal convertibility, it was possible for traders to start importing [and exporting] goods on their own. They were not forced to wait until a big state organization imported the first bananas. So this part of shock therapy was visible; goods started to be available from one day to the next."

Third, he continued, "The radical opening of the Polish market happened at the very time when most of the monopolies were very weak as pressure groups" because of the total discrediting of the old party hierarchy in the Solidarity years. And this, in turn, meant that, "contrary to [what happened in] almost all of the former Soviet countries, the first government after 1989 was not driven by the ex-nomenklatura, which often in the former Soviet Union tried to delay the changes." This created far less high-level resistance to liberal reforms than Russia experienced—and it also did not allow Red managers to "privatize" their own plants and become the new oligarchs.

No, Kostrzewa added, he did not think that Poland, Hungary, the Czech Republic, "and, I believe, even Slovakia" would repeat the old Latin American cycle of swinging back and forth between democracy and authoritarianism over a long period. Their "robust economic growth" was legitimizing democracy, and the "democratic system seems to overcome many childhood diseases of the system." These countries were building up their middle class and small and medium-sized firms, and they did not have, on the Russian pattern, "huge disproportions between the megarich and the megapoor."[27]

To be sure, Poland, like Russia and like Hungary, started its reforms in the early 1990s in the face of a skeptical to hostile popular mind-set. As Hungarian philosopher G. M. Tamas summarized the situation at the time:

> All the surveys and polling data show that public opinion in our region rejects dictatorship, but would like to see a strong man at the helm; favors popular government, but hates parliament, parties, and the press; likes social welfare legislation and equality, but not trade unions; wants to topple the present government, but disapproves of the idea of a regular opposition; supports the notion of the market (which is a code word for Western-style living standards), but wishes to punish and expropriate the rich and condemns banking for preying on simple working people; favors a guaranteed minimum income, but sees unemployment as an immoral state and wants to punish or possibly deport the unemployed.[28]

The western Slavs broke out of that rut; initially, at least, the eastern Slavs did not.

The Ukrainian Example

The best foil for exploring the divide is Ukraine. This was the one eastern Slav country that had a good chance, if its elites had really wanted to do so, to become more European and eventually, perhaps, become associated with the European Union. Its population of 50 million made it a more manageable size than Russia's 147 million, and more comparable to Poland's 39 million (or France's 57 million). It did not have the extremes of a Russia, spread over the Eurasian continents. It was more homogeneous and less sprawling than Russia, with ethnic Ukrainians and Russians making up the large bulk of its population.

Moreover, many Ukrainians, both inside the country and in the large émigré communities in the United States and Canada, thought that Ukraine had been exploited by Russia in the Soviet Union and that it would flourish economically once it threw off its Muscovite masters and achieved independence.[29] In both the nineteenth and twentieth centuries, after all, the black Ukrainian earth had been the primary source of grain for Russia. In Soviet times Ukraine had been a center for the manufacture of missiles, tanks, and sturdy turbines; and its skilled scientists and engineers were more oriented toward practical applications than their more theoretical Russian counterparts.[30] Its standard of living (partly because of privileges it enjoyed over three decades as the power base of Soviet leaders Nikita Khrushchev and Leonid Brezhnev) was higher than that in Russia. Besides, Kyiv could count on the secret weapon of the diaspora in North America. Throughout their generations in exile, the fiercely nationalist émigrés in Canada and the United States, who came from the part of western Ukraine that was not incorporated into the Soviet Union until after World War II, had nurtured the Ukrainian culture and mystique. They would, it was thought, bring investment and entrepreneurial and democratic expertise back to the land of their ancestors. So widespread was the conviction of Ukraine's economic advantage that an overwhelming majority of the population—including most of the 11 million ethnic Russians in the land—voted in favor of independence in the 1991 referendum.

Psychologically, too, the nationalist Ukrainians in the west around Lviv considered themselves much more Western than the Russians (or the Russian-speaking eastern Ukrainians, for that matter). Kyiv had brought Christianity to the eastern Slavs, after all, and, much later, imported whatever Enlightenment ideas came to the region. Western Ukraine had also been at different times part of the Austro-Hungarian Empire and of Poland, and its primary religious allegiance was not to the Orthodox Church, but to the Uniate Church under the pope in Rome. With this background, what could be more natural than for Ukraine to strengthen its weak sense of any identity as distinct from Russia, reclaim its unique heritage, assume a more Western character, and at the same time persuade the rich West to bolster its still fragile independence from Russia? This indeed was the strategy of the policy elite around President Leonid Kuchma, the surprise winner in the 1994 presidential election. It looked promising.

To understand why the strategy initially succeeded brilliantly in foreign policy but failed to establish a domestic and economic foundation for this policy, it is necessary here, too, to look at the devil of the details. The burden of tradition may suggest broadly why a Western course was even more difficult for Kyiv than for Warsaw. But history is not fate. Only by examining the interplay of the authoritarian inheritance with specific players and their shifting perception of policy choices can one come to an approximate explanation of events.

The account, then, begins properly with the new Ukraine's first president, Leonid Kravchuk. He was a communist apparatchik who had stolen the nationalists' clothes just in time to get elected by popular vote as the Soviet Union crumbled. He brought his old apparat with him to govern the new state. He introduced no Russian-style privatization—as late as 1994 there was not a single private bakery in Kyiv—but his cronies still managed to make personal fortunes in paler imitation of Russia's instant capitalists, buying petroleum and metals at old Soviet ruble prices for sale abroad at world dollar prices. No Ukrainian Boris Berezovsky or Mikhail Khodorovsky would make the Forbes list of billionaires, but less flamboyantly, parts of the Ukrainian nomenklatura, too, still preserved their power and converted their privilege into cash. Under this malign neglect, the economy went into a tailspin, with hyperinflation of 10,000 percent, a drop of 60 percent in GDP within three years, and what seemed at the time to be peculiarly egregious arrears of several months' unpaid wages.

Despite the communist continuity and economic calamity, the West appreciated Kravchuk's initial consolidation of Ukrainian independence, which shut the door on any near-term Russian temptation to revert to imperialism. Russians of all political persuasions might still think that after three centuries of union Ukraine rightfully belonged to Russia and should return, but this union would not be restored unless Ukraine's many ethnic Russians and Russophile eastern Ukrainians wanted it. And if Russia did not reabsorb its Slavic soulmates in Ukraine, it was unlikely to have an undemocratic appetite whetted for reabsorbing other parts of the "near abroad." The longer the question of reassimilating Ukraine could be kept off the active agenda in Moscow, then, the better.

Kravchuk also won Western respect for the tolerance Ukraine showed its Russian, Polish, Romanian, Jewish, and other minorities. With this mix of peoples in a country lacking a tradition of nationhood, any ethnic concept of citizenship, rather than uniting the country, would have split it. It therefore made sense to strive for a civic concept; anyone living on Ukrainian territory on the day of independence was declared a citizen.

Finally, the West was grateful to Kravchuk for acceding to strong U.S. pressure over three years and forfeiting the nuclear weapons

Ukraine had inherited from the Soviet Union. The informal quid pro quo was an American security assurance that was worded ambiguously enough that Kyiv could interpret it as a hint of protection, while the United States could interpret it as a repetition of more general OSCE pledges.

In addition, once Kravchuk's successor started economic reform, Washington rewarded Kyiv with grants and credits that elevated Ukraine to the third-largest recipient of U.S. aid, after Israel and Egypt. Various Ukrainian-Canadian and Ukrainian-American businessmen flocked to the old country to start computer consultancies in Kyiv or supermarkets in Dnipropetrovsk. Compatriots explained the unique, flourishing system of ethnic Ukrainian financial cooperatives in the United States and Canada that might be adopted to channel a plethora of small savings into equitable investment. With funding from philanthropist George Soros, émigré educators also established a graduate school of public administration to rush civil servants through crash courses, while Western economists and political scientists advised parliament and government exhaustively on legislation and policy. North American lawyers helped educate fledgling jurists, compiled and translated a dictionary of Anglo-Saxon legal terms and concepts directly into Ukrainian (without the intermediation of Russian), published the corpus of (previously often secret) Ukrainian legislation, and computerized university law schools to give them online access to statutes.

With this start, Ukraine established its independence for the second time, following in the footsteps of the short-lived Ukrainian regime that emerged from World War I to be crushed by the Bolsheviks in brutal civil war. And it avoided the repeat civil war that the U.S. Central Intelligence Agency feared might break out.[31] Tension between ships of the Black Sea Fleet apportioned to the Russian and Ukrainian navies did escalate so far in the spring of 1994 that officers of the Russian vessel *Cheleken*—which had seized navigational equipment from the port of Odessa—gave orders to the 318th Division of the Russian fleet to fire on pursuing Ukrainian boats. The orders were never carried out, though, and the incident passed.

Similarly, although some leaders of the ethnic Russian majority on the Crimean peninsula agitated for secession to Russia once it became clear that the depressed Ukrainian economy would not pump money into their Black Sea resorts, no blood was shed there. (At least, what blood was shed did not involve Ukrainians, but only Russians and those Tatars finally returning to their native Crimea after Stalinist exile in Siberia, or else the respective Russian and Tatar mafias in Crimea.) Nor was there in Kyiv any Russian-style shootout between president and parliament. There was no Chechen war, and Ukraine had no imperial ambitions. When Leonid Kuchma, an old industrial apparatchik who had managed what was touted as the largest missile factory in the world, was unexpectedly elected president over the incumbent in 1994, there was a peaceful succession.

In his first years in office Kuchma finally introduced macroeconomic stabilization and rudimentary economic reforms. He reconciled eastern and western Ukrainians (with substantial help from Moscow, as the war in Chechnya made any Ukrainian reunion with Russia repugnant, especially to parents of draft-age sons). He displayed some unexpected political skills as well, courting individual members of parliament on key issues in a way Yeltsin never tried to do in Moscow, forging a power-sharing arrangement with a hostile parliament dominated by the old left, writing a constitution that many Ukrainians took as their nation's badge of maturity, and, under the stern eye of the central bank, introducing a new currency that stayed stable for several years. The United States and Germany, in particular—other Europeans focused on the former superpower of Russia to the exclusion of Ukraine—approved and supported Kuchma's efforts.

In his early reform period Kuchma followed the Russian model, timidly, rather than the Polish model. Warsaw might have offered Kyiv a helpful example, especially since Poland was already succeeding, economically and democratically, by the time Ukraine began its reforms. Some Poles, in fact, even urged the Ukrainians to use the seventeenth-century Polish republic that Ukrainian lands had been part of as a prototype and to build on that.[32] But the old Ukrainian peasant antipathies toward Polish landlords and memories of mutual butchery as recently as the 1940s remained too strong for that idea to be popular. In the early 1990s would-be Ukrainian reformers sometimes cited the rather inappropriate Estonian model of transformation as their ideal, but never the Polish. Ukraine never had the "bench depth" of successive sophisticated Polish finance ministers and economists, in any case.[33] Despite all the top-down efforts to achieve Polish-Ukrainian reconciliation—and despite the availability in Kyiv of willing Polish economic advisers—Poland had little influence on its neighbor beyond spreading Western fashions through the bustling cross-border suitcase trade.

Russia's energetic young reformers in the mid-1990s also had little impact on Ukraine. The brain drain of ambitious Ukrainians over centuries to glittering Moscow had taken its toll; so had this century's four exterminations of Ukrainian elites in the Red-White civil war, induced famine, Stalin's purges, and World War II. There was no pack of hot-shot reformers in Ukraine with an education in basic market economics comparable to Anatoli Chubais and Boris Nemtsov and their colleagues in Moscow. And not even Grigory Yavlinsky had any desire to return to the small pond of his native Ukraine to become a politician there.[34]

For the North American diaspora, it was a surprise to find that western Ukrainians failed to become a strong transmission belt for modernization and Westernization in independent Ukraine. The émigrés certainly did not expect fraternization with the Poles by those Ukrainians who took over vacated Polish houses in Lviv in 1945, even as the expelled Lviv Poles took over the bombed-out cellars of German expellees in Breslau in western Poland as the postwar borders shifted. They did, however, anticipate, that their Galician cousins would naturally think more the way Americans and Canadians thought. And they expected the Rukh movement in western Ukraine, which had agitated so effectively for independence in the 1980s, to have much more influence in the Ukraine of the 1990s than its minority vote ultimately accorded it. Yet the Galicians turned out to have little interest in pressing for a market economy—and their voice was in any case muffled by the atomization of politics in a country with little national consciousness and by the monopolization of Kyiv politics by the regional clans of Dnipropetrovsk and Donetsk.

The Death of Reform

These two old bureaucratic and geographical clans left over from communist days set the course of Ukrainian politics. The large majority of Kuchma's senior appointees came from Dnipropetrovsk, and originally he had a certain claim to leadership of that city's clan. By the time he lost interest in economic reform in 1995–96, though, Dnipropetrovsk's industrial and monetary power had essentially flowed to Petro Lazarenko, prime minister in the mid-1990s. Under the patronage of Lazarenko, the United Energy Systems empire quickly

cornered some 80 percent of Ukraine's natural gas supply, then par-
layed this near-monopoly into ownership of a network of other companies, accounting for an estimated eighth of the country's GDP.
Lazarenko and the Hromada party he founded (after he was fired as
prime minister in mid-1997 amid charges of corruption) clearly had
no interest in changing a system that had been so good to them—nor
did other political-business conglomerates.[35]

In the new era of elections the Donetsk clan did form the Liberal
party, but this was little more than the old power struggle in 1990s
dress. The international colleagues whom the Ukrainian Liberal party
seemed to admire most were the Japanese Liberal Democrats, and
their special attraction lay less in any distinct platform than in their
enormous success in staying in power virtually uninterrupted for half
a century.[36]

Under the circumstances, those Ukrainians in a position to profit
from the new commerce generally focused their attention on making
money today, at the expense of setting up durable institutions for tomorrow or doing the necessary nation building in an infant state. And,
unlike the Russian oligarchs, they preferred shutting out Western competition to attracting new investment that they might get a percentage
of. No megadeals comparable to Russia's Caspian Sea energy projects
were waiting to be made in any case, since Ukraine was less endowed
with raw materials. But initially several smaller direct equity investors
came in, with the hope that Ukraine's ubiquitous chicanery, demands
for bribes, taxes that often exceeded 100 percent of profits, and ever-
shifting laws with arbitrary application were just temporary teething
problems. Within a few years these companies had been chased away.

The British JKX Oil and Gas firm, for one, informed Kyiv that it
could produce 20 percent of Ukraine's domestic gas needs from its
Poltava fields and thus help correct the country's chronic trade deficits
from imported energy. Yet it was barred by Ukrainian rivals from feed-
ing its stock into the domestic pipeline. The sugar giant Tate & Lyle
had to forfeit delivery contracts to Coca-Cola and other customers in
Russia and close its Odessa refinery after Ukrainian bureaucrats suddenly banned import of sugar cane and export of the company's fine
white sugar, apparently in a clumsy attempt to benefit domestic producers of lumpy, gray beet sugar. Similarly, Kiev Atlantic and other
Western firms that had helped farmers finance seed, fertilizer, and other
inputs nonetheless failed to get their contracted grain when the state

abruptly expropriated harvests (at prices less than half the world price). In the telecommunications sector that is so crucial for the future, Motorola finally wrote off its substantial initial investment on a contract for mobile phones after the rules and exorbitant fees for frequencies kept shifting, Ukrainian competitors were awarded prime wavelengths under opaque circumstances—and, according to one executive, Motorola refused to deliver a $1 million payoff.

One Canadian investor who abandoned projects in Kyiv and other graft-ridden cities and moved to what was then a better-run Odessa spoke for many of his colleagues in complaining that "former communists" who have hung on to bureaucratic posts "lie, do not tell the truth, deceive you, [and] tell you that they are working to assist your project, when in fact they work against you." This makes Ukraine "a very pathetic and sick place to do business." More personally, a Ukrainian-American businessman in Kyiv recalls that growing up he was not sure whether he was American or Ukrainian, "but after one week here I knew I was American!"[37]

Even as the big-name companies, in frustration, pulled out close to half of the $2 billion that was all the investment Ukraine had been able to attract in the 1990s, there seemed to be little awareness in Kyiv that the sure penalty for killing the golden goose would be repulsion of potential future investors. On the contrary, there was a common feeling that the country had an innate right to foreign investment and a resentment of Westerners who willingly plowed money into the corrupt Philippines (as one of Kuchma's aides phrased it) but then cited corruption as an excuse not to invest heavily in Ukraine.[38] There was suspicion, in what was seen as a zero-sum game, that wily Westerners would use their unfair advantages in wealth and knowledge of capitalist rules of the road to cheat inexperienced Ukrainians. Often enough there was indignation at middle-level ranks when stingy foreigners would not cough up the few-thousand-dollar payoffs they so clearly could afford—or at higher levels, when Westerners who had already made their bundle cited contract law to muscle out Ukrainians who just wanted to make their bundle too. In a government of low pay and high turnover, there was also an urge by various ministers and deputy ministers to line their own pockets fast, as their predecessors had done, before they got fired or lost access. The legal risk was negligible; as Vyacheslav Pikhovshek, director of the Ukrainian Center for Independent Political Research, pointed out, "There has not been a single trial in Ukraine for corruption."[39]

In this atmosphere, periodic antigraft campaigns never flushed out the stables, but remained at the level of wars of sometimes true, sometimes false, accusations of corruption by rivals. The few officials who seemed intent on a real cleanup, like Justice Minister Serhiy Holovaty, soon found themselves out of office.

For a few years Ukraine's driving out of foreign direct investment did not seriously harm the country. Portfolio investment flowed in, eager to snap up undervalued firms as they privatized. When privatization also bogged down, however—and especially as the Asian and Russian crises made investors wary—the hot money flowed out again. The government repeatedly overshot its promised budget deficits, triggering suspension of IMF loans. It received from Moody's the lowest credit rating in all of eastern Europe and the former Soviet Union. When it launched its first Eurobonds in early 1998—just to raise money to service debt on the Western loans that had been heavily front-loaded in the advance vote of confidence in Kuchma—it had to offer a spread double that for Russian government paper. A month after Moscow defaulted on its debt in August 1998, Kyiv had to reschedule its domestic government debt. By then its hard-currency reserves were exceeded by debt coming due. Its wage arrears, like Russia's, now ran into billions of dollars.[40] Its pensioners were receiving $19 a month, if they got paid at all.[41]

The upshot was that Ukraine's shadow versions of Russia's oligarchs blocked both reform and Western investment, without any real battle. The Ukrainian economy set one of the worst records in the region. Debts for Ukraine's profligate import of energy from Russia and Turkmenistan piled up. Land reform on the bankrupt collective farms was not begun until the first timid authorization of land sales in 2001, and grain harvests in this once-upon-a-time breadbasket dropped to half what they used to be in the Soviet era. The old Communist party apparatchiks, who now called themselves businessmen, were still plundering the state. Structural reforms that were essential for the economy to start growing again were nowhere to be seen. Arbitrary taxes were not being rationalized to draw the shadow economy into legitimacy. Russian and Ukrainian mafias, rather than imitating Italian or Colombian mafias in at least reinvesting their profits in the economies they leech, were diligently exporting more capital than their countries have been receiving in Western aid.[42] Gangland murders, while not on a Russian scale, also plagued Ukraine.

Politically, there was no concept of government as a neutral provider of the common good or as umpire; instead, it was seen as the first in line to bleed the state. The strongest incentives to getting elected to parliament or taking government office still tended to be immunity from prosecution or having the inside advantage to manipulate licenses, contracts, and state credits. And Ukrainian, like Russian, business was both over- and underregulated: overregulated in the number of stamps (and therefore bribes) required for every franchise; underregulated in the lack of protection for the anonymous consumer or for honest firms.[43] After he was reelected in 1999, President Kuchma again announced that he would pursue liberal reforms, but skeptical Western investors continued to wait for deeds instead of words.

Paradoxically, Kyiv's short-sighted and self-destructive domestic policy in the 1990s was coupled with a foreign policy that was highly effective in enhancing Ukraine's security. Together, Kravchuk and Kuchma steered Ukraine through the fluid first years when rival Ukrainian politicians might have been tempted to make common cause with Moscow. Today, with new power bases solidified, few players would willingly trade their positions even in a smaller, poorer Ukraine for a bit role in richer Russia. But beyond ensuring the sheer longevity of Ukraine's independence, for the longest period in the country's entire history, the two first presidents also managed to thwart Russia's attempt to marshal a common foreign policy and defense in a Moscow-led Commonwealth of Independent States—that is, the old Soviet Union minus the Baltic states. Ukraine initially declared itself "bloc-free," in a politically correct rubric for slipping out from the droit de regard Russia sought to exercise in its "near abroad." Kuchma then went further in applauding Polish entry into NATO and even speculating that one day Ukraine, too, might join the alliance. Simultaneously, he outmaneuvered ethnic Russian politicians in Crimea who were trying to turn the peninsula's autonomy into accession to Russia; and he also wrested control of Sevastopol away from the Russian military command, which had been running it de facto as a closed city. By 1995–96 Ukrainian officials were describing their overall policy choice as one between good (Western) integration and bad (Soviet/Russian) disintegration. Or they declared (by implicit contrast to Russia) that "Ukraine is European, and its future is European."[44] One Kyiv journalist was even blunter. "The U.S. should occupy Ukraine and teach it democracy the way America occupied Germany and taught Germany democracy!" he exclaimed.[45]

The official sentiment found some resonance among the Ukrainian policy elite.[46] And Russian nationalists inadvertently helped the progression by periodically claiming the naval port of Sevastopol and demanding as a right the indefinite berthing of the Russian Black Sea Fleet there. Repeatedly, the more strident Russian assertions forced even the Soviet loyalists in the very unreconstructed Ukrainian Communist party to swear their patriotism and steadfastness to Ukrainian sovereignty over Sevastopol.

Whatever back-handed help Kuchma had from Moscow, though, it was his own considerable accomplishment to effect the Western reorientation of foreign policy in an eastern Slav peasant land with an army, an ex-KGB security service, and a former communist hierarchy steeped in Soviet thinking. The fact that he brought off the shift so smoothly owed much to quiet U.S.-Ukrainian diplomacy and to the skill of a few key Ukrainian diplomats, like Borys Tarasyuk, ambassador to Belgium and NATO in the mid-1990s and later foreign minister. By 1997 Kyiv had fulfilled the preconditions of resolving or neutralizing border disputes with Romania and other neighbors—without backlash from the old Ukrainian hierarchies. It was rewarded with the "distinctive partnership" with NATO that it sought—and this high-profile Western recognition of Ukraine at last jolted Yeltsin into recognizing Ukraine's borders.

The chronic schizophrenia between a Western-oriented foreign policy and domestic entropy doomed Kyiv's dogged efforts to gain admission to the European Union. Both the United States and Germany, Ukraine's strongest Western backers, finally gave up on the country. The disillusionment was mutual. Lazarenko, having quarreled with his boss and retired to a $6 million California estate that he paid for in cash, was under criminal indictment in the United States and out of the picture. Kuchma fired his West-leaning foreign minister, Tarasyuk, and also, in parliamentary maneuvers, Prime Minister Viktor Yushchenko, the one Ukrainian economic reformer the West trusted. Kuchma himself also finally parted ways with the hectoring West. His relations with the United States and Europe soured especially after critical journalist Georgi Gongadze was found beheaded in 2000, and an electronics specialist on the president's security staff quit and released a tape—spliced, Kuchma contended—in which Kuchma's voice suggested getting rid of Gongadze. He reverted to pan-Slav fraternity and struck a deal Moscow had long coveted, trading Ukrainian energy debts to Russia for Russian equity in Ukrainian industry. Many Westerners could only agree when Volodymyr Horbulin, then Kuchma's closest adviser, confided to a Russian interviewer in the late 1990s that "the biggest enemy in Ukraine today is ourselves."[47]

Russia—with residual claims to special influence in the "near abroad" of neighboring states, an exhilarating energy and volatility, a hybrid political system that was far more open than in communist times in requiring competing clans to clear the new hurdle of elections, and a hybrid economic system of bandit oligarchs, stranglehold mafias, and incipient market disciplines—also chose a non-Western path in the 1990s. It developed more external links with the West than Ukraine did in its institutionalized participation in the Group of Seven (now Eight) annual "economic" summits and the NATO-Russian Permanent Joint Council, and with its oil, gas, nickel, and other raw-materials deals with Western corporations. It initiated regular summits with Germany and France; and it of course received more deference from the West than did less powerful, nonnuclear nations. But until the twenty-first century it seemed unlikely to qualify, or want to qualify, for membership in the EU-NATO system.

2001

The judgment that the Russians, Ukrainians, and Belarusians were no more than bystanders at the rebirth of Europe at the turn of the millennium prevailed in the West until 2001; it still does for Ukraine politically and for Belarus both politically and economically.

In Belarus, President Alexander Lukashenko, sometimes disparaged as "the last dictator in Europe," was reelected in 2001 in what OSCE monitors deemed a rigged election. His country's unreformed economy still depends on annual Russian largesse of some $1 billion, plus arms exports to Islamist end users and others on a scale that keeps the country among the world's top ten weapons exporters.[48] Russian officials tolerate his adoration, but basically regard Lukashenko as an anachronism.

In Ukraine, ministries still tend to be regarded as money-spinners for those holding the top positions in them. Politics and business have not disaggregated even to the extent they have begun to in Russia; there is little party coherence in the Supreme Rada, and many candidates for parliament still seem less interested in passing laws than in acquiring immunity from prosecution for questionable business dealings. Investigative journalism continues to be an unhealthy profession; a dozen reporters from the ranks of those who criticize the government have vanished or turned up murdered in the past decade.

Economically, Ukraine has been doing much better since President Leonid Kuchma finally struck his debts-equity deal with Moscow. Since then, bilateral relations have warmed, as personified by the arrival in Kyiv of the high-powered Russian ambassador Viktor Chernomyrdin, former Russian prime minister and former head of Gazprom.[49] The microeconomic reforms effected in 2000–01 by Prime Minister Viktor Yushchenko and by one-time gas oligarch turned industry and energy minister, Julia Timoshenko, broke the energy cartel and squeezed it for $4 billion in back taxes, or a significant 13 percent of the country's GDP. In 2001 economic gowth reached some 9 percent.

Swedish economic analyst and sometime reform adviser to both Moscow and Kyiv Anders Åslund argues that with basic macroeconomic liberalization and privatization finally in place, new market competition is already functioning to crowd out the notorious rent seekers of the 1990s. Victor Pinchuk, Ukraine's forty-year-old steel mogul, for example, "wants to play within the established legal framework" and sees Russia's Alfa Group as his ideal. The slow land reform has also brought 50 percent of land into private ownership by now, though huge holdings remain "a problem." The question now is, he suggests, whether rule of law in property and contractual rights, in particular, will be enforced. In retrospect, he sees the first "explosion of individual crime" in both Ukraine and Russia as lasting from 1989 to 1994, before becoming "centralized" in the hands of the "oligarchs with their private security forces." After 1998, he contends, "crime became institutionalized," with police, customs, and court officials the most corrupt. Yet in Ukraine, Kuchma's firing of the minister of security after the murder of investigative journalist Gongadze greatly weakened the police's "centralized organized crime apparatus." As a result, the Ukrainian elite "can't steal any longer—they're blocking each other from stealing." This at least offers the hope of a new start.[50]

However, it is Russia that has undergone the most radical change since the turn of the century, both in the new leadership style of President Vladimir Putin and in the West's image of him. Putin is now widely perceived not as a lowest common denominator KGB bureaucrat, but rather as the kind of pragmatic modernizer Russia has not had since the early twentieth century. Domestically, he has set the clear goal of making the economy function, has methodically gone about winning Duma approval of the reforms that are needed for this transformation—and has amassed enough power to be able to impose his views from above. He was rewarded with a turnaround to positive economic growth that reached 7.6 percent in 2000 and 5 or 6 percent in 2001.[51] In Åslund's view, what delayed Russia for so long was not only the sweetheart deals that privatized Russia's mineral wealth and delivered it into the hand of rent seekers, but also—by contrast with conventional wisdom in the West—too little rather than too much shock therapy.

In this analysis, the main reason Poland succeeded so fast was that Balcerowicz's shock therapy was radical enough to destroy the old system and let the new economy grow in its place. The main reason Russia floundered for a decade was that its reforms were only half-hearted. It took the financial crash of 1998 to impose reality, in the form of a two-thirds ruble devaluation, pricing of Western imports out of the Russian market—and therefore, at last, an incentive to Russian entrepreneurs to manufacture real goods rather than just profiteer from buying oil in cheap rubles and selling it in expensive dollars. The crash also brought home to at least some of the oligarchs, finally, that they had far more to gain both by protecting their newfound fortunes by rule of law and by investing their wealth in productive output than by continuing to strip assets and exploit raw materials.

In 2000, his first year as president, Putin rose to popularity by renewing the savage war in Chechnya after some bombings in Moscow were attributed under murky circumstances to Chechens. Otherwise, he concentrated on building a strong state; neutralizing the political power of the oligarchs, the regional barons, and the "family" power network he had inherited from his patron Yeltsin; and, via surrogates, closing down the NTV station that reported on him so negatively. With the tycoons, he eventually struck an uneasy deal in which he promised not to renationalize the bounty they had acquired in insider privatization if they paid their taxes and stayed out of politics. He delivered on his promise, cutting income tax to a flat 13 percent and corporate taxes down from 34 to 25 percent, to elicit more tax compliance. As revenues came in, he also began paying up on the state's huge arrears in pensions and wages. In terms of personnel, he appointed, ambivalently, both economic reformers and would-be recentralizers to his own staff and government posts.

Boilerplate aside, however, Putin initially paid little attention to broader economic policy. He failed to harmonize and simplify the welter of taxes, to reform the banking sector, or to create conditions that would curb the steady capital flight, which grew to an estimated $25 billion in 2000, or five times foreign direct investment. Nor did he reform the corruption-prone administration. Many outside observers, in fact, formed their overall picture of Putin not from his policies, but rather from his insensitive handling of the sinking of the Kursk submarine in the Barents Sea—and from the clumsy official attempts in subsequent months to blame the tragedy on a nonexistent collision with some intruding Western submarine.

But then suddenly, in his State of the Nation address in April 2001, Putin set out an ambitious program of structural reforms to achieve sustained 8 percent annual growth in the first decade of the century. To avoid "sliding to the second, possibly the third echelon of world states"—and this "for the first time in the past 200, 300 years"—he warned, Russia would have to make strenuous efforts to return from the communist "blind alley" to the "main stream of civilization." It must constitute a law-based, federative state. It must institute comprehensive judicial reform and fight crime and corruption. It should strive to meet the requirements for entry into the World Trade Organization. Market mechanisms could help the country conquer its "progressive backwardness" in the economy. Russia should have a "strong state power" with a regulatory and legal framework. And it had to invest in its decaying railroads and electricity grids and other outmoded infrastructure. Tiny Finland, the president noted, had five times the $50 billion stock capitalization of huge Russia; indeed, Nokia's capitalization alone equaled Russia's. Russian firms would have to start increasing their capitalization by playing by market rules.[52]

Putin then moved to oust the cozy management of Gazprom, Russia's largest firm, holder of a third of world natural gas reserves, worth $40 billion, producer of 7 percent of Russia's GDP, source of 40 percent of all Russian tax revenues (when it pays up), and hijacker of the weak

Russian state in the early 1990s. The Duma passed a land code that allowed urban private land to be bought and sold and used as collateral for the first time in three-quarters of a century; a restructuring of the power sector and telecommunications; a code of corporate governance, with greater transparency and minority shareholders' rights; and a criminal procedure code that would shift the right to issue search warrants from prosecutors to courts and introduce trial by jury. The hard budget restraints that the 1998 crash had imposed on Moscow and on the regions continued as a matter of policy, as did the sharp cuts in subsidies. Russia serviced its sovereign debts and even paid back $350 million to the International Monetary Fund two years early. Officials promised more transparency, with the participation of foreign bidders, in the next wave of privatization in 2005–10. The number of licenses required to start a new business was reduced, and a "one-stop shop" was opened to aid fledgling entrepreneurs. It even began to look as if Putin might move on some of the microeconomic changes that were now crucial, especially establishment of a real commercial banking system and perhaps even the judicial reform that is a prerequisite for rooting out the pervasive corruption. Reduction of housing and utilities subsidies, breakup of energy and raw-materials monopolies, and fundamental decriminalization of politics, however, still seemed far off.

With these shifts, Putin's image began to change in the West. U.S. president George W. Bush, who had scorned Bill Clinton's overemphasis on personal relations with Kremlin leaders, met his Russian counterpart and told the world afterwards that he had looked into Putin's soul and been reassured.

As if to encourage reform, Russia's economy began looking up. Not only was there positive growth for the third successive year in 2001; the trade surplus reached $47 billion, investment rose 9 percent, and income rose 6 percent. The stock market was 60 percent above values a year ealier, and Standard and Poor's added a plus to the country's B rating for sovereign debt. Gazprom reported export profits of $14.5 billion and gas contracts worth $250 billion to supply a fourth of EU consumption over the next decade and a half.[53]

The gratifying figures failed to convince the skeptics. Russia's low base, the two-thirds devaluation of the ruble after 1998, and, above all, the deus ex machina trebling in oil prices between mid-1998 and 2000 accounted for the success, the doubters said, and not the actions of the Russian government. Political skeptics further noted Putin's coercive reduction of dissent from the media and whistleblowers and other autocratic proclivities and stressed that Russia remained far removed from a liberal democracy under any definition.

Germans, having fifty years earlier escaped faith in the exceptionalism of their superior collective "culture" over the West's soulless "civilization"—and Poles, having just escaped the exceptionalism of martyrology—looked eastward and asked if Russians too might now be slipping away from historical destiny and graduating from the status of glorious empire to become, simply, a messy nation.[54]

The next clue to this riddle would come on September 11, 2001.

CHAPTER EIGHT

EU *"Domestic"* Policy

The forces that impelled Europe's unprecedented integration in the second half of the twentieth century were the deterrent horror of Auschwitz, the gulag, and the bomb; economic reconstruction; the magnetic attraction of a long peace and attendant prosperity; a globalized interdependence that has made statelets even as large as Germany far too small to cope alone with pollution and capital flows; German remorse and nightmares; and, in central Europe, a yearning for what is perceived as Western "normality."

Would these dynamics still prevail once Europe entered the twenty-first century, with the overarching Soviet threat and the post–cold war fluidity both gone? Could capitalism's animal spirits of self-interest and personal gain continue to drive the European project further? And could this still delicate process be insulated against potential Russian or Balkan disorder?

Pessimists, the true conservatives, argued from manifold lessons of history that the answer was no. To them it was obvious that the impulses to integration arose in a period of unusually mobile politics. That period was over. Ordinary clashes of interest were back.

Optimists, the true radicals, had an intimation instead that rationality, habit, and institutions could all prolong the newfound impetus to cooperation. In this view, the benefits of joint endeavor had already become so internalized that members would continue to pay the cost, however painful, of disciplined budgets and progressive loss of sovereignty. A new pragmatism reigned. If anything, the threat of chaos from the east would force (western and central) Europeans to accelerate their integration for their own protection. Put baldly, the institutions of monetary union and the EU Council, however imperfect, would have to succeed for sheer lack of any tolerable alternative.

It would be a mistake, optimists further suggested, to measure the decade-old sapling of the European Union against the two-century-old oak of the United States. The 1990s had made clear that the EU would continue to be a confederation-plus for decades to come—and despite Kohl's best efforts in the early 1990s, probably never would become a real federation. Its genius, unlike the American genius, to judge from the post–cold war evidence, was expressed less in powerful competing institutions than in ongoing process. And as long as the U.S.-sponsored peace prevailed in Europe, a consensual confederation process should suffice both to generate mutual commitments and to give member nations the confidence that they could maintain their own identities without being assimilated into a bland homogeneity that no one wanted.

Indeed, the corollary of this rare social optimism was that equally rare mode of decisionmaking that projected the domestic consensus politics of Germanic, Scandinavian, and Benelux Europe onto the European plane and made it work—in many cases—even without the glue of national solidarity. This approach was manifest in the 1990s in treating crisis as opportunity, uncertainty as fluidity, and anxiety about the future in general and Germany in particular as an energizing disequilibrium. Repeatedly, compromise was tipped into mutual resolve rather than deadlock; interdependence led to pooling of sovereignty rather than scapegoating; inertia was turned into the kinetics of cumulative movement rather than inertness.

Out of this came a process of growing commonality in addressing political, economic, and social problems that Harvard's J. H. H. Weiler, borrowing from Albert O. Hirschman, identifies as the shift from "exit" to "voice"—and that Cologne University's Wolfgang Wessels calls "ratchet fusion." European Community members first pooled part of their sovereignty conditionally, in what they thought was a revocable choice, then discovered that they became so inextricably bound up with their partners that "exit" would have brought unacceptable costs. This realization, in turn, repeatedly prompted member states to demand more "voice" within the consensus web and thus to consolidate the supranational institution.[1] Wessels applies this insight to analyze EU treaty revisions in both a "dynamic macro perspective" and "micro" national behavior in the half century of "supranational communi-tarisation." The yearly rate of reaching binding decisions, he finds, has more than doubled since the early 1980s in an "integration cas-cade" as EU members identify "the EU system as the optimal problem solving area."[2] Specifically, Stefan Collignon of the London School of Economics flags the role of the euro in creating new public goods that then require maintenance by the transfer of more decisionmaking to the common European level.[3]

Against such expectation of a continuing integration dynamic must be cast the sophisticated agnostic view of Johns Hopkins's David P. Calleo. Rhetorically, Calleo asks what is the difference between today's "triumphant" and "imperial" liberalism and that of a hundred years earlier that was so cruelly betrayed by the twentieth century's wars and totalitarian systems? Europe's cold war practice of cooperation he sees as merely an atypical "frozen parenthesis" in Europe's history. He is suspicious of U.S. hegemony and overstretch in central Europe, as in the world at large, and he hopes that Europe has used the paren-thesis to build an EU that can now offset "diminishing American he-gemony." But he doubts it.[4]

In Weiler's and Wessels's context, the processes that modernized and integrated West European societies and economies after World War II turned out to be less exceptional feats than a continuing trans-forming pattern. Thus Spain and Portugal effected their evolution from authoritarian to democratic systems in the 1970s and 1980s with the aid and tutelage of the EC in general and of the German Social Demo-cratic party in particular. By now they are even beginning to commu-nicate with each other across a border that for 700 years divided rather than united them, and are turning the new Euroregion there into a model of cooperation.[5] The self-confidence that Ireland acquired as it found in the EC an alternative orientation to England, moved into high-tech manufacture, and generated one of the fastest growth rates in Europe, was instrumental in boosting the republic's self-image enough to end, provisionally, the cycle of killings in Northern Ireland in the 1998 peace settlement.[6] And Italy and Greece jacked themselves up to become members of the European Monetary Union in good standing.

This mutual benefit is repeated variously in the experience of virtu-ally all EU members. The French National Assembly fumes about and defies the EU ban on shooting migratory birds during nesting sea-son—but France owes to the benign EC environment in the 1970s and

1980s the fact that its per capita income today almost equals that of united Germany. Germans pay the most, but, as their political leaders keep reminding them, their exporters also profit greatly from the huge single market, and their real average earnings sextupled in the past half century, for a healthy average annual increase of 4.7 percent. Such tangible progress is a powerful incentive for elites to continue and deepen integration, even at the cost of making some uncomfortable national concessions for the greater weal. It lets the Danes put up with the indignity of not getting their favorite little apples certified by Brussels, lets the French tolerate EU requirements that traded cheese be pasteurized, and forces the Germans to accept imported beer that does not meet their sixteenth century purity standards.

Yet voters who take for granted such fruits of cooperation tend to ask politicians, "What have you done for me lately?" And in this century's fast-changing world, the answer to that question will depend on the answers to several clusters of further questions—about EMU, EU governance, Germany, the French-German connection, assimilation of the central Europeans, and security. In brief:

—What will be the long-term effects of monetary union? Will the euro's 25 percent drop against the dollar in the first three years of its existence damage the EU economically or politically?

—Will the Germans make the necessary economic reforms to stay competitive in a globalized world? Or has a consensus system that is admirably suited to incremental change reached its natural limits and shown itself incapable of more radical metamorphosis?

—Can the French-German special relationship survive the change of generation in leaderships? How doggedly will France try to claw back political control of the European (and French) central banks?

—Will the EU knock heads together sufficiently to adapt institutions and rules made for six members to an EU of almost thirty members? Is the premise that crisis impels change in fact correct? Will the Bavarians accept cuts in the Common Agricultural Policy? Will the French accept cuts in German contributions to the EU budget that Paris would have to compensate for? How can the sense of mutual benefit be sustained when the necessary painful decisions are so often blamed on Brussels?

—Will the central Europeans continue without political backlash, despite the agonies of transformation, on their course of crafting democracies and market economies?[7] Might they in fact provide a fresh raison d'être to a jaded western Europe? And how far east will the EU aura radiate into countries that will not soon qualify for double membership in the EU and NATO?

—Finally, can some approximation of civility slowly be restored in the former Yugoslavia? Will armistice last long enough for European financial assistance to become an effective lever there? How can NATO, the EU, the UN, and the OSCE together best contain or stop war in the Balkans? How can Europe export security rather than import insecurity?

EMU

The European Monetary Union was the first great post–cold war test of the conflicting hypotheses in attempts to answer the host of questions. As measured in January 2002—when the euro graduated from being a virtual currency to become the coin of the realm in the pockets of 300 million Europeans—the EMU record offered some vindication to pessimists, some vindication to optimists. Pessimists pointed to the devaluation of the euro since its inception—and observed that EMU's prophesied 0.5 percent bonus to economic growth never materialized. Optimists countered that the numerous disaster scenarios never materialized either, and they credited the euro with mitigating the economic slump in 2001. Both noted that in realizing the vision of the Treaty of Rome, free movement of capital and services still lags well behind free movement of goods and people.

As the euro became real, consumers, despite initial misgivings—in Germany the *Bild* boulevard newspaper ran long lists of sauerkraut and camcorder and airline prices under the headline "€r macht alles teurer"—got used to the new money.[8] Travelers appreciated the convenience of not having to carry six wallets on a holiday drive from Amsterdam to Venice, or to lose constantly in conversion fees. All Europeans welcomed the novel transparency of pricing—and the pressure to equalize prices across borders—as equivalent items were quoted in easily compared euros rather than in a confusion of francs, lire, and guilders. Germans discovered that they could buy Volkswagens more cheaply in Milan than in Munich. The Greeks, having embraced neoliberal orthodoxy and reduced inflation, budget deficits, and government debt in the interim, rejoiced at finally being among the European front runners and did not mourn the loss of their 2,600-year-old drachma.[9] And even in Sweden and Denmark (if not yet in Britain), by the launch date a majority had turned around to favor joining EMU.[10] The previous criticism of the European Central Bank for its slowness in lowering interest rates faded. And the whole massive undertaking of introducing 15 billion new banknotes and 50 billion new coins overnight turned out to be about as exciting as a zipcode revision, concluded chief Deutsche Bank economist Norbert Walter.[11]

In the U.S. media the reviews ranged from neutral to dismissive. The Giant supermarket chain may have mounted a campaign to collect leftover schillings and pesetas from American travelers to feed Washington's neediest. But veteran economics commentator Robert J. Samuelson still feared that monetary union would set off a backlash, as "local and global economic discontent" blamed all woes on Frankfurt, Brussels, and "Europe."[12]

Yet the record of EMU in the three years of the virtual euro is impressive for a new-born currency. Within the eurozone, where the bulk of Europe's trade occurs, EMU cut transaction costs and exchange rate risks for both exporters and investors; improved competitiveness, efficiency, and allocation; and generally facilitated cross-border investment and trade. The sheer predictability of the currency yielded major advantages; two-thirds of the increase in German wage costs from the late 1980s to the late 1990s, for example, came from appreciation of the deutsche mark.[13]

From this perspective the devaluation of the euro, while embarrassing, was irrelevant. When the euro began as an accounting unit in 1999, it was worth just over $1.18. As the overall European economy continued to trail the American powerhouse, however, the euro lost 14 percent of its initial value against the dollar in its first year, and by January 2000 had dropped below dollar parity. Yet with internal European exchange rates locked together, the European Central Bank held a relaxed view of the fall and let the continent benefit from the resultant stimulus to exports. Smaller euro nations, especially those that had brought weaker currencies into EMU, prospered from their assured stability; Ireland grew by 10 to 11 percent, Luxembourg by 8.1 percent, Spain and Belgium by 4 percent. Between 1998 and 2000 Europe's overall growth averaged 3 percent, double the rate from 1992 to 1997, and created 2.5 million jobs. Overall unemployment dropped from 11.5 percent in 1996 to 8.3 percent in 2001—its best performance in a decade—thanks to

7.6 million new jobs in the eurozone. Before joblessness again rose in 2002, Europe's unemployment rate remained stubbornly higher than the United States' 5.4 percent, however. A particular benefit from the kind of structural shift that monetary union encouraged came in growth of new, flexible part-time jobs at three times the rate of full-time positions.[14]

Productivity per man-hour increased in the eurozone by a respectable 1.6 percent per year between 1996 and 2000, even if not at the American rate of 2.1 percent. Most significant, perhaps, when the 2001 slowdown hit the euro held internally; there was no repetition of the crisis in the European Monetary System in the early 1990s, no strain of the deutsche mark pushing upward and the lira falling out of the bottom. Indeed, this stabilization in the world's biggest exporter and largest single market of rich consumers was so much taken for granted that the achievement hardly merited comment.

What did not respond as anticipated, however, was the persistent gap between Europe's 3 percent and America's 4 and 5 percent growth—and the dive in the world economy in mid-2000, as the United States, Europe, and Japan headed toward synchronous recession for the first time in a quarter century. Economists may have marveled at how undervalued the euro was as the U.S. trade deficit soared in 2000 to a record 4.5 percent of national income, at $450 billion; as U.S. consumers blithely assumed household debts at 100 percent of income; and as the technology bubble burst and merger and acquisition inflows dried up—all without denting the greenback. But European investors still trusted the dollar and America's Midas touch and kept sending their money to the U.S. regardless of the contrary "fundamentals." The net outflow of direct and portfolio investment from Europe reached €162.3 billion ($140 billion) in 1999 and €158 billion in 2000.[15]

Moreover, the tripling of oil prices administered an external shock to Europe—and oil continued to be denominated in dollars, as did half of world exports, including even the European Airbus. Huge outlays as EU livestock was slaughtered wholesale to eradicate BSE (bovine spongiform encephalopathy, or "mad cow disease") and foot-and-mouth disease in 2000 added to the pressure. So did the U.S. slide into cyclical recession in March 2001; Europe turned out to be far more dependent on insatiable American consumers than had been thought, and the years that were supposed to see European exceed

American growth at long last produced only a puny estimated European increase of slightly over 1 percent for 2001 and 2002.

Under the circumstances, the euro manifestly did not impinge on the dollar as a world reserve currency; by the late 1990s, the dollar had risen from below 60 percent in the early 1990s to provide 68.2 percent of world reserves, as against the euro's 12.7 percent, while more than four-fifths of all foreign exchange transactions involved the dollar.[16] Nor did continental financial centers impinge on non-euro London, which retained 30 percent of global spot foreign exchange turnover and 36 percent of over-the-counter derivatives.[17]

On the other hand, the speed with which the euro money market sprang up, especially for very short-term liquidity, surprised everyone. In its first three years the new currency established itself as the world's second most important currency, accounting for 35 percent of all transactions on international capital markets, as against the dollar's 45 percent.[18] With EMU's stringent budgets, sovereign bond issuance is falling by an estimated $50 billion, but the underdeveloped category of corporate bonds—which in the past funded only a third of business debt in the eurozone, compared with 80 percent in the United States—is growing fast. In the first year alone euro debt issuance more than doubled, from €254 billion to €536 billion.[19] As the volume increases and instruments become more varied and more liquid, the overall cost of debt should decrease, thereby aiding entrepreneurs seeking capital—and giving more choice and flexibility, and therefore higher yields, to insurance and pension funds that were previously confined to fragmented national markets.[20]

In the euro's first year, Eurobonds shot up 285 percent, with a quarter of these issued in amounts exceeding €1 billion.[21] By 2000 a third of all international bond and note issues were denominated in euros, according to the Bank for International Settlements; by 2001 the figure had risen to 47 percent.[22] In June 2001 companies borrowed more in euro-denominated bonds ($50 billion) than in dollar-denominated bonds ($35 billion).[23] Deutsche Bank economist Walter expects the eurozone bond markets to reach the U.S. size of some $3 trillion in a relatively short time.[24]

The European equity market will be slower to match its $139 trillion American counterpart. At the euro's launch in 1999 the total eurozone stock market capitalization was only half that of the United States' as a percentage of GDP, but it should approximate its American counterpart within a decade or so, according to Walter. The euro-12 bourses traded only a third, the EU-15 less than half of the U.S. figure, since corporate financing on the continent has traditionally come much more than in the United States from in-house banks that hold seats on borrowers' boards.[25] Here, too, however, Europe is moving toward a shareholder pattern more like that of the United States, with the trend led by divestment of enormous noncore holdings by German banks and insurance companies under the tax reform that took effect in January 2002. The first cross-border European stock exchange was founded in 2000, as the Paris, Amsterdam, and Brussels bourses fused to form Euronext—and went on in 2002 to buy London's Liffe derivatives exchange and become the front runner to form the dominant pan-European stock exchange.

In the infant years of the euro, European mergers and acquisitions quickly became livelier, reaching $707 billion in 1999, double those in 1998. Before the worldwide slump in merger activity in 2001 there were even a few huge fusions, such as Vodafone's $190 billion take-over of Mannesmann in telecommunications—so far the only success-ful hostile bid in Germany—and the Rhone-Poulenc-Hoechst merger to form Aventis, in pharmaceuticals. European law firms have also recently begun merging across national and language borders to pro-duce giants like Clifford Chance, with $1.3 billion revenues in 2000, and Freshfields Bruckhaus Deringer, with more than 2,000 lawyers in nineteen countries.

Before the dot.com bubble burst and stocks on Germany's Neuer Markt collapsed, the impulse provided by the euro also increased the continent's notoriously scarce venture capital for a heady year and a half.[26] At its height in 2000 the Neuer Markt had over 300 listings and had raised a total €23.5 billion, according to Deutsche Börse AG.[27] As of 2001, though, there was still five times more venture capital per capita available in the United States than in Europe.[28]

Even more important than the various market readouts is the rapid development of a new equity culture as a byproduct of EMU. By the launch of the euro, the number of directly held equities in Europe had already doubled from €1,873 billion in 1996 to €3,631 billion ($3,429 billion) in 1999. Some projections anticipated that this figure would double again, to €6,291, or a quarter of Europeans' savings and in-vestments, by 2004. Mutual funds grew proportionally, from €938 billion in 1996 to €2,023 billion in 1999. And within the virtual euro's lifetime the number of European shareholders increased sharply.[29]

Regionally, too, as monetary union gradually creates for the first time a true single market in which alternative costs can be easily measured by both consumers and entrepreneurs—by small firms as well as by large businesses with greater analytical capability—the capital shakeup is reinforcing the trend of an investment flow to EMU countries that have low wage scales and are most in need of development. Ireland and Spain are attracting significant funds—Ireland's GNP per capita is now higher than Britain's—and despite its high unemployment, Spain is turning in what is being called its best economic performance in two centuries.

Both the successes and the disappointments of the fledgling euro economy moved the European Council, meeting in Lisbon in March 2000, to apply EMU-style benchmarking to other tasks. The summit set the goal of overtaking the United States and giving the EU the most competitive and dynamic knowledge-based economy in the world by 2010—not by administrative fiat, but by such means as liberalization, deregulation, encouragement of entrepreneurship, tax and welfare cuts, pension reform, transparency and accountability in corporate management, improved respect for shareholders' rights, technological modernization, the dismantling of intra-European market barriers, the forcing of competition on oligarchies, and the shaking up of rigid labor markets.[30] Specifically, this entailed achieving by the end of 2001 a European patent and a "fully integrated and liberalised telecommunications market"; by 2003, an open, integrated securities market; and by 2005, an open, integrated financial market—all of which were originally supposed to have been realized back in 1992, when the single market arrived. Liberalization was to be speeded up "in areas such as gas, electricity, postal services and transportation," and there was to be "rapid progress on the long-standing proposals on takeover bids"— that is, an end to management's practice of protecting itself with "poison pills" in negotiations, often without the approval or even the knowledge of shareholders. As with EMU benchmarking (and, in a very different area and under a different name, NATO peer review of allies' defense planning), members were to set long-, medium-, and short-term goals for inspection and monitoring by colleagues.

The targets implied, improbably, that the necessary implementing legislation would be passed by the deadline of late 2002. Legislation was indeed passed in 2000, requiring telecommunications providers to open up the last "local loop" to rivals to assure competitive prices for access to high-speed Internet services.[31] Further laws in 2001 standardized rules for Europe's telecommunications and media sector in a way that should "complete the single market on information, with more competition," in the judgment of European commissioner for telecommunications Erkki Liikanen.[32] The European Commission took on the automobile giants by ordering an end to exclusive dealerships (and therefore of price differentials of up to 50 percent across the EU) by 2003.[33] But other legislation greatly watered down the liberalization of postal services, and by early 2002 there still was no European patent, largely because of Madrid's insistence that Spanish join English, French, and German as a mandatory language for documents.[34]

The EU has finally agreed on specifications for a Europe-registered company—and on changes in insurance guidelines that make it easier for firms to establish branches inside Europe. In technology it leads the United States in establishing an agreed cell phone standard. In information technology (IT) and e-commerce in general it lags the United States by only twelve months, not its earlier eighteen, according to the Accenture IT consultancy; and computer ownership in Germany more than doubled between 1993 and 2000, to equip every second household with a computer.[35] But despite all the technological improvement, there are still only 25 computers per hundred people in the EU, as against 52 in the United States and 29 in Japan; only 45 percent of primary and 80 percent of secondary schools in the EU have Internet access, as against 95 percent in the United States, according to Unice, the federation of EU employers' organizations.[36]

Moreover, in this more nebulous world of myriad large and small demands, it seems, benchmarking works less effectively than it did for the clearcut Maastricht criteria for entry into EMU. After the Lisbon summit, Britain, Spain, and Portugal, the initiators of the liberalizing targets, continued to push for the Lisbon agenda—but Germany and France, hearing the siren call of their 2002 elections and ignoring the dozen years of tough negotiations that had almost produced consensus on a new EU takeover code, scuppered both that regulation and the long-planned opening up of utilities markets. Within a year the Lisbon momentum dissipated. Efforts to produce a standard European prospectus for raising money from investors failed. Bitter feuds raged over rules to let pension funds operate across borders. Protectionist labor unions and industrial lobbies enjoyed renewed influence.[37] The manifold remaining national and even regional barriers—Germany, alone, still has eight decentralized bourses—made a mockery of the Rome Treaty's aspiration to free movement of capital.

In February 2001 former European Monetary Institute chief Alexandre Lamfalussy, now chairing a committee of wise men commissioned by Ecofin to recommend ways to free financial services, tried to recover the momentum. His report deplored the "remarkable cocktail of Kafkaesque inefficiency" in Europe's fragmented securities markets, which made equity transactions cost an average eight times more in Europe than in the United States, kept the average size of a European investment fund at only a sixth of its American counterpart, gave European pension funds an average return from the late 1980s to the late 1990s of only 6.3 percent, as against America's 10.5 percent— and generally raised formidable barriers to Europe's ever achieving the kind of capital market that might one day approach the U.S. market in size, liquidity, and flexibility. Lamfalussy's report urged adoption of American-style disclosure rules, an end to national protectionism for investment and pension funds, harmonization of national regulations, acceleration of EU decisionmaking, compression of the subsequent national implementation period from two years to eighteen months; and consolidation of Europe's forty different financial regulatory agencies into one for each country. With exquisite symbolism, his report was itself shelved for the next year, while the European Parliament and the Commission fought a turf war.[38]

As E-day for issuance of real euro money approached, EU officials and outside observers joined in chastising European governments for their lethargy. The European Commission—in a role contradicting its reputation in America as an imposer of bureaucratic red tape rather than a dismantler of government meddling in the economy—scolded EU member states for failing to open up markets to take advantage of the euro. Commission president Romano Prodi called delays in completing the single market "very expensive for Europe."[39] Internal Market Commissioner Frits Bolkestein declared that if member states did not implement in 2002 at least ten of the forty-two specific measures needed to create integrated financial and securities markets, this would be a "political and economic failure"; in particular, he rebuked Germany for "corporatist reflexes" and "nationalist feelings."[40] The Commission chastised Germany and France for doing too little to make labor markets less rigid and, exasperated by Paris's and Berlin's stonewalling on policy, threatened to use existing antitrust law to break up utilities in these countries.[41]

For good measure, the International Monetary Fund, U.S. Federal Reserve chairman Alan Greenspan, the Association of European Chambers of Commerce, and the European Round Table of Industrialists joined the chorus of critics, fretting that the economic upswing of 1999–2000 had lulled governments into complacency and inaction.[42] The last IMF annual report on the eurozone economy before E-day lauded the arrival of the bills and coins as a "major milestone in European integration," but warned that the "competition and dynamism" released by the euro could be stymied by "continuing sluggishness in reform."[43]

At this point, the political trick for the euroland governments will be to get past the job-killing stage of restructuring as fast as possible (even in a period of retrenchment), to reach the second stage of releasing capital to generate new employment. A clash within and among countries could arise as telecommunications, banks, and IT firms alike fire employees and the first serious post-EMU recession works its way into electoral politics. Surprisingly, so far no Europe-wide protest à la Ross Perot has coalesced to complain about the great sucking sound of jobs being flushed south and east within euroland, or within an enlarged EU.

In the neoliberal view, further privatization, deregulation, and other liberalization measures are already under way in euroland, and they should pick up speed as younger generations (whether they call themselves right or left) inherit power. The portion of GDP controlled by the state should drop. Pensions will be trimmed. Retirement funds will, in any case, have to shift from pay-as-you-go to fully funded systems as populations age. The social safety net of unemployment payments and universal health benefits is already being trimmed; full pay for sick Mondays and regular spa mudbaths is unsustainable. After more than a decade of airing these issues ad nauseam, the consensus for change is present, even if politics is slow to follow. Significantly, the Netherlands, the main exponent in the 1970s of the "Dutch disease" of expansive socialist redistribution and wage costs 20 percent higher than Germany's, turned around fifteen years later to produce the "Dutch miracle" of flex-time work, job creation, and wage costs 20 percent lower than Germany's.[44] A footnote of history will surely record that one of the politicians who brought this about, as he himself changed from Keynesian to "pragmatic monetarist," was none other than the ECB's first chief, Willem F. Duisenberg.

Yet Europe's emerging labor flexibility is unlikely ever to reach American levels of mobility, either geographically or financially. The bulk of Greeks, Italians, and Poles who flock to Germany for work will go back to their home countries as living conditions improve there—and they will themselves compound that advance with their savings and the small shops they start. And even Germans who live in Schwäbisch Gmünd will, by and large, want to stay there instead of moving to Frankfurt.

Besides, for all their admiration of American openness and exuberance, Europe's more homogeneous nations still value solidarity and regard America's extreme individualism as callousness toward life's unfortunates. Even the continent's conservative–social democratic consensus in favor of neoliberalism at the turn of the millennium retained enough elements of the old social democratic–conservative consensus of solidarity to ensure that while the social safety net could be slackened, it would not be torn down. Notably, in the 1990s Chancellor Kohl frequently made the point by asking American conservatives critical of "Rhine capitalism" if they really thought that Chancellor Otto von Bismarck was a socialist when he introduced social payments in the nineteenth century.[45]

Obversely, Sir Leon Brittan, the EU's trade commissioner in the 1990s, long stressed to opponents of liberalization that Europe will not have to give up its social model. Instead, he turned the question around and asked how the continent could possibly afford to maintain decent social protection if it did not regain competitiveness and a healthy economy and end "the seduction of inflationary policies."[46] Warnfried Dettling, the conservative prophet of a new social contract above partisanship, argues that Germany can both modernize and attract investment, because of its political stability, labor peace, and craftsmanship; and still defend the young, elderly, sick, and unemployed.[47] This devotion to basic social welfare is even stronger now, in the overwhelmingly left-governed EU.[48] Tellingly, the Lisbon free market targets were deliberately paired with a "social agenda" of "more and better jobs and social cohesion."

In the narrower context of the governance of the European Monetary Union, issues of jobs and social cohesion will never influence EMU decisions to the extent the French would like, of course. But already the Germanic premise of the supremacy of technocratic economic rationality over social or political considerations is being modified to take more account of such concerns in the present lean economic times. In early 2001 the European Commission activated the stability pact's discipline system in reprimanding Ireland for overheating. Dublin took offense—and the row contributed to the subsequent debacle as Irish voters rejected the Nice Treaty in referendum.[49] A few months later, when the understood limits were again overshot, this time by Prime Minister Silvio Berlusconi's increasingly Euroskeptical Italy—a big player that could not be pushed around—the EU reacted with no more than embarrassed silence. In this case the corrective to excessive exuberance was left to the market impact of the U.S. decrease in European imports.[50] And when Germany's growth rate, the worst in the EU at 0.6 percent in 2001, pushed its budget deficits perilously close to the stability pact's 3 percent ceiling, the Germans were hardly in a position to be strict with others about the pact they had once dictated. The ECB signaled that it would be more flexible and give governments more time to meet the original target of zero budget deficits by 2003—and noted that the prescribed 1996 guidelines could be "intelligently adapted" if governments needed to take fiscal countermeasures. Within the EU as a whole, finance ministers also agreed to increase the approved fiscal flexibility under their nonbinding Broad Economic Policy Guidelines.[51]

Complaints about lack of transparency and accountability are more commonly directed at the EU as a whole than at EMU, of course, but the old EU culture of secrecy probably reaches its zenith in the rarefied world of the European Central Bank, which goes so far as to insist that the minutes of its meetings must remain under lock and key for decades to come. Central banks, critics argue, should at the least subject their broad policy strategies to the scrutiny of elected officials.[52] In this context various assessments of the Bundesbank as the model for the ECB have noted that over decades the German government in fact exerted far more informal influence over the largely independent Bundesbank than either party ever admitted publicly. And by comparison with the United States, critics continue, the requirement that the ECB president testify regularly before the weak and heterogeneous European Parliament is inadequate; it does not begin to match the demand that the chairman of the Federal Reserve testify before the far more powerful U.S. Congress.

The economic aspect of potential nonaccountability is the awkward division between monetary and fiscal policy, with the ECB controlling monetary policy and national governments controlling fiscal policy— subject to the constraints of the stability pact, and to the worry that rivals could begin a tax war to gain unfair advantages. The French and Germans, following the familiar cycle of seeking solutions in increasing "voice" within the EU, see the only way out of the dilemma as increased harmonization of tax and other financial regimes among EU members. Britain vehemently rejects this course.

The political aspect of potential nonaccountability is linked to the broader misgiving about a "democratic deficit" in the EU, the extreme depoliticization of the ECB, and its insulation from the outside world in what ECB board member Tommaso Padoa-Schioppa calls an uncomfortable "loneliness."[53] Very briefly, the argument pits the advantages derived from "output" of the public good in regulation and stabilization of the European economy—and the efficiency with which closed old-boy networks of specialists can produce this output when they operate beyond the public, nationalized glare—against the disadvantages of lack of democratic transparency and accountability.

A key riddle here is the anomaly that—despite Kohl's best efforts to drum up a European political union at the same time as monetary union— there is no governmental counterpart to the ECB as there is to the U.S. Federal Reserve. The EU is not a government, but a highly instutionalized system of supranational cooperation. And even if a dozen EU finance ministers from varying financial traditions could somehow agree on timely collective action in a way that would not destabilize volatile markets, the delicate question would still arise as to which ministers would be the appropriate policymakers. Britain, along with Sweden and Denmark, has blocked the French desire to have a euro-12 "Council" with decisionmaking powers, which would exclude non-EMU members and would formally decommunitize EU economic solidarity. (The European Commission, which can hardly exercise inside the European Monetary Union its traditional right of exclusive initiation of common EU economic legislation, raises similar complaints.) Yet by the same token, the EU-15 Ecofin, with three non-EMU participants, cannot reasonably prescribe policy for the euro-12.

So far, the attempt to square the circle has been to give some informal policy oversight to the consultative Euro "Group" of the twelve EMU finance ministers, as advised by the secretive Economic and

Financial Committee, composed of one official from each member country's finance ministry and central bank, along with two representatives from the ECB and two observers from the European Commission. This arrangement invites its own controversy, however, in the arcane world of "comitology." No one expects a central bank to be steered by opinion polls, but even central banks must ultimately be accountable to the public they serve via elected officials. And the forerunner of the Economic and Financial Committee, the Monetary Committee, which coordinated policy for the European Monetary System, carried secrecy to the extreme. No minutes were ever taken of its meetings; for years even the names of members were unavailable; and in its later years the committee did not publish so much as an annual report.[54]

Conceivably, several more years of the euro's smooth functioning as the common currency might convince European voters that the loss of democratic "input," transparency, and accountability is justifiable. More likely in the search for legitimacy are growing checks on the ECB through an increase in concerted action by EMU finance ministers.[55]

Germany, France, and Britain

Clearly, the sanguine theory that EMU will in fact act as a powerful catalyst to trigger needed reform and enhanced competitiveness in Europe will be tested first and foremost in Germany and France—in their domestic economies, their resolution of EU finances, and their commitment to continuing their joint coordinating role in the EU. Germany has the third-largest economy in the world and is the main financier of the EU. France has an economy second only to Germany's in Europe and is the world's third-largest exporter of capital and its sixth-largest trader. Moreover, in their joint impact on the EU, even if France and Germany do not constitute a directorate, their bilateral policy clashes often reflect more general contradictions between (roughly, northern and southern) EU members. If Paris and Berlin can reach satisfactory compromises, these often point the way to solutions that will be acceptable to others.[56]

Internally, the French and German economies are already less encrusted than they might appear on the surface—as Germany's steady trade surpluses and France's leading growth rates in Europe in the late twentieth and early twenty-first centuries would suggest.[57] Rudi Dornbusch may still fear that Europe will now be too fatigued by its epic fights over grand monetary union to muster the energy for the nitty-gritty of reform.[58] But out of the exhaustive public discussions of Europe's loss of competitiveness, at least a grudging consensus has been emerging among German business, political, and labor elites—and in French business, if not yet all political, labor, and countryside elites—that there is simply no alternative to painful reform.[59]

At the turn of the century the Germans were shocked to discover that after five decades of leading Europe, they were near the bottom in the EU league. Their economic growth was the worst; their capital productivity was 30 percent below America's; their labor productivity was relatively low. Even worse, they barely made it into the top twenty nations in the Program for International Student Assessment's international study of the educational accomplishments of teenagers in 2001.[60]

The shock was all the greater, because Germany was not used to thinking of itself as a loser—or as the restrictive state that neoliberals now claimed it was. Back in the 1950s the father of the German economic miracle, Ludwig Erhard, had, after all, insisted on "social market" solutions to the postwar impoverishment, in a system that was distinctly freer than France's dirigisme. The subsequent success of the Federal Republic's big conglomerates and those famed small- and medium-sized family concerns that today constitute more than 99 percent of enterprises, hire 70 percent of all workers, and produce 57 percent of GDP, quickly coalesced into a cozy system nicknamed "Germany, Inc." Banks and insurance companies maintained multiple cross-holdings; capital came primarily from those banks whose directors sat on company boards and saw to it that "their" firms remained solvent. Returns on investment may have been lower than in the United States, but Germans prided themselves on avoidance of America's dog-eat-dog rivalry. The assured bank financing—and often government-guaranteed credits for the third of GDP that was exported—allowed executive boards to elevate responsible long-term planning above short-term profits. Social peace reigned, with contracts negotiated within an overall consensus among employers, labor unions, and government, and workers sharing in management through "codetermination," holding secure jobs even in recessions, and enjoying an enviable social safety net.

Yet there were many distorting subsidies, in props for the Ruhr coalfields, for example, or in regional government guarantees that allowed the twelve *Länder* banks to undercut commercial interest rates, or in *Länder* bailouts of big local industries that were threatened with collapse. There was a stranglehold on many jobs by guild regulations that excluded newcomers. And the compulsory nonwage social welfare costs for hiring new workers were so high that they discouraged any American-style burgeoning of low-paying service jobs; indeed, the whole service sector remained underdeveloped in comparison with other modern economies. There were prerequisites of formal diploma training for opening a restaurant or founding a computer chip company; the common jibe was that it would have been illegal for Hewlett, Packard, and Gates to tinker in their garages in Germany.

And then there were all those fusty laws from as far back as 1909, decreeing that shops had to close their doors at 6:30 p.m. (or, after the laws were relaxed, at a generous 8 p.m. on specified days). Detailed "unfair trade" regulations prohibited discounts above 3 percent. Furniture stores might have discreet Sunday visiting hours, allowing young couples to examine the baroque "bed landscapes" on offer, but no money could change hands, nor could contracts be signed. Convenience stores in gas stations and train stations might stay open at odd hours to meet the needs of travelers—and the concept of emergency rations might expand well beyond lubricating oil and butter and schnapps—but the distinction would remain. A new subscriber to *Die Zeit* might get the bonus of a Black and Decker home drill—but only if a friend who lived at a different address nominated him for this dispensation. In Germany Land's End could not advertise—as it did in 174 other countries—unconditional guarantees on its merchandise. As late as 2002 clothing retailer C&A was enjoined to desist from giving 20 percent rebates to customers who helped ease currency changeover during the brief deutsche mark–euro overlap by using credit cards.[61]

What eroded Germany, Inc., more than anything else was the combination of globalization, the "new economy" of accelerating innovation in information and communications technology, America's unprecedented decade-long boom in the 1990s—and, of course, the enormous drain on the Federal Republic's resources as it pumped a trillion dollars, or 5 percent of its GDP, into its indigent new eastern regions after unification. While New York yuppies became dot.com millionaires overnight and inflated the bubble that would burst in 2000–01, German manufacturers began to find themselves increasingly undercut in costs and prices. Globalization, by shaving margins worldwide, exposed just how inefficient and expensive capital was in Germany.

Under these conditions, frustrated neoliberals contended, the Germans were not shocked nearly enough by their poor showing. They dabbled with reforms, but as soon as the economy began to pick up, they sloughed off and turned complacent. In this judgment, the conservatives were just as culpable as were the Social Democrats. Thus, throughout the 1990s the center-right government of Chancellor Kohl, watching the swift adaptation of the more supple U.S. economy to globalization, preached the need for root-and-branch transformation in Germany too. Indeed, the conservatives did establish a coherent legal framework for the digital age in replacing the old-style regulatory framework with the model Telecommunications Law, the Information and Communication Services Act, and the Media Services Interstate Agreement of 1996/97.[62]

Yet the conservatives never really had the stomach to push through what the business world increasingly regarded as the indispensable broader liberation of the economy from the heavy hand of the state. Kohl's heart lay elsewhere: in German unification and European integration. He did successfully fence off the most important reform of all—EMU—by refusing to blame monetary union for high unemployment in the initial restructuring that was its inevitable corollary. Unlike the French, he deliberately compartmentalized the two questions, and those Germans who lost their jobs never made a scapegoat of the euro. Kohl did not, however, exert his leadership to transform the ossifying German economy.

Without waiting for belated government action, then, the private sector plunged into the age of globalization. Daimler-Benz bought Chrysler; Volkswagen bought the Rolls-Royce motor car division; Deutsche Bank, conforming to the requisite accounting and transparency standards, listed on the New York Stock Exchange. Executives introduced U.S. accounting methods and began moving slowly away from collective management toward clear lines of personal responsibility.[63] Several German corporations set up incubator venture funds; by 1999 overall European venture capital investment reached $25 billion, or 13.5 percent of GDP, by comparison with the $45 billion in the United States, or 37 percent of GDP.[64] The public slowly joined the trend; share and fund holders multiplied two-and-a-half times from 1997 and 2001 to reach 13.4 million.

Given the lateness of reforms and the hard-edged politics of downsizing, numerous observers inside and outside the country asked whether cumbersome consensus politics in Germany had finally reached its limits.[65] But those voices inside the country were less evidence of stagnation than a sign that a consensus on the urgent need for change was finally emerging.[66]

Ironically, the neoliberal breakthrough did not come with Christian Democratic chancellor Helmut Kohl, but had to await the 1998 election of Social Democratic chancellor Gerhard Schröder, with an action program that his party's shrinking left wing deemed a betrayal of hallowed principles and the growing centrist wing deemed a repetition of the party's historic role in modernizing Germany at crucial junctures. To the cheers of businessmen, Finance Minister Hans Eichel instituted austerity, cutting the budget by an announced DM30 billion ($15 billion), and set the goal of bringing state spending as a share of GDP back below the 50 percent level it had reached between 1993 and 1996, to the preunification "state quota" of 46 percent—and perhaps even to an Anglo-Saxon 40 percent by 2006.[67]

Most important, punitive capital gains taxes on financial institutions' sales of cross-holdings to other domestic financial institutions were removed, thus inviting a shift away from the old cross-holding system of stakeholders to a more competitive structure, favoring shareholders.[68] In the biggest tax cuts in half a century, the government also lowered the rates on corporate profits from 52 to 38 percent and on the top income bracket from 52 to 48 percent, on the way to an even lower 42 percent by 2005.[69] With a view to Germany's aging population, the government further introduced the first stage of reform of the expensive pay-as-you-go pension system, shaving benefits from 70.7 percent to some 69 percent of wages by 2010, trimming the state's 75 percent funding of pensions (as against 40 percent in the United States), and nudging retirement funds toward self-financing by allowing employees to invest privately a small percentage of their gross wages that previously automatically went into the state pension system. The government cut the high 42.3 percent nonwage labor costs of 1998 to 40.8 percent by the transfer of some pension costs to the general budget, and aimed for an ultimate target of under 40 percent (though these costs subsequently crept up again).

The Schröder government also yielded, at last, to five years of pressure from Brussels to phase out by 2005 special preferences for 560 savings banks and the twelve *Landesbanken*, regional public sector banks, with their 40 percent share of the domestic deposit market. The Bundestag repealed the Nazi-era law limiting discounts to 3 percent. Eichel announced that Germany's "closed system" was over.[70] Further legislation is being planned to set up a single supervisory authority for financial markets; restructure the Bundesbank to streamline decisionmaking; increase investor protection by requiring greater disclosure of management holdings and punishing manipulation or insider trading more severely; limit interlocking boards; cut red tape; reduce the time it takes new companies to come onto the stock market from the present average of forty years to something approaching the fourteen years that is the U.S. norm; and shift passive welfare for the rustbelt jobless to more active training for modern employment in a high-tech era.[71]

To be sure, in deference to the Social Democrats' labor-union constituency, Schröder displayed a certain ambiguity about his neoliberal orientation from the beginning, bailing out the bankrupt Holzmann construction firm that critics argued should have been allowed to fail, piling job-deterrent social security costs onto previously exempt low-paying positions, railing against the loss of Mannesmann to the British (if not the British loss of Bentley to Volkswagen), and mounting a last-ditch defense of government underwriting of Germany's *Landesbanken*.[72]

Moreover, Schröder's commitment to reforms waned as respectable growth in 2000 eased the sense of crisis—and as the 2002 election loomed, critics charged. Most perversely, while EMU "cruelly exposed structural weaknesses in Germany," its initial successes actually reduced pressure to reform.[73] In some of the most highly publicized instances, the German government not only reneged on banning "poison pills" in the EU takeover code and joined France in postponing compulsory privatization of utilities in 2001, but even toughened Germany's own protectionist legislation against unsolicited bids. It again increased workers' sickness benefits, expanded standard worker codetermination in businesses to include part-time employees, and encumbered rather than eased the dismissal of workers by small businesses (with five to ten employees).[74] The German cartel office blocked three takeover deals by foreign companies, eliciting from one bidder the comment that the process was reminiscent of dealing with a "banana republic."[75]

However mixed Berlin's record, E-day in 2002, which introduced euro cash and simultaneously brought the new tax, pension, and takeover laws into force, tolled the end of Germany, Inc. A once-in-a-generation chance opened for financial institutions that no longer wanted to be industries' cash cows to disinvest. In a bear market, the sell-offs began cautiously—but they signaled a new era and a new economic system for Germany.

Like their German counterparts, the French elites were convinced that reforms were essential. The French government's lingering dirigisme in still disposing of more than 50 percent of GDP in 2001 surpassed Germany's level, was equaled only by Denmark and Sweden—and soared above America's 30 percent.[76] The state had to reduce this share, withdraw from its pervasive intervention, and let private entrepreneurship flourish if French firms were to remain competitive and attractive to all-important foreign capital in an age of globalization.

Just because a paternalistic state was so central a part of France's republican identity, however, the would-be reformers decided they must adopt tactics that were the exact opposite of Germany's. Faced with farmers and strike-prone workers enraged by loss of privilege and of France's precious uniqueness, the governing elites shrank from arguing the case on its domestic merits. Instead, they justified practices that starkly contradicted the French tradition and would lead to more unemployment before less by saying this was the necessary price to carry EMU and the EU forward—and thereby to keep the power of unified Germany in check. The rhetoric continued to be "rear-guard interventionism," but the underlying process was "Europeanization of the French State," in the analysis of David Howarth.[77] True to form, Chirac's own party refused to vote for ratification of monetary union, and French workers repeatedly demonstrated against EMU and associated austerity in the late 1990s. Also true to form, France's allies complained, while Paris was pushing EU energy liberalization as far into the future as possible, the powerful nonprivatized Électricité de France was using the breathing space to gobble up electricity providers in more open markets abroad.

The whole adaptation to Europe's "quasi-federal structures and quasi-pluralist processes" is far more difficult for unitary countries like France and Britain than for Germany, with its long-time "federal structures and corporatist processes" and experience with the kind of "semi-sovereignty" that characterizes the EU, notes Boston University's Vivien Schmidt.[78] A country with one of the proudest histories in Europe finds it hard to leave history behind. Paris has not yet made its peace with its diminished role and Berlin's enhanced strength since German unification. During this transition France has lost historical certitude, and "it is not easy being medium," in Dominique Moïsi's trenchant judgment of his compatriots.[79]

The initial reaction of Paris to the fall of the Berlin Wall had been to lull itself with the assumption that the edifice of the EC and the French-German reconciliation would continue to let France be the star architect of Europe, as it had been for three decades. When the changes instead transformed Bonn/Berlin into Europe's main collaborative architect, France, in Moïsi's analysis, turned "melancholy" and "morose," as globalization, unemployment, American supremacy, and European merger eroded French culture and identity. Prime Minister Lionel Jospin avoided ratifying the 1997 Amsterdam Treaty as long as possible because of the aversion of the National Assembly and the Senate to surrendering French sovereignty on immigration. And President Chirac gave every indication of regarding the molding of the European Central Bank in the image of the Bundesbank as the final blow, shattering French pretensions. The president might impose France's will on the fourteen other EU members once, in naming the head of the ECB for the second half of the first eight-year term, but only at the terrible cost of Europe's mocking laughter. "On ne rit pas"— as Chirac vainly lectured reporters in his postmidnight debriefing at the Brussels summit in May 1998—would be the epitaph for that French dream.[80]

Nonetheless, EMU in particular is forcing the French political class to recognize how modern France has actually become by now, how much "more like the others," in Mitterrand's phraseology. In his early years in office, Prime Minister Jospin was pragmatic in leading reform, and was rewarded until the recent global slowdown by the best economic performance in Europe, with an associated decline in unemployment, a reduction in the inefficient multitude of French banks, and adoption by many large French companies of Anglo-Saxon standards of accounting and corporate governance.[81] Jospin dropped his campaign vow to stop privatization of France's large state sector and proceeded to sell off chunks of France Télécom and Air France, he further backed Air France's management against the 1998 strike by pilots, and France has quietly offset the compulsory thirty-five-hour work week with flexibility.[82] On the other hand, as France's economy, too, slowed and opinion polls presaged a Chirac victory over Jospin for the 2002 presidential election, the prime minister all but stopped privatization and other liberal reforms—and he swiftly gave in a month before E-day to the blackmail of an illegal strike by policemen to force their public sector pay hike above guidelines.

In some areas domestic politics has thus brought Paris and Berlin together in braking EU liberalization, despite the two countries' basic acceptance of neoliberal inevitability. In other areas domestic politics has separated the two, especially in the issues of farm subsidies, overall funding of the EU, and what the Germans regard as their "brutal" treatment by Chirac when the six-year schedule of upcoming contributions was last apportioned in 1999. At that point the French president would not permit reductions either in the exorbitant 40 percent of the EU budget that goes into farm subsidies or in Berlin's burden of EU funding.

Today, under the financial pressures of globalization, EMU, and EU enlargement to the east, the Germans will no doubt increasingly pull away from the original EC bargain of high subsidies for French food and lesser subsidies for German industrial manufactures. A modest start was made in trimming the common agricultural policy with initial cuts in cereal and beef support in 1992. And Germany has been signaling that the next budget deal that is to be struck after the admission of new, heavily rural central European members must devolve CAP payments from the EU to national capitals in good measure. This change is seen by German policymakers as essential if the European Union is not to bankrupt itself by extending its present lavish subsidies to Poland's 10 million farmers.[83] Speeches by the Bavarian president of the German national farmers' association, Gerd Sonnleitner, suggest that the German agrarian lobby is resigned to inevitable cuts in its handouts.[84] Bavarian officials are already planning how to renationalize farm subsidies, paying income support rather than the EU's outdated price support—and probably making farmers richer in the process.[85] Certainly such a shift would be easier for the center-left government in Berlin, which is far less beholden to domestic farmers, than it ever was for German conservatives. And personally it would be easier for Schröder, who has no special Gallic attachment, than it was for Kohl, who still felt a special postwar obligation to France and the "community of fate" with his own war generation in France.

Other bilateral quarrels concern Paris's reluctance to privatize government defense holdings and let joint ventures with German firms proceed autonomously; liberalization of trade, and especially the goal of a transatlantic free trade zone; and the treatment of Turkey.[86] Enough of a habit of bilateral coordination of European policies has built up in the past two decades, though, to keep conflict over raw national interests in check. In September 1998, France's European minister, Pierre Moscovici, at least admitted publicly for the first time that France could not indefinitely continue to pay only a fraction of what Germany pays the EU, even if his president hardly acted on this admission.[87] All told, the bilateral *"entente élémentaire,"* or basic alliance, as the French call it, seems likely to continue, if with more reserve.[88]

How smoothly the evolutionary process works in Europe at large will depend to a considerable extent on how well the French-German team operates—and perhaps, too, on how fast Britain becomes a real player in the EU. The personal bruises in the relationship between Kohl and Chirac have not been transmitted to the next generation of leaders, but neither has the sense of special German deference to France. With Kohl's electoral defeat, Paris lost "one of the best German chancellors the French have ever had."[89]

The less predictable question is how far the United Kingdom will choose to reengage in pan-European affairs and, possibly, expand the French-German duo to a trio.[90] Even Britons who are not anti-European remain wary of having the British identity submerged in ever closer union and see the current French-German drive for tax harmonization as a threat to London's financial market.[91] But City bankers do not want to be shut out of the financial single market, Prime Minister Tony Blair has said he intends to lead the United Kingdom into the European Monetary Union, with a referendum on the issue—and, perhaps most significantly, Harrod's has been accepting payment in euros from the first day of the new currency.

London also welcomes the new German emphasis on the British precept of "subsidiarity," following European Commission restrictions on German industrial subsidies and corporate merger plans, and it approves the European Court of Justice rulings on the EU-wide applicability of health insurance, which now requires German companies to pay for eyeglasses bought in Manchester or Ibiza, say, as well as in Hamburg.[92] German businessmen, like Martin Kohlhaussen of the Commerzbank Board, openly call for the pragmatic British to join EMU and exert more influence in the sometimes overtheoretical European Union, and Berlin has left the door of the euro-12 ministerial group more open to future British participation than Paris would have wished.

Deepening

In its assigned task of reforming decisionmaking in EU institutions to accommodate a doubling of members without seizing up, the Nice summit of December 2000 was a disaster. Beforehand, it had been hoped that the multiple crises of abrupt resignation by the entire European Commission and war in Kosovo in 1999, the entry of Carinthian governor Jörg Haider's radical right Freedom Party into Austria's ruling coalition in 2000, and the impending accession of new central European members to the Union would shock the EU into effective action. They didn't.

The Commission's resignation followed some minor scandals over nepotism and loose accounting in various commissioners' offices and a subsequent showdown in the European Parliament. The confrontation did not, as it turned out, advance the powers of the Strasbourg legislature as much as Europarliamentarians had hoped, since the subsequent low turnout in Europe-wide elections (and the usual magnification of unrelated domestic protests in a European vote) conferred little legitimacy on that body. The one effect the institutional confrontation did have was to galvanize the European Council in Berlin in early 1999 to act with unwonted speed to name Romano Prodi successor to the invisible Jacques Santer as president of the Commission, and to name the very visible Javier Solana as high representative for common foreign and security policy, reporting to the intergovernmental Council rather than the supranational Commission.

The Freedom Party's gain of 27 percent of Austrian votes in October 1999 to become the second-largest party in the country posed an even more unexpected challenge to the EU: to define what behavior should disqualify a member state from exercising rights and privileges in the Union—and to stipulate just how far the EU might go in meddling in the domestic politics of a member state. To be sure, the remarkable tolerance for EU intervention in what used to be considered sovereign domestic affairs could be regarded as the hallmark of the European Union. But it was one thing to tell Slovak voters aspiring to join the EU that they first had to dump their autocratic prime minister, Vladimir Mečiar; it was quite another thing to tell the voters of a Western member in good standing that they had made the wrong choice in domestic elections and the entire country would now be punished for the entry of the Freedom Party into the government. As the fairplay Scandinavians in particular stressed, the Freedom Party—however nasty Haider's periodic slurs on various Balkan and other nationalities—had violated neither Austrian nor EU law. After five months of ostentatiously "isolating" Austrian officials bilaterally and in Council of Ministers meetings, the other EU members and Vienna found a face-saving way to normalize relations again before the Nice summit.[93]

EU members were less successful, however, in the critical issue of adopting mechanisms that could force their interminable talking shop at some point to stop talking and act, even with twenty-five or thirty loquacious interlocutors. Nor did they do anything to redress the EU's infamous democratic deficit. At Nice the mercurial French summit host, Jacques Chirac, had other priorities and grandly ignored the iron rule that the holder of the EU presidency must be a neutral facilitator rather than promote its own interests. He infuriated the smaller countries (and Commission president Prodi) by riding roughshod over them.[94] He rejected the simplest escape from capricious Council vetoes offered by the German-proposed "double majority" of both member nations and the size of their populations. Instead, he subordinated all else to maintaining Paris's equality with Berlin in the Council's weighted votes, even though there were now 40 percent more Germans than French in the EU. As a result, the "qualified majority voting" that was supposed to have been expanded at Nice to simplify decisionmaking became instead even more complicated under arcane new counting rules of a triple majority that not even the signers understood. The fifteen assembled leaders did endorse the lofty rhetoric of a nonbinding Charter of Fundamental Rights, but otherwise made little progress in wrapping up the "leftovers" of the Amsterdam Treaty, which was itself supposed to have wrapped up the leftovers of the Maastricht Treaty. So acrimonious was the summit that it spilled over not only to its customary 6 a.m. close after the last scheduled meeting day, but to the wee hours of the second day after the programmed conclusion.

London was pleased with this minimal outcome, especially since Britain managed to preserve its veto on EU tax harmonization, at least temporarily. Madrid was happy that its threat to veto admission of new Central European members into the club, should enlargement subtract one penny from Spain's bountiful EU subsidies, seemed to be paying off. And Chirac, of course, was elated by his success in blocking the 83 million Germans from getting any more Council votes than the 59 million Frenchmen.

Everyone else, however, was sour. Rome was upset, as usual, because Italy was not treated as a big power, despite its size as one of the five largest EU states and its history as one of the six founders of the European Community. Berlin was distressed that the Nice Treaty failed to solve so many institutional bottlenecks that needed resolution to avoid paralyzing the EU once new central European members were added. The German *Länder* were rebelling against the loss of their powers vis-à-vis both Berlin and Brussels over the previous half century and were threatening not to ratify the Nice Treaty in the Bundesrat unless this erosion were reversed. France and Germany were quarreling openly. The European Parliament, sotto voce, threatened to reject the Nice Treaty because its own powers remained marginal in the document. And in the final insult, the EU-loving Irish—who had arguably benefited more than anyone else from the EU and who regularly told pollsters that an astounding 75 to 85 percent of them liked the EU—rejected the treaty in a low turnout for the mandatory referendum.

In the hangover that followed, the Germans expressed a common view, concluding that Nice proved that the intergovernmental method had reached its limits. An informal consensus process designed for a club of six could be stretched—barely—to work with fifteen. It could not possibly work with two or three dozen members as diverse as Sweden and Malta, as vivid lingering memories of Malta's obstructionism at the 1975 Helsinki Conference on Security and Cooperation in Europe suggested.

Under the pressure of the urgent need for action, the Germans began to probe how they might turn their own domestic necessity into a virtue. Berlin, too, stood accused of national egoism—of having put narrow internal quarrels with the *Länder* above the broader European weal at Nice in insisting that yet another treaty conference be called for 2004 to follow in the weary wake of Maastricht, Amsterdam, and Nice to prescribe a binding "catalogue of competences" for the EU, nation-state, and regional levels.

To escape the post-Nice malaise, German diplomats now chose a "flight forward" that quickly shot well beyond the general opinion of other European elites. In a bolt out of the blue a year earlier, in April 2000, German foreign minister Joschka Fischer had resurrected the whole vexed question of the EU's *finalité*, or end goals, and in a talk at Berlin's Humboldt University, called for a federal Europe. At the time, his appeal had been widely seen as an anachronism, a throwback to the days of the founding fathers and pro-European demonstrations by idealistic young Germans. In response, French foreign minister Hubert Védrine had complimented his colleague, then gone on to deflate any federal fancies and praise instead the present dominance in the EU of intergovernmental authority wielded by nation-states over the supranational European Commission. In a noteworthy performance for a neo-Gaullist, French president Jacques Chirac had also lauded Europe effusively in the German Bundestag—but had skirted the idea of a federation and praised instead Fischer's parallel vision of an elite avant-garde that would integrate faster than laggard EU members wanted. British prime minister Tony Blair had countered by calling for a European "superpower but not a superstate."[95] German Chancellor Gerhard Schröder had remained conspicuously silent.

To those steeped in the EU's unique "Monnet method" of rolling consensus, Fischer's summons threatened the familiar system under which Spanish fish quotas are casually traded for Swedish allowances for Arctic farms, or huge subsidies for French peasants are prolonged in return for institution of German anti-inflation canons at the European Central Bank. As long as the *finalité* of the EU was left unaddressed and vague—and as long as Berlin was still willing to bankroll the growing number of deals—such logrolling could continue to function. The various European leaders could still stick together, while dreaming their different dreams. But once Fischer described his own federal dream and forced others to do the same, France and Germany would clash. And Blair, who was hard pressed as it was to bring Britain into the European Monetary Union, would have to fend off the redoubled wrath of British Euroskeptics over the dreaded f-word.

By the Nice summit, it seemed that the incremental pragmatists had succeeded in sidelining Fischer's grand debate. But in the wake of Nice the Germans revived the call for a federation—a goal that to them was entirely compatible with subsidiarity, given the German domestic federal system. In a speech to the European Parliament in April 2001, German president Johannes Rau proposed "a new European constitution" for a "federation of nation-states." This opaque formulation, which is about as logical as "hot snow," had been coined by former EU Commission president Jacques Delors in the rather different context of an avant-garde federation of the six founding members of the European Community. In its legislative function, Rau added, the Council of Ministers should become an upper house to complement the European Parliament. He was promptly seconded by Carlo Ciampi, now the Italian president and, in more restrained fashion, by Belgian officials.

Then in May, to the astonishment of almost everyone, the German chancellor—who had prided himself on having avoided the topic of Europe altogether in his 1998 election campaign and had subsequently volunteered little about the EU—suddenly stepped forward as the newest cheerleader for a federal Europe. His chosen instrument was a resolution drafted under his chairmanship for the Social Democratic Party's convention in the fall of 2001 and personally promoted by him at the spring conference of European Socialists in Berlin. "German Social Democracy will take on itself the role of being a party of European unification," Schröder proclaimed.

The resolution further called for the European Commission to become a "strong European executive" and for the European Parliament to be granted full budget authority. The Council should indeed become the upper parliamentary chamber to guard the prerogatives of member states against encroachment by EU bureaucrats in the same way that the German Bundesrat guards the prerogatives of the German *Länder* against encroachment by Berlin. Under the "subsidiarity principle" of assigning powers to the lowest appropriate level of governance, those competences that nations could exercise better than the EU should be returned from Brussels to the member states. In particular, the agricultural subsidies that together with aid for regional infrastructure account for 80 percent of the EU budget should be partly shifted down one level by joint national-EU "cofinancing."

Furthermore, Europol should be turned into an operative Europe-wide police force, the EU's exterior perimeter should be patrolled by a joint border police, and the Nice Charter of Fundamental Rights should be incorporated into the EU treaties and made legally binding. Such an evolution, Schröder argued, would help redress the democratic deficit by making the murky EU institutions more transparent and accountable.[96]

German feuilletons appeared, comparing the current primitive state of EU cooperation with American disarray before the constitutional convention of 1789. Various commentators became fascinated by the chaos in the eighteenth-century American confederation prior to the constitutional convention, by the audacity with which those convention delegates exceeded their instructions, and by the passionate and deep philosophical debate in the *Federalist Papers.*

And suddenly the magic word *convention* was in the air. A drafting committee made up not only of bureaucrats and experts, but also of governmental, national legislative, and European Parliament representatives had been successful in writing the Charter of Fundamental Rights for Nice. Why couldn't that process be repeated to compose a full-blown single constitution? Indeed, why couldn't that charter become a bill of rights for the new EU constitution? It was all well and good to agree with the European Court of Justice that the scattered elements of supranational governance in successive EC/EU treaties formed a constitutional equivalent. But a single, spare summation of those treaty elements might prove far more attractive to the public than the impenetrable prose of the Maastricht, Amsterdam, and Nice Treaties and those 90,000 accumulated pages of the sacrosanct *acquis communautaire.*[97]

This time around, the potent German brew could not simply be damned with faint praise as Fischer's Humboldt speech had been. The Italians and Europarliamentarians welcomed the Social Democratic paper and its attempt to overcome the EU's democratic deficit—but few others did. Austrian chancellor Wolfgang Schüssel and a spokesman for the ruling Danish Social Democrats joined Blair in warning against erecting some "superstate." One Tory backbencher sputtered that the German proposal recalled Hitler's design for Europe. The

British press once again condemned "centralization" and reminded readers that the English-invented democracy had worked splendidly for 800 years without the straitjacket of a written constitution.

In Latin Europe, a spokesman for the Spanish government told *El Pais* that Madrid was "unpleasantly surprised" by the German initiative, especially by the attempt to reduce the EU's financial responsibility for regional development by pushing these costs in part back onto national governments. Indeed, the Spanish went on the offensive, objecting to and reopening the whole package agreed on in 1999 by the Spanish government as well as all other EU member states. In that deal regional funds were automatically reserved for member states' regions that fall below 75 percent of the average EU wealth. Under this formula the combination of Spain's rising prosperity after twenty years of EU subsidies with the accession of a dozen poor central European countries would disqualify all but the very poorest Spanish regions and require Madrid to share with the central Europeans the EU largesse it so long enjoyed. Numerous other EU members regarded the Spanish threat of a veto on new members as blackmail.

More suavely, French president Chirac and prime minister Lionel Jospin immediately rejected any devolution of farm subsidies from Brussels to Paris, the prime beneficiary of the EU's Common Agricultural Policy. Such a move, they said, would be an undesirable renationalization and retreat from EU solidarity. They further told Schröder at their next bilateral summit that the German chancellor's ideas for institutional reform were not acceptable "in this form" and again lauded the intergovernmental process. French finance minister Laurent Fabius ruled out any downgrading of the intergovernmental European Council to no more than an upper parliamentary chamber. (So did EU president Prodi, for that matter, along with Schröder's own foreign minister, who quickly adopted what was by now the catchword, never defined, of "federation of nation-states.") French European minister Moscovici counseled sticking to the current balance between Council, Commission, and Parliament, and observed primly that national governments were the proper "expression of the will of the people."

Some German reporters in Paris noted further that the French government cedes its own National Assembly so little control over the French budget that it would hardly tolerate ceding more power over the EU budget to the European Parliament. Others described French officials as spurning enhanced powers for the European Parliament because of the "disproportionate weight" of Germany in the European Parliament—that is, the additional EP seats that French president François Mitterrand had grudgingly accorded Kohl after unification instantaneously expanded the Federal Republic's population. The clear French preference was to perpetuate the intergovernmental method of peripatetic European Council summits and Council of Ministers' meetings in which those equal voting weights for France and Germany that President Chirac had nailed down at Nice would apply. And while Paris did not necessarily oppose compiling a coherent EU constitution, it wanted any draft to be written by a more steerable commission of experts, not by some unpredictable convention.

Adding to the negative reactions to the constitutional idea, pragmatists of various nations shrank from the unraveling of all the tortuous multilateral package deals of the past decade that would inevitably follow from the German-proposed isolation and repackaging of those segments that addressed "constitutional" questions.

On the face of it, then, Schröder's initiative appeared to be doomed. It might have been written off as just another domestic political ploy, an attempt to steal the pro-Europe clothes of the Christian Democrats as neatly as his Social Democrats had stolen the conservatives' clothes of liberal economic reform. Indeed, at the time, chancellery staff had downplayed the specifics of the Social Democratic proposal and highlighted instead Schröder's political preemption in neutralizing an issue that might otherwise have favored the Christian Democrats in the 2002 national election.

Yet once ideas are released, they do not always return to their bottles. What initially looked like abstract philosophizing quickly developed surprising momentum. Having set the agenda, the Germans began the deal making and quotidian bureaucratic follow-up to carry the idea further. By February 2002 a convention of elder statesmen, government representatives, and European and national parliamentarians of EU member-states and the ten top candidate states began meeting under the chairmanship of former French president Valery Giscard d'Estaing. Its mandate was to draft constitutional arrangements, delineate competences, and recommend the kind of institutional reform that would keep even a greatly enlarged Union capable of acting. Recommendations were to be passed on to the treaty summit of 2004 for decision.[98]

What was involved here, in the analysis of Oxford University's Kalypso Nikolaïdis, was a change in five paradigms: (1) from allocative outcomes to the process of change of allocation, with a stress on flexible and open-ended dynamics; (2) from distribution of competences to shared competences, by such means as networking, cooperation, and proportionality; (3) from separation of powers to power checks, with procedural subsidiarity, mutual control, and asymmetric federalism; (4) from transfer of power to empowerment, away from zero-sum thinking to proactive subsidiarity and positive sum allocation; and (5) from multilevel to multicentered governance, with nonhierarchical models, mutual recognition, and shared identity.[99] Not every delegate would have been able to articulate the convention's tasks as eloquently. But these historic changes in fact describe the accelerating dynamic of the EU as it matures in the post–cold war world.

Unusually, this time around, the opinions of ordinary citizens about the future of their EU are actually being solicited. And this time around, the European on the street, as she jangles novel non-national euros in her purse, might just look with favor on the oddity of a constitution for the nonstate of Europe. Or so the Germans, the Belgians, and some former French officials hope.

CHAPTER NINE

EU Foreign Policy

For Americans, September 11, 2001, was an existential provocation. The instant murder of 3,000 civilians and felling of the World Trade Center's twin towers disabused them of their firm conviction that the world's sole superpower was invulnerable. In addition, it gave the lie to the prevalent assumption that the twenty-first century's autonomous globalized markets largely obviated the need for activist politics and diplomacy.

For Europeans, too, that suicidal al-Qaida mission sparked existential angst, not only because their own open cities and civilization itself seemed threatened, but also because global U.S. leadership was suddenly at risk. The Europeans' immediate solidarity arose from heartfelt sympathy and horror—but also from a wish to avert any U.S. reflex of bombing the perpetrators or their surrogates and then withdrawing from the hostile world. Such abdication would have been a disaster. Like it or not, George W. Bush was the only common leader the industrialized democracies had. His forfeiture of this role would have left them rudderless, at the worst possible moment.

"We are all Americans now," *Le Monde* famously proclaimed on September 12. "New York is the symbol for millions of emigrants fleeing persecution of life and limb. The symbol of refuge, the chance to make a new start, a promise of hope for the persecuted and the oppressed," Chancellor Gerhard Schröder eulogized in offering his condolences.[1] For his part, Prime Minister Tony Blair circumnavigated the globe as an eloquent avenging angel, to the ovation of Americans and the embarrassment of the British. And for the first time in its half century of existence, the NATO Council invoked Article 5 of the 1949

Washington Treaty, deeming an attack on one alliance member an attack on all.

In the event, there was no quick spasm of American overreaction. Instead, the Bush administration took the time to forge an antiterror-ist coalition of the willing, avoided falling into al-Qaida leader Osama bin Laden's trap and summoning forth a clash between Christian and Islamic civilizations, differentiated between Islam and Islamist extrem-ism, compelled Pakistan to renounce its decade-long support of vio-lent Islamist groups, and welcomed Vladimir Putin's unexpected embrace of the West. An administration that had been at pains not to be trammeled by the United Nations nonetheless paid its UN dues and sought and received Security Council endorsement of an American military response, even as it stressed that no Security Council man-date was required.

Reminded of the dangers should al-Qaida associates ever go be-yond turning hijacked jetliners into manned cruise missiles and esca-late to nuclear weapons, the Bush administration also restored some money it had previously suspended from old programs to help Russia destroy military-grade plutonium. Leading a campaign to freeze ter-rorist funds around the world, it reversed its previous opposition to tougher international antilaundering agreements that might hurt U.S. competitiveness in financial services and agreed to shore up the role of the twenty-nine-nation Financial Action Task Force. [2] Further, it be-came active once more in multilateral efforts to restart world trade negotiations in Doha and acknowledged to some extent the long-term importance of global economic growth in depriving terrorists of breed-ing grounds in stagnant poverty.

Initially, it seemed to the Europeans that America's loss of innocence, however tragic the circumstances, was salutary. The city on a hill real-ized that it did need the rest of the world after all. The Bush administra-tion dropped the solipsism of its first eight months in office. The Europeans applauded—and they applauded even more at the swift vic-tory of America's precision targeting of al-Qaida and Taliban hideouts, the consequent demystification of al-Qaida and of Islamist extremism in Pakistan, and the execution of the war in such a way that the fa-mously antiforeign Afghans welcomed the Americans as liberators, while condemning fanatic "Arab Afghans" as the outsiders.

And then, in retrospect, the Europeans counted the transatlantic cost. They had lined up to offer troops and ships and planes for the common fight against terrorism. Reversing the roles in the 1990s quarrels about whether equitable burden sharing meant NATO must assume responsibilities outside its own theater, the formerly reluctant Europeans had volunteered such service—and had been rebuffed by the former passionate U.S. advocates of out-of-area missions for the alliance. A few British and Australian commandos and planes did join the fray. Germany had its second moment of reckoning after the Kosovo war, buried its post-1945 military inhibitions for good, and authorized dispatch of Bundeswehr troops to combat in Afghanistan.

Yet the military alliance of NATO was absent in this war, apart from deploying eight frigates to the eastern Mediterranean and seven E3 airborne early warning and control system (AWACS) aircraft to patrol U.S. airspace while their American equivalents flew to Asia.[3] Otherwise, the brutal fact was that the Europeans were irrelevant. The United States conducted its coalition of the willing unilaterally. Europe was at peace, and therefore had little claim on American attention in competing with the clear and present danger of terrorism.

Moreover, the gap between Europe's dumb weapons and America's smart missiles (some British systems excepted), it turned out, was wider than ever. With its precision-guided bombs and missiles, the United States was already far advanced in the celebrated "revolution in military affairs." It had a monopoly on the global positioning satellites in stationary orbit that were all-important for pinpointing the location of personnel and targets. It had abundant satellite intelligence—which it was reluctant to share with its allies—that it could utilize for real-time targeting. Nor would the European allies have been able, for sheer lack of military hardware, to act on America's centimeter-accurate intelligence images had they seen them. In the years since the 1999 Kosovo war the United States had upgraded its planes and munitions to all-weather capability. For the first time it now had operational attack drones that did not risk pilots' lives, along with a mix of platforms that in combination could loiter over battlefields to provide real-time intelligence; it had the kind of integrated battlefield management computer system that could let the captain on a ridge use the intelligence for devastating tactical targeting—and let the overall commander conduct the whole campaign from his headquarters in Florida. It was now obvious that American air power—triumphant after decades of accusations that it was indiscriminate, inefficient, and even psychologically counterproductive—would rule future wars, along with special forces spotters armed with laser pointers, Pashto or (fill in the blank) phrasebooks, and iron constitutions.

Not even the modernized light infantry that the Europeans had never really gotten around to funding in their rush to cut defense spending in the 1990s would have been useful in Afghanistan. The transatlantic gap from the accelerating American digitalization of war promised to grow as the United States—which already accounted for more than a third of world military outlays—topped off its $350 billion annual Pentagon budget with another $20 billion in the wake of the Afghan campaign, for something like 40 percent of world military appropriations, or a level equal to the defense budgets of the fifteen next highest spending countries combined.[4] The question already raised in Kosovo of whether Europeans would again be able to fight alongside the high-tech Americans became more acute than ever.

Even the traditional function of Europe as America's continental aircraft carrier was downgraded as U.S. planes flew to Afghanistan from real aircraft carriers, from Diego Garcia, and from Missouri, halfway around the globe. Turkey may have been a main staging area; Europe proper was not. In the end, Europe contributed less to the war in Afghanistan than it had to the Gulf War a decade earlier. More broadly, while the U.S. had indeed needed allies in its campaign, common values had less to do with their choice than did geography. Washington's crucial partners were not the European democracies, but personal fiefdoms in Central Asia, as blessed by Putin; a military regime in Pakistan; and those flexible Pashtun tribes that could be persuaded to defect from the Taliban.

Thus, the Americans were happy enough to get the quick German police tips that there had been a twentieth would-be accomplice of the September 11 hijackers. They increased secret service exchanges of information somewhat, to add the Europeans' better human intelligence in Islamist circles to America's awesome signals and imaging capabilities. But when the Bush administration dealt with the Europeans, it made no pretense of talking with equals. Once the Taliban and al-Qaida were routed, the United States could, without consultation, bar the British from deploying peacekeeping troops in Afghan warlord precincts that might interfere with America's military hunt for mastermind Osama bin Laden. It could unilaterally abrogate the 1972 Anti-Ballistic Missile (ABM) Treaty and abort international inspections for the 1972 Biological Weapons Convention that the 144 signatories had all but agreed on after six years of negotiations. And it could decide solo that it would not actually destroy U.S. nuclear warheads in any informal deal on deep cuts with the Russians, but only put them into reversible storage. After all, as Clark S. Judge formulated it in a Hoover Institution essay on the benevolence of America's hegemony in the world, "Since the attacks, the earth's major nations—ranging from the NATO countries to Russia to China to Japan—and so many others have put aside their differences with the United States."[5] More pugnaciously, curmudgeon William Safire made the same point in concluding that when America acts firmly enough, all its critics shut up.[6] What the *Economist*, a long-time American cheerleader, called "the doctrine of seeking national security through military might" prevailed in Washington.[7]

Under the circumstances, such imperturbable transatlantic stalwarts as Stanley Sloan and François Heisbourg now worry more about an alliance crisis than they ever did during all the past NATO brawls about nuclear targeting, burden sharing, or life after the cold war. Sloan, long the encyclopedic NATO specialist at the Library of Congress and now a private consultant, sees a stark choice looming between "deepening" or else "dissipating" NATO and urges negotiation of a new, overarching Atlantic Community Treaty, with biannual summits of all NATO and EU members and candidates.[8] More bluntly, Germany's leading opinion weekly, *Die Zeit*, already sees NATO as being "pushed into its grave" and concludes, "Since September 11 NATO has fallen into an identity crisis. Washington prefers to act alone in the world, while the Europeans can't even keep their own house in order. What still holds the alliance together?"[9]

François Heisbourg, chairman of the International Institute for Strategic Studies Council, expresses the same concerns about "America's unilateralist drift, moving towards institutional practices and foreign-policy profiles akin to those of the first 150 years of the US Republic." Washington's "pick and choose" response to NATO offers of assistance under Article 5 hollowed out this solemn pledge of mutual support to "the presumption (not the obligation) of active military assistance." American aversion to multilateral cooperation, combined with Europe's refusal to take its due share of security responsibility in the world, is thus "leading to a situation of *de facto* division of labour between the US and Europe, eroding the traditional NATO ethos of risk-sharing." We are witnessing the death of the old NATO, he contends—though he attributes its demise not just to the Afghan war, but also to the confirmation this war gave to the transatlantic split that first became apparent during the Kosovo war in 1999.[10]

Indeed, that prior war was a turning point, in part because of its very different significance for Europe and for the United States

The Kosovo Harbinger

For Europeans, the eleven-week war in Kosovo and its preceding crisis were as existential as today's terrorist threat, if for different reasons. They put to the test all the continent's gains of the previous fifty years, and especially of the post–cold war 1990s. They challenged the assumption that at last, at the end of a terrible century, voluntary cooperation had triumphed over Nazi and communist coercion. They exhumed the savage ethnic Balkan wars of a bygone era even before the forgotten Great War.

The earlier failure of Europe (as of America) to stop atrocities in Bosnia at the beginning of the 1990s had been different. That lapse could be, and was, attributed to surprise, to residual abhorrence of upsetting the nuclear cold war balance, to the murkiness of measuring the relative cruelty of reciprocal murders by Serbs, Croats, and Bosniaks. "Bosnia came too early," was the common excuse. The European Community had not yet bestirred itself after two decades of Eurosclerosis to finish building the single European market of 1992 or the Maastricht design of monetary union. The Russian legions that would remain in central Europe and Germany until 1994 made governments reluctant to test Moscow's sensitivities in foreign policy. The French and the British were still queasy about German unification and still flirting with the idea of a return to nineteenth-century balance-of-power politics in backing the Serbs against the "German" Croats. Passive Europeans were still too accustomed to letting the American superpower make security decisions for its transatlantic protégés.

Besides, back in 1991 and 1992 the Balkans just were not part of the mental map of Europe. In Bismarck's lingering words, they were not worth the bones of a single Pomeranian grenadier. The whole aim of diplomacy in Bosnia was simply to wall off barbaric Yugoslavia and prevent the conflagration from jumping over to civilized Europe.

By 1999, however, the old alibis no longer applied. Europe did not need to fear any backlash from a Russia whose GDP had shrunk to less than the capitalization of Wal-Mart, whose armies had retreated a thousand miles to the east and degenerated after the disastrous slaughter in Chechnya. The European Union had had time to realize that it was, in fact, more than just an emergency cold war artifact, and even to anticipate a brave "common foreign and security policy" prescribed in the Amsterdam as well as the Maastricht Treaties. Virtually all of the postcommunist governments of the small nationalities perennially suspended between the powerful Russians and Germans were now drawn ineluctably to the magnets of the EU and NATO, eschewing Russian dysfunction and aspiring instead to a German-style transformation from a hierarchical to a democratic mind-set.

Most important, perhaps, the West could no longer plead ignorance. It had seen the fruit of its earlier malign neglect in the Serb massacre of Bosniaks at Srebrenica, the worst mass murder in Europe since 1945. This had answered definitively the question of comparative evil and identified the Serbs as the most bloodthirsty offenders in ex-Yugoslavia—and it had altered the pacifist reflexes of the '68 generation of European protesters against the Vietnam War, who now ruled most of the continent. Joschka Fischer, foreign minister in Germany's very new red-green government, was only the most eloquent in Europe's new-wave left cabinets in expressing agony at the growing conflict between his two basic principles of "no more war" and "no more genocide." For him and his colleagues in crisis, the latter precept had to prevail, even at the cost of NATO's first hot war. In Europe, in this day and age, they could not acquiesce in Yugoslav president Slobodan Milosevic's brutality. They could not be like all those good Germans who had looked the other way in 1938—and failed to prevent worse—as their Jewish neighbors were persecuted in Kristallnacht. The Germans, in particular, could not look the other way during their presidency of the EU in the first half of 1999.

Moreover, a generation that had grown up thinking on a European scale now subconsciously put Bismarck behind it and took it for granted that even the recalcitrant Balkans must be part of the new Europe.[11] The contest, said Javier Solana, secretary-general of NATO and future foreign policy spokesman for the EU, was "between two visions of Europe. One vision—Milosevic's vision—is of a Europe of ethnically pure states, a Europe of nationalism, authoritarianism and xenophobia. The other vision—that of the NATO Allies, the European Union and of our Partners—is a Europe of integration, democracy and ethnic pluralism."[12]

The war in Kosovo was a just war, added British prime minister Tony Blair, a moral crusade that was all the more legitimate because there was no conceivable material or exclusive cultural interest involved. There was no oil to be had. The Connecticut-size region was a backwater rather than any strategic crossroads. The people whose human rights NATO was defending were not Christians but Muslims.

What was at stake, then, was no more—but also no less—than the identity of twenty-first-century Europe. Now the Albanians, too, were brothers, and the Europeans were obliged to be their brothers' keeper. There was strong public support for this stance except, notably, in Greece.[13]

For the Americans, by contrast, the war in Kosovo represented only a derivative interest. To be sure, especially after the airstrikes began, Washington had its own strong incentive: to avoid humiliation as the West's guarantor of last resort and destruction of the NATO core of future coalitions of the willing. And tactically, the United States was the main initiator and actor and the undisputed commander-in-chief. Yet its stake remained derivative.[14] Because stability and decency in Kosovo were important to Europe, they were also important to Washington, but they did not have the inherent urgency of, say, preventing Iraq from developing a nuclear bomb that could devastate Israel and detonate American politics. Indeed, one of the many black scenarios, as NATO verged on losing the war of nerves and strategy in Kosovo throughout the month of May, was that Americans might wake up one day and ask why they were providing three-quarters of the planes for this operation when it really was, or should have been, Europe's responsibility.[15]

It was a close call, but in the end the West did not lose in any of the multiple ways it might have.[16] Not a single American body bag came back from combat to haunt President Bill Clinton. He did not have to make any fateful decision to commit ground troops or else abandon the fight. Russia was not irreconcilably alienated from the West and proved amenable, if grumpily, to becoming part of the solution rather than part of the problem. The more than a million Kosovo Albanian refugees did not destabilize Albania or Macedonia, did not have to live in tent cities over winter, did not become a permanent diaspora and breeding ground for terrorists or lose their will to return home and take charge of their own lives. It was Milosevic's determination that buckled, even though the Yugoslav army still felt unvanquished. NATO's extraordinary solidarity held up over seventy-eight long days of bombing, despite an errant strike on the Chinese embassy, heart-rending television images of Serb as well as Albanian victims, and total Greek public opposition to the airstrikes.

And because the West did not lose in the end, there was relatively little angry postwar recrimination among the allies. NATO did not disintegrate after all. The Clinton administration was bolstered in its conviction that alliances enhance rather than diminish the effectiveness of the world's sheriff. The Europeans, though stunned by the stark evidence of the growing gap between them and the United States in military technology and of their continued dependence on American leadership long after the end of the cold war, gained a sense of purpose in the formidable task of modernizing southeastern Europe and cleaning up Ottoman as well as communist debris. All the central European and Balkan neighbors who had bandwagoned to offer NATO their airfields or airspace, on the wager that the alliance would eventually win, were rewarded in the new Southeast European Stability Pact with more Western money and attention than they had dreamed possible.

In retrospect, NATO's containment of Milosevic in Kosovo turned the tide. It demonstrated that intimidation of Serbia's neighbors brought suffering rather than victory to Serbia itself, and sufficiently demystified Milosevic that voters became disillusioned and voted against him. The Serb opposition parties, now in government, exhumed enough ethnic Albanian corpses to show Serbs that accusations of war crimes were based on fact and sent Milosevic to The Hague to be tried. The crucial conditions were created for opportunists in the region to opt for reconciliation as more profitable than nationalist extremism. Prime Minister Zoran Djindjic began preaching reason and nonviolent economic solutions to the festering problems of Kosovo's status, Montenegro's status, and the Serbs' vengeful sense of having been victimized by history—and reaped an immediate $1.3 billion in aid from the West. The black hole of Yugoslavia, in the center of the Balkans, was filled. Normal overland and Danube River traffic resumed. Serious economic development in the region could begin. Bulgarian trucks could transit neighboring Serbia and no longer had to detour 500 miles through eastern Romania to bring their produce to west European markets.

Moreover, Belgrade's example set off a political chain reaction. On the heels of Milosevic's extradition, the Srpska Republic in Bosnia passed a resolution at least formally mandating cooperation with The Hague tribunal. The moderate Croatian government sent two Croatian generals, heroes of the wars of the early 1990s, to answer indictments in The Hague, and when adamant nationalists quit the coalition and demanded a parliamentary vote of nonconfidence, there was no lingering crisis. The government remained in power. And in Kosovo itself, moderate Albanians won both local and Kosovo-wide elections over militants.

The way has thus been cleared for all Balkan nations that want to cease being "Balkan" to become instead "Southeast European" and aspire to the ultimate bliss of membership in the EU. The soft power of Europe can come into full play, with its magnetic attraction and therefore the strong incentive it gives candidate members to conform their practices to West European standards. The Balkans too, in the words of Bulgarian deputy foreign minister Konstantin Dimitrov, can now demonstrate that they need not be "an accursed part of Europe," but can become, instead, "civilized," "European," and even "transatlantic."[17]

The lessons the two sides of the Atlantic drew from this experience were quite different. The United States concluded from trying to conduct an allied military campaign in Kosovo—as would become apparent in Afghanistan—that it must never again subject itself to "war by committee" of nineteen NATO members. In particular, it complained about French vetoes of targets it wished to strike and about the slowness of decisionmaking. Nor did the barely veiled tensions between the American supreme allied commander, Wesley K. Clark, and his superiors in Washington help—or the even less veiled tensions between President Clinton's first commandment of avoiding any GI ground deployment and Prime Minister Blair's contrary conviction that eschewing ground troops would lose the war.

By contrast, the lesson the Europeans began to draw from Kosovo was that in the post–cold war world they could not count indefinitely on American patience with keeping 100,000 troops on the old continent and relieving the Europeans from having to solve their own security problems. A U.S. reinsurance policy against any misuse of Russia's nuclear arsenal was one thing; any future bailout by American forces in the troubled Balkans was quite another. Europe would have to play a more autonomous European role, variously described as a "common foreign and security policy" (CFSP), a "European security and defense identity" (ESDI, later ESDP or CESDP, with the P standing for policy and the C for common), or a strengthened "European pillar" for NATO.

It had become a cliché after the Soviet collapse, of course, to acknowledge that the United States was the world's sole remaining superpower, but the enormity of the military and leadership gap that Kosovo revealed between the United States and its European allies still shocked the Europeans. They provided few of the 1,100 aircraft used in the airstrikes, fewer of the 23,000 bombs and missiles, and fewer still of the 7,000-plus precision-guided munitions. Major-General Klaus Naumann, general inspector of the Bundeswehr and the chairman of NATO's Military Committee in the mid-1990s, had for years warned of the increasing transatlantic gap in capability. Now proof of the disparity was painfully obvious.[18] "Kosovo was two or three sizes too big for us," observed one senior German diplomat ruefully.

The equally painful corollary was that there could be no substitute for leadership by what Secretary of State Madeleine Albright called "the indispensable nation." Washington's demonstrated willingness to fire its high-tech weapons conferred an unparalleled credibility on U.S. deeds and words. Milosevic had nothing but scorn for the economic embargoes or credits that constituted the EU's main tools. And if he thought he could call America's bluff by exceeding agreed ceilings on his military and paramilitary forces in Kosovo in late 1998 and brazenly starting ethnic cleansing in February 1999, there was no way that he might have been deflected from his chosen course by Europe's flabbier sanctions or cajoling. Ever since the Clinton administration reengaged the United States in the Balkans issue at the Dayton conference in 1995, the Europeans had known that without the United States they were helpless in their own Balkan backyard. They had contemplated no move in the region without American participation. The sole exception, the Italian-led pacification of anarchic Albania in 1997, was in essence less a restoration of domestic law and order than a glorified evacuation of northwestern European nationals out of harm's way.

To be sure, once NATO's bombing failed to produce the expected results in the first few days and, instead of forcing Milosevic's swift capitulation, accelerated the Serb expulsion of more than half of the Kosovo Albanian population, the neat schema of American hawks and European doves vanished. The American president was among the most timid of the allies, resisting any commitment of the ground troops that alone could flush Serb troops and armor out of hiding. But still, it was the American president whom the more hawkish European, British prime minister Tony Blair—and General Wesley K. Clark—had to convince of the need for this step. And in retrospect, especially after it became apparent that Serb army losses of materiel to an air bombardment unsupported by ground troops were far less than NATO thought, Western analysts concluded that it was civilian destruction in Serbia plus the ultimate threat of NATO ground forces—along with the actual flushing operations of the Kosovo Liberation Army—that finally triggered Milosevic's withdrawal from Kosovo.

NATO's near failure in Kosovo thus only emphasized European impotence in any robust peacemaking. Europe's leaders looked over the abyss of what might have happened had Milosevic hung on for even two more weeks and prevented return of the Albanian refugees before the next winter—and they shuddered. Milosevic might well have burst the strained NATO cohesion, alienated the United States from Europe, left Kosovo refugees as a time bomb in Albania and Macedonia over the winter, filled the emptied Kosovar houses with Serb settlers, and demonstrated to other local bullies that violence does pay in a complaisant Europe. Instead, Kosovar Albanians got a chance to start over.

America's unique credibility in deterrence therefore remains indispensable for the preservation of stability in Europe. And so does the U.S. role as primus inter pares, for the same reasons that required American engagement when NATO was founded half a century ago. U.S. leadership in European security continues to be the only device for avoiding leadership by the richest, most populous, and most energetic country in Europe: Germany. And no non-German—nor any German in public life today—wishes to repeat the fatal experiments with German preeminence of 1870, 1914, and 1939, even with the convinced democrats of contemporary Germany.

Moreover, whatever the frustrations of the other partners, the structural leadership of one country is often essential to force closure on policy debates in the alliance. After (or sometimes before) due deliberation among allies, only the United States can end the debate and compel a decision to act. And, as the crucial last stages of the Kosovo settlement showed yet again, only the Americans possess the authority to commit the entire alliance to an agreement in tough bilateral negotiations with the still-nuclear Russians. "The U.S.A. is in a weight class of its own, a superheavyweight," Fischer told *Der Spiegel* inter- viewers who were trying to goad him into describing Europe as a for- eign policy rival to the United States. "The Europeans are in the process of forming, gradually, out of various lighter classes, [only] a heavy middleweight."[19]

The final distinctive characteristic of the United States as leader of NATO is the reassurance that American dominance provides for the new democracies in central Europe. Poland, the largest of the three freshman members admitted to the alliance two weeks before the war in Kosovo began, would have been leery of entrusting its security to an alliance led by Germany—and without tacit American oversight it would also have been reluctant to accept reconciliation and a benefi- cial special relationship with Germany in the early 1990s. The Poles' faith in America may be the extreme example, but it represents a phe- nomenon common to central Europeans. By popular acclaim in the region, NATO is already the core of hard security in post–cold war Europe; and both the new democracies that hope to join the alliance soon and those that qualify only for NATO's looser Partnership for Peace are striving above all for close association with U.S. power.

What special niche, then, remains for the Europeans in their continent's security? This was the question that Kosovo forced the European Union to face before it was ready to do so. Originally the EU had intended to postpone difficult decisions on common foreign and security policy until after it had met the three major initial chal- lenges of launching the euro, agreeing on the controversial institu- tional and agricultural reforms that are urgently needed to prevent paralysis or insolvency of an enlarging Union, and preparing for the first round of admission of new central European members in the early twenty-first century. Instead, in spring 1999 the EU—including even its neutral members—was suddenly required, for the first time in its history, to approve a NATO military operation. At the summit level it complied and went on to name political heavyweight Javier Solana as high representative for EU foreign policy; to commit five times as many European troops to Kosovo peacekeeping as the U.S. contingent; to foot the lion's share of the costs of political, economic, and social development in the Balkans over the next ten years; to absorb the security tasks of the orphan Western European Union; and to trans- form the French-German-Belgian-Spanish-Luxembourg Eurocorps into

Europe's first joint "rapid reaction force." The intervention force of 60,000, it was agreed at the Helsinki summit in December 1999 at the urging of the British and French, should be ready by 2003 for deployment on sixty-days' notice, for a two-year mission "where NATO as a whole is not engaged." In the interim the EU countries assumed the main responsibility for NATO's KFOR (Kosovo Forces), for the peacekeeping forces in Macedonia that were suddenly required in 2001 to end Albanian-Slav military clashes, and for the long-term Southeastern Stability Pact for economic development in the Balkans as a whole.

Expectations differed about just how fast the EU initiatives might evolve into an authentic European voice in foreign policy. The most zealous cheerleaders in France and on assorted op-ed pages throughout Europe called for European emancipation from American hegemony.[20] Despite all the contrary evidence, this view often misread Kosovo as a second Iraq, with Washington pushing reluctant allies into attacking Serbia and turning NATO into the world's policeman, and with Europe winning the peace through its special negotiator, Finnish president Martti Ahtisaari.[21] The thesis was dramatic, easy to grasp, and seemed well on its way to becoming conventional wisdom even in sporadic American commentary on the mood in Europe.[22] It was, however, unrepresentative of the more sober attempts by Europe's major governments to achieve just the opposite goal in the wake of Kosovo, that is, to keep an increasingly inward-looking United States engaged in Europe a decade after the end of the cold war.[23]

A prerequisite for keeping the U.S. engaged, of course, had to be organizing and equipping European forces in a way that could prevent the transatlantic gap in capacity from widening and rendering the Europeans incapable of fighting alongside the Americans in the future. And this necessity, in turn, required major changes in European procurement, configuration of forces, and—for those that did not yet have professional armed forces—conscription. Christoph Bertram, director of the German Institute for International and Security Affairs, summarized the first requirement: "We want to keep up sufficiently to make interoperability possible and avoid a division of labor in which the U.S. provides the air power at 15,000 feet and the Europeans provide the body bags on the ground."[24] To achieve such interoperability, however, a laggard Europe would have to overtake a moving target.

The second need—to alter troop configuration—arose from the changed nature of the threat. During the cold war, large divisions with heavy firepower were required to hold NATO's shallow east-west territory against the kind of massed attack planned in Soviet military doctrine. With the end of the cold war and the shrinkage of the Russian army, however, the main danger came from local despots on the periphery of heartland Europe. The military response required in such cases, should diplomacy fail, would be a "rapid reaction" by more mobile and lightly armed forces, on the pattern of the U.S. 82d Airborne. Britain had begun this shift under the direction of Defense Secretary George Robertson, before he moved on to become NATO secretary-general; other countries were only beginning to catch up.

The third imperative was as strong—and as awkward—as the first two in the minds of officials. It followed from the probable dispatch of rapid reaction forces outside the strict NATO treaty area to the EU periphery; only volunteers, not draftees, could be sent to these zones.[25]

Summarizing contemporary thinking on defense reform in France and Germany—and therefore in the EU as a whole—Heisbourg, then president of the Center for Security Policy in Geneva, wrote that it was now urgent to convert the recommendations that had been circulating in the strategic community for a decade into policy and to build up European military capability.[26] The shock of Kosovo and "the three years of humiliation of Europe in Bosnia" compelled this response. As his call for embedding a "Europe of defense" in the Atlantic alliance indicated, Heisbourg was no Gaullist. He wanted to keep the U.S. superpower engaged in Europe and he argued that only a stronger Europe that pulled its weight could attract Washington's flagging attention in the post–cold war world. He repeated the British-French appeal at St. Malo in 1998 in calling on the Europeans to increase and focus defense spending to give themselves the "credible military means" to police their own continent as necessary. He deplored the fact that a rich Europe allocated a combined $145 billion for defense, or 55 percent of the then U.S. defense budget of $264 billion, but got only a paltry return on this investment. It spent only half as much as the United States on procurement, only a third as much on indispensable research and development, he objected.[27] Moreover, even with 1.9 million men in uniform—500,000 more than the United States—Europe could field only 2 percent of these as the crucial rapid reaction forces.

Heisbourg's proposed remedies were to nudge Germany and Italy to adopt professional armed forces; to improve Europe's institutional ability to respond swiftly to crisis and to converge disparate national defense policies toward active intervention; to acquire the requisite satellite surveillance, military electronics, heavy airlift, more versatile aircraft, and precision-guided weapons; to consolidate European defense industry and establish two or three large producers that would be competitive worldwide; to spend more on equipment and merge national weapons acquisition programs into a pan-European procurement agency that could correct the existing wasteful duplication through economies of scale; and to internationalize bids (on the condition that "Fortress America" also opened its procurement to non-Americans). These measures could stretch current European budgets to pay for much more of the necessary high-tech weaponry, he contended, even without raising taxes.

In conjuring up European rapid reaction forces, most EU members confined their vision to establishing mechanisms for steering any military operation on a day-to-day basis under priorities set by the European Union. Missions, while they might push far toward the coercive end of the spectrum, would hew essentially to the "Petersberg tasks" of humanitarian rescues, peacekeeping, and peacemaking outlined by the Western European Union in 1992. French defense minister Alain Richard, however, reflecting his country's tradition of power projection, entertained even grander hopes of forging a "defense union," complete with a European general staff that would be independent of American command.[28]

Such proposals illustrated the unleashing of the European defense imagination after Kosovo. German generals no longer protested—as they had when the Eurocorps forerunner, the French-German brigade, was sprung on them by politicians in the mid-1980s—that the old German general staff would not have deigned to mix even the military cultures of German-speaking Saxons and Bavarians in the same company and that multinational units could never work. Nor did anyone ask, as some did when the Berlin Wall fell, if members of the European Community might not revert to the habits of the previous two millennia and resort to battle against each other. Nor were there now any serious challenges, it seemed, to the principle that Europeans should be able to borrow U.S. NATO assets for operations without direct

American participation, under the Combined Joint Task Force guidelines painstakingly worked out in NATO in the mid-1990s.

In this new climate, much of the old reluctance to fold the Western European Union into the EU evaporated. Objections by neutral EU members vanished; given Milosevic's provocation, they had no qualms about joining with EU members that were also members of NATO in endorsing Western military action in Yugoslavia in March 1999, even without a prior mandate by the UN Security Council or the Organization for Security and Cooperation in Europe. Indeed, the concept of the legitimacy of intervention by regional alliances against the will of a sovereign state that perpetrates human rights abuses was increasingly gaining favor in interpretations of international law.[29] As far back as the Amsterdam summit of 1997, Finland and Sweden had in any case called for a pan-European "crisis-management" army (to act under UN or OSCE auspices), and in the wake of the Kosovo war, Finnish prime minister Paavo Lipponen renewed the appeal. Ireland's neutrality was always instrumental, intended primarily to distance Dublin from London, and was obsolescent. That left Austria, whose attachment to neutrality was equally instrumental—distancing Vienna from Berlin—and equally obsolescent. "There are no neutrals any more," concluded a German diplomat.

Discussing the European Union's assumption of an overt defense role, the diplomat continued, "Of course, the big problem is, how do you make sure that countries like Turkey" do not veto EU action by blocking use of NATO assets? "Turkey is close to a lot of trouble spots that may call for European crisis reaction."[30] Ankara, as a veteran member of NATO but a second-class applicant for EU membership, would indeed try to trade its veto power on release of NATO assets to extract a higher position in the queue for the EU. A two-year deadlock would result, before British and American brokers in December 2001 worked out a compromise guaranteeing that the EU rapid reaction force (with Greece as an understood but unspecified participant) would never be used against a NATO ally (Turkey), while the force would have assured access to NATO planning staff and other assets, but only on a case-by-case rather than blanket basis.[31]

American skeptics pointed to other problems as well. While they were astonished that the NATO and EU allies hung together for almost three months of airstrikes in Yugoslavia (and that France under

President Jacques Chirac dropped its old affinity for the Serbs), they did not expect such exemplary solidarity to survive the crisis. They doubted the efficacy of EU crisis management by committee when there was no single dominant partner to force decisions. They anticipated the resurgence of rival assertions of national advantage and recalled the vain pleas by Italy's partners a few years back that Rome not pay Milosevic's cronies $950 million for a share in the privatization of Yugoslavia's telecommunications. For all the remarkable surrender of sovereignty by the obsolescing European nation-states, they scoffed at the notion that the Europeans might actually pool their armies as they were pooling their currencies. And even in more limited regional foreign policy that fell short of that ultimate commitment of blood, many American critics faulted European priorities; the Europeans, they objected, were concentrating far too much on parochial issues of reshuffling EU institutions and were neglecting the more necessary project of swift admission of the fledgling central European democracies to membership in the club.

Despite all the brave talk, many Europeans, too, remained highly doubtful about the development of a pan-European crisis reaction force, even one borrowing American NATO assets. By now Europeans were already persuaded that they were permanent allies, that they did not need to fear each other or fear recidivism to Europe's constant "civil wars." But there was still a long way to go to translate that conviction into a pan-European rationalization of defense efforts, into a Dutch decision that the Netherlands does not need a tiny air force when Germany has a bigger and better one, or into British reliance on Belgian ammunition (given that Brussels might again withhold needed supplies as it did during the Gulf War).[32]

Nor were voters eager to forfeit the "peace dividend" of sharply reduced defense budgets that they had enjoyed since the end of the cold war, no matter how humiliated the narrow foreign-policy elites felt. The most crucial country, Germany—which would have to finance any new French reconnaissance satellite, serious defense R&D, or major advances in laser-guided munitions or electronic countermeasures—was already feeling strapped. Its sluggish economy before mid-2000 was a major reason for the fall of the euro against the dollar in the first eighteen months of the new currency. Germans were already grumbling about the belt tightening and structural change that the government of Gerhard Schröder was finally demanding of them in order to render Germany fit for the globalized competition of the information age. Ironically, no sooner had Germany finally broken beyond post–World War II taboos and become "normal" enough to join allies in sending combat troops outside the NATO perimeter to Kosovo, than the Bundeswehr had its budget slashed by more than 8 percent. Appropriations fell from the DM48 billion originally guaranteed to Defense Minister Rudolf Scharping for 2000 to DM45 billion, with a further drop to DM44 billion ordered by 2003. Such allocations hardly allowed for the planned expansion of the key German rapid reaction forces from 37,000 to 63,000—the number deemed essential to allow rotation and meet Germany's promised commitment of troops to KFOR and SFOR.[33] And the additional costs as Berlin assumed command of the peacekeepers in Macedonia in 2001 certainly left no extra funds even for operational equipment, let alone military research.

That remained the dispiriting situation as the Europeans tried to pull themselves together after September 11, 2001.

Common European Security and Defense Policy

In September and October 2001 the Europeans initially displayed little advance in formulating a common EU foreign policy over their improvisations in Kosovo in 1999. For the first time an American secretary of state did know which phone number to call for Europe and reached High Representative Solana on his mobile in the Trieste airport to announce that the United States was about to commence bombing in Afghanistan. But in Europe the resort to national rather than EU reflexes was conspicuous. All their fine words about a common foreign and security policy fell to dust as British, French, German, and Italian leaders competed with one another to be awarded George W. Bush's blue ribbon in the "beauty contest," as it was sardonically called, of displaying solidarity with the United States. NATO issued its common invocation of Article 5 within a day of the attacks; but at first the European Union could not even get its prime ministers or foreign ministers together to hammer out an agreed statement.

Chancellor Schröder tried on September 11 and 12 to drum up such a meeting, phoning Blair, Chirac, and, since Belgium held the EU presidency, Prime Minister Guy Verhofstadt. The attempt failed. "Verhofstadt's first reaction was positive, and he called around. The reaction in Europe was negative," recounted a member of the chancellor's staff. "I was absolutely stunned. The argument of Chirac was that if we do that, we give a sign of nervousness. I think we missed an opportunity. . . . Not for results, but for confronting this new phenomenon from a European level." By the time a summit finally took place several weeks later, "so many heads of state and government had made the pilgrimage to Washington that it took away a chance for Europe."[34]

In his very public pilgrimage, Prime Minister Blair breathed new life into the special Anglo-Saxon relationship and was rewarded by getting some of Britain's planes and special forces admitted to the action in Afghanistan. President Chirac flubbed his lines by warning in Washington against any American "arrogance" and otherwise triggering his hosts' memories of the French propensity to veto or betray targets selected by the world's hyperpower—and French forces did not participate in the initial assault. Chancellor Schröder fought a knock-down, drag-out battle with his own Social Democrats and his Green coalition partners and won the left's historic approval for Bundeswehr participation in combat on the far side of the globe—but without substantially increasing Berlin's risible defense budget. And Prime Minister Berlusconi, who was dropping Italy's traditional Euroenthusiasm as fast as he could in any case, banked on personal bonding with his fellow conservative, Bush.

In policy terms, there was nothing intrinsically wrong with this rush to be first to set foot in the White House and to be photographed in grim determination at Ground Zero. But it was unseemly. It belied all the protestations of desire for a common European foreign policy, commonly arrived at. The whole exercise degenerated into squabbles as the leaders of the main potential military contributors to the anti-terrorism campaign, Britain, France, and Germany, tried to meet à trois just before an EU summit and triggered smaller nations' angry suspicions that they were trying to form a directorate. And it degenerated into farce as word got out that Chirac and Schröder had been invited to a quiet working dinner at 10 Downing Street, and Italian, Spanish, Belgian, and Dutch gatecrashers—and Javier Solana—lined up to share in the soup.

Nor could the EU's embryonic foreign policy structure operate to bring European leaders together. The EU member states have every intention of keeping control of foreign policy in their national capitals; both High Representative Javier Solana, reporting to the intergovernmental European Council, and Commissioner Chris Patten, reporting to the supranational European Commission, are authorized only to be implementers, not political initiators of foreign policy. The two have worked well together—in tandem with NATO—in defusing lesser crises, like the flareup of fighting in Macedonia in 2001. They have no autonomous authority, however, especially in any global crisis. And even in nonoperational analysis, if the EU's Joint Situation Center in Brussels so much as formed any Crisis Cell after September 11, this was a well-kept secret. Nor did Solana's Political and Security Committee, supported by the EU Military Committee and its 120-person military staff under Finnish general Gustav Hägglund, play any public role. As for Solana's Policy Planning Staff and Early Warning Unit, this has only twenty officials, with no more than an administrative and liaison function.

And yet, despite the apparent disarray in European foreign policy after September 11, it was significant that the content of that policy was in fact congruent in the various capitals. To be sure, the provocation was so great that a unanimous reaction might have been expected. But it was still noteworthy that the Greeks did not demur at the coordinated EU stance this time, as they had done in favoring the Serbs during the wars in ex-Yugoslavia in the 1990s, and that the French did not curry exceptional favor with the Arabs, as they had done in the 1970s and 1980s. And there was no question but that neutral Sweden, Finland, and Austria would fully back the European rejection of terrorism and support of the United States. This degree of harmony was not accidental; a good deal of prior coordination went into it, especially between German foreign minister Joschka Fischer and French foreign minister Hubert Védrine.

More unexpected, perhaps, was the new European resolve in the sphere of home affairs and justice that had hitherto been zealously kept as a preserve of national sovereignty. Theoretically, EU members had earlier sanctioned communitarizing this field, too, at some point in the future, but in practice all had been dragging their feet. As evidence mounted of terrorist use of Europe as a safe haven and recruiting ground for radicalizing middle-class Arab students, however, fourteen members of the EU agreed on a Europe-wide arrest warrant by 2004, quick extradition in the interim, development of a cross-border Europol with real police powers, and (probably) establishment in 2002 of a Eurojust office of European prosecutors. The basis would be mutual recognition of domestic judicial decisions—and out of it could come something approaching a restoration of Europe's medieval Roman "jus commune."[35] Only the new maverick, Berlusconi, stalled until he could win some concessions; cabaret comics attributed his diffidence to fears that Spanish prosecutors might emulate Italian prosecutors and haul the billionaire prime minister before their courts, too, to answer charges of corruption and bribing judges.[36]

Below the surface, then, there has in fact been a real convergence of European foreign policy, Bertram points out, comparing this evolution with the process that led up to the European Monetary Union. The rudimentary "European political cooperation" of regularizing commonalities in members' sovereign foreign policies that started back in the 1970s—and had one signal success in getting human rights standards written into the Helsinki Final Act of 1975, despite U.S. skepticism—is now maturing into a far more generative European foreign policy. Bertram contrasts the "fantastic" French accusations that Germany was trying to rebuild a Habsburg zone of influence in the Balkans in the early 1990s with today's closeness, "when very little light shines between the French, British, German, Italian, Spanish, and Dutch" positions. Their policies toward China, India, and Afghanistan are comparable. "They have had an extraordinary alignment. . . . These fuzzy institutions set up since [the] Helsinki [summit of 1999 that launched the EU rapid-reaction force] have already created a common habit of thinking. There has been increased cooperation, and officials of the EU's fifteen nations now talk constantly to each other in a way they never did earlier." A striking part of this alignment has been Germany's shift away from the pacifist inclinations of the post–World War II baby boomers and toward French and British readiness to project military power.

"The other extraordinary development is the feeling that if any of us wants to be taken seriously internationally, we have to have Europe as the force multiplier, as an influence multiplier," continues Bertram. "European action in Macedonia [in damping down ethnic war in 2001] was not unimpressive. Solana [joined in writing] the Mitchell Commission Report," under the chairmanship of former U.S. senator George Mitchell, to try to restart the Mideast peace process. There is an almost surprised recognition that, "By God, we have similar interests!" What is still lacking, however, Bertram notes, is a member-nation that actively campaigns to rally other members behind a foreign policy consensus in the way Germany and France often rally others on behalf of a domestic EU agenda. Germany still shrinks from high-profile involvement in the outside world, while France, for all its global rhetoric, does not lobby others for a common foreign policy either.[37]

In this broader context of a congruent European foreign policy, it might even be said that Blair was speaking for all of Europe in his activism after September 11. Security policy was his chosen way to keep Euroskeptical Britain linked to Europe, pending his campaign to bring the country into EMU. If he had better access to the White House than others in presenting European points of view, then his interventions served the common European cause. Most conspicuously, he represented all his European colleagues in warning Bush that any attempt to dethrone Saddam Hussein by air assault tactics in the flush of Afghan victory would only destabilize the region, since Iraq did not have Afghanistan's preconditions. Back of this position was explicit behind-the-scenes coordination between Blair, Chirac, and Schröder—and appreciation that Blair, as a fellow elected politician, could speak to Bush as a peer, with more authority than those Bush advisers who were also pressing, in administration infighting, for restraint. Similarly, precisely because of its Anglo-Saxon solidarity, London could warn Washington, as no other European capital dared to do, that human rights must be respected, even for suspected al-Qaida prisoners held at America's Guantanamo Bay naval base in Cuba. Only this way, the British pointed out, could America lay any claim to moral superiority over the terrorists.

In less dramatic foreign policy issues, the EU has been making a quiet success of exporting stability to its sometimes unruly "near abroad." So great is the success, in fact, that it is no longer even thought of as foreign policy but rather as domestic policy, as the EU moves toward incorporating the new democracies in central Europe into its system, while helping them overcome old hostilities among themselves. Even in the problematic Balkans—after a start in the 1990s that was anything but united—European policy in promising these states that they, too, can eventually qualify for and join the EU is a powerful normative incentive for democratic and market transformation and local cooperation in Europe's least developed corner.

The near abroad of the Mediterranean is a trickier area, given the Mideast's confrontations and complexities. In the 1980s the European

Community was not a player; its precept of "land for peace," coupled with its willingness to extend recognition to a Palestinian entity before the Palestinians had acknowledged Israel's right to exist, was viewed by Israel and the United States as inimical to Israel's interests. The EC became more of a player, if still a subordinate one, as land for peace in fact became the framework of the post–cold war peace process. Europe deliberately kept its role nonpolitical, but EU trade concessions, investment, technical and humanitarian assistance, and, after the 1993 Oslo Accords, funding of the Palestinian Authority's administration, hospitals, police, higher education, and transport projects allowed it on several occasions to help moderate adamant Palestinian Authority positions. For this reason Israel expressly welcomed the EU financing of the Palestinians. Since 1995 the EU's "Barcelona Process," while focusing on trade and economic cooperation, has also provided a forum for discreet contacts between Israelis and Palestinians during breakdowns of their peace process—and the EU has on occasion been an intermediary between the Palestinians and the United States. In addition, the EU Association Agreements giving aid, along with access to European markets, to the three Maghreb states have helped boost economic growth and provide plausible alternatives to Islamism in these countries.[38]

In the main show in the Mideast, the Europeans are under no illusion that anyone other than the United States has the power to force the Israelis and Palestinians toward a peace settlement or even, at a minimum, to manage the crisis to avert all-out war. In the period when the young Bush administration basically abdicated from Mideast involvement, German foreign minister Fischer and High Representative Solana did manage on several occasions to help the parties deescalate the degree of violence—but their intent was only to keep America's seat warm while urging Washington to again intervene vigorously in the region.[39] Bilaterally, Germany and Israel have also had a special intelligence and military relationship for decades, as the Germans have sought to atone for the sins of the Nazi era.[40]

Farther afield in the region, the Europeans, and especially the Germans—to the periodic irritation of the United States—have kept their lines open with an Iran that is evolving, however unevenly, away from the fundamentalism of the revolutionary ayatollahs, is developing the yeast of a civil society, and in the estimate of some observers is exploring new paths as the first "post-Reformation" Islamic state in the region. After September 11 the British, too, had direct talks with Iranian officials and encouraged the modest cooperation that Tehran offered Washington in the war on al-Qaida and the Taliban.

In addition, the EU and its member states together donate 55 percent of humanitarian and development aid in the world. The EU has been instrumental in setting international environmental standards and in getting agreement by 120 states (though not the United States, China, Iraq, or Israel) on an International Criminal Court. And the example of the EU in turning a once warring continent into a zone of cooperative peace and prosperity is increasingly seen as a model worthy of emulation in South America, Asia, and Africa. All told, Skidmore's Roy Ginsberg concludes in the first academic empirical study of common European foreign policy, the EU had far more impact on the outside world in the decade after the end of the cold war than is generally recognized.[41]

Russia

In the area of Russian relations with the West, the EC/EU has usually been subordinate to the American superpower, but Europe has also had an autonomous or sometimes even alternative attraction for Moscow. As long as Germany was divided in the cold war, the Russians held a tacit "German card" that periodically provoked American suspicion that Moscow might lure Bonn away from the West by offering reunifcation of East and West Germany as an enticement. In the 1980s in particular, the United States worried that Mikhail Gorbachev's enthusiasm for a "European house" that would include Russia (but apparently not the United States) could seduce the West Germans. That worry was laid to rest as Gorbachev realized how much he needed Western help for his domestic modernization and paid for such aid by relinquishing Moscow's World War II trophies of the German Democratic Republic and central Europe and letting the Germanies reunite unconditionally, with eastern Germany fully incorporated into NATO.

As this shift occurred, relations with Russia finally ceased to be an emotional issue in Germany or in Europe as a whole. Reunified Germany gladly paid Moscow billions of dollars to help repatriate the Soviet troops that had been billeted in central Europe for half a century, constructing housing and retraining tens of thousands of officers for civilian jobs, but without high expectations of systemic transformation. In Europe there was no angry backlash as Russia fell into bandit capitalism, and no recrimination comparable to the U.S. polemics about who "lost" Russia.

Today the EU accounts for a third of Russia's trade—and is seen by some Russians as a more appropriate economic and social model for Russia than is superpower America—but Putin's insistence that Russia is part of Europe is no longer viewed by Washington as an attempt to split up the U.S.-European alliance. Nor are there major transatlantic differences in analyzing contemporary Russia. Both Americans and Europeans eyed the new Russian president skeptically as he built his popularity on reviving the brutal war in Chechnya in early 2000; increasingly cut back the political power of rival regional governors, constitutional institutions, and oligarchs; and emasculated the Federation Council, the legislative upper house. After Putin's proreform speech in April 2001, however, both Americans and Europeans essentially concluded that this president, like Gorbachev, was serious about wanting to drag the Russian economy into the twenty-first century and would sacrifice Russian great power claims to this mundane task. As an earnest of his intent, Putin closed Russia's naval base in Vietnam and surveillance post in Cuba, dropped his earlier insistence on the primacy of the UN Security Council (and of a Russian veto) in conflict resolution, and acquiesced in further NATO enlargement and the establishment of U.S. bases in his backyard of Central Asia. Putin was no democrat, but he was a pragmatist the West could work with.

Under these circumstances, unlike in the 1980s, there is no American accusation that the Germans and Europeans are becoming dangerously dependent on Russian gas, despite long-term supply contracts. Nor does the mooted potential "common European economic space," which would include Russia, presage anything more to Europeans than persuading Moscow to raise its customs, auditing, oversight, transparency, and other commercial standards to European levels. They know that the United States will always be more important to Moscow than Europe will be, both as the only other possessor of a major intercontinental nuclear arsenal and as the only possible certifier of Russia as a major world actor. Yet they know, too, that in practice Europe remains more influential than the United States in the impact of its daily economic and social intercourse with Russians. In the end, it will be up to the EU, not the United States, to decide whether Russia is as European as Putin contends.

Or, more accurately, perhaps, it will be up to Russia, by its own choice, to decide just how far east "Europe" will now extend. For seven decades, following the trumpet call of Aleksandr Blok in his poem "The Scythians," Russia prided itself on being the anti-West and the anti-Europe. Today Dmitri Trenin, deputy director of the Carnegie Center in Moscow, summons Russians instead to make the positive European choice that they alone can make. "Russia's entry into Europe will not be the result of a deal made in Moscow and Brussels," he counsels. "It will be 95, 97, 98 percent made at home. It's the extent of Russia's 'Europeanization,' the depth and breadth of Russia's economic transformation, social restructuring, political [and] legal evolution that will turn Russia eventually—and I believe it will—into a European country."[42]

Transatlantic Relations Today

The September 11 terrorist attack on the U.S. brought home to Europeans not only the Americans' vulnerability, but also their own. The collapse of the Soviet empire, army, and ideology did not turn Europe into a risk-free zone after all. Europeans now know viscerally that they too face threats that come from outside their own geographical area, argues David C. Gompert, president of RAND Europe.[43] This realization has shifted the decades-old debate about alliance "burden sharing," in part in the direction that Washington has long advocated. As magnificent as the European feat has been in banning war altogether from a bloody continent—and as valuable as this accomplishment has been for American as well as European interests—it is no longer enough. In a world in which knowledge, trade, investment—and terrorism—have all gone global, the Europeans must help the United States in creating and preserving the common good of security in Asia as well as in Europe and the Mideast.

If Europe is to accept some global coresponsibility with the United States, however, there are two corollaries. The first is that the Europeans, contradicting their reflexes in the post–cold war era, must develop and pay for the military means to sustain their share. The second is that the United States must maintain, in François Heisbourg's phrase, the "ethos of risk-sharing" that succeeded brilliantly in post–World War II Europe in signaling U.S. resolve to shield fragile democracies, economies, and societies. That is, contradicting its own reflexes, the Bush administration must realize that however powerful the United States is militarily, it cannot protect itself from the fanaticism and violence of the have-nots without the help of allies and multilateral institutions—and that it therefore has a strong stake in working together with Europe in Balkan "nation building" as well as in constructing international systems and norms of good behavior.

In one sense the rewriting of the grand transatlantic bargain that brought so much benefit to Europe and America over the past half century is easier after September 11. Most obviously, we have all been reminded of the centrality of the core values we share. From this renewed perspective, in our common security efforts, fights over the particular form of EU-NATO military cooperation no longer seem as important as the need to overcome the two institutions' fifty-year practice of ignoring each other—and to increase the kind of formal and informal cooperation that worked in smothering violence in Macedonia in 2001.

In economic relations, acrimonious trade wars no longer seem to be the overwhelming measure of the transatlantic relationship (even if the U.S. steel lobby immediately used the postattack crisis to claim special protection). What businessmen have dubbed "coopetition"—the mix of cooperation and competition between companies in a particular sector—applies to transnational as well as to commercial playing fields. The American and European world trade negotiators and friends Robert Zoellick and Pascal Lamy have been able to work out a reasonable compromise on the decades-old bananas feud. And when the World Trade Organization took up the long-running European appeal in 2001 and again ruled U.S. tax breaks for exporters illegal, the Bush administration, instead of immediately threatening to pull out of the WTO, at least considered beginning the congressional spadework needed to change the tax legislation.[44] Moreover, despite some fireworks over EU rejection in 2001 of the $43 billion all-American General Electric takeover bid for Honeywell, it must be acknowledged that by and large U.S. and European competition authorities and other regulatory agencies work well together, even if their philosophies diverge somewhat.[45]

In another sense, however, the security component of the transatlantic bargain will be very hard to calibrate in a period when NATO's whole raison d'être has been hollowed out, the U.S. and European armed forces are growing farther and farther apart in capability, and the White House is occupied by the most unilateralist president in the past fifty years. During the apocalyptic cold war, NATO fully served U.S. interests—and U.S. self-definition—in shielding western Europe against intimidation by the Soviet superiority in heavy ground weapons offensively deployed in central Europe. After the end of the cold war, a changing NATO continued to serve Europe's interests in adapting to become the rather narrower security enforcer for western Europe against local bullies in ex-Yugoslavia.

However, this latter purpose was insufficient for a superpower with global responsibilities in a more unstable Asia and Middle East. Two years after Kosovo, the United States fulfilled its vow never again to rely on the entangling NATO alliance as a partner in major military operations. Heisbourg observes that Washington's "don't call us, we'll call you" reply on September 27, 2001, to NATO's offer of Article 5 support made the American viewpoint crystal clear. At this point NATO's residual operations consist of running three peacekeeping projects in the Balkans "of the sort that used to be done by the UN." Thus, "NATO is no longer a defence organisation, but a security and defence-services institution."[46] And the downgrading of NATO is only being exacerbated by the expansion of the alliance to the east—Putin is even musing about eventual Russian membership—as so many new, passive central European members join.

Nor does some facile division of labor promise a healthy solution to the dilemma. Any arrangement that left European foot soldiers facing future bullets on the ground while American pilots flew safely five miles above them would be no more acceptable than an arrangement that pitted the American bad cop against the European good cop (and let Europeans reap commercial profits from nations the U.S. was boycotting). Alternatively, assigning hard-power combat missions in Asia to the United States and soft-power peacekeeping and nation building missions to the Europeans would lead to lose-lose results, warns RAND's Gompert. With Europe becoming ever more stable and Asia less so, the United States could find itself loaded with inequitable burdens and dangers, while Europeans could find their global security slipping increasingly out of their control. Each could then feel morally

superior to—and betrayed by—the other. The present arguments between a Europe that wants a voice without providing capabilities and
a United States that wants European capabilities without a European
voice would be aggravated. The Atlantic alliance would atrophy. France
might welcome such an outcome as emancipation from American hegemony, but Britain, Germany, and every other EU member nation
would be appalled. The best partnership, Gompert concludes, must be
both more equal and more global.[47]

Devising an equitable strategy will be especially difficult because
the life-shaping experiences of the responsible political actors in the
United States and Europe differ in many respects. For sixty years the
United States has been both the ultimate producer of security in the
world and the arbiter of the definition of security. The intensely patriotic Americans, even if they have not always been wise in the battles
they have chosen, see themselves as generous with their might in a
dangerous world. Washington finds its use of military and other power
legitimate not only because of America's benevolent intentions, but
also because the United States has the most open democracy in the
world, and its unilateralism finds strong approval among its citizens.

Today's European leaders, by contrast—give or take a few wise or
unwise power projections by Britain and France—have generally been
consumers of American security. And their miraculous realization of
Kant's dream of peace in Europe arises not only from U.S. military
deterrence, but also from progressive renunciation among themselves
of the use of force and even of traditional national interest.[48] They
have invented, and are still inventing, a postmodern, postnational form
of governance, with pooled sovereignty and rules that are equally binding for all participants; they have been extending to a broader supranational commonwealth the kind of social trust Americans assume
only in their domestic sphere. Many Europeans, while grateful for the
U.S. military operation to defeat al-Qaida and the Taliban, regard
Washington's go-it-alone instincts as a damaging reversion to anarchy
and might-is-right in international relations.

"In a curious symmetry these changes [in Europe] have come partly
as a result of the second thirty years' war: 1914–1945," explains Robert Cooper, the diplomat who headed the British antiterrorist effort
after September 11, 2001.[49] The first paroxysm led to the rejection of
religion as an organizing principle on the continent, and instead to

adoption of the state system as codified in the Peace of Westphalia of 1648. The second paroxysm, aided by the prod of globalization, has now led to another revolutionary systemic change in Europe, based on reconciliation, postnational pooling of sovereignty, blurring of the distinction between domestic and foreign affairs, and hourly meddling in each other's business. A peculiar European Union has evolved that will never be a federation but is vastly more than a confederation or even a concert of nations.

This European Union is imperfect and therefore open to change. As its practitioners like to say, it is less an institution than a process. It is lean in bureaucracy and budget. Yet it still determines three-quarters of member states' contemporary legislation and interprets this body of law authoritatively in the European Court of Justice. And despite a consensus system that theoretically should ensure deadlock, it repeatedly wrestles out common positions on economic issues and aspires to do the same for security issues. It throws itself into crises that force it to "flee forward" as a less risky alternative to sticking with the status quo. It is flexible enough to allow for constant readjustment of the division of competencies and for a flow of authority back to states or regions as political moods shift. It bridges the political and the technocratic by increasingly assigning economic decisions to experts. In tandem with NATO, the European Union rests its security on unprecedented acceptance of interdependence, transparency, and mutual vulnerability.[50] The emerging European governance has nothing to do with a "new *world* order." It is a "postmodern," postnational island—albeit a large one—in a world that consists primarily of "modern" nation-states (like China, Iran, and the United States) and still "premodern" chaos, in Cooper's analysis.[51]

The interaction of this EU creature with a not-yet-postmodern America that also takes pride in inventing itself every day will challenge the imagination and tolerance of both sides. Europe is certainly becoming more American, through the U.S. cultural and linguistic hegemony, the new economic orthodoxy of Anglo-Saxon neoliberalism, and the dominance on the continent of a Germany that grew up in the image of the United States. Yet Europe is also beginning to take on an American-like self-confidence, and it will increasingly wish to exercise its expanding financial power, for example, in ways that may impinge on the U.S understanding of its own world leadership. Already former German chancellor Helmut Schmidt is calling for a single coordinated European "financial policy toward the rest of the world" in the International Monetary Fund, the World Bank, and globalized markets.[52]

As the only military superpower, the United States has not yet been compelled to internalize interdependence in the way Europe has had to. The United States still tends to want to establish rules of international law that will bind others but not itself. It champions the cause of Chinese dissidents but resents others telling it not to convict and execute a Paraguayan immigrant who has not received adequate legal defense. Its boisterous ethnic and single-cause politics leads to national legislation that blithely orders other countries to ban or limit their trade.[53] Individual states in the U.S. set their own foreign policy in decreeing boycotts of Swiss banks and Italian insurance firms that are judged too miserly in paying heirs to Jewish victims of the Nazis. Yet Texas governors, after pro forma objections by Europeans as yet another death row inmate is consigned to the electric chair, write retorts telling the Europeans to stop sticking their noses into other people's business.[54] Sharing sovereignty is not a strong superpower instinct.

Thus the Europeans, seeing in the international war crimes tribunal at The Hague the slow victory of rule of law over barbarism, would like to extend this judicial tool to the Rwandas and Congos of the world. The United States, by contrast—feeling itself the particular target of the world's dispossessed and of al-Qaida's not-so-dispossessed—sees in an International Criminal Court the danger that America's officers, righteously engaged in bringing order to a disorderly world, might be brought before the court frivolously or maliciously. Similarly, Europeans incline to seek the antidote for pre-modern, dysfunctional, and failed states in long-term development and education and fear that America's diffusion of the military fight from Afghanistan to other al-Qaida havens will make hostages to fortune of every U.S. consulate and library in the third world. For their part, Americans tend to worry more about the short-term security risks.

Moreover, European governments fear that America's ostentatious unilateral scrapping of the ABM Treaty well before U.S. tests would have violated it will encourage proliferation of weapons of mass destruction and induce China, the country that has the most to lose from comprehensive U.S. missile defense, to multiply its warheads and decoys in destabilizing ways to counter the U.S. shield and maintain its own deterrence. The Europeans worry even more about Washington's unilateral decision to store rather than destroy decommissioned nuclear warheads and dispense with inspections—and thus leave Russia's reciprocally unchecked warheads as tempting targets for future al-Qaida terrorists. The Bush administration, on the contrary, regards the ABM Treaty as an objectionable restraint on American freedom of action. Similarly, Europe's governments tend to fret that American rejection of inspections to monitor observance of the Biological Weapons Convention will encourage cheating, while the Bush administration frets instead that inspections would allow intrusive espionage in American pharmaceutical firms and armed forces. Europeans also want to give teeth to the Chemical Warfare Convention and the Missile Technology Control Regime, while the United States is leery of further international constraints on its own military forces.

The same rifts divide Washington from Europe (and from many other countries in the world) on the biodiversity treaty, the Kyoto protocol on reducing greenhouse gases and global warming that the United States has pulled out of, the Comprehensive Test Ban Treaty that the U.S. Senate has never ratified, and bans on antipersonnel land mines and small-arms exports that the United States opposes. International votes ran 142 to 0 for approval, with 18 abstentions, on the land mine ban; 120 to 7, with 21 abstentions on the International Criminal Court; and 178 to 1 on the Kyoto protocol vote in 2001. Transatlantic differences over the Kyoto protocol on global warming can further be measured by the contrast between per capita energy consumption of 6.2 and 3.1 tons of oil equivalent per year in the United States and Europe, respectively.[55]

More broadly, the Europeans (explicitly including the Anglo-Saxon British) perceive a need to overcome the poverty and sense of hopelessness and injustice that make breeding grounds for terrorism in many parts of the Islamic and third world. The Bush administration tends to dismiss such concerns; well after September 11 it was still seeking deep cuts in international financial aid to developing countries—and it still scorned "nation building" by international military and police forces as unworthy of America's warriors. Typically, Europe contributes 37 percent of the United Nations' basic budget and 50 percent of the UN's special program costs, whereas the United States donates only 22 percent and 17 percent, respectively.[56] Add to this the clash of various values that go beyond pragmatic interests—the morality of the death penalty, hormone-treated meat, genetically modified organisms, data protection, and prohibitions on pornography and Nazi propaganda on the Internet—and the potential for U.S.-European strains increases.[57]

For a time, September 11 muted European alarm over U.S. withdrawal from the series of international treaties that an overwhelming number of other states had endorsed. But as the image of the collapsing World Trade Center faded and was supplemented by other images—of diminishing but still present "collateral damage" in poor villages from invisible planes, and of U.S. marines forcing al-Qaida suspects in Guantanamo Bay to kneel in cages in "sensory deprivation" headgear—European concern again mounted. Europeans fear an American abdication from the Western leadership that only the U.S. can provide—but they equally fear American leadership when it is defined as unilateralism. The proper transatlantic balance in foreign policy looks as hard to achieve as is the proper domestic balance, on both sides of the Atlantic, between freedoms and the necessary restraints to defend those freedoms against attack. In searching for the right foreign policy equilibrium, many Europeans now hope for an atmosphere in which policy debates across a spectrum of opinions will be viewed not as conflicts of opposing U.S. and European national interests, but rather as joint explorations—just as legitimate and just as "domestic" as interagency wrestling in Washington—to find the best common policies in what has already become a conterminous transatlantic community.

Presidential candidate George W. Bush summarized the dilemma well when he said of non-Americans, "If we are an arrogant nation, they will resent us," and added, "If we're a humble nation, but strong, they'll welcome us." Midway through his term, at a point when the administration's unilateralist instincts seemed to have survived or even been strengthened by the September 11 trauma, Europeans are not sure that President Bush remembers the words of candidate Bush. Nor are they sure that they are, themselves, ready to assume the kind of global responsibility and fund the kind of military muscle that might convince Washington that close allies are a help rather than a hindrance. A common European security and defense policy is still in its infancy.

CHAPTER TEN

Epilogue

The original scorched memory of Hitler and Stalin and the craving for obverse reconciliation no longer drive the process of European integration as they once did. Nor do the tectonic upheavals that followed the end of the cold-war epoch.

Nor, after sixteen tumultuous years, is Helmut Kohl there to steer Europe into the third millennium. In retrospect, after Kohl so thoroughly discredited himself and his party by blatantly violating campaign funding laws, it is tempting to diminish the role that the longest-serving German chancellor in the twentieth century played in shaping post–cold war Europe. Yet the accomplishments of this outsized figure remain. Looking back, he must surely think that events justified his instinct that the next generation would have less of a compulsion than his contemporaries had to unite Europe—and that he must therefore lock Germany into irreversible monetary union while he still ruled. Chancellor Schröder now accepts EMU as a given, but he would never have toiled to produce it as Kohl did, and EMU would never have been born without that German engagement. Speaking for those in their fifties, Schröder says bluntly that the time has come for Berlin to pursue its own national interest just as vigorously as Paris and London do. His generation is European, he adds, but this is a matter of choice, not obligation.[1] This choice—with the corollary risk that Germans might one day again make the wrong choice—is precisely what Kohl wanted to ban forever.

With monetary union and the pan-European cooperative network in place, though, Kohl in effect won his historic gamble, even as he lost his personal reputation. He precluded any other option. Five decades of peace and prosperity in Europe have permanently redefined the way national interest is perceived in heartland Europe.

Much reconstruction remains to be done in the EU, of course. Its astonishingly low number of bureaucrats—30,000, or less than the administration of the single city of Cologne—can probably continue to run EU affairs without expanding greatly. But the number of allotted European commissioners must be slimmed down. Means must be found—possibly by shifting weights among its various directorates general—to decrease the Commission's vulnerability to special-interest pleading.[2] Institutional and agricultural reforms are still needed to facilitate the entry of central Europeans into the Union.[3]

Furthermore, parliamentary oversight of policies and actions must be strengthened, both in the European Parliament and in national legislatures. Transparency and democratic accountability must increase in a Union that, for an association of democracies, has been shamelessly secretive in its decisionmaking and horse trading, and lacking in verifiable lines of responsibility. The chattering class may have exaggerated the popular backlash following the Maastricht summit and overlooked the fundamentally positive feeling for Europe below surface reactions. But the EU remains a project of the elites, not of the grass roots. The European Central Bank is doubly remote from citizens, both in its transnationality and in the deliberate depoliticization of monetary management. The ECB has inherited some of the Bundesbank's prestige, but its dearth of political accountability imposes a special need to prove itself to citizens. National governments will similarly have to prove to voters that a Europe that is growing and overhauling its economy as a unit can produce jobs better than each country can do separately. If they fail, there will be a crisis not only of economics but of political legitimacy.[4]

Yet the blueprints for all of these alterations are already on the table. They do not have to be conjured up out of a void. However startling various innovations might have seemed when they were proposed at Maastricht in 1991, they are now taken for granted. The revolutions of monetary union and accession of the central Europeans to the European system are already underway. The required reconstructions will be accomplished step by step in the period of consolidation that now follows the convulsions.

In this new century, the impulse to further integration will come from stimuli other than the familiar longing for reconciliation, the earthquakes at the end of the cold war, and the ardor of one German chancellor for exorcising the demons of the past. The impetus will arise essentially from the exigencies of interdependence and globalization, as reinforced by institutions and habit—and now from the threat of spillover from Balkan, or global, chaos. These could not have carried on the dynamics alone had the EC not awakened from its stagnation to shape the single European market in the late 1980s. But that single market was formed, with monetary union as its final target, in time to absorb the shocks of German unification and to embed united Germany in a sturdy European structure. In any number of crises, the only alternative to painful integration has been predictable disaster; the only solution has therefore been, in the German phrase, to "flee forward." The successful habit of consultation has its own momentum, in any case, and institutions tend to perpetuate themselves. Pooling of sovereignty has brought tangible benefits to participants in the past, and there is a widespread expectation of common good to come, as well as a growing trust in the process itself. Monetary union, in order to function smoothly, will require much more intra-European economic coordination. And cooperation by euro-12 finance ministers in the Euro Group will in turn require more prior cooperation by heads of government.

Combined, these forces of consolidation should continue to energize rather than enervate Europe, should provide synergy instead of entropy, benchmarks instead of lowest common denominators, mutual empowerment instead of scapegoating. Europe remains a work in progress. So far, it seems condemned to succeed.

Notes

Preface

1. World Bank, *The World Bank Atlas, 2001* (Washington, 2001), pp. 44ff, pegs European gross national income at about $8.2 trillion, U.S. GNI at $8.9 trillion. This figure understates the size of the European economy, however, since it reflects what economists regard as the excessive 25 percent devaluation of the euro between 1999 and 2001.

Chapter One

1. Francis Fukuyama, *The End of History and the Last Man* (Free Press, 1992). For the purposes of this book, "Europe" is most often used not in its geographic but in its political sense. It refers to the heartland Europe of the EU and the widening sphere of states in the region that share its democratic and market values, including Switzerland, Norway, and most of the central European states that are candidates to join the EU.

2. This book does not address the many arguments about the nature of globalization, but it assumes that in the computer age the phenomenon goes far beyond the high international capital flows and trade of the pre–World War I system of a gold standard and antagonism among still bellicist European nation-states. For an exploration of how globalization affects international relations, see Jean-Marie Guehenno, "Globalisation and Its Impact on International Strategy," paper presented at the International Institute for Strategic Studies (IISS) annual conference, Oxford, September 3–6, 1998; and Paul Krugman's inaugural column for the *New York Times*, "Once and Again," January 2, 2000; throughout this book, references to the *New York Times* are generally taken from the paper's website (www.nytimes.com).

3. Interview, Bonn, 1996.

232 / NOTES TO PAGES 4–14

4. Founding father Konrad Adenauer, in the midst of West Germany's economic miracle, won a unique absolute majority in 1957 with the simple slogan "No experiments." For four decades thereafter, as the mark rose and kept on rising, the Christian Democrats revived this effective electoral appeal to the Germans' penchant for predictability.

5. See Robert Bideleux and Ian Jeffries, *A History of Eastern Europe: Crisis and Change* (New York: Routledge, 1998).

6. This concept appears in virtually every Kohl speech on Europe. See, for example, "Erklärung der Bundesregierung," speech in the Bundestag, December 12, 1996, in *Bulletin* no. 103, p. 1113, of the Press and Information Service.

7. Kohl used this phrase many times. The most famous occasion was in his speech in Louvain, Belgium, on February 2, 1996; excerpts in *Internationale Politik*, vol. 52, no. 8 (August 1996), p. 82.

8. Robert Cooper, *The Post-Modern State and the World Order* (London: Demos, 1996); interviews in February and May 1998, and in May, June, August, and November 1997, when Cooper was deputy chief of mission in the British Embassy, Bonn. See also Robert Cooper, "The Meaning of 1989," *Prospect,* December 1999, pp. 26–30.

9. For one description of how internalized transnational approaches have become, even in traditionally domestic ministries, see Wolf-Dieter Eberwein and Karl Kaiser, eds., *Germany's New Foreign Policy* (Houndmills: Palgrave, 2001), esp. pp. 38–57.

10. Interview, November 1997.

11. Interviews: telephone, November 1997; Davos, January 1998.

12. Telephone interview, November 1997.

13. There are, in fact, formal restrictions on crossing the border. But virtually any Pole can get a three-month German visa for the asking. Anecdotal evidence suggests that most of the cleaning women in Berlin today are Poles who live in cramped rooms in the German capital during the week and return to their families in Poland on weekends. Even as far west as the Rhineland or Belgium there is a steady stream of Polish cleaning women, construction workers, and crop pickers who stay their three months, then pass their jobs on to cousins or friends in rotation.

14. Interview, Bonn, 1994.

15. The Maastricht conference of heads of government or state took place in December 1991; the treaty was formally signed February 7, 1992.

16. See, for example, John J. Mearsheimer, "Back to the Future: Instability in Europe after the Cold War," *International Security,* vol. 15, no. 1 (Summer 1990), pp. 5–56; John J. Mearsheimer, "The False Promise of International Institutions," Working Paper 10 (John M. Olin Institute for Strategic Studies, Harvard University, November 1994); Kenneth N. Waltz, "The Emerging

Structure of International Politics," *International Security,* vol. 18, no. 2 (Fall 1993), pp. 44–79; Michael Mandelbaum, *The Dawn of Peace in Europe* (Twentieth Century Fund Press, 1996); Charles A. Kupchan, "Reviving the West," *Foreign Affairs,* vol. 75, no. 3 (May/June 1996), pp. 92–104; Rudi Dornbusch, "Euro Fantasies," *Foreign Affairs,* vol. 75, no. 5 (September/October 1996), pp. 110–24; Tony Judt, *A Grand Illusion? An Essay on Europe* (Hill and Wang, 1996); Milton Friedman, "Why Europe can't afford the euro. The danger of a common currency," *Times* (London), November 19, 1997; interview with James Tobin, "Ein schlimmes Beispiel," *Die Zeit,* March 28, 1998, p. 31; and virtually all the American media reporting on the EU Intergovernmental Conference of 1996–97.

Different though they are, these works all reflect the premises sketched here. Judt regards European cooperation from 1945 to 1989 as no more than a "parenthesis"—and notions of "Europe" as no more than a "mantra" to avoid facing real problems like unemployment. Mandelbaum mentions the European Union only three times in a 169-page text (excluding footnotes), once to point out its failure in Bosnia, the other two times to urge central European states' entry into the EU as a better alternative to NATO membership. Kupchan, although he proposes a new institution of an "Atlantic Union" that would combine the functions of the EU and NATO, does so because he is convinced that the pursuit of the "cold war legacies" of NATO expansion, "monetary union, a common foreign and security policy, and centralized governance of Europe" will fail. Expectations of the worst from European monetary union on sheer economic grounds—especially the lack of regional adjustment by labor mobility—also predominate in the analysis of leading American economists like Dornbusch or Friedman.

Exceptions, curiously, to what the *Economist* identifies as the prevalent American "genre" of Europessimism ("Diplomatic baggage," *Economist,* November 15, 1997, p. 7 of review section) are two analysts who are more noted as eastern European than as western European specialists. Martin Malia, "A New Europe for the Old?" *Daedalus* (Summer 1997), flags the current steps toward European integration as the most significant since the time of Charlemagne. Zbigniew Brzezinski, *The Grand Chessboard* (Basic Books, 1997), notes that while the European enterprise may be "lukewarm, lacking in passion and a sense of mission," it is nonetheless surging forward on the commitment of the French and German elites to it.

For illustration that the dismissive U.S. view of the EU continues, contrast the mocking American coverage with the serious European reporting of the Laeken EU summit that authorized an EU constitutional convention in December 2001: "Zukunftsweisender EU-Konvent?" *Neue Zürcher Zeitung,* December 17, 2001; Peter Norman, "EU sets course towards new era,"

Financial Times, December 17, 2001; Thomas Fuller and Barry James, "EU Bickering Snarls Summit," and John Vinocut, "On Both War and Peace, the EU Stands Divided," *International Herald Tribune,* December 17, 2001, p. 1; and Edmund L. Andrews, "In Push for European Unity, Leader Finds Fissures," *New York Times,* December 15, 2001.

17. The *World Bank Atlas, 2001* (Washington: World Bank, 2001), pp. 44 ff., estimates Polish gross national income at $157 billion, Russian GNI at $329 billion.

18. Wolfgang Schmale, *Scheitert Europa an seinem Mythendefizit?* (Bochum: Winkler, 1997).

19. Joseph S. Nye Jr., *Bound to Lead: The Changing Nature of American Power* (Basic Books, 1990), and *The Paradox of American Power* (Oxford University Press, 2002).

20. This point is argued most cogently in Peter Katzenstein, ed., *Tamed Power: Germany in Europe* (Cornell University Press, 1998). In this book Katzenstein also proposes a theoretical synthesis of neorealism and neofunctionalism. While the theory of international relations is well outside the scope of the present book, it is worth noting that Katzenstein thus challenges the strong Euroskeptic bias of the neorealist school in the United States. See also Michael Mertes, "Germany's Social and Political Culture: Change through Consensus?" in Michael Mertes, Steven Muller, and Heinrich August Winkler, *In Search of Germany* (New Brunswick: Transaction, 1996).

21. Bruce Blair, "Loose Cannon," *National Interest,* no. 52 (Summer 1998), pp. 87–98; "Russia's National Security Concept," *Nezavisimoye Voennoye Obozrenie* (Moscow), January 14, 2000, translation in David Johnson List #4051, January 20, 2000 (davidjohnson@erols.com); and Mark Kramer, "What Is Driving Russia's New Strategic Concept," Harvard Program in New Approaches to Russian Security, in David Johnson's CDI Russian Weekly #84, January 14, 2000.

22. Martin Feldstein, "EMU and International Conflict," *Foreign Affairs,* vol. 76, no. 6 (November/December 1997), pp. 60–73.

23. John Newhouse, *Europe Adrift* (Pantheon, 1997).

24. Philip Stephens, "Intellectual gulf," *Financial Times,* January 19, 1998, p. 14.

25. Irving Kristol, "Petrified Europe," *Wall Street Journal Europe,* February 2, 1998.

26. William Safire, "Alice in Euroland," *New York Times,* April 30, 1998. In fairness, it should be noted that the United States was not altogether alone in its dismissal of EMU. In Britain, too, "many politicians and financial commentators and most of the news media displayed an almost spectacular misjudgment of the events that ensured EMU's scheduled launch," according to Wolfgang Münchau. "Some of the more visceral critics totally misread the

German institutions, in particular the Bundesbank and the German constitutional court, hoping that they might block the project at the last minute. They mistook German skepticism on EMU for a general Euroskepticism," and still "predict that the project will collapse." "Prepared for EMU? It's time to live with the euro," *Financial Times*, April 28, 1998, p. 3.

27. See, for example, Richard W. Stevenson, "Euro Could Eventually Rival the Dollar," *New York Times*, April 28, 1998; and Anne Swardson, "Europe Banks on a 30-Year Dream," *Washington Post*, April 28, 1998; throughout this book, references to the *Washington Post* are generally taken from the paper's website (www.washingtonpost.com).

Chapter Two

1. Dean Acheson, *Present at the Creation* (W. W. Norton, 1987), especially p. 231. See also Dennis L. Bark and David R. Gress, *A History of West Germany*, vol. 1: *From Shadow to Substance: 1945–1963* (Oxford: Basil Blackwell, 1989), pp. 128–40; and Theodor Eschenburg, "Jahre der Besatzung, 1945–1949," in DVA/Brockhaus, *History of the Federal Republic of Germany*, vol. 1 (Stuttgart/Wiesbaden: Deutsche Verlags-Anstalt/F. A. Brockhaus, 1981), pp. 265–69.

2. *Der Spiegel*, September 10, 1984. Mitterand's quote is cited in several works, including Bark and Gress, *A History of West Germany: vol. 2: Democracy and Its Discontents*, p. 460.

3. In a memo to British prime minister Anthony Eden, February 7, 1956. Cited in Hans-Peter Schwarz, *Die Ära Adenauer 1949–1957* (Stuttgart/Wiesbaden: Deutsche Verlags-Anstalt/F. A. Brockhaus, 1981), p. 340.

4. The European Council was established by the 1957 Treaty of Rome but was not institutionalized until 1974. From then on, summits were held regularly and increasingly took on the role of initiator and arbiter in policies. From the early 1980s, the European Council moved beyond "conventional" summitry to a system in which "conclusions of the European Council possess quasi-legal authority," says Peter Ludlow, founder of the Centre for European Policy Studies in Brussels. He contends that the Council system that developed, "far from killing supranationalism," as was widely thought in the early years after the Treaty of Rome, "rescued it by making its member states themselves responsible, through the Council, for the management of the new system." He maintains, in effect—against the thesis of Alan S. Milward in *The European Rescue of the Nation-State* (London: Routledge, 1992)—that the nation-state was coopted into progressively expanding the scope and powers of collective decisionmaking in Europe in a way that was neither federalism nor the traditional diplomacy of sovereign states. Peter Ludlow,

236 / NOTES TO PAGES 24-29

"Recasting the European Political System, 1950–1996," *CEPS Review,* no. 1 (Summer 1996), pp. 25–33.

5. Fiona Hayes-Renshaw and Helen Wallace, *The Council of Ministers* (St. Martin's, 1997), pp. 1, 211. The authors add dryly that the council is also the focus for the 800-strong Brussels press corps, "through which ministers address their domestic publics." For an ABC of the European Union, see John Pinder, *The European Union: A Very Short Introduction* (Oxford University Press, 2001).

6. See especially Schwarz, *Die Ära Adenauer,* pp. 94–118, 288–96.

7. Ibid., p. 289.

8. TREVI is an acronym for terrorism, radicalism, extremism, and internal violence.

9. Anthony Forster and William Wallace, "Common Foreign and Security Policy," in Helen Wallace and William Wallace, *Policy-Making in the European Union,* 3d ed. (Oxford University Press, 1996), pp. 411–35.

10. Ibid., p. 61.

11. The bizarre transatlantic banana war began in the early 1990s as a skirmish between the Germans, who dote on cheaper and tastier Latin American bananas and free trade, and the French, who dote on their former colonies and intervention in the market. The French won, and the EU, to encourage African and Caribbean imports of the fruit, set quotas on "dollar bananas" from Latin America. From 1993 on, African, Caribbean, and Pacific bananas could enter the EU duty free, but dollar bananas had to pay a tariff of about 24 percent on the first 2 million tons, and more than 200 percent over this "quota." In its initial ruling, the European Court of Justice turned down a German government petition to declare the regime illegal, since the quota was flexible enough not to cause "serious and irreparable damage" to Germany. See Christopher Stephens, "EU Policy for the Banana Market," in Wallace and Wallace, *Policy-Making in the European Union,* pp. 325–51.

12. J. H. H. Weiler, "The Transformation of Europe," *Yale Law Journal,* vol. 100, no. 8 (1991), pp. 2403–83; and J. H. H. Weiler, *The Consititution of Europe* (Cambridge University Press, 1999). See also J. H. H. Weiler, "A Quiet Revolution: The European Court of Justice and Its Interlocutors," *Comparative Political Studies,* vol. 26, no. 4 (January 1994), pp. 510–34; Andre Bzdera, "The Court of Justice of the European Community and the Politics of Institutional Reform," *West European Politics,* vol. 15, no. 3 (July 1992), pp. 122–36; Mary L. Volcansek, "The European Court of Justice: Supranational Policy-Making," *West European Politics,* vol. 15, no. 3 (July 1992), pp. 109–21; Karen J. Alter and Sophie Meunier-Aitsahalia, "Judicial Politics in the European Community," *Comparative Political Studies,* vol. 26, no. 4 (January 1994), pp. 535–61; Robert Rice, "States breaking EU laws may have to pay damages," *Financial Times,* November 29, 1995, p. 18; "France rapped over

farmers," *Financial Times,* December 16, 1997, p. 10; and Josephine Shaw, *The Law of the European Union* (Basingstoke: Macmillan, 1996).

13. For a protean exploration of this phenomenon, see Weiler, *The Constitution of Europe.*

14. For complaints about the European Court of Justice, see Andrew Adonis and Robert Rice, "In the hot seat of judgment," *Financial Times,* April 3, 1995, p. 15; Robert Rice, "German judge attacks European court," *Financial Times,* August 21, 1995, p. 2; editorial, "European law in the dock," *Financial Times,* August 21, 1995; Robert Rice, "EU liability ruling turns spotlight on Court," *Financial Times,* November 29, 1995, p. 2; Günter Hirsch, "Keine Integration ohne Rechtseinheit," *Frankfurter Allgemeine Zeitung,* October 9, 1996, p. 15; Uwe Wesel, "Ausgerechnet Bananen," *Die Zeit,* April 4, 1997, p. 44; "Biased referee?" *Economist,* May 17, 1997, pp. 35ff; and "Bonn to defy European Court," *Financial Times,* June 6, 1998, p. 2.

15. Brigid Laffan and Michael Shackleton, "The Budget," and Helen Wallace and Alasdair R. Young, "The Single Market: A New Approach to Policy," both in Wallace and Wallace, *Policy-Making in the European Union,* pp. 71–96 and 125–55.

16. David Allen, "Competition Policy: Policing the Single Market," Janne Haaland Matlary, "Energy Policy: From a National to a European Framework?" and Stephen Woolcock and Michael Hodges, "EU Policy in the Uruguay Round," all in Wallace and Wallace, *Policy-Making in the European Union,* pp. 157–83, 257–77, and 301–24.

17. Interviews. See also Alberta Sbragia, "Environmental Policy: The 'Push-Pull' of Policy-Making," in Wallace and Wallace, *Policy-Making in the European Union,* pp. 235–55.

18. Interviews. See also Dominique Moïsi, "End in sight for Mr Eternity," *Financial Times,* March 10, 1998, p. 18; and Gilbert Ziebura, *Die deutsch-französischen Beziehungen seit 1945* (Stuttgart: Günther Neske, 1997).

19. On Mitterrand's efforts to forestall unification, see Elizabeth Pond, *Beyond the Wall* (Brookings, 1993); Horst Teltschik, *329 Tage* (Berlin: Siedler, 1991); and Philip Zelikow and Condoleezza Rice, *Germany Unified and Europe Transformed* (Harvard University Press, 1995). Kohl's affection for Mitterrand shines through the laudatio for this "great European" that he gave *Le Monde* on Mitterrand's retirement from office on May 11, 1995. German Government Bulletin 41 (May 1995), pp. 356ff.

20. See Pond, *Beyond the Wall,* pp. 33–55, 65–68; and Catherine McArdle Kelleher, *The Future of European Security* (Brookings, 1995), pp. 57–63.

21. See Valerie Guerin-Sendelbach, "Ein Tandem für Europa? Die deutsch-französische Zusammenarbeit der achtziger Jahre," Working Paper on International Relations 77 (Bonn: German Society for Foreign Policy, September 1993).

Chapter Three

1. The East German Politburo had intended to allow much freer travel outside the German Democratic Republic, but only later and only with official exit stamps. An ambiguous televised press conference during prime-time evening news led many East Berliners to think they could suddenly visit West Berlin at will, however, and they quickly massed at the crossing points. Border guards initially blocked their way, but—without orders—finally chose to let the East Berliners through rather than shoot. See Hans-Hermann Hertle, *Chronik des Mauerfalls* (Berlin: Ch. Links, 1996); and Elizabeth Pond, *Beyond the Wall* (Brookings, 1993). For an account of the Leipzig demonstration a month earlier that established the precedent that East German security forces would not shoot demonstrators, see David Schoenbaum and Elizabeth Pond, *The German Question and Other German Questions* (London: Macmillan, 1996), pp. 146–49.

2. Patricia Clough, *Helmut Kohl* (Munich: DTV, 1998); Klaus Dreher, *Helmut Kohl* (Stuttgart: Deutsche Verlags-Anstalt, 1998).

3. Kai Diekmann and Ralf Georg Reuth, *Kohl: Ich wollte Deutschlands Einheit* (Berlin: Propyläen, 1996), p. 483.

4. For some Anglo-Saxon premonitions of the pending French revaluation, see Richard Bernstein, "The French Revolution: Right or Wrong?" *New York Times Book Review*, July 10, 1988, pp. 1ff.; and the special section on the French Revolution in the *Economist*, December 24, 1988, pp. 119ff.

5. For evaluations of the bilateral relationship in this period, see Valerie Guerin-Sendelbach, *Ein Tandem für Europa?* (Bonn: Europa Union Verlag, 1993); Ingo Kolboom and Ernst Weisenfeld, eds., *Frankreich in Europa* (Bonn: Europa Union Verlag, 1993); Patrick McCarthy, ed., *France-Germany 1983–1993* (St. Martin's, 1993); and Philip H. Gordon, *Die Deutsch-Französische Partnerschaft und die Atlantische Allianz* (Bonn: Europa Union Verlag, 1994).

6. For a sampling of the flood of literature in this vein predicting or advocating the demise of NATO after the collapse of the Berlin Wall, see Ronald Steel, "NATO's Last Mission," *Foreign Policy*, vol. 76 (Fall 1989), pp. 83–95; Christopher Layne, "Superpower Disengagement," *Foreign Policy*, vol. 78 (Spring 1990), pp. 3–25; and Richard H. Ullman, *Securing Europe* (Princeton University Press, 1991).

7. See especially Lily Gardner Feldman's chapter, "The European Community and German Unification," in Leon Hurwitz and Christian Lequesne, eds., *The State of the European Community, 1989–90* (Boulder, Colo.: Lynne Rienner, 1991); Lily Feldman, "Germany and the EC: Realism and Responsibility," *Annals of the American Academy* (January 1994), pp. 25–43; and Helen Wallace and Alasdair R. Young, "The Single Market," in Helen Wallace and William Wallace, *Policy-Making in the European Union*, 3d ed. (Oxford

University Press, 1996), pp. 125–55. Peter Ludlow, founder of the Center for European Policy Studies, contests the common perception of stagnation in the EC after the mid-1960s. He argues that these decades constituted instead a period of "consolidation of the EU's political system and the laying of the bases of the dramatic advances which occurred in the decade following 1986. Peter Ludlow, "Recasting the European Political System, 1950–1996," *CEPS Review,* no. 1 (Summer 1996), pp. 25–33.

8. French finance minister Dominique Strauss-Kahn's summary of this strategy can be found in Craig Whitney, "Euro-Ready France Pleases a Guide with Vision," *New York Times,* April 19, 1998.

9. This reading is based on interviews, consistency with Kohl's later positions on EMU, and the dynamic of allied acceptance of German unification. The received wisdom is that Kohl agreed to give up the deutsche mark as payment for unification. However, this version was categorically denied by Wilhelm Schönfelder, the Foreign Ministry's point man in the issue from the mid-1980s on and currently the German ambassador to the EU Committee of Permanent Representatives (COREPER), in interviews in 1997 and 1998; by Dietrich von Kyaw, then the German ambassador to COREPER, in interviews in 1998; and by Horst Teltschik, national security adviser to Kohl during the process of German unification, in interviews in 1990 and 1997. Their interpretation—that Kohl supported EMU, but only under stringent conditions—is in any case more consistent with Kohl's later fierce defense of EMU than is the view that his opposition inexplicably turned to advocacy as the going got tough. Finally, it is clear from other evidence that the shift of initial French and British resistance into acquiescence with unification reflected less an EMU trade-off than American pressure on Paris and London to accede to the inevitable. *Der Spiegel* purported to show from official minutes of a Kohl meeting with Secretary of State James Baker in early 1990 that the chancellor thought then that monetary union would run counter to German national interest—but the magazine omitted the sentence after its chosen quote, which made clear Kohl was referring to the arguments of those in the Bundesbank and elsewhere that he would have to refute to win EMU. See Hanns Jürgen Küsters and Daniel Hofmann, eds., *Deutsche Einheit. Sonderedition aus den Akten des Bundeskanzleramtes. Dokumente zur Deutschlandpolitik* (Munich: R. Oldenbourg, 1998), document 120, pp. 636–41; and an article by the political scientist who has written the first history of the economic aspects of German unification based on the opened documentation, Dieter Grosser, "Der Euro war nicht der Preis für die deutsche Einheit," *Welt am Sonntag,* May 17, 1998, p. 9. David Howarth ("The French State in the EuroZone," paper presented at the biennial meeting of the European Community Studies Association [ECSA], Madison, Wis., May 31–June 2, 2001) contends that the French motivation for desiring EMU was essentially

domestic; it was seen as a way to force France to move away from its habitual dirigisme toward liberalization in a "*self-imposed* 'semi-sovereignty' game" (emphasis in the original). For other evaluations of the French-German dynamic, see David M. Andrews, "History as Destiny: The Committee of Governors and the Origins of EMU," paper presented at the annual meeting of the American Political Science Association, Atlanta, September 2–5, 1999; and Madeleine O. Hosli, "Negotiating the European Economic and Monetary Union," paper presented at the ECSA meeting, May 31–June 2, 2001.

See also Wilhelm Schönfelder and Elke Thiel, *Ein Markt—Eine Währung* (Baden-Baden: Nomos, 1996); Thomas Hanke and Norbert Walter, *Der Euro* (Frankfurt: Campus, 1998), p. 18; Peter Norman, "EMU's broody hen," *Financial Times*, May 2, 1998, p. 7; Joachim Bitterlich, "Anfangs frostig, später europäisch," *Die Zeit*, May 7, 1998, p. 4; Thomas Hanke and Wolf Proissl, "Die Dolchstosslegende," *Die Zeit*, May 7, 1998, p. 5; and for the American role in unification, Philip Zelikow and Condoleezza Rice, *Germany Unified and Europe Transformed* (Harvard University Press, 1995); and Pond, *Beyond the Wall*, pp. 138ff. Most English-language literature, by contrast, accepts the conventional wisdom. See, for example, the analysis by Loukas Tsoukalis, "Economic and Monetary Union," in Wallace and Wallace, *Policy-Making in the European Union*, p. 293; and Anne Swardson, "Europe Banks on a 30-Year Dream," *Washington Post*, April 28, 1998, p. A1. For one last polemic against the euro on the eve of its adoption, see Rudolf Augstein's argument that EMU is a "chimera in the desert" and cannot work unless one changes human nature. "Neue Menschen, neue Menschen," *Der Spiegel*, April 27, 1998, pp. 102ff.

10. Reinhard Bettzuege, ed., *Aussenpolitik der Bundesrepublik Deutschland. Dokumente von 1949 bis 1994* (Bonn: German Foreign Ministry, 1995), pp.776ff. The phrasing is taken from Kohl and Mitterrand's summary of their April meeting to the Italian president of the EC on December 6, 1990.

11. Bettzuege, *Aussenpolitik*, pp. 729ff.

12. See, for example, Timothy Garton Ash, "Germany's Choice," *Foreign Affairs*, vol. 73, no. 4 (July/August 1994), pp. 65–81.

13. Europol was in fact not launched until 1998.

14. Bettzuege, *Aussenpolitik*, pp. 846ff.

15. Group interview with the German-American Workshop, May 1998, Bonn.

16. December 5, 1991.

17. For one example of the economic argumentation against EMU, see Manfred J. M. Neumann, "Die Mark ist ein Wohlstandsfaktor," *Die Zeit*, October 16, 1992, p. 32.

18. Kolboom and Weisenfeld, *Frankreich in Europa*, p. 75.

19. As translated from the German translation from the French in ibid., p. 79.

20. Strictly speaking, this was not in the same league as Adenauer's flout-

ing of public opinion, since more nuanced polls in the 1980s in Germany, unlike those in the Netherlands, never showed a majority against the deployment. See Pond, *Beyond the Wall*, chap. 4.

21. See, for example, "From Here to EMU," *Economist*, October 23, 1993, pp. 29ff.

22. Lionel Barber, "EU warned budget cannot grow to pay for expansion," *Financial Times*, October 23, 1995, p. 1; and Rudolf G. Adam, "Wo ein Wille ist, gibt es viele Wege," *Frankfurter Allgemeine Zeitung*, December 5, 1995, pp. 16ff. The Visegrad states—the name derives from the city where they first met to try coordinate their approaches to the West—were originally Poland, Hungary, and Czechoslovakia. After Czechoslovakia split into the Czech Republic and Slovakia, there were four members of the group.

23. After Austria, Belgium, Denmark, and Luxembourg, and only slightly above France and the Netherlands, as measured in purchasing power parity in the annual pamphlet *OECD in Figures*. One indicator of the sensitivity of this issue was the unavailability for many years of any official EU figures for net contributions.

24. Representative discussions from the ubiquitous contemporary coverage of the phenomenon include the insert section "Politikverdrossenheit," *Das Parlament*, July 30, 1993; and "Doch wie Weimar?" *Der Spiegel*, December 20, 1993, pp. 38ff.

25. Wallace and Wallace, *Policy-Making in the European Union*, pp. 375ff.

26. Ibid., p. 371.

27. Deutsches Institut für Wirtschaftsforschung, "Bananenfestung Europa," weekly report, April 8, 1992, pp. 175–79; Wallace and Wallace, *Policy-Making in the European Union*, chap. 13.

Chapter Four

1. According to megahistorian Paul Johnson, the present peace is the longest in history. He maintains that "the fifty years of peace between the Great Powers is a significant landmark in human history. Never before, and indeed never since there have been great powers to fight each other, has a general peace lasted so long. . . . As a historian, I can confidently say that this is unique: There is no precedent in world history for war being ruled out of forward calculations at such a high level." "World War II and the Path to Peace," *Wall Street Journal Europe*, May 8, 1995, p. 6. See also John Gaddis, *The Long Peace* (Oxford University Press, 1987).

It would go well beyond the scope of this book to address the broader academic debate about the thesis that democracies tend not to go to war with other democracies. This controversy can be followed in Michael Doyle, *Ways* of *War and Peace* (W. W. Norton, 1997); in the fall 1994 issue of *International Security*, vol. 19, no. 2; and in Pierre Hassner, "Beyond the Three Traditions: The Philosophy of War and Peace in Historical Perspective," *International Affairs*, vol. 70, no. 4 (October 1994). What is indisputable, however, is that war in western Europe is now unthinkable.

2. See, for example, Ian Davidson, "Atlantic Alliance fails to read the writing on the wall," *Financial Times*, July 12, 1990, p. 2; Daniel T. Plesch and Daniel Shorr, "NATO, Down and (Soon) Out," *International Herald Tribune*, July 24, 1992; and even John Lukacs, *The End of the Twentieth Century and the End of the Modern Age* (Ticknor and Fields, 1993).

3. Robert Mauthner and Lionel Barber, "U.S. seeks EC defence pledge," *Financial Times*, November 8, 1991, p. 1.

4. Vera Tolz measures the shift in Yeltsin's abandonment of the adjective "Rossiiskaya" in favor of the traditional "Russkaya" for "Russian." The latter refers to common blood, the former (in 1990s usage), to a nation united instead by common institutions. This analysis was presented in "What Is Russia: Post-Communist Debates on Nation-Building," at the annual conference of the British Association for the Advancement of Slavic Studies, Cambridge, April 5, 1998.

5. Frank Umbach, "The Role and Influence of the Military Establishment in Russia's Foreign and Security Policies in the Yeltsin Era," *Journal of Slavic Military Studies*, vol. 9, no. 3 (September 1996), pp. 467–500. For application of this doctrine to the largest Russian exercises since the breakup of the Soviet Union, see Michael R. Gordon, "Maneuvers Show Russian Reliance on Nuclear Arms," *New York Times*, July 10, 1999.

6. See Anatol Lieven, *Chechnya: Tombstone of Russian Power* (Yale University Press, 1998).

7. NATO London Declaration, Press Communiqué S-1(90)36, July 6, 1990.

8. Laura Silber and Allan Little, *Yugoslavia: Death of a Nation* (New York: TV Books, 1996), p. 159.

9. See Susan L. Woodward, *Balkan Tragedy* (Brookings, 1995); Silber and Little, *Yugoslavia*; Warren Zimmermann, *Origins of a Catastrophe* (Times Books, 1996); Richard Holbrooke, *To End a War* (Random House, 1998); David Rohde, *Endgame* (Farrar, Straus and Giroux, 1998); and Mark Danner's series of articles in the *New York Review of Books*, November 20, 1997, December 4, 1997, December 18, 1997, February 5, 1998, February 19, 1998, March 26, 1998, and April 23, 1998. For a rather different European perspective on the "endgame" in Bosnia, see Carl Bildt, "The search for peace" (review of Holbrooke's book), *Financial Times*, July 2, 1998, p. 16.

10. Silber and Little, *Yugoslavia*, p. 201.

11. Probably the most influential book to view the Yugoslav bloodletting as an outbreak of ancient ethnic hatreds—it was famously read by President

Clinton in the early 1990s—was Robert Kaplan's *Balkan Ghosts* (Vintage, 1994). For refutations of this view, see the books on Yugoslavia already cited, plus Michael Ignatieff, "The Politics of Self-Destruction," *New York Review of Books*, November 2, 1995, pp. 17ff; and Brian Hall, "Rebecca West's War," *New Yorker*, April 15, 1996, pp. 74–83.

12. Holbrooke, *To End a War*, pp. 65–68.

13. Ibid., p. 67.

14. "NATO beyond Bosnia," Congressional Research Service Report for Congress 94-977 S (December 7, 1994).

15. The atmosphere in Dayton was captured in one sputtering British cable from the airbase that began, according to an American diplomat who saw it, "The Americans let the animals out of the cage today." "Animals" refers to all the non-Americans and their perceived treatment by Holbrooke.

16. Countries participating under Partnership for Peace were Albania, Austria, Bulgaria, the Czech Republic, Estonia, Finland, Hungary, Latvia, Lithuania, Poland, Romania, Russia, Slovakia, Slovenia, Sweden, and Ukraine. Additional IFOR personnel came from Argentina, Egypt, Ireland, Jordan, and Morocco.

17. See the summary in the International Institute for Strategic Studies, *Strategic Survey 1993–1994* (London: Brassey's, 1994), pp. 117–25.

18. Volker Rühe, "Shaping Euro-Atlantic Policies—A Grand Strategy for a New Era," Alastair Buchan Memorial Lecture, delivered at the International Institute for Strategic Studies, London, March 26, 1993; copy distributed by German Defense Ministry.

19. Interviews with Onyszkiewicz, February 1998 (Munich) and February 1997 (Warsaw).

20. Geremek speech in Aachen on May 21, 1998, provided by the Polish Embassy in Cologne. For the current state of the special Polish-German relationship, see especially Roland Freudenstein, "Poland, Germany and the EU," *International Affairs*, vol. 74, no. 1 (January 1998), pp. 41–54. For earlier descriptions, see Dieter Bingen, *Die Polenpolitik der Bonner Republik von Adenauer bis Kohl: 1949–1991* (Baden-Baden: Nomos, 1998); Roland Freudenstein, ed., *VII. Deutsch-Polnisches Forum* (Bonn: Europa Union Verlag, 1993); Hans-Adolf Jacobsen and Mieczeslaw Tomala, eds., *Warschau-Bonn* (Cologne: Wissenschaft und Politik, 1990); and Michael Ludwig, *Polen und die deutsche Frage* (Bonn: Europa Union Verlag, 1990.)

21. Interviews; James Goldgeier, "NATO Enlargement: Anatomy of a Decision," *Washington Quarterly*, vol. 21, no. 1 (Winter 1998), pp. 85–102; and Jonathan Eyal, "NATO's Enlargement: Anatomy of a Decision," *International Affairs*, vol. 73, no. 4 (October 1997), pp. 695–719.

22. A striking feature of the American debate was the overwhelming opposition to enlargement among columnists and opinion writers. The crusade

was led by Thomas L. Friedman of the *New York Times*. See, for example, his "Gulf of Tonkin II," *New York Times*, March 31, 1998, and numerous other columns; Jim Hoagland, "From NATO to the Real World," *Washington Post*, May 3, 1998; Charles A. Kupchan, "Expand NATO—And Split Europe," *New York Times*, November 27, 1994; Michael Mandelbaum, "Preserving the New Peace," *Foreign Affairs*, vol. 74, no. 3 (May/June 1995), pp. 9–13; John Lewis Gaddis, "The Senate Should Halt NATO Expansion," *New York Times*, April 27, 1998, and "History, Grand Strategy and NATO Enlargement," *Survival*, vol. 40, no. 1 (Spring 1998), pp. 145–51; William Pfaff, "European Security Isn't Broken. So Why Try to Fix It Now?" *International Herald Tribune*, February 18, 1997, p. 8. See also "Expanding NATO: Will It Weaken the Alliance?" transcript of a debate between Richard C. Holbrooke and Michael E. Mandelbaum at the Council on Foreign Relations in New York, December 9, 1996.

23. The pro-enlargement campaign was spearheaded initially by RAND Corporation analysts in a flurry of articles. See, for example, Ronald D. Asmus, Richard L. Kugler, and F. Stephen Larrabee, "Building a New NATO," *Foreign Affairs*, vol. 72, no. 4 (September/October 1993), pp. 28–40; and Ronald D. Asmus, Robert D. Blackwill, and F. Stephen Larrabee, "Can NATO Survive?" *Washington Quarterly*, vol. 19, no. 2 (Spring 1996), pp. 79–101. See also NATO's own "Study on NATO Enlargement," September 1995. For a discussion of civilian-military relations in the candidate countries, see Reka Szemerkenyi, "Central European Civil-Military Reforms at Risk," Adelphi Paper 306 (London: International Institute for Strategic Studies, December 1996).

24. Strobe Talbott, "Why NATO Should Grow," *New York Review of Books*, August 10, 1995, pp. 27–30. See also Richard C. Holbrooke, "America, a European Power," *Foreign Affairs*, vol. 74, no. 2 (March/April, 1995), pp. 38–51.

25. See, for example, Madeleine Albright, "Bringing New Democracies into the NATO Fold," *International Herald Tribune*, July 8, 1997, p. 8.

26. Obversely, Kaliningrad was a special concern of Poland and Lithuania in the early 1990s because of the concentration there of Soviet troops withdrawing from eastern Germany and Poland. For German interest in helping to develop the Kaliningrad special economic zone as a link between Russia and the West rather than a bone of contention, see Heike Dörrenbächer, *Die Sonderwirtschaftszone Jantar' von Kaliningrad (Königsberg)* (Bonn: Europa Union Verlag, 1994).

27. Jonathan Eyal, "NATO's Enlargement," specifies that the Baltics could be defended only if there were prepositioning of materiel there. Prepositioning would be seen as so provocative by Russia that it is not a serious NATO option.

28. Interviews with Onyszkiewicz, February 1998 (Munich) and February 1997 (Warsaw). Other Poles argued as well that it was only after NATO

finally decided to admit Poland to membership that the Russians began talking to Poles directly and seriously about their bilateral relationship, rather than expecting to negotiate with the West about Poland over the heads of the Poles.

29. Bartolomiej Sienkiewicz, "A Gentle Russia," *Gazeta Wyborcza*, July 1, 1998; English translation in David Johnson List #2251, July 7, 1998 (davidjohnson@erols.com).

30. "The Baltic Revolution," *Economist*, April 18, 1998, pp. 30ff. In interviews, Finnish diplomats who closely monitor regional developments in cooperation with the three Baltic foreign ministries also note a sharp decrease in Russian attempts to ride roughshod over Baltic preferences following the final decision to enlarge NATO.

31. Interview, February 1997.

32. Olga Alexandrova, "Perzeptionen der auswärtigen Sicherheit in der Ukraine," paper for the Federal Institute for Eastern Studies, Cologne, August 1993.

33. Interview, Warsaw, 1995.

34. The best analyses of Ukrainian security issues and the Russian-Ukrainian agreements have been written by James Sherr and Sherman Garnett. See James Sherr, "Russia-Ukraine Rapprochement?" *Survival*, vol. 39, no. 3 (Autumn 1997), pp. 33ff; James Sherr, "Russia and Ukraine: Towards Compromise or Convergence?" Conflict Studies Research Center, Royal Military Academy, Sandhurst, August 1997 (gopher://marvin.nc3a.NATO.int/00/secdef/csrc/f60all.txt%09%09%2B); Sherman W. Garnett, *Keystone in the Arch: Ukraine in the Emerging Security Environment of Central and Eastern Europe* (Washington: Carnegie Endowment for International Peace, 1997); Stephen A. Cambone, "NATO Enlargement: Implications for the Military Dimension of Ukraine's Security," *Harriman Review*, vol. 10, no. 3 (Winter 1997), pp. 8–18; and Christian F. Wehrschütz, "Die ukrainisch-russischen Beziehungen: Ungewisse Partnerschaft," Working Paper 3066 (Berlin: Stiftung Wissenschaft und Politik, April 1998).

35. Interview, Brussels, June 1998.

36. Interviews in Kyiv and Warsaw, March 1997.

37. Interview, Warsaw, 1996.

38. The Eurocorps began in the late 1980s as a French-German brigade and then added troops from Belgium, Spain, and Luxembourg.

39. The WEU was born in 1948—before NATO existed—as the Brussels Treaty Organization of Britain, France, and the Benelux countries. It was intended as a defense pact against any return to German aggression, and when it admitted Germany and Italy as members in 1954 it barred Bonn from acquiring certain classes of weapons; these restrictions would not be lifted until the 1980s and 1990s. The WEU ceased to have any serious function once NATO

was founded, but it was revived as part of the renewed French-German rapprochement in the 1980s. Its ten current full members include also Portugal, Spain, and Greece. The eighteen others in the organization are associate members Iceland, Norway, and Turkey; associate partners Poland, Hungary, the Czech Republic, Slovenia, Estonia, Slovakia, Latvia, Lithuania, Bulgaria, and Romania; and observers Austria, Denmark, Finland, Ireland, and Sweden. For discussion of ESDI, see Michael O'Hanlon, "Transforming NATO: The Role of European Forces," *Survival*, vol. 39, no. 3 (Autumn 1997), pp. 5ff.

40. See Charles Barry, "NATO's Combined Joint Task Forces in Theory and Practice," *Survival*, vol. 38, no. 1 (Spring 1996), pp. 81-97; and Philip H. Gordon, "Europe's Uncommon Foreign Policy," *International Security*, vol. 22, no. 3 (Winter 1997/98), pp. 74-100.

41. Solana speech at the annual Munich Security Conference, February 1998.

42. Interview. Article 5 of NATO's 1949 founding treaty designates an attack on any NATO member as an attack on all alliance members; this is the basis for the "spine" of NATO's continuous political consultations and the integrated command that was activated in Bosnia.

43. Speech at NATO's Defense Planning Committee, June 11, 1998, NATO press release.

44. For an overview of the shrinking of commands, see Thomas-Durell Young, ed., *Command in NATO after the Cold War: Alliance, National, and Multinational Considerations* (Carlisle Barracks, Pa.: Strategic Studies Institute, U.S. Army War College, 1997).

45. For overviews of the aborted French-NATO rapprochement, see Bruno Racine, "Für ein transatlantisches Gleichgewicht. Frankreich, NATO und europäische Verteidigungspolitik," *Internationale Politik*, vol. 53, no. 2 (February 1998), pp. 19-24; Jonathan Marcus, "Adjustment, Recrimination: Franco-U.S. Relations and the New World Disorder," *Washington Quarterly*, vol. 21, no. 2 (Spring 1998), pp. 17-32; and Gilles Andreani, "Frankreich und die NATO," *Internationale Politik*, vol. 53, no. 7 (July 1998), pp. 27-32.

46. The Euro-Atlantic Partnership Council replaced the North Atlantic Cooperation Council after the Soviet Union split into fifteen states.

47. Interview.

48. Solana speech at the University of Warsaw, April 18, 1996; NATO press release.

49. James Goodby, citing Alexander George and Kenneth Boulding, explores the difference between stable peace, conditional peace, and precarious peace in "Europe Undivided," *Washington Quarterly*, vol. 21, no. 3 (Summer 1998), pp. 191-207. He also notes Hedley Bull's distinction between the Hobbesian view of international politics as a state of war, the Kantian view of it as a potential community of mankind, and the Grotian view of it as relations within an international society.

50. Interview.

51. Interview, Brussels, 1996.

52. Paul Cornish, *Partnership in Crisis: The U.S., Europe and the Fall and Rise of NATO* (London: Royal Institute of International Affairs, 1997). See also the upbeat assessment after NATO bit the bullet in Bosnia and hammered out a CJTF agreement in Stanley Sloan, "Negotiating a New Transatlantic Bargain," *NATO Review*, vol. 44, no. 2 (March 1996), pp. 19–23. For the contrary argument that NATO will "be reluctant to use force to manage or settle disputes that do not involve its members' territories"—and that this "would be politically embarrassing and ultimately perhaps dangerous for NATO," see Joseph Lepgold, "NATO's Post–Cold War Collective Action Problem," *International Security*, vol. 23, no. 1 (Summer 1998), pp. 78–106. Lepgold advocates instead a "decentralization" of the alliance that would push military planning and responsibility further down the chain of command and devolve more responsibility and accountability onto Europeans.

Chapter Five

1. For one of the few written references to this modus operandi by an actor, see Tommaso Padoa-Schioppa, "The Euro and Politics," *Transatlantic Internationale Politik*, vol. 1, no. 4 (Winter 2000), pp. 11ff.

2. "Germany's Europe," *Financial Times*, April 28, 1994.

3. Scott Sullivan, "Down in the Dumps," *Newsweek*, April 12, 1993, pp. 10–15; *International Herald Tribune*, April 20, 1994.

4. John Andrews, survey of "The European Union: Family frictions," *Economist*, October 22, 1994.

5. George Steiner, "Sind unsere Kräfte erschöpft?" *Frankfurter Allgemeine Zeitung*, August 27, 1994.

6. Peter Ludlow, "Beyond Maastricht: Recasting the European Political and Economic System," Centre for European Policy Studies Working Document 79 (Brussels, July 1993). See also Stanley Hoffmann on Europe's "serious crisis" in "Goodbye to a United Europe?" *New York Review of Books*, May 27, 1993, pp. 27ff; Stanley Hoffmann, "Europe's Identity Crisis Revisited," *Daedalus* (Spring 1994), pp. 1–23; and Hans Arnold, *Europa am Ende?* (Munich: Piper, 1993).

7. Kohl's speeches from 1996 to 1998 are available on the Internet at (www.bundesregierung.de). His earlier speeches are available in the regular print issues of the government "Bulletin."

8. The "democratic deficit" is the conspicuous lack of direct accountability to voters in all the EU institutions. The European Commission and the European Council cut their deals behind closed doors in a kind of secrecy

that no European national parliament would tolerate. The European Parliament, while it suddenly flexed its muscles in propelling the premature expulsion of the European Commission in 1999, is not in a position to force disclosure or transparency on either. See Neil Buckley, "Brussels 'must break tradition of secrecy,'" *Financial Times*, July 23, 1999, p. 1; Christopher Lord, "Assessing Democracy in a Contested Polity," *Journal of Common Market Studies*, vol. 39, no. 4 (2001), pp. 641–61; Christopher Lord and David Beetham, "Legitimizing the EU: Is There a 'Post-parliamentary Basis' for Its Legitimacy?" *Journal of Common Market Studies*, vol. 39, no. 3 (2001), pp. 443–62; Philippe C. Schmitter, *How to Democratize the European Union . . . and Why Bother?* (Lanham, Md.: Rowman and Littlefield, 2000); Dimitris N. Chryssochoou, *Democracy in the European Union* (London: I. B. Tauris, 2000); Larry Siedentop, *Democracy in Europe* (London: Penguin, 2000); and Karlheinz Neunreither and Antje Wiener, eds., *European Integration after Amsterdam* (Oxford University Press, 2000).

9. For a discussion of the conflict between widening and deepening, see the survey of the European Union in the *Economist*, October 22, 1994. For one of the earliest statements of the German position—even before the fall of the Berlin Wall—see Michael Mertes and Norbert J. Prill, "Der verhängnisvolle Irrtum eines Entweder-Oder," *Frankfurter Allgemeine Zeitung*, July 19, 1989, p. 8. For a discussion of it in the post-Maastricht period, see Rudolf Seiters, deputy chairman of the Christian Democratic Union/Christian Social Union (hereafter CDU/CSU) parliamentary caucus, "Welches Europa wollen wir?" *Frankfurter Allgemeine Zeitung*, April 28, 1995, pp. 8ff.

10. CDU/CSU Parliamentary Group, "Reflections on European Policy," September 1, 1994. Quotations here are from the CDU's English translation.

11. For one study of these exchanges, see Guido Hartmann, *Sozio-kulturelle Probleme deutsch-französischer Ministerialkooperation* (Berlin: Wissenschaftlicher Verlag, 1997).

12. For Lamfalussy's own summation of EMI activity, see his interview, "Der Weg wird noch unruhig," *Die Zeit*, December 22, 1995, p. 19; and Andrew Fisher and David Wighton, "EMI sets out options on euro," *Financial Times*, January 11, 1997, p. 1.

13. Quentin Peel, "Kohl warns on EU contributions," *Financial Times*, May 18, 1994, p 2.

14. Kinkel speech at the German Society for Foreign Policy, August 24, 1994; see also Kohl speech at the thirtieth-anniversary celebration of the Elysée Treaty, January 21, 1993; Reinhard Bettzuege, ed., *Aussenpolitik der Bundesrepublik Deutschland. Dokumente von 1949 bis 1994* (Bonn: German Foreign Ministry, 1995), pp. 1081–86 and 899–902.

15. CDU/CSU, "Reflections on European Policy."

16. "Back to the drawing-board," *Economist*, September 10, 1994.

17. David Marsh argued in *Die Zeit*, for example, that the whole experiment in monetary union in fact threatened to split Europe wide open. Sardonically, he predicted that a single currency would indeed come—and that it would probably be called the deutsche mark. "D-Mark für alle?" *Die Zeit*, September 23, 1994; and "Spaltpilz Einheitswährung," *Die Zeit*, March 1, 1996. See also Ian Davidson, "Chord of disunity," *Financial Times*, October 2, 1996, p. 2.

18. Karl Lamers, "Germany's Responsibilities and Interests in the Field of Foreign Policy," paper presented to the CDU/CSU parliamentary caucus executive committee, August 23–24, 1993.

19. For differences over joint airplane production, see, for example, Bernard Gray and David Buchan, "France pulls out of air project," *Financial Times*, February 24, 1996, p. 1; and Michael Lindemann and Andrew Jack, "Germany, France to discuss military transport," *Financial Times*, August 8, 1996, p. 2.

20. See Wernhard Möschel, "Europapolitik zwischen deutscher Romantik und gallischer Klarheit," *Aus Politik und Zeitgeschichte*, B 3-4/95 (January 13, 1995), pp. 10–16; and Stanley Hoffmann, "French Dilemmas and Strategies in the New Europe," in Joseph S. Nye, Robert O. Keohane, and Stanley Hoffmann, eds., *Europe after the Cold War* (Harvard University Press, 1993).

21. CDU/CSU, "Reflections on European Policy."

22. "CDU und CSU wollen Kerngruppe in der EU stärken," *Frankfurter Allgemeine Zeitung*, February 9, 1994, p. 1.

23. See also the tracing of Kohl's fingerprints on the paper in "Kinkel widerspricht Europa-Konzept," *Frankfurter Allgemeine Zeitung*, September 3, 1994, p. 1; and "Verstimmung über Europapapier der Unionsfraktion," *Frankfurter Allgemeine Zeitung*, September 6, 1994, p. 1.

24. For a plea for continued French-German coordination just before the election, see Deutsche Gesellschaft für Auswärtige Politik and others, *Handeln für Europa* (Opladen: Leske + Budrich, 1995).

25. The other two signatories were Austria and Italy. Greece later acceded to the accord as well.

26. For suppressed German irritation over these and other surprises, see, for example, "Kohl will mit Chirac über Frankreichs Atom-Politik sprechen/ Bonner Unbehagen," *Frankfurter Allgemeine Zeitung*, July 11, 1995, p. 2; "Deutsch unerwünscht," *Frankfurter Allgemeine Zeitung*, November 3, 1995, p. 6; "Millon verspricht Abstimmung mit Bonn," *Frankfurter Allgemeine Zeitung*, February 21, 1996, p. 5; Günther Nonnenmacher, "Auf dem Weg zur Berufsarmee," *Frankfurter Allgemeine Zeitung*, February 23, 1996, p. 1; "Unklarheiten in der deutsch-französischen Sicherheitspolitik," *Frankfurter Allgemeine Zeitung*, March 2, 1996, p. 1; "Französiche Soldaten verlassen Deutschland bis 1999," *Frankfurter Allgemeine Zeitung*, July 18, 1996, p. 1; "Diesmal ohne Jubel," *Frankfurter Allgemeine Zeitung*, July 18, 1996, p. 1.

27. For one of the clearest expositions both of the French logic and of the breach with the past that this decision required, see Michel Rocard, "Wir sollten mehr auf die anderen hören," *Die Zeit*, September 6, 1996, p. 8. See also the interview with Jean-Pierre Chevènement, "Angst vor Deutschland?" *Die Zeit*, August 2, 1996, p. 39. For a sampling of media coverage tracing Chirac's evolution, see, for example, David Buchan, "Schengen stand ignites French Euro debate/Doubts grow over Pres. Chirac's commitment," *Financial Times*, July 1, 1995, p. 2; "Chirac becomes Balladur," *Economist*, November 4, 1995, p. 45; David Buchan, Andrew Jack, and John Ridding, "France backs Germany on EMU penalties plan," *Financial Times*, November 13, 1995, p. 20; David Buchan, "France and Germany gear up for next IGC," *Financial Times*, December 2, 1995, p. 2; "Verworrene französische Maastricht-Debatte," *Neue Zürcher Zeitung*, February 3, 1996, p. 3; "Die Handlungsfähigkeit der Europäischen Union verbessern," *Frankfurter Allgemeine Zeitung*, December 8, 1995, p. 1; Erik Hoffmeyer, "Bystanders at the infighting," *Financial Times*, February 9, 1996, p. 22; "Juppé-bekenntnis in Bonn zur Europäischen Währungsunion," *Frankfurter Allgemeine Zeitung*, February 13, 1996, p. 13; David Buchan, "EMU back on French lips," *Financial Times*, February 20, 1996, p. 2; David Buchan, "France wants to rein in non-EMU states," *Financial Times*, February 21, 1996, p. 2; Peter Norman, "Paris and Bonn agree EU foreign policy opt-out pact," *Financial Times*, February 28, 1996, p. 2; David Buchan, "Paris-Bonn accord on EMU 'ins' and 'outs,'" *Financial Times*, March 27, 1996, p. 2; Klaus Kinkel and Hervé Charette, "Es muss eine echte europäische Identität entstehen," *Frankfurter Allgemeine Zeitung*, March 29, 1996, p. 7; "Staatsminister besucht Slowakei," *Frankfurter Allgemeine Zeitung*, July 1, 1996, p. 2; Werner Hoyer and Michel Barnier, "Gemeinsam zu europäischen Zielen," *Die Zeit*, July 12, 1996, p. 8; and "Kohl und Chirac planen für ein Europa des 21 Jahrhunderts," *Frankfurter Allgemeine Zeitung*, September 2, 1996, p. 1. So much has been published on this and other issues discussed in chapters 5 and 8 especially that notes can only be indicative.

28. Compare, for example, Kohl's evocation of Churchill on April 29, 1991, and June 18, 1992, with his statement on October 5, 1993, that he would no longer use Churchill's formulation because of the "misunderstandings" it aroused. "Im Bewusstsein der europäischen Idee als Werte- und Kulturgemeinschaft," Federal Press Office Documentation Bulletin, April 29, 1991; and "Helmut Kohl. Bilanzen und Perspektiven" (Bonn: Federal Government Press and Information Service, 1997), pp. 60, 192.

29. See "Bonn und Paris rufen nach europäischer Identität," *Frankfurter Allgemeine Zeitung*, March 29, 1996, p. 1; "Die letzte Entscheidung bleibt bei den Regierungen," interview with Kinkel, *Süddeutsche Zeitung*, March 7, 1996.

30. Robert Graham, "Paris, Bonn seek to bring EU institutions closer to

citizens," *Financial Times*, May 8, 1998, p. 2; and Lionel Barber, "A punctured image," *Financial Times*, June 15, 1998, p. 17.

31. Karl Kaiser and Hanns W. Maull, eds., "Die Zukunft der europäischen Integration: Folgerungen für die deutsche Politik," Working Paper 78 (Bonn: Research Institute of the German Society for Foreign Policy, October 1993).

32. CDU/CSU, "Reflections on European Policy."

33. Rudolph G. Adam, "Wo ein Wille ist, gibt es viele Wege," *Frankfurter Allgemeine Zeitung*, May 12, 1995. For subsequent recognition of this shift, see also "Reality dawns in Tralee," editorial, *Financial Times*, September 9, 1996, p. 17; Neil Buckley, "Dehaene to present EMU budget," *Financial Times*, September 30, 1996; "'Der euro ist mehr als eine Münze," *Die Zeit*, interview with Lamers, September 5, 1997, p. 7; and "Goodbye, Federal Europe," *Economist*, November 15, 1997, pp. 27ff.

34. Interview, Bonn, 1999.

35. Ernst-Moritz Lipp, member of the Dresdner Bank board, and Hans-Olaf Henkel, president of the Federal Association of German Industry (BDI), at the German-Italian Colloquium, Bonn, April 1998; Jeffrey Sachs, "The Last Resort," *World Link*, March/April 1998, pp. 6ff.

36. The most sensational formulation of this concern was the book by a British employee of the European Commission who was subsequently disciplined, Bernard Connolly, *The Rotten Heart of Europe* (London: Faber and Faber, 1995). More sophisticated and qualified concern was expressed by Timothy Garton Ash, "Back to Europe," *Prospect* (June 1996), p. 25.

37. Ludlow, "Beyond Maastricht," p. 43.

38. See, for example, Holger Schmiedling, "Price worth paying," *Financial Times*, December 19, 1995, p. 12.

39. For Mundell's own evaluation as it became clear that EMU would proceed, see his articles, "Great Expectations for the Euro," *Wall Street Journal Europe*, March 24, 1998, p. 10; "Great Expectations for the Euro—Part II," *Wall Street Journal Europe*, March 25, 1998; and "Making the Euro Work," *Wall Street Journal Europe*, April 30, 1998. The United States exports 11.4 percent of its GDP, as calculated from 1996 statistics in the brochure "OECD in Figures," 1998 edition, supplement to *OECD Observer*, no. 212, June/July 1998. Counting both exports and imports, the share of foreign trade in GDP was just below 20 percent for the U.S. and 25 percent for the euro area, according to Sirkka Hämäläinen of the ECB Executive Board in her talk, "The Role of the Euro in the International Monetary System—Reserve Currency, Trade Currency and Investment Currency," presented at the European Central Bank, February 5, 1999.

40. For an overview of this and other issues, see the 26-page "EMU" survey in the *Economist*, April 11, 1998; the insert section, "The Birth of the Euro," in the *Financial Times*, April 30, 1998; and Horst Siebert, "Monetary Carrots and Fiscal Sticks," *WorldLink*, March/April 1998, pp. 4ff.

41. Angel de la Fuente and Farael Domenech, "The Redistributive Effects of the EU Budget," *Journal of Common Market Studies*, vol. 39, no. 2 (2001), pp. 307–30.

42. Gabriele Tondl, "Fiscal Federalism and the Reality of the European Union Budget," in Colin Crouch, ed., *After the Euro* (Oxford University Press, 2000), pp. 229–73.

43. "Scharping verzichtet auf 'Manifest'/Schröder: Währungsunion als nationales Thema der SPD," *Frankfurter Allgemeine Zeitung*, October 30, 1995; Peter Norman, "Schroeder upsets SPD euro consensus," *Financial Times*, October 30, 1995, p. 2; Alan Friedman, "Vision of a Single EU Currency Collides with German Politics," *International Herald Tribune*, October 31, 1995, p. 1; "Stabilität ist nicht alles," interview with Schröder, *Der Spiegel*, December 25, 1995; "Mover and shaker," interview with Schröder, *Financial Times*, March 17, 1997, p. 16; Peter Norman, "Pressure mounts on Bonn to delay EMU" [with subsequent correction attributing the quotes in the story to Bavarian premier Edmund Stoiber, not Finance Minister Theo Waigel], *Financial Times*, July 7, 1997, p. 1; Ralph Atkins, "EMU divisions hit Kohl's party," *Financial Times*, July 29, 1997, p. 1; "Ein Tausch von Sicherheit gegen Hoffnung," *Handelsblatt*, April 22, 1998, p. 3; and Günter Bannas and Hans-Jörg Heims, "Im Zweifel lieber doch keinen Putsch," *Süddeutsche Zeitung*, April 24, 1998, p. 3. Tellingly, a more frontal German dissent had to come from outside the country, from Lord (Ralf) Dahrendorf in Oxford, in an interview in *Der Spiegel*, "Alle Eier in einen Korb," November 12, 1995, pp. 27ff.

44. For an overview of the criteria from the German perspective, see "Wie wichtig sind die finanzpolitischen Konvergenzkriterien?" *Deutsches Institut für Wirtschaftsforschung Wochenbericht* (hereafter *DIW*), February 8, 1996, pp. 93–99.

45. Tietmeyer, group interview, Gütersloh, March 1995; Oliver Schumacher, "Kulturkampf der Geldhüter," *Die Zeit*, November 17, 1995, p. 25.

46. Lionel Barber and John Kampfner, "Germany sets hard terms for EMU deal," *Financial Times*, December 13, 1995, p. 1. See also "Die Debatte um den EU-Haushalt," *DIW*, October 2, 1997; "'Wir müssen den Spielraum beschränken,'" interview with Otmar Issing, *Der Spiegel*, January 15, 1996, pp. 85–87; "Gut für Deutschland," *Der Spiegel*, January 15, 1996. pp. 84ff; Robert Chote, "Tietmeyer warns on one currency," interview, *Financial Times*, February 3, 1996, p. 2; "Tietmeyer nennt die Europäische Währungsunion 'im wirtschaftlichen Sinne nicht absolut notwendig,'" *Frankfurter Allgemeine Zeitung*, March 21, 1996, p. 5; Andrew Fisher and Peter Norman, "Bundesbank outlines plans for EU currency stability," *Financial Times*, April 11, 1996, p. 10; Tietmeyer interview, "Finding way through ins and outs," *Financial Times*, April 11, 1996, p. 2; Reimut Jochimsen, "Der Euro verzeiht keine Tricks," *Die Zeit*, April 19, 1996, p. 6; Peter Norman, "Pöhl cautions

on cost of EMU 'mistakes,'" *Financial Times*, April 19, 1996, p. 2; Andrew Fisher, "Issing warns on euro and competitiveness," *Financial Times*, December 18, 1996, p. 3; Nina Grunenberg, "Prediger der harten Mark," *Die Zeit*, January 24, 1997, p. 3; Samuel Brittan, "How Bundesbank sees EMU," *Financial Times*, February 12, 1997, p. 18; Peter Norman and Andrew Fisher, "German row over EMU deepens," *Financial Times*, May 30, 1997, p. 1; and Hans Tietmeyer interview, "Der Euro—ein entnationalisiertes Geld," *Die Zeit*, December 12, 1997, p. 24.

47. See, for example, Ian Davidson, "A divisive destiny," *Financial Times*, January 24, 1996, p. 12. *Die Zeit* shared this suspicion: Oliver Schumacher, "Unter mittelständischen Unternehmen in Deutschland grassiert die Angst vor der europäischen Währungsunion," *Die Zeit*, January 29, 1995, pp. 21ff. See also Tom Buerkle, "A European Slowdown Chills Prospects for Single Currency," *International Herald Tribune*, November 23, 1995, p. 1; "A dying deadline?" *Economist*, January 20, 1996, p. 31; John Schmid, "Can Bonn Pass EMU Test? 2 Reports Raise New Doubts That It Will," *International Herald Tribune*, January 27, 1996, p. 1; Tom Buerkle, "Maastricht Criteria on Ropes," *International Herald Tribune*, January 27, 1996, p. 9; Terence Roth, "Economic Woes Oblige Bonn to Consider Delay in EU Single Currency," *Wall Street Journal Europe*, February 5, 1996, p. 1; and Tom Buerkle, "Skittish, Europeans Won't Part with Their Money," *International Herald Tribune*, February 19, 1996, p. 1.

48. "Bonn sind die Ausgaben für Brüssel zu hoch," *Frankfurter Allgemeine Zeitung*, July 25, 1995, p. 11; Marcell von Donat, "Europa braucht einen Plan," *Die Zeit*, August 12, 1995, p. 16; Joseph Fitchett, "Good for Germans, Good for Europe," *International Herald Tribune*, December 5, 1995, p. 1; Tom Buerkle, "An Apparent Dead End for European Centralization," *International Herald Tribune*, December 6, 1995, p. 5; Alan Friedman, "Devotion to DM Dictates Europe's Sacrifice," *International Herald Tribune*, December 6, 1995, p. 5; George Graham, "Payment system hurries the pace in debate on EMU," *Financial Times*, July 19, 1996, p. 2; "Grössere Ausgewogenheit angestrebt," *Frankfurter Allgemeine Zeitung*, July 22, 1996, p. 5.

49. Emma Tucker, "Schengen group backs France," *Financial Times*, September 6, 1995, p. 2; Peter Norman, "Germany urges measures to guarantee EMU discipline," *Financial Times*, September 12, 1995, p. 1; "Eurosceptic markets," editorial, *Financial Times*, September 16, 1995, p. 8; Emma Tucker, "Market turmoil over EMU fear," *Financial Times*, September 22, 1995, p. 1; Lionel Barber, "Europe in new currency split," *Financial Times*, September 29, 1995, p. 1; Lionel Barber, "Bonn sets agenda for monetary union," *Financial Times*, October 2, 1995, p. 2; Lionel Barber, "EMU hits stumbling block," *Financial Times*, October 6, 1995, p. 22; "Vor 'Maastricht Zwei'

eine deutsch-französische Initiative," *Frankfurter Allgemeine Zeitung,* October 9, 1995, p. 4; and Tom Buerkle, "A French-German Feud Festers on Currency Plan," *International Herald Tribune,* November 27, 1995, p. 1.

50. "'Monsieur X' für die EU-Aussenpolitik?" *Frankfurter Allgemeine Zeitung,* September 13, 1995; Quentin Peel, "Germans seek 4-year agenda on EU reform," *Financial Times,* September 13, 1995. For the companion wish list of the Reflection Group, which was writing the official agenda for the forthcoming Intergovernmental Conference, see Peter Hort, "Materialsammlung für eine EU-Reform an Haupt und Gliedern," *Frankfurter Allgemeine Zeitung,* September 8, 1995, p. 9.

51. See, for example, Dr. Ludolf von Wartenberg, director-general of the Federation of German Industry, "UK needed at the heart of Europe," *Financial Times,* August 24, 1994; and the interview with Percy Barnevik, chief executive officer of the Swedish-Swiss engineering firm ABB, "The Moment of European Truth," *Time,* September 19, 1994, pp. 40ff.

52. Peter Norman, "Waigel spells out plan for EMU stability," *Financial Times,* November 8, 1995, p. 2; "Stabilitätspakt soll die Währungsunion sichern," *Frankfurter Allgemeine Zeitung,* November 11, 1995, p. 13; and Peter Norman, "Germany proposes fines to regulate EMU states," *Financial Times,* November 11, 1995, p. 1.

53. "In Paris keimt Unbehagen über Deutschland und die Währungsunion," *Frankfurter Allgemeine Zeitung,* November 11, 1995, p. 18. Beyond specific policy differences, there was a basic philosophical difference in the two countries' approach to democracy. For the Germans there are some issues that are exempt from populist decision; over the decades the pursuit of low inflation had become one of these sacrosanct areas. This violated the principles of the more republican heirs of the French revolution, who regarded every issue as subject to political choice.

54. "Federal Government Statement," Bulletin 103 (December 1995), pp. 1011-15.

55. For one of the many episodes in the long-running banana opera, see Frances Williams, "US to seek WTO ruling on EU banana plans," *Financial Times,* July 24, 1998, p. 6.

56. No one took this statistical shortfall as a serious breach of financial rectitude by model Germany; everyone understood that it was a temporary deviation in the 1990s, brought about by Bonn's assumption of East Berlin's debts and the $100 billion a year transfers to the east. This lapse by the preacher of strictness was, however, embarrassing. See Terence Roth, "Economic Woes Oblige Bonn to Consider Delay in EU Single Currency," *Wall Street Journal Europe,* February 5, 1996, p. 1; Robert Chote, "Germany and France may miss Maastricht targets," *Financial Times,* June 21, 1996, p. 14; and Peter Norman, "Bonn increases deficit forecast to 2.9 percent," *Financial Times,* January 27, 1997, p. 1.

57. See Robert Rice, "German judge attacks European court," *Financial Times*, August 21, 1995, p. 2; Andrew Adonis and Robert Rice, "In the hot seat of judgment," *Financial Times*, April 3, 1995, p. 15; Manfred Zuleeg, "Ein Gericht jenseits von Gesetz und Recht?" *Frankfurter Allgemeine Zeitung*, March 17, 1994, p. 13; and J. H. H. Weiler, "A Quiet Revolution: The European Court of Justice and Its Interlocutors," *Comparative Political Studies*, vol. 26, no. 4 (January 1994), pp. 510–34.

58. The relevant figures at that point showed only six net contributors in 1994, after receipts from the EU were subtracted from contributions to it: Germany, Luxembourg, Italy, France, the Netherlands, and Belgium. Bonn's net contribution ran to 0.65 percent of German GNP, Luxembourg's to 0.46 percent, Italy's to 0.23 percent, and France and the Netherlands's to only 0.17 percent. Greater equalization would begin with the accession of net payers Austria, Sweden, and Finland to the EU in 1995, a subsequent adjustment to the British rebate, and the modest reductions in farm subsidies in the late 1990s. By 2000 Germany's net contribution was reduced to 0.47 percent of its GNP and was roughly matched by Sweden's 0.50 percent, the Netherlands's 0.44 percent, and Luxembourg's 0.35 percent; France's contribution was even lower than in 1994, at 0.10 percent; and Italy and Finland were net recipients. European Commission, "Allocation of 2000 EU Operating Expenditure by Member State," 2001, p. 126 (http://europa.eu/int/comm/budget/agenda2000reports_en.htm).

59. Edward Mortimer, "The wrong priority," *Financial Times*, January 17, 1996, p. 10; William Pfaff, "Progress Doesn't Just Run Ahead, You Have to Help It," *International Herald Tribune*, January 2, 1996, p. 6; and Brian Beedham, "Germany Has a Plan for Europe That Goes Too Far Too Fast," *International Herald Tribune*, January 9, 1996, p. 8.

60. See Kohl's speech in Louvain, Belgium, February 2, 1996. This was a theme he would repeat again and again, as, for example, when he quoted Mitterrand to Lower Saxony voters in early 1998: "Nationalism—that is war." (Christian Wernicke, "Der euro-fighter," *Die Zeit*, April 29, 1998.) Actually, although Kohl's use of the phrase set off the greatest public commotion, German connoisseurs point out that German president Roman Herzog had used it before Kohl did, and that Mitterrand was its "real inventor" in one of his last speeches before the European Parliament. Officials on Kohl's staff were surprised by the reaction to a phrase that he had often used before. They attributed this to the fact that Kohl was speaking in Belgium; the Brussels reporters had not previously heard his one-liner.

Substantively, it should be noted here that various German civil servants who have been working the issue of European integration contest the interpretation that Kohl gave up the goal of political union. They ask what political union actually is and argue that the possible spectrum is so wide that the concept of "giving up" on it is meaningless. Nonetheless, it should also be noted that Kohl's rhetorical shift was sufficient to raise British hopes of a common German-British understanding on the issue.

61. Renate Köcher, "Kühle Realisten," *Frankfurter Allgemeine Zeitung*, November 15, 1995. Allensbach observed, "A good 90 percent are not especially interested in the topic." Resignation that the euro was going to come anyway was growing, Köcher pointed out. See also "96 percent gegen Bonn/ Hände weg von unserer Mark," *Bild*, December 7, 1991; "Umfrage: Wir wollen unsere Mark behalten," *Bild*, June 20, 1992; and Herbert Kremp, "Mit der DM verlören die Deutschen mehr als ihre Währung," *Welt an Sonntag*, November 5, 1995, pp. 24–25.

62. Ian Davidson, "Beyond the catcalls," *Financial Times*, February 7, 1996, p. 10.

63. Including, most strikingly, a joint appeal by parliamentary majority leaders Wolfgang Schäuble and the same Philippe Seguin who had branded Bonn's Maastricht negotiators worthy successors of Hitler. Other examples were the joint statements by the two foreign ministers and the two defense ministers. See, for example, Kinkel and Charette, "Es muss eine echte europäische Identität entstehen"; Peter Norman, "Paris and Bonn agree EU foreign policy opt-out pact"; "The Helmut and Jacques Show," *Economist*, April 6, 1996, pp. 29f; "Frankreichs Staatspräsident Chirac besucht Bundeskanzler Kohl," *Frankfurter Allgemeine Zeitung*, May 11, 1996, p. 2; "Kohl und Chirac vereinbaren gemeinsames Vorgehen," *Frankfurter Allgemeine Zeitung*, June 7, 1996, p. 1; David Buchan, "Kohl and Chirac plan to push EU," *Financial Times*, June 7, 1996, p. 3; Peter Norman, "Paris and Bonn vow to meet EMU date," September 18, 1996, p. 1; and "Paris und Bonn," editorial, *Frankfurter Allgemeine Zeitung*, December 9, 1996, p. 1. For a German insider's view of the stability pact, see Wilhelm Schönfelder and Elke Thiel, "Stabilitätspakt und Euro-X-Gremium—Die stabilitätspolitische Untermauerung der WWU," *Integration* (Bonn), vol. 21, no. 2 (April 1998), pp. 69–76.

64. Group interview, June 1996. Other convergence statistics are given in "Europäische Währungsunion: Reale Konvergenz unentbehrlich," *DIW*, August 1, 1996, pp. 515–24.

65. Lionel Barber, "EU nations underspend on regional aid by $24bn," *Financial Times*, July 29, 1996, p. 1.

66. Lionel Barber and Robert Graham, "UK, Germany block financing for EU transport networks," *Financial Times*, June 25, 1996, p. 16; Robert Chote, "Germany isolated over IMF gold sales," *Financial Times*, June 26, 1996, p. 4; and "Cut and grow—hope and woe," *Economist*, July 27, 1996. pp. 25ff.

67. Andrew Hill, "Italian PM begins preparing lira's re-entry into ERM," *Financial Times*, June 11, 1996, p. 1.

68. Peter Norman, "France wants G7-style club for single currency," *Financial Times*, June 18, 1996, p. 14; and Robert Chote, "Welcome for EMU policy 'club' proposal," *Financial Times*, June 20, 1996, p. 2.

69. Neil Buckley, "Brussels fury over cash for VW," *Financial Times*, July 31, 1996; "Ein Rechtsbruch als Antwort auf einen Rechtsbruch?" *Frankfurter Allgemeine Zeitung*, July 31, 1996, p. 4; "Bonn und Brüssel wollen den Streit um die VW-Subventionen beilegen," *Frankfurter Allgemeine Zeitung*, September 4, 1996, p. 15; Wolfgang Münchau, "VW aid fight part of wider battle," *Financial Times*, September 6, 1996, p. 12.

70. For an overview, see Joe Rogaly and others, "Britain: The rogue piece in Europe's jigsaw," special section, *Financial Times*, June 12, 1996. The ban would not be lifted until the end of 1998.

71. "In Santer's style," *Economist*, July 1, 1996, p. 32. In an academic analysis of budgetary and regulatory data from the late 1990s and early 2000s, however, Mark Pollack found little evidence to support the thesis of greater European Commission restraint. Mark Pollack, "The End of Creeping Competence? EU Policy-making since Maastricht," *Journal of Common Market Studies*, vol. 38, no. 3 (2000), pp. 519–38.

72. John Tagliabue, "European Monetary Union Hits New Snags," *New York Times*, August 30, 1996.

73. Rudi Dornbusch, "Euro Fantasies," *Foreign Affairs*, vol. 75, no. 5 (September/October 1996), pp. 110–24; Martin Feldstein, "EMU and International Conflict," *Foreign Affairs*, vol. 76, no. 6 (November/December 1997), pp. 60–73; interview with James Tobin, "'Ein schlimmes Beispiel,'" *Die Zeit*, March 28, 1998, p. 31. However, in person Dornbusch was much more relaxed about EMU prospects at the Davos Economic Summit in January 1998, telling journalists that he had meant only that EMU would not solve unemployment, not that inflexible labor would sabotage the unified European economy. For two other fiercely negative American readings shortly before final adoption of EMU plans in 1998, see Irving Kristol, "Petrified Europe," *Wall Street Journal Europe*, February 2, 1998; and William Safire, "Alice in Euroland," *New York Times*, April 30. 1998. For a critical German view that EMU could not work unless human nature changed, see Rudolf Augstein, "Neue Menschen, neue Menschen!" *Der Spiegel*, April 27, 1998, pp. 102ff.

74. Carola Kaps, "Die Währungsunion ist ein Vorhaben ohne ökonomische Vernunft," *Frankfurter Allgemeine Zeitung*, December 18, 1996, p. 18. For U.S. skepticism about visions of EMU in the early 1990s, see Mark N. Nelson, "Transatlantic Travails," *Foreign Policy*, vol. 92 (Fall 1993), pp. 75–91.

75. See, for example, John Newhouse, *Europe Adrift* (Pantheon, 1997).

76. Robert A. Mundell, "The International Impact of the Euro and Its Implications for the Transition Countries," paper presented at the fourth Dubrovnik Conference on the Transition Economies, June 23–26, 1998. See also Martin Wolf, "Euro's world test," *Financial Times*, July 7, 1998, p. 16. Others who held a positive view of EMU included Fred Bergsten and Randall Henning of the Institute for International Economics.

77. See, for example, Martin Wolf, "Strange love/Or how I have not stopped worrying but learned to love the euro," *Financial Times*, May 5, 1998, p. 20.

78. World Economic Forum, Davos, February 1998.

79. For the traditional German point of view fiercely defending the independence of the ECB against any encroachment by the then-euro-11 finance ministers, see Schönfelder and Thiel, "Stabilitätspakt und Euro-X-Gremium."

80. Lionel Barber and Neil Buckley, "Germany pushes EU into tough pact over euro," *Financial Times*, December 14, 1996, p. 1; Lionel Barber, "France and Germany struggle to turn their European dreams into reality," *Financial Times*, December 14, 1996, p. 2; "EMU after Dublin," *Economist*, December 21, 1996, p. 15; Lionel Barber, "The cracks appear," *Financial Times*, April 29, 1998, p. 14.

81. For a sophisticated reading of the Amsterdam outcome in social policy and subsidiarity, see Carl Lankowski, ed., "Break Out, Break Down or Break In?" AICGS Research Report 8 (Washington, 1998), especially Lankowski's own essay, pp. 39–52. For a study of the *Länder* use of their new constitutional voice in European policy, see Michael J. Baun, "The *Länder* and German European Policy: The 1996 IGC and Amsterdam Treaty," *German Studies Review*, vol. 21, no. 2 (May 1998), pp. 329–46.

82. John Peet, "Europe's Mid-Life Crisis," special section, *Economist*, May 31, 1997; Robert Leicht, "Kleinmut vor dem grossen Sprung," *Die Zeit*, June 6, 1997, p. 1; "Is Europe's Currency Coming Apart?" editorial, *Economist*, June 7, 1997, pp. 15ff; "Towards EMU/Kicking and Screaming into 1999," special section, *Economist*, June 7, 1997, pp. 21–25; "Amsterdam is no Maastricht," editorial, *Financial Times*, June 14, 1997, p. 6; and "Euro-divisions," *Economist*, June 14, 1997, pp. 33ff.

83. "France Still Trapped," *Economist*, July 5, 1997, pp. 23ff.

84. "Advent of EMU Means Europeans Must Make Reforms," October 21, 1997; text provided by U.S. Embassy, Bonn.

85. Malta was originally on this short list, but the newly elected Labour party withdrew its application for membership in 1996. When the Nationalist party returned to power in 1998, it reinstated the application.

86. Until then, the EBRD had been a French fief, and Chirac expected it to continue as such. The other nations that had set up the bank in the early 1990s were sufficiently angered by Chirac's stonewalling, however, that they left the post vacant for more than half a year and then finally appointed Köhler.

87. "The euro could hardly have had a worse start," scolded Eberhard Wisdorff in "Schwere Hypothek," *Handelsblatt*, May 4, 1998, p. 2. The leaders "gambled away a chance to convince citizens that the new money will be hard," asserted Peter Hort in "Schatten auf der Währungsunion," *Frankfurter Allgemeine Zeitung*, May 4, 1998, p. 1. Kohl "leaves the Euro-

battle defeated," and the decision "gives German Euroskeptics [a] boost," concluded Andreas Oldag in "Schwere Geburt," *Süddeutsche Zeitung*, May 5, 1998, p. 4. The boulevard *Bild* joined the chorus in "Euro: The Dirty Compromise," May 4, 1998, p. 1—but kept the proper perspective by placing this story below its announcement of the simultaneous, ignominious fall of Cologne's First Football Club into the second league. In the event, German markets seconded *Bild*'s priority and rose helpfully, despite what Kohl called his "dogfight" with Chirac. See also Lionel Barber, "Wim-Claude Trichenberg," *Financial Times*, May 4, 1998, p. 15; "The euro: single currency, multiple injuries," *Financial Times*, May 5, 1998, p. 2; and Michael Stabenow, "Nur Santer und Blair können beim Familienfoto mühelos lächeln," *Frankfurter Allgemeine Zeitung*, May 4, 1998, p 3. For unconvincing denials that Tietmeyer ever threatened to resign, see "Bundesbank dementiert Tietmeyer-Rücktritt," *Süddeutsche Zeitung*, May 6, 1998, p. 30; and Christian Wernicke, "Der Sündenfall von Brüssel," *Die Zeit*, May 7, 1998, pp. 2ff. A few days later, Chirac apologized to Kohl at their own bilateral summit, saying, according to one German official, that he had not realized his implicit veto against the fourteen other EU heads of government would bring such domestic political trouble for Kohl. The French president is "an unguided missile," asserted another German official in an interview in May 1998, fastidiously quoting the *Economist*.

88. "Keeping up the pace in the EMU race," *Financial Times*, March 26, 1998, p. 2.

89. "The verdict on EMU members," *Financial Times*, March 26, 1998, p. 11. Three years later, new doubts did arise about Italian legerdemain with swap contracts to understate Rome's budget deficit in 1998, but the European Commission and Eurostat, the EU statistics office, rejected these as unfounded. See Rebecca Bream, James Blitz, and Peter Norman, "Doubts over way Italy qualified for euro," *Financial Times*, November 5, 2001, p. 1; James Blitz, "Italy rebuts swap contract claims," *Financial Times*, November 6, 2001, p. 6; and Peter Norman, "Rome 'did not cheat over deficit,'" *Financial Times*, November 6, 2001, p. 6.

90. The Lombard rate is one of the rates at which banks get overnight loans from the central bank.

91. See also Alberta Sbragia, "Italy Pays for Europe: Political Leadership, Political Choice, and Institutional Adaptation," in Maria Green Cowles, James Caporase, and Thomas Risse, eds., *Transforming Europe* (Cornell University Press, 2001), pp. 79–96.

92. Andreatta at the German-Italian Colloquium on "Europe and the Challenge of Globalization," Bonn, April 1, 1998. See also Friedhelm Gröteke, "Märchen von Alice im Wunderland," *Die Zeit*, April 23, 1998, p. 28; the interview with Italian finance minister Ciampi, "Problem erkannt," *Die Zeit*,

April 23, 1998, p. 29; James Blitz and Martin Wolf, "Ciampi defies odds on monetary union," *Financial Times*, May 7, 1998, p 3; "Promoted to Europe's premier league," *Financial Times*, June 15, 1998, p. 1 of survey of Italy; "Italy's Government Soldiers On, but For How Long?" *Economist*, July 4, 1998, pp. 25ff.

93. Barry Riley, "Aim for bourse without borders," *Financial Times*, May 18, 1998, p. 15.

Chapter Six

1. As used here, "central Europe" refers to the ten central European states that have "Europe agreements" promising membership in the EU—Poland, Hungary, the Czech Republic, Slovakia, Bulgaria, Romania, Slovenia, Estonia, Latvia, and Lithuania—plus Albania, which has a trade and cooperation agreement with the EU. It thus includes the Baltics, but excludes other Soviet successor states as well as the Yugoslav successor states other than Slovenia.

2. Interview, October 1997.

3. Leszek Balcerowicz, "Fallacies and other lessons," *Economic Policy*, December 1994, p. 47. See also his article "The Interplay between Economic and Political Transition," *Polish Quarterly of International Affairs* (Summer/Autumn 1996), pp. 9–28.

4. When the Polish communist leadership softened somewhat and entered "round table" talks with Solidarity representatives in the spring of 1989, the two sides agreed on a free election for a new upper house and for 35 percent of the seats in the lower house, the Sejm. To the astonishment of both sides, opposition candidates won all but one of the contested seats. The communists then offered to give some less-important cabinet posts to Solidarity nominees, but in a move that electrified the Soviet bloc, Walesa scrapped the brokered deal and got small parties that had previously been satellites of the communists to give Solidarity a majority for forming a new government. In the resulting coalition the communists held on to the military and police ministries, but Solidarity's Tadeusz Mazowiecki became prime minister in fact as well as in name. It was the first time in seventy years that communists had surrendered power peacefully in any country.

5. Polish statistics and IMF estimates given in Stanislaw Gomulka, "The IMF-Supported Programs of Poland and Russia, 1990–1994," Studies and Analyses Working Paper 36 (Warsaw: Center for Social and Economic Research, 1995), p. 33.

6. See Joseph A. Schumpeter's classic, *Capitalism, Socialism, and Democracy* (1942; London: Allen and Unwin, 1976); and Larry Diamond and Marc F. Plattner, eds., *Capitalism, Socialism, and Democracy Revisited* (Johns Hopkins University Press, 1993). One of Schumpeter's central points was the

need for the creative destruction of inefficient economic structures to make way for efficient capitalist ones.

7. The Poles were acutely aware of the repeated failures of free markets to stabilize and produce rising tides for all in South America and, as they then saw it, in Greece. But forging a liberal economy was for them as much a question of Western identity as it was of economic system. For the argument that capitalism works only in the West, see Hernando de Soto, *The Mystery of Capital: Why Capitalism Triumphs in the West and Fails Everywhere Else* (London: Bantam, 2000).

8. Interviews at CBOS (Centrum Badania Opinii Spolecznej) polling organization, 1993 and 1994. On the Catholic Church in the early years of Polish transition, see Leszek Nowak, "Essay on the Church," and Andrzej Gierech, "Will Messianism Reduce Our Distance to Europe?" *Polish Western Affairs* (Poznan), vol. 33, no. 1 (1992), pp. 3–11, 13–26.

9. Commission of the European Communities, *Central and Eastern Eurobarometer no. 2* (Brussels, February 1992). In answers to the more concrete question about the coming year, only 17 percent expected things to improve, 32 percent thought things would get worse, and 33 percent expected no significant change from their current discomfort.

10. For discussion of the Polish mind-set, see Stanislaw Gomulka and Antony Polonsky, eds., *Polish Paradoxes* (London: Routledge, 1990). For a sociological analysis of the choices in the transition, see Andrzej Rychard, *Reforms, Adaptation, and Breakthrough* (Warsaw: IFiS, 1993).

11. Cited in Richard F. Staar, ed., *1990 Yearbook of International Communist Affairs* (Stanford: Hoover Institution Press, 1990), p. 374.

12. Interview with Balcerowicz associate, October 1997.

13. Ben Slay, "The Polish Economic Transition," *East-Central European Economies in Transition*, Joint Economic Committee, 103 Cong. 2 sess. (Government Printing Office, 1994), pp. 463–79; Ben Slay, "The Dilemmas of Economic Liberalism in Poland," *Europe-Asia Studies*, vol. 45, no. 2 (1993), pp. 237–57.

14. The OECD notes both the shallowness of Polish poverty—that is, the large number of those in the category who fall just under the threshold—and the resulting discrepancy in results of between a tenth and a quarter of the population classified as poor, depending on the method of calculation. Organization for Economic Cooperation and Development, *OECD Economic Surveys: Poland 1997* (Paris, 1996), p. 89ff.

15. Even Balcerowicz lost his nerve for fiscal and monetary rigor in mid-1990, charged his deputy, Marek Dabrowski, and tried "to bend the economy to fit promises of imminent relief after six months of shock therapy." Quoted in Slay, "The Dilemmas of Economic Liberalism in Poland," p. 241. Subsequent statistics are taken from Gomulka, "The IMF-Supported Programs of

Poland and Russia"; Slay, "The Polish Economic Transition"; *OECD Economic Surveys: Poland 1997*; "Poland," *Business Central Europe*, annual, 1997/98, p. 26; John Hardt, "External Economic Relations with Particular Focus on Regional Cooperation," Janima Witkowska, "Foreign Capital as a Factor of Structural Changes in the Polish Economy," and Zofia Wysokinska, "Evaluation of Structural Changes in Polish Industry and in Foreign Capital Flow to Poland in the Period of Systemic Transformation," from the NATO Economic Colloquium, Brussels, June 25–27, 1997; World Bank "Transition" newsletters; and Grzegorz W. Kolodko and D. Mario Nuti, "The Polish Alternative," paper prepared for the United Nations University World Institute for Development Economics Research, Helsinki, March 1997.

16. Cited in Brooke Unger, "Against the Grain: A Survey of Poland," *Economist*, April 16, 1994, p. 5.

17. Kolodko and Nuti, "The Polish Alternative," table 1.

18. This assessment summarizes the mainstream Western evaluation to be found in, among others, Deutsche Bank Research, "Eastern Europe: Heading for Reform: Issue 4: Poland" (1993); Jeffrey D. Sachs, *Poland's Jump to the Market Economy* (MIT Press, 1993); *OECD Economic Surveys: Poland 1997*; Slay, "Polish Economic Transition," pp. 463ff; and Gomulka, "The IMF-Supported Programs of Poland and Russia." Kolodko, a severe critic of Balcerowicz, rejects this characterization, maintaining that while Balcerowicz's shock therapy led to severe recession and relatively high inflation until mid-1993, his own strategy for Poland had led to the sustained growth since 1993. See Kolodko and Nuti, "The Polish Alternative"; Grzegorz Kolodko, *From Shock to Therapy* (Oxford University Press, 1999); and Grzegorz Kolodko, "Russia Should Put Its People First," *New York Times*, July 7, 1998. For an analysis arguing that Poland's growth derived from an evolutionary process arising from the old communist system rather than a revolutionary scrapping of that system, see Kazimierz A. Poznanski, *Poland's Protracted Transition* (Cambridge University Press, 1996).

19. Kolodko and Nuti, "The Polish Alternative," table 1; and *East-Central European Economies in Transition*.

20. *OECD Economic Surveys: Poland 1997*, p. 153. Although the bazaars are declining in importance as wealth spreads, the fifteen largest bazaars still accounted for turnover of $2.2 billion in 1997, according to official figures. "Poland: Cross-Border Trade with Neighbors Declines," *RFE/RL Magazine* (Radio Free Europe/Radio Liberty), July 16, 1998 (www.rferl.org/nca/features/).

21. Simon Johnson and Gary W. Loveman, "State Enterprise Restructuring: A Tale of Two Shipyards," in Simon Johnson and others, *Starting Over in Eastern Europe: Entrepreneurship and Economic Renewal* (Harvard Business School Press, 1995).

22. Interviews, Warsaw, February 1997; 1995.

23. See Elizabeth Pond, "The Polish Election," *Harriman Review*, vol. 8, no. 4 (December 1995), pp. 35–40.

24. Interview, Warsaw, November 1995.

25. Kolodko and Nuti, "The Polish Alternative," table 1 and p. 39; Christopher Bobinski, "Poland finds feel-good factor," *Financial Times*, February 5, 1996, p. 2.

26. *Business Central Europe*, 1997/98.

27. Ibid.; Kolodko and Nuti, "The Polish Alternative," pp. 6, 30; Jan Winiecki, "The Polish Generic Private Sector in Transition: Developments and Characteristics," *Europe-Asia Studies*, vol. 54, no. 1 (January 2002), pp. 5–29.

28. For a study proposing that insider deals, exclusion of foreign competition, and the resulting "culture of dishonesty" also played a major role in the Czech debacle, see Mitchell Orenstein, "Vaclav Klaus: Revolutionary and Parliamentarian," *East European Constitutional Review* (Winter 1998), pp. 46–55. Orenstein concludes that Klaus's legacy is likely to be less that he once built the strongest neoliberal party in central Europe than that he demonstrated "the limits of neoliberal economics in practice."

29. European Commission, *Central and Eastern Eurobarometer no. 8* (Brussels, March 1998).

30. Cited in Kolodko and Nuti, "The Polish Alternative," p. 7.

31. Eurobarometer questionnaires further revealed that popular evaluation of the overall "direction of the country" was far more positive than it had been five years earlier, with 40 percent judging their direction "right" and 33 percent "wrong" (1995 surveys), as against verdicts of only 20 percent "right" and 58 percent "wrong" in 1991, the worst evaluation of the nine countries polled (including Czechoslovakia, Hungary, the three Baltic states, Albania, Bulgaria, and Romania).

32. Malachi Martin, *The Keys of This Blood: The Struggle for World Dominion between Pope John Paul II, Mikhail Gorbachev and the Capitalist West* (Simon and Schuster, 1990.)

33. Polish newspaper reports November 4–7, 1997, carried in English translation in the *Polish News Bulletin*.

34. Pieronek was replaced in 1998, but the shift did not change church policy on the EU.

35. In the summer of 1998 the Polish Association of War Victims, vociferously backed by Radio Marija, erected more than a hundred crosses next to the death camp in an explicitly antisemitic gesture. The government put pressure on the church hierarchy to order removal of the crosses. The church suspended priest Ryszard Krol for putting up one of the crosses, but otherwise moved slowly. The Sejm finally passed legislation establishing one-hundred-meter "conservation zones" around former concentration camp sites, and riot police removed all the crosses except for one eight-meter-high "papal

cross" in 1999. The most militant squatter on the property, Kasimierz Switon, was convicted in January 2000 of inciting hatred against Jews and fined a token amount. For ongoing coverage of Jewish-Polish strains, see especially the *New York Times* and *Washington Post*, and the Radio Free Europe/Radio Liberty daily *Newsline* at (www.rferl.org/newsline/search/). Examples are Jane Perlez, "A Polish Playgound Has Plenty of Ghosts to Go Around," *New York Times*, June 24, 1998; Alessandra Stanley, "Chief Rabbi of Poland Is Asking a Favor of 'Mr. Pope,'" *New York Times, June* 12, 1999; Christine Spolar, "Settling the Right to Poland's Jewish Past," *Washington Post*, April 22, 1998, p. A27; Nora FitzGerald, "In Warsaw, a Jewish Street Reborn," *Washington Post,* July 13, 1999, p. C1; Bogdan Turek, "Tension Rises over Crosses in Auschwitz," *RFE/RL Magazine*, August 10, 1998.

36. The church suspended Jankowski for a period. While this hardly muzzled him, Poles took the action as serious discipline.

37. See Elizabeth Pond, "'Shoah' Stirs Painful Memories for Poles," *Christian Science Monitor*, December 13, 1985, p. 1.

38. Interview, 1996.

39. Telephone interview, November 1997.

40. Jan T. Gross, *Neighbors* (Princeton University Press, 2001), also published in Polish in 2000.

41. Daniel Jonah Goldhagen, *Hitler's Willing Executioners* (Knopf, 1996).

42. Eva Hoffman, *Shtetl* (Boston: Houghton Mifflin, 1997). pp. 248, 257. For accounts of the Polish reaction to the Jedwabne revelations, see Adam Michnik, "Wie schuldig sind die Polen?" *Die Zeit*, March 22, 2001, p. 7; Helga Hirsch, "Befreiende Wahrheit," *Die Zeit*, April 19, 2001, p. 43; Johanna Tokarska-Bakir, "Vergangenheit, die nicht vergehen will," *Frankfurter Allgemeine Zeitung*, May 2, 2001, p. 10; Michael Ludwig, "'Die Weichsel hat einst jiddisch gesprochen,'" *Frankfurter Allgemeine Zeitung*, May 3, 2000; "Polens Bischöfe zum Mord von Jedwabne," *Neue Zürcher Zeitung*, May 5, 2001 (www.nzz.ch/al/index.html); Michael Ludwig, "Nestbeschmutzende Staatsanwälte nehmen keine Rücksicht auf die Nationalität der Täter," *Frankfurter Allgemeine Zeitung*, May 9, 2001, p. 3; Elizabeth Pond, "Poland Becomes Normal," *Wall Street Journal Europe*, May 17, 2001, p. 6; Gabriele Lesser, "Vergiftete Vergebung," *Die Woche*, May 25, 2001, p. 10; the review of *Neighbors* by Istvan Deak, "Heroes and Victims," *New York Review of Books*, May 31, 2001, pp. 51ff., and the subsequent exchanges of letters in the *New York Review of Books*, September 20, 2001, pp. 91ff., and November 15, 2001, pp. 64ff.; Thomas Urban, "Neue Thesen zum Massaker von Jedwabne," *Süddeutsche Zeitung*, June 6, 2001, p. 8; "Streit um neuen Gedenkstein in Jedwabne," *Neue Zürcher Zeitung*, June 9, 2001; John Reed, "Poland's president seeks to lay country's war guilt to rest," *Financial Times*, July 7, 2001, p. 2; Helga Hirsch, "Tief verborgene Wahrheit," *Die Zeit*, Sep-

tember 20, 2001; and "Unklarheiten um das Pogrom von Jedwabne," *Neue Zürcher Zeitung*, December 22, 2001. For more general discussion of Polish-Jewish relations, see Elizabeth Pond, "The Polish-Jewish Dialogue," *Harriman Review*, vol. 9. no. 3 (Summer 1996), pp. 65–68; Andrew Nagorski, "'Schindler's List' and the Polish Question," *Foreign Affairs*, vol. 73, no. 4 (July/August 1994), pp. 152–57; Piotr Wrobel, "Double Memory: Poles and Jews after the Holocaust," *Eastern European Politics and Societies*, vol. 11, no. 3 (Fall 1997), pp. 560–74; H. H. Ben-Sasson, ed., *A History of the Jewish People*, English trans. (Harvard University Press, 1976); and Peter Novick, *The Holocaust in American Life* (Boston: Houghton Mifflin, 1999).

43. Interviews with Janusz Reiter, formerly ambassador to Germany and later director of the Warsaw Center for International Relations, and others in Warsaw, Poznan, Wroclaw, Bonn, and Berlin. See also the interview with Polish foreign minister Bronislaw Geremek, "Heimweh nach Europa," *Die Zeit*, July 30, 1998, p. 7. Although German-Polish rapprochement was initially top-down, driven by the two governments and disliked by much of their populations, by the late 1990s it was taken for granted by ordinary citizens as well. One CBOS survey found that Germans surpassed even Americans when Poles were asked whom they most liked to work with in business and in politics: Germans ranked 77 percent and 74 percent respectively, Americans 58 percent and 67 percent. Cited in Steve Crawshaw, "Germany Looks East," *Prospect* (January 1997), pp. 50–53. The best single source on post–World War II German-Polish relations is Dieter Bingen, *Die Polenpolitik der Bonner Republik von Adenauer bis Kohl 1949–1991* (Baden-Baden: Nomos, 1998). See also Josef Füllenbach and Franz J. Klein, *Bonn und Warschau* (Bonn: Europa Union Verlag, 1977); Hans-Adolf Jacobsen and Mieczyslaw Tomala, *Bonn Warschau 1945–1991* (Cologne: Verlag Wissenschaft und Politik, 1992); the English-language journal *Polish Western Affairs* published by the Institute for Western Affairs in Poznan; issue on "The New Germany, Poland, and the Future of all-European Cooperation," *Polish Review* (New York), vol. 37, no. 4 (1992); Ewa Kobylinska, Andreas Lawaty, and Rüdiger Stephan, *Deutsche und Polen, 100 Schlüsselbegriffe* (Munich: Piper, 1992); Thomas Urban, *Deutsche in Polen* (Munich: C. H. Beck, 1993); Stephen E. Hanson and Willfried Spohn, eds., *Can Europe Work?* (University of Washington Press, 1995); Krzysztof Skubiszewski, "Deutschland: Anwalt der MOE-Staaten," *Internationale Politik* (February 1997), pp. 29–33; and Elizabeth Pond, "A Historical Reconciliation with Poland," *Transition* (Prague), February 9, 1996, pp. 9ff. For German advocacy of swift EU enlargement to bring in central European members, see Ann L. Phillips, *Power and Influence after the Cold War: Germany in East-Central Europe* (Lanham, Md.: Rowman and Littlefield, 2000).

44. Text provided by the Polish Embassy, Cologne.

45. Interview, Davos, Switzerland, January 1998.

46. Czech president Vaclav Havel also calls NATO membership "the least expensive way to guarantee security." See the *Annual Survey of Eastern Europe and the Former Soviet Union: 1997* (Armonk, N.Y.: M. E. Sharpe, 1999).

47. For a more reserved view of the status of the armed forces of NATO candidates in central Europe, see James Sherr's four-part series, "Armed Forces in Central Europe: Reform without Direction," June 1996, Conflict Studies Research Center, Royal Military Academy, Sandhurst; the first essay is at (gopher://marvin.nc3a.nato.int/00/secdef/csrc/g53.1%09%09%2B).

48. *OECD Economic Surveys: Poland 1997*, p. 120. The OECD also notes, however, that if the measure is consumer durables, then Poland is just about equal to Greece. Specifically, Poland soars with cable TV hookups in a quarter of all households. "Telly Addicts," *Business Central Europe*, vol. 7, no. 68 (February 2000), p. 47.

49. *OECD Economic Surveys: Poland 1997*, p. 120; "Facing the Future: A Survey of Poland" and "Facts and Figures," *Business Central Europe*, vol. 7, no. 68 (February 2000), pp. 43–52, 55. The current figures illustrate the speed of transformation, as well as the enormity of the problem; statistics from the mid-1990s showed a quarter of the population in agriculture producing 6.5 percent of GDP on farms averaging seven hectares in size.

50. Interview with Werner Hoyer, member of parliament and state minister in the German Foreign Ministry, Salzburg, June 1998.

51. Bank Austria, *East-West Report 2/2001* (June 13, 2001), p. 29; and *World Bank Atlas 2001* (Washington: World Bank, 2001), pp. 44ff.

52. European Commission, "Making a Success of Enlargement," November 13, 2001 (http://europa.eu.int/comm/enlargement/report2001/index.htm).

53. Aleks Szczerbiak, "Polish Public Opinion: Explaining Declining Support for EU Membership," *Journal of Common Market Studies*, vol. 39, no. 1 (2001), pp. 105–22; John Reed, "Worried in Warsaw," *Financial Times*, January 10, 2002, p. 12.

54. For an assessment that gives high grades to the vigorous Polish press, see Wojciech Sadurski, "Freedom of the Press in Postcommunist Poland," *East European Politics and Societies*, vol. 10, no. 3 (Fall 1996), pp. 439–56.

55. *OECD Economic Surveys: Poland 1997*, p. 19. For a projection of the likely impact of entry into the EU on the Polish economy, see Zenon Wisniewski, "Effekte des EU—Beitritts auf den Arbeitsmarkt in Polen," *Osteuropa-Wirtschaft*, vol. 42, no. 3 (September 1997), pp. 293ff.

56. *OECD Economic Surveys: Poland 1997*, pp. 132ff.

57. Ibid., p. 67.

58. For dissent from this mainstream view and the argument that the transition has in many respects worsened conditions in central Europe, see *East European Politics and Societies*, vol. 15, no. 2 (Spring 2001), edited by Kazimierz Poznanski.

59. For studies of the EU's normative influence in terms of magnetic appeal and explicit conditionality for EU membership, see Milada Anna Vachudova, "The Leverage of International Institutions on Democratizing States: Eastern Europe and the European Union," Working Paper RSG 2001/33 (Florence: European University Institute, 2001); Mark K. Dietrich, "Legal and Judicial Reform in Central Europe and the Former Soviet Union" (Washington: World Bank, August 2000); Michael Danderstädt,. "EU-Osterweiterung: Wirkungen, Erwartungen und Interessen in den Beitrittsländern," *Integration*, vol. 21, no. 3 (July 1998); Heather Grabbe. "How does Europeanization Affect CEE Governance? Conditionality, Diffusion and Diversity," *Journal of European Public Policy*, vol. 8, no. 6 (2001), pp.1013-31; Barbara Lippert, Gaby Umbach, and Wolfgang Wessels, "Europeanization of CDD Executives: EU Membership Negotiations as a Shaping Power," *Journal of European Public Policy*, vol. 8, no. 6 (2001), pp. 980-1012; and Beate Sissenich, "State-Building by a Nonstate: EU Enlargement and Its Effects on State Capacity Building in Poland and Hungary," and Michelle Egan, "Joining the Club: The Impact of Europeanization on Czech Economics and Institutional Reform," papers presented at the European Community Studies Association conference, Madison, Wis., May 31-June 2, 2001. For background on EU aid to central Europe, see Ulrich Sedelmeier and Helen Wallace, "Policies towards Central and Eastern Europe," in Helen Wallace and William Wallace, eds., *Policy-Making in the European Union*, 3d ed. (Oxford University Press, 1996), pp. 353-87; and Barbara Lippert and Peter Becker, eds., *Towards EU-Membership: Transformation and Integration in Poland and the Czech Republic* (Bonn: Europa Union Verlag, 1998). For accounts of Polish-EU negotiations, see Klaus-Peter Schmid, "Ein netter Starrkopf," *Die Zeit*, March 26, 1998, p. 2; and Lionel Barber, "The Poles' position," *Financial Times*, July 30, 1998, p. 12. For an overview of the first decade of economic change in both central and eastern Europe, see the World Bank, "Transition: The First Ten Years," released in January 2002 (www.worldbank.org/eca).

60. See, for example, Alan Mayhew, *Recreating Europe: The European Union's Policy toward Central and Eastern Europe* (Cambridge University Press, 1998); and Heather Grabbe, "Profiting from EU Enlargement" (London: Centre for European Reform, June 2001). For consideration of the impact of the EU's enlarged external border, see Jan Zielonka, "How New Enlarged Borders Will Reshape the European Union," *Journal of Common Market Studies*, vol. 39, no. 3 (2001), pp. 507-36.

61. Two-way trade for 1994 was worth more than DM150 billion. "Kräftiger Zuwachs im Osthandel," *Frankfurter Allgemeine Zeitung*, March 31, 1995; "Osteuropa erreicht als deutscher Handelspartner das Niveau Amerikas," *Frankfurter Allgemeine Zeitung*, April 8, 1995.

62. *OECD Economic Surveys: Poland 1997*, p. 120.

63. The EU's financial aid to central Europe is modest—$3.3 billion a year for the entire region to help speed adjustment in the pre-accession period. This is only a fraction of the $50 billion to $100 billion a year that western Germany has been pouring into eastern Germany. The assistance, unlike Germany's, is not intended as investment or consumer subsidies, however. The EU sees the only effective way toward organic growth in the region as being to create the conditions to attract private investment, as Poland, Hungary, and the Czech Republic have done.

For lessons from the Iberian transformation about what builds or destroys democracies, see Juan J. Linz and Alfred Stepan, *Problems of Democratic Transition and Consolidation* (Johns Hopkins Univerity Press, 1996); Guillermo O'Donnell, Philippe C. Schmitter, and Laurence Whitehead, eds., *Transitions from Authoritarian Rule* (Johns Hopkins University Press, 1986), especially Philippe C. Schmitter, "An Introduction to Southern European Transitions from Authoritarian Rule: Italy, Greece, Portugal, Spain, and Turkey," pp. 3–10, and Adam Przeworski, "Some Problems in the Study of the Transition to Democracy," pp. 47–63; and Adam Przeworski, *Democracy and the Market: Political and Economic Reforms in Eastern Europe and Latin America* (Cambridge University Press, 1991). For other general studies of the difficulty of introducing democratic systems, see Ernest Gellner, *Conditions of Liberty: Civil Society and Its Rivals* (New York: Penguin, 1994); Giuseppe Di Palma, *To Craft Democracies* (University of California Press, 1990); and Robert D. Putnam, *Bowling Alone: The Collapse and Revival of American Community* (Simon and Schuster, 2000). The *Journal of Democracy* consistently carries essays exploring the hard work required to progress from formal elections to real liberal democracy, especially in light of the repeated failure to do so in South America. *East European Politics and Societies*, vol. 10, no. 3 (Fall 1996) also explores this issue in articles by Vladimir Tismaneau, "The Leninist Debris, or Waiting for Peron," pp. 504ff; and Daniel Cirot, "Why East Central Europe Is Not Quite Ready for Peron, but May Be One Day," pp. 536ff. See also Martin Krygier, "Virtuous Circles: Antipodean Reflections on Power, Institutions, and Civic Society," *East European Politics and Societies*, vol. 11, no. 1 (Winter 1997), pp. 36–88; Stephan Haggard and Robert R. Kaufman, *The Political Economy of Democratic Transitions* (Princeton University Press, 1995); Mary Kaldor and Ivan Vejvoda, "Democratization in Central and Eastern European Countries," *International Affairs*, vol. 73, no. 1 (1997), pp. 59–82; Josef Novak, "The Precarious Triumph of Civil Society," *Transition*, January 10, 1997, pp. 11ff; Fareed Zakaria, "The Rise of Illiberal Democracy," *Foreign Affairs*, vol. 76, no. 6 (November/December 1997), pp. 22–43; Ellen Comisso, "Is the Glass Half Full or Half Empty?" *Communist and Post-Communist Studies*, vol. 30, no. 1 (March 1997), pp. 1–21; Jakob Juchler, "Probleme der Demokratisierung in den osteuropäischen Transformations-Ländern," *Osteuropa*, vol. 47, no. 9 (September 1997), pp. 898–913.

For broad early studies of the transformation in central Europe, see John Pinder, *The European Community and Eastern Europe* (New York: Council on Foreign Relations Press, 1991); John R. Lampe, ed., *Creating Capital Markets in Eastern Europe* (Washington: Woodrow Wilson Center Press, 1992); Bundesinstitut für ostwissenschaftliche und internationale Studien (Cologne), *Aufbruch im Osten Europas* (Munich: Carl Hanser, 1993); Jerzy Hausner and Grzegorz Mosue, eds., *Transformation Processes in Eastern Europe: Western Perspectives and the Polish Experience* (Krakow: Friedrich Ebert Stiftung and Polish Academy of Sciences, 1993); A. E. Dick Howard, ed., *Constitution Making in Eastern Europe* (Washington: Woodrow Wilson Center Press, 1993); Romuald Holly, ed., *Political Consciousness and Civic Education during the Transformation of the System* (Warsaw: Polish Academy of Sciences, 1994); and Joan M. Nelson, ed., *Precarious Balance* (San Francisco: Institute for Contemporary Studies, 1994).

64. The classic checklist of minimal democratic requirements is to be found in Robert A. Dahl, *Democracy and Its Critics* (Yale University Press, 1989).

65. For a thoughtful discussion of "Ethnic Conflict and International Security" as viewed at the height of the atrocities in the former Yugoslavia and before NATO intervention there, see *Survival*, vol. 35, no. 1 (Spring 1993). For a musing about why the phenomenal success story of the transformation in central Europe has received so little academic credit, see Grzegorz Ekiert, "Ten Years After: An Optimistic View," *East European Politics and Societies*, vol. 13, no. 2 (Spring 1999), pp. 278–84.

66. On the sometimes trickier issue of Hungarian efforts to provide cultural and economic assistance to Hungarians living abroad, note the peaceful resolution with Romania in "Ungarisch-rumänischer Kompromiss/Einigung über das Status-Gesetz," *Neue Zürcher Zeitung*, December 24, 2001.

67. David Rohde, "Meanwhile, Back in Bosnia, "*New York Times*, July 18, 1999.

68. Interview with Wolfgang Ischinger, then political director in the German Foreign Ministry, January 1998; David Buchan, "U.S. planning reward for Milosevic," *Financial Times*, February 23, 1998, p. 2; Reuters, "Hoping to Change Its Image, Bosnian Serb Party Expels Karadzic," *New York Times*, December 25, 2001.

69. The fragile nature of gains was illustrated, however, when more ultra-nationalist Serbs won subsequent elections in September 1998.

Chapter Seven

1. Andrei Piontkovsky, head of the Moscow Center for Strategic Studies, made this point explicitly in "Window of Opportunity: How Russia Might Fit into the International Scheme," *Jamestown Foundation Prism* 22, part 2,

November 13, 1998, carried in David Johnson List #2479, November 16, 1998 (davidjohnson@erols.com).

2. Timothy Heritage, "Analysis: What Next for Russia after Starovoitova?" Reuters, Moscow, November 24, 1998.

3. Clifford Gaddy and Barry Ickes, "Beyond a Bail-Out: Time to Face Reality about Russia's 'Virtual Economy,'" Brookings, 1998 (www.brook.edu/fp/w-papers/gaddy/gaddick1.htm).

4. Geoffrey Hosking, "We Must Stop Demanding of Russians What We Would Never Tolerate Ourselves," Independent, August 29, 1998, in David Johnson List #2322, August 29, 1998.

5. Anders Åslund vehemently contests the validity of these standard statistics, primarily because of, on the one hand, the bias toward overstating output in the communist command economies, and on the other hand, the bias toward understatement as the growing shadow economies of the 1990s evaded confiscatory taxes—and as the old statistical systems simply failed to measure new private output. Russia "hardly saw any decline in output," he states, while Ukraine experienced only "a moderate slump." Anders Åslund, Building Capitalism: The Transformation of the Former Soviet Bloc (Cambridge University Press, 2002), pp. 8, 121–40. Robert A. Mundell, by contrast, treats the reported drops as real in his chapter in Mario I. Blejer and Marko Skreb, eds, Macroeconomic Stabilization in Transition Economics (Cambridge University Press, 1997), according to a note by George Washington University's James A. Millar in David Johnson List #5167, March 24, 2001.

6. See Martin Wolf, "Caught in the Transition Trap," Financial Times, June 30, 1999, p. 11.

7. These are pre-1998 figures. Anders Åslund calculates that the financial crash, which wiped out not only Russia's infant middle class but also much of the oligarchs' fortunes, resulted in a less dramatic ratio of 10.5 between the wealthiest and poorest tenths of the population. For his further conclusion that the 1998 crash—despite the jolting drop of 4.6 percent in GDP and 30 percent in standard of living—has benefited the local economy by wiping out imports and introducing more realism. See Anders Åslund, "The Battered Bear," WorldLink, July/August 1999, pp. 36ff; and "The Problem of Fiscal Federalism," Journal of Democracy, vol. 10, no. 2 (April 1999), pp. 83–86.

8. For an even more dire calculation that 50 million were living below "a ridiculously low poverty line" in Russia, see the keynote address by then World Bank chief economist Joseph Stiglitz at the bank's annual Conference on Development Economics, April 28–30, 1999. See also Robert Lyle, "World Bank Asks if Economic Transition Has Failed Former USSR," Radio Free Europe/Radio Liberty (RFE/RL) report, in David Johnson List #3236, April 28, 1999.

9. Poverty figures are from "Transitions 1999," published by the UN Development Program. Other statistics are all taken from Brown University's Stephen Shenfield, in "On the Threshold of Disaster: The Socio-Economic Situation in Russia," in David Johnson List #3245, July 2, 1998.

10. President Yeltsin told a conference on crime in February 1993 that two-thirds of private companies and 40 percent of businessmen were involved in corruption. Viktor Ilyukhincho of the Duma Security Committee said in May 1994 that 55 percent of capital was in mafia hands. Cited in James Sherr, "Russia, Geopolitics and Crime," Conflict Studies Research Center, Royal Military Academy Sandhurst (gopher://marvin.nc3a.nato.int/00/secdef/csrc2.1%09%09%2B). The *Economist* identified "criminal infiltration of state bodies that have the power to snoop and confiscate" as "one of the most sinister developments in Russia" ("The Russian Mafia Means Business," July 4, 1998, p. 64). And Transparency International, on the basis of questionnaires given to international businessmen and others, ranked Russia just behind Nigeria as second worst on its list of corruption in 1996; Russia improved on Transparency International's 1998 list for a ranking of tenth worst.

For representative discussions of the intertwined criminal, economic, and political worlds and some comparisons with Poland, see also Antoni K. Kaminski, "The New Polish Regime and the Specter of Economic Corruption" (Washington: Woodrow Wilson Center, April 3, 1996); Dieter Bingen, "Zwischen Raum und Wirklichkeit," *Internationale Politik*, vol. 52, no. 1 (January 1997), pp. 69–72; Kurt Schelter, "Bedrohung durch die russische Mafia," *Internationale Politik*, vol. 52, no. 1 (January 1997), pp. 31–36; and David Satter, "The Rise of the Russian Criminal State," *Jamestown Foundation Prism*, September 4, 1998 (brdcast@mx.jamestown.org); Ol'ga Kryshtanovskaya, "Russia's Illegal Structures," and Igor' Sundiev, "Criminological Components of the Current Social Dynamics in Russia," in Klaus Segbers and Stephan De Spiegeleire, eds., *Post-Soviet Puzzles*, vol. 3 (Baden-Baden: Nomos, 1995), pp. 591–614, 615–34; and Donald N. Jensen, "How Russia Is Ruled—1998" (www.rferl.org/nca/special/ruwhorules/index.html).

11. For a comprehensive look at mafia criminality, see Federico Varese, *The Russian Mafia* (Oxford University Press, 2001).

12. Fred Hiatt, "Russia's Iron Lady," *Washington Post*, November 16, 1998.

13. Clay Harris and Jeremy Grant, "World's exposure exceeds $200bn," *Financial Times*, August 28, 1998, p. 3. By 1999, some estimates of capital flight from Russia ran as high as $150 billion. See Simon Pirani, "$150 billion Capital Flight Ravages Russia," *Guardian*, May 16, 1999, in David Johnson List #3289, May 17, 1999.

14. Thomas E. Graham Jr., "A World without Russia?" paper presented at Jamestown Foundation conference, Washington, June 9, 1999, in David Johnson List #3336, June 11, 1999.

15. "Wäre George Soros nicht gewesen, hätten wir es in Russland geschafft," *Frankfurter Allgemeine Zeitung*, August 24, 1998, p. 17.

16. Susan Eisenhower, "A Summit for Listening," *Washington Post*, September 1, 1998, p. A19.

17. *Esquire,* October 1998, cited without headline in David Johnson List #2394, September 24, 1998.

18. Gaddy and Ickes, "Beyond a Bail-Out."

19. Martin Malia, "The Haunting Presence of Marxism-Leninism," *Journal of Democracy,* vol. 10, no. 2 (April 1999) pp. 41–46. Also see this special issue on "What Went Wrong in Russia?" for additional views by Michael McFaul, Peter Reddaway, and others.

20. Dmitri K. Simes, "Don't Mess with Russia's Self-Rule," *Newsday*, September 23, 1998.

21. Richard Pipes, "Russia's Past, Russia's Future," *Commentary* (June 1996), pp. 30ff.

22. Anders Åslund, "Post-communist report card," *Financial Times*, August 5, 1998, p. 10.

23. Ernest Gellner, *Conditions of Liberty: Civil Society and Its Rivals* (New York: Penguin, 1994), p. 148 (emphasis in the original). Examining why the Enlightenment notion of civil society was revived among humanist dissidents in central Europe in the 1980s, Gellner defines civil society as "that set of diverse non-governmental institutions which is strong enough to counterbalance the state and, while not preventing the state from fulfilling its role of keeper of the peace and arbitrator among major interests, can nevertheless prevent it from dominating and atomizing the rest of society" (p. 5). See also Francis Fukuyama, *Trust: The Social Virtues and the Creation of Prosperity* (Free Press, 1995); and Bronislaw Geremek and others, *The Idea of a Civil Society* (Research Triangle Park, N.C.: National Humanities Center, 1992).

24. John Thornhill, "Moscow mayor blames IMF advice for Russia's woes," *Financial Times*, September 24, 1998, p. 2.

25. See David Marples, "Belarus: An Analysis of the Lukashenka Regime," *Harriman Review* (Spring 1997), vol. 10, no. 1, pp. 24ff; Kathleen J. Mihalisko, "Belarus, Moldova, and Ukraine," in Karen Dawisha and Bruce Parrott, eds., *Democratic Changes and Authoritarian Reactions in Russia, Ukraine, Belarus, and Moldova* (Cambridge University Press, 1997), pp. 223–81; and running *RFE/RL Newsline* reports.

26. Salzburg, June 1998.

27. Interview, Warsaw, September 1997.

28. G. M. Tamas, "Socialism, Capitalism, and Modernity," in Larry Diamond and Marc F. Plattner, *Capitalism, Socialism, and Democracy Revisited* (Johns Hopkins University Press, 1993), p. 67.

29. The earliest serious economic study to reach this conclusion was Ivan Koropeckyj, ed., *The Ukraine within the USSR: An Economic Balance Sheet* (Praeger, 1977).

30. George Gamota, "Science, Technology and Conversion in Ukraine," MITRE Corporation, March 1993.

31. See Daniel Williams and R. Jeffrey Smith, "U.S. Intelligence Sees Economic Plight Leading to Breakup of Ukraine," *Washington Post*, January 25, 1994, p. 7.

32. Antoni Kaminski, interviews, Warsaw, March 1997 and earlier.

33. The U.S. ambassador to Poland, Nicholas Rey, used this analogy with football teams with good substitute players in February 1997, as one excellent finance minister was suddenly succeeded by another in Warsaw.

34. To be fair, Yavlinsky does not regard his choice solely as one between being a big fish in a provincial pond and being a small fish in the more exciting Russian pond. He explains that as a Jewish politician he would be targeted as a scapegoat for hardship in Ukraine in a way that he is not in Russia.

35. For a description of how Ukrainian gas companies make huge profits by monopolizing sales to bankrupt companies and manipulating barter payments, see Alexander Pivovarsky, "Ukraine's Virtual Economy," conference paper, June 30, 1999, in Dominique Arel's Ukrainian List #50, July 1999 (darel@brown.edu). Lazarenko's basic mistake, according to Kyiv politicians, was not that he milked the state, but rather that he did not share the cream with other leading politicians as expected. After what was clearly a tip-off by Ukrainian security forces, Lazarenko was detained as he crossed the Swiss border on a Panamanian passport in late 1998, with a bundle of money to add to his $20 million Swiss bank account. The Ukrainian parliament stripped him of his immunity as a parliamentary deputy in early 1999, and he was subsequently arrested in the United States. As of this writing, he was fighting extradition to Switzerland, had settled his family on a $6.75 million estate in northern California, and was accusing the Kuchma government of having diverted IMF funds to personal and political uses. See Timothy O'Brien, "A Palace Fit for a Fugitive and Ukraine's Ex-Premier," *New York Times,* September 1, 1999, p. 1; and Thomas Catan and Charles Clover, "Ukrainian funds affair stirs debate on US ties," *Financial Times*, January 28, 2000, p 2.

36. Vladimir Shcherban, then Donetsk governor, head of the Liberal party, and member of parliament, interview, Donetsk, 1996.

37. Interviews, Kyiv, February and March, 1997.

38. Yevhen P. Kushnariov, presidential chief of staff, interview, Kyiv, February 1998.

39. Interview, Kyiv, September 1997.

40. One of the more bizarre comparisons is that wage arrears accounted for only 35 percent of GDP in Russia but well over 100 percent in Ukraine.

41. Peter K. Cornelius and Patrick Lenain, eds., *Ukraine: Accelerating the Transition to Market* (Washington: International Monetary Fund, 1997), p. 98. See also Michelle Riboud and Hoaquan Chu, "Pension Reform, Growth, and the Labor Market in Ukraine," Policy Research Working Paper 1731 (Washington: World Bank, February 1997); and TACIS, *Ukrainian Economic Trends*, quarterly issues and updates (Brussels: European Commission, August 1998).

42. See Louise Shelley, "The Price Tag of Russia's Organized Crime," *Transition* 8 (World Bank, February 1997), pp. 7ff; and Kevin Done, "Investors give Europe a miss," *Financial Times*, April 15, 1997, p. 2.

43. See Elizabeth Pond, "Letter from Kiev: Crisis, 1997 Style," *Washington Quarterly*, vol. 20, no. 4 (Autumn 1997), pp. 79–87; Ilya Prizel, "Ukraine between Proto-Democracy and 'Soft' Authoritarianism," in Dawisha and Parrott, *Democratic Changes and Authoritarian Reactions*, pp. 330–69; F. Stephen Larrabee, "Ukraine's Balancing Act," *Survival*, vol. 38, no. 2 (Summer 1996), pp. 143–65; the issue of *Harriman Review*, vol. 10, no. 3 (Winter 1997) on "Ukrainian National Security"; and Taras Kuzio, *Ukraine under Kuchma* (Basingstoke: Macmillan, 1997).

44. Volodymyr Mukhin, chairman of the Defense and Security Committee of the Ukrainian Supreme Rada, on a visit to Bonn in 1996.

45. Conversation, Kyiv, 1995.

46. For an analysis of the most focused elite opinion poll, see Evgenii Golovakha, "Elites in Ukraine: Evaluation of the Project's Elite Survey," in Segbers and De Spiegeleire, *Post-Soviet Puzzles*, pp. 167–241.

47. Interview in *Nezavisimaya gazeta*, February 5, 1997; translated into English in Foreign Broadcast Information Service, February 6, 1997.

48. Jan Maksymiuk, "Should Lukashenka Be Regarded as a Legitimate President?" *RFE/RL Newsline,* vol. 5, no. 170, September 11, 2001, back issues available at ⟨www.rferl.org/newsline/search/⟩; and Mark Lenzi, "Europe's Armory for Terrorism," *Washington Post*, January 3, 2002, p. 17.

49. For an astute analysis of Russian-Ukrainian relations, see Tadeusz Andrzej Olszanski, "Ukraine and Russia: Mutual Relations and the Conditions That Determine Them" (Warsaw: Center for Eastern Studies, November 2001).

50. Martin Hutchinson, interview with Åslund, "Building Capitalism," January 10, 2001, carried in David Johnson List No. 6018, January 12, 2001; Anders Åslund and Georges de Menil, eds. *Economic Reform in Ukraine: The Unfinished Agenda* (Armonk: N.Y.: M. E. Sharpe, 2000).

51. Åslund, *Building Capitalism*; Brigitte Granville and Peter Oppenheimer, eds. *Russia's Post-Communist Economy* (Oxford University Press, 2001); Clifford G. Gaddy and Barry W. Ickes, "The Virtual Economy and Economic Recovery in Russia," *Transition Newsletter* (World Bank/William Davidson Institute), vol. 12, no. 1 (February/March 2001), pp. 1ff.

52. John Hardt, "Putin's Economic Strategy and U.S. Interests," Report for Congress RL31023, Congressional Research Service, June 19, 2001.

53. Heinrich Vogel, "The Putin System," *Transatlantic Internationale Politik*, vol. 3, no. 1 (Spring 2002); and Allen C. Lynch, "Roots of Russia's Economic Dilemmas: Liberal Economics and Illiberal Geography," *Europe-Asia Studies*, vol. 54, no. 1 (January 2002), pp. 31–49.

54. See Dominic Lieven, *Empire: The Russian Empire and Its Rivals* (Yale University Press, 2000); and Michael McFaul, *Russia's Unfinished Revolution: Political Change from Gorbachev to Putin* (Cornell University Press, 2001).

Chapter Eight

1. J. H. H. Weiler, *The Constitution of Europe* (Cambridge University Press, 1999), especially pp. 58ff.; Albert O. Hirschman, *Exit, Voice, and Loyalty* (Harvard University Press, 1970).

2. Wolfgang Wessels, "The Evolution of the EU System/Amsterdam and Nice/Ratchet Fusion in the Making," paper presented at the biennial European Community Studies Association (ECSA) conference, Madison, Wis., May 31–June 2, 2001. See also, from the same conference, Simon Bulmer, "Policy Transfer in the European Union: An Institutionalist Perspective."

3. Stefan Collignon, "Quo Vadis Europa?" *Transatlantic Internationale Politik*, vol. 3, no. 1 (Spring 2002). See also the abundant theoretical literature on neofunctionalism.

4. David P. Calleo, *Rethinking Europe's Future* (Princeton University Press, 2001), pp. 1–11.

5. David White, "New connections start to bring change to an ancient frontier," *Financial Times*, June 16, 1998, p. 3; and "Iberische Kooperation statt Konkurrenz," *Neue Zürcher Zeitung*, November 23, 2001 (www.nzz/ch/al/index.html).

6. Fintan O'Toole, "Peace in Northern Ireland Moves into the Realm of the Possible," *Washington Post*, April 12, 1998, p. C1; John Lloyd, "Good Traitors," *Prospect*, January 2000, pp. 36–40; R. O'Donnell, ed. *Europe: The Irish Experience* (Dublin: Institute for European Affairs, 2000); and Michael Cox, Adrian Guelke, and Fiona Stephen, eds., *A Farewell to Arms?* (Manchester University Press, 2000).

7. Giuseppe Di Palma, *To Craft Democracies* (University of California Press, 1990).

8. "It makes everything more expensive." *Bild*, November 27, 28, and 29, 2001, p. 6.

9. Christiane Karweil, "Das Wunder von Athen," *Die Zeit*, November 22, 2001, p. 33.

10. Christopher Brown-Humes, Clare MacCarthy, and Andrew Parker, "Sweden may vote on euro in 2003," *Financial Times*, January 10, 2002, p. 1; Clare MacCarthy, "Danes switch in favour of eurozone," *Financial Times*, January 11, 2002, p. 2.

11. Norbert Walter, "Euro:Dollar = Airbus:Boeing," *Transatlantic Internationale Politik*, vol. 2, no. 4 (Winter 2001), pp. 25ff.; and Norbert Walter, "Second to (N)One," German Issues 23 (Washington: American Institute for Contemporary German Studies, 2000.)

12. Robert J. Samuelson, "Ready or Not, Here Comes the Euro," *Washington Post*, December 26, 2001, p. 31; "Here Comes the Euro," *New York Times*, January 1, 2002; T. R. Reid, "Common Currency Builds on Common Culture," *Washington Post*, January 1, 2002, p. 1; Max Berley, "Money Won't Buy Them Unity," *Washington Post*, September 9, 2001, p. B1; David Ignatius, "Europe Needs a Good Crisis," *Washington Post*, December 16, 2001, p. B7; Edmund L. Andrews, "Hoping a Euro in the Hand Will Be Worth More," *New York Times*, December 26, 2001.

13. Estimated by the Federal Association of German Industry (BDI); cited in Thomas Hanke and Norbert Walter, *Der Euro—Kurs auf die Zukunft*, 3d ed. (Frankfurt: Campus, 1998), p. 116.

14. Tony Barber, "Work wanted," *Financial Times*, November 7, 2001; Martin Wolf, "A catalyst for further change," *Financial Times*, January 2, 2002, p. 13.

15. Martin Wolf, "Europe's capacity for weakness," *Financial Times*, July 4, 2001, p 13.

16. Wilfried Herz, "Kratzen am Großen Vorbild," *Die Zeit*, November 22, 2001, p. 30; Christopher Swann, "Euro fails to make ground on the dollar," *Financial Times*, October 20, 2001, p. 6; "A Global Euro?" *Economist* July 28, 2001, p. 68.

17. Christopher Swann, "Capital 'still dominant as a financial centre,'" *Financial Times*, October 10, 2001, p. 10.

18. Tony Barber, "Political currency," *Financial Times*, December 31, 2001, p. 8.

19. Robert H. Dugger, "Euro-Strengthening—Notes on Demographics, Restructuring and One-Time Adjustment," paper presented at the European Institiute Roundtable on Financial and Monetary Affairs, Washington, April 30, 2001.

20. Edward Luce and Vincent Boland, "Retreat from Moscow takes investors back to German safe haven," *Financial Times*, September 1, 1998, p. 2; Simon Davie, "Powerful force for change," *Financial Times*, "The Birth of the Euro" special section, April 30, 1998, p. 6.

21. Elke Thiel, "Wirtschaften unter Euro-Bedingungen," *Stiftung Wissenschaft und Politik* (Berlin), October 2001, p. 18.

22. "A Global Euro?"

23. Aline van Duyn, "Euro corporate bonds give the dollar a run for its money," *Financial Times*, June 29, 2001.

24. Telephone interview, April 1998.

25. For a sampling of discussions about the need for Germany and Europe to shake up their rigidities, but also of the problems this will trigger in social security, see Robert Taylor, "New strategies called for," *Financial Times*, April 30, 1998, "The Birth of the Euro" special section, p. 2; Dirk Meyer, "The Provisions of the German Charitable Welfare System and the Challenge of the Free Market," *German Studies Review*, vol. 20, no. 3 (October 1997), pp. 371–98; and Jürgen von Hagen, "Von der Deutschen Mark zum Euro," *Aus Politik und Zeitgeschichte Beilage zu Das Parlament*, B24, June 5, 1998, pp. 35–46.

26. Hugo Dixon, "EMU's capital consequences," *Financial Times*, April 30, 1998, p. 17. For the portrait of a rare German venture capitalist of the new breed and his pioneer listing on the new Neuer Markt for innovative companies, see Ralph Atkins, "An upwardly mobile star," *Financial Times*, April 30, 1998, p. 14. For the broad German shift away from family-owned and bank-financed firms to equity financing, see Graham Bowley, "Corporate Germany reaping the rewards of risk-taking," *Financial Times*, August 11, 1998, p. 14.; Marc Brost and others, "Mut, Schweiß, und Tränen," *Die Zeit*, August 16, 2001, pp. 15ff.

27. David B. Audretsch, and others, "The New Economy in Germany and the United States: Policy Challenges and Solutions," New Economy Study (Washington: American Institute for Contemporary German Studies, January 2002), pp. 4, 18.

28. "A Ragbag of Reform," *Economist*, March 3, 2001, pp. 67–69.

29. "Survey—Europe reinvented: The cult of equity," *Financial Times*, Jan. 26, 2001, p. 26; Bertrand Benoit, "Germany's courts chase after its companies," *Financial Times*, Nov. 27, 2001, p. 14.

30. Dernot Hodson and Imelda Maher, "The Open Method as a New Mode of Governance: The Case of Soft Economic Policy Co-ordination," *Journal of Common Market Studies*, vol. 39, no. 4 (2001), pp. 719–46. The basic text of the Lisbon decisions can be found in the documentation section of *Transatlantic Internationale Politik*, vol. 1, no. 3 (Fall 2000), pp. 116–28.

31. Daniel Dombey, "Brussels in local loop legal action," *Financial Times*, December 21, 2001, p. 8.

32. Daniel Dombey, "Breakthrough on EU telecoms," *Financial Times*, December 13, 2001, p. 6.

33. Francesco Guerrara and Tim Burt, "Brussels push to make car dealers more competitive," *Financial Times*, January 10, 2002, p. 1.

34. Daniel Dombey, "Brussels tries new tack in drive for liberalisation," *Financial Times*, December 4, 2001, p. 4.

35. Paul Abrahams, "Europe closing IT gap with US," *Financial Times*, October 18, 2001, p. 7; Hugh Williamson, "Data signal Germany's transformation to IT society," *Financial Times*. October 5, 2001, p. 8.

36. Peter Norman, "Stockholm or bust," *Financial Times*, March 22, 2001, p 12.

37. "Fair weather reformers," *Financial Times*, December 11, 2001, p. 16.

38. "A Ragbag of Reform"; Thiel, "Wirtschaften unter Euro-Bedingungen"; and Peter Norman, "Hopes reviving for EU securities reform," *Financial Times*, December 21, 2001, p. 8.

39. Peter Norman, "Prodi says EU states lack the will to deliver results," *Financial Times*, December 13, 2001, p. 1.

40. Birgit Jennen, "Bolkestein fordert Reformanstoß für europäischen Finanzmarkt," *Financial Times Deutschland*, December 3, 2001, p. 12; Christian Wernicke, "Die teutonische Agenda," *Die Zeit*, January 6, 2001, p. 11.

41. Daniel Dombey, "Brussels in call to free more labour markets," *Financial Times*, November 30, 2001, p. 8; Francesco Guerrera and Hugh Williamson, "Experts reignite Brussels bid for EU takeover code," *Financial Times*, January 11, 2002, p. 1.

42. Peter Norman, "Brussels and industry call for speedier liberalisation," *Financial Times*, December 11, 2001, p. 8; Michael Mann, "Business leaders urge EU to revive reform process," *Financial Times*, January 11, 2002, p. 2.

43. David Turner, Nicholas George, and Clare MacCarthy, "Opposition to the euro wanes as hard cash creates converts," *Financial Times*, December 24, 2001, p. 1.

44. World Economic Forum, Davos, February 1998.

45. Wolfgang Streeck, "German Capitalism: Does It Exist? Can It Survive?" in Colin Crouch and Wolfgang Streeck, eds., *Modern Capitalism or Modern Capitalisms?* (London: Francis Pinter, 1995).

46. "Sir Leon Brittan," *World Link*, March/April, 1998, pp. 12ff.

47. Warnfried Dettling, "Koalition der Ideen," *Die Zeit*, May 7, 1998, p. 11.

48. See also Adair Turner, *Just Capital: The Liberal Economy* (Basingstoke: Macmillan, 2001).

49. Peter Norman, "Brussels disciplines Ireland," *Financial Times*, January 25, 2001, p. 2. The Commission, rather than the Euro Group, is the watchdog here; in one of the oddities of the European Monetary Union, the stability pact applies to all EU members in a moral sense, but only the twelve EMU members may be fined for overstepping it.

50. Peter Norman, "Italy's budget makes monkey of euro-zone pact on fiscal policy," *Financial Times*, July 13, 2001, p. 2; James Blitz, "A rift at the heart of Rome," *Financial Times*, January 4, 2002.

51. Claus Hulverscheidt and Daniel Dombey, "Eichel puts case for changes to EU stability pact," *Financial Times*, August 17, 2001, p. 1; Lionel Barber, "Eichel's second thoughts," *Financial Times*, August 21, 2001, p. 13; Haig Simonian, "Call for redefinition of EU's stability pact," *Financial Times*, October 24, 2001, p. 6; Christian Wernicke, "Hart am Limit," *Die Zeit*, October 25, 2001, p. 22; Tony Barber, "ECB set to relax budget targets," *Financial Times*, November 22, 2001, p. 1; "Instability pact," *Financial Times*, December 5, 2001, p. 14; Marco Buti, Werner Roger, and Jan In't Veld, "Stabilizing Output and Inflation: Policy Conflicts and Co-operation under a Stability Pact," *Journal of Common Market Studies*, vol. 39, no. 5 (2001); Alasdair Murray, "The Euro Comes of Age," *CER Bulletin*, no. 21 (December/January 2001/2002) (www.cer.org.uk/articles/n_21_murray.html).

52. O. Issing, "The Eurosystem: Transparent and Accountable or 'Willem in Euroland,'" *Journal of Common Market Studies*, vol. 37, no. 3 (1999), pp. 503–19; Jakob de Haan and Sylvester C. W. Eijffinger, "The Democratic Accountability of the European Central Bank: A Comment on Two Fairy-Tales," *Journal of Common Market Studies*, vol. 38, no. 3 (2000), pp. 393–407; Jakob de Haan, "Independence and Democratic Accountability of the ECB," paper presented at the ECSA conference, Madison, Wis., May 31–June 2, 2001; Alan Blinder and others, "How Do Central Banks Talk?" Geneva Reports on the World Economy 3 (London: Centre for Economic Policy Research and International Center for Monetary and Banking Studies, 2001).

53. Tommaso Padoa-Schioppa, "The Euro and Politics," *Transatlantic Internationale Politik*, vol. 2, no. 4 (Winter 2000), pp. 11–16.

54. Thomas Christiansen and Emil Kirchner, eds., *Europe in Change: Committee Governance in the European Union* (Manchester University Press, 2000), especially p. 140.

55. Kenneth Dyson, *The Politics of the Euro-Zone* (Oxford University Press, 2000); Christian Taylor, "The Role and Status of the European Central Bank: Some Proposals for Accountability and Cooperation," in Colin Crouch, ed., *After the Euro* (Oxford University Press, 2000), pp. 179–202. For a proposal that the Euro Group get more powers and that EMU members "coordinate" but not "harmonize" or force "convergence" of their policies, see Pierre Jacquet and Jean Pisani-Ferry, "Economic Policy Co-ordination in the Euro Zone; What Has Been Achieved? What Should Be Done?" (London: Center for European Reform, January 2001).

56. Interviews, Bonn. See also "Franco-German fractures," editorial, *Financial Times*, May 6, 1998, p. 13.

57. Organization for Economic Cooperation and Development, *OECD Economic Surveys: Germany* (Paris, 1998). Germany's visible trade surplus hit record highs of more than $60 billion in 1997 and 1998; its current account

deficit plunged sharply in 1998. *Deutsche Bank Monthly Report,* March 2000, p. 55 (www.bundesbank.de/de/monatsbericht/bericht03/textteil/00/zabi99.pdf). See also "Europe's Start-up Stampede," *Economist,* January 15, 2000, pp. 67ff.; Terence Roth, "New Economy Spurs Germany to Break Its Corporate Mold," *Wall Street Journal Europe,* January 28, 2000, p. 1; Tony Barber, "German chiefs draft code to do business by," *Financial Times,* February 1, 2000, p. 2; Geoff Nairn, "Poised to deny America much of the IT pie," *Financial Times,* February 3, 2000, p. 9; Ralph Atkins and others, "Mannesmann is on verge of surrender to Vodafone," *Financial Times,* February 4, 2000, p. 1; John Plender, "Whirlwinds of change," *Financial Times,* February 4, 2000, p. 12; Philip Stephens, "Blind to the new Europe," *Financial Times,* February 4, 2000, p. 13; "A deal that will change Europe," *Financial Times,* February 5, 2000, p. 6; and "Europe's New Capitalism," *Economist,* February 12, 2000, pp. 75–78.

58. World Economic Forum, Davos, January 1998.

59. See, for example, the consultants' report on competitiveness written for the European Commission in 1998. It found that GDP per capita in Europe is a third lower than in the United States because of the failure to create service jobs. Emma Tucker, "Europe outpaced by US on competition, says report," *Financial Times,* November 16, 1998, p. 18. See also the widely noted speech by German president Roman Herzog at the Hotel Adlon, Berlin, April 26, 1997, available at (www.bundespraesident.de/txt/vi-00.htm).

60. Uwe Jean Heuser, "Fröhliches Mittelmaß," *Die Zeit,* January 3, 2002, p. 1.

61. Bertrand Benoit, "Defiant C&A reignites debate on German shopping laws," *Financial Times,* January 9, 2002, p. 2.

62. Audretsch and others, "The New Economy in Germany and the United States," pp. 22–24.

63. See, for example, Tony Major and Thibaut Madelin, "Deutsche executive shake-up to defy consensus tradition," *Financial Times,* January 17, 2002, p. 1.

64. Audretsch and others, "The New Economy in Germany and the United States," p. 16; Bertrand Benoit, "Germany embraces venture capitalism," *Financial Times,* January 7, 2000, p. 25.

65. "Goldilocks on speed," editorial, *Financial Times,* April 25, 1998, p. 6.

66. For a broader survey of the embrace of neoliberalism by the European left as a whole, see "Europe's New Left," *Economist,* February 12, 2000, pp. 19–23.

67. Wolfgang Schäuble at the German-Italian Colloquium, Bonn, April 1998.

68. Haig Simonian, "Christmas comes early for German board rooms," *Financial Times,* December 24, 1999, p. 3; Tony Major, "Corporate Germany in preparation for shake-up," *Financial Times,* February 4, 2000, p. 20.

69. Businessmen campaigning for the reductions cited an even higher corporate tax of 60 percent, including a 45 percent federal tax on undistributed profits plus a roughly 15 percent local tax on large businesses.

70. "No great harm, no good either," *Economist*, July 14, 2001, p. 31; Stefan von Borstel, "Müller rudert bei Lohnnebenkosten zurück," *Die Welt*, July 23, 2001, p. 4; Terence Roth, "New Economy Spurs Germany to Break Its Corporate Mold," *Wall Street Journal Europe*, January 28, 2000, p. 1.

71. Tony Barber and others, "Survey—Germany: Banking and Finance," *Financial Times*, October 15, 2001; Bertrand Benoit, "Germany's courts chase after its companies," *Financial Times*, November 27, 2001, p. 14.

72. Werner A. Perger, "Reformer leben gefährlich," *Die Zeit*, August 2, 2001, p. 4; Oliver Schumacher, "Eichel steht noch, aber er wackelt," *Süddeutsche Zeitung*, October 22, 2001, p. 4; Robert Leicht, "Der deutsche Patient," *Die Zeit*, January 3, 2002, p. 1; Werner A. Perger, "Vom Elend der kleinen Schritte," *Die Zeit*, January 3, 2002, p. 3.

73. Peter Norman, "Currency pioneers get ready for euro's big day," *Financial Times*, December 27, 2001, p. 3.

74. Paul Betts and Deborah Hargrave, "No way in," *Financial Times*, May 3, 2001, p. 12; Josef Joffe, "Kanzler kraftlos," *Die Zeit*, May 31, 2001, p. 1; Michael Mann, "Brussels tries again on common takeover rules," *Financial Times*, September 5, 2001, p. 2; "Poisoned bill," editorial, *Financial Times*, November 13, 2001, p. 16; "Ein Land voller Tabus," *Die Zeit*, November 29, 2001, p. 29; and Paul Betts, "Buyers beware," *Financial Times*, December 20, 2001, p. 16.

75. James Harding and Bertrand Benoit, "German regulator's blow for deals," *Financial Times*, November 30, 2001, p 1.

76. "Economic and Financial Indicators," *Economist*, August 4, 2001, p. 82.

77. David Howarth, "The French State in the Euro Zone: 'Modernization' and Legitimizing Dirigisme in the 'Semi-Sovereignty Game,'" paper presented at the ECSA conference, Madison, Wis., May 31–June 2, 2001.

78. Vivien Schmidt, "Policy, Discourse, and Institutional Reform: The Impact of Europeanization on National Governance Practices, Ideas, and Discourse," paper prepared for the European Consortium for Political Research workshop on Policy, Discourse, and Institutional Reform, Grenoble, April 6–11, 2001. See also Gisela Müller-Brandeck-Bocquet, "Frankreichs Europapolitik unter Chirac und Jospin," *Integration*, vol. 24, no. 3 (July 2001), pp. 258–73; and Robert Graham, "Dose of realism for France," *Financial Times*, August 17, 1998. Graham cites the annual report of the Bank of France by Jean-Claude Trichet in late 1998 as pressing for a reduction of the 54.1 percent share of public spending in GDP toward the EU average of 48.2 percent and the G-7 average of 38.3 percent.

79. Dominique Moïsi, "The Trouble with France," *Foreign Affairs*, vol. 77, no. 3 (May/June 1998), pp. 94–104; Dominique Moïsi, "A fresh direction,"

Financial Times, May 11, 1998, p. 14; Robert Graham, "France cuts working week to 35 hours," *Financial Times,* May 20, 1998, p. 2; Sophie Pedder, France Survey, *Economist,* June 5, 1999.

80. "It's no laughing matter."

81. Victor Mallet, "Global troubles overshadow liberal project," *Financial Times,* "France: Banking and Finance" survey, October 22, 2001, p. I.

82. See also Robert Graham, "Turning back the clock," *Financial Times,* July 29, 1999, p. 15.

83. OECD figures, reported in the *Economist,* August 8, 1998, p. 87. See also Lionel Barber, "Brussels sees EU eastward expansion without budget rise," *Financial Times,* June 26, 1996, p. 1. Poland is specifically demanding full and equal access to the EU's huge farm subsidies if the system is not reformed before Warsaw joins the EU. See Michael Smith and Stefan Wagstyl, "Frontrunners demand farm subsidies," and "East European states under pressure from farmers to fight for full EU benefits," *Financial Times,* January 4, 2000, p. 4; and "Eastern farming," *Financial Times,* January 7, 2000, p. 14.

84. He spoke in this vein, for example, at the EU Commission representation office in Bonn, December 3, 1997.

85. For an overview of EU farm policy, see K. A. Ingersent, A. J. Rayner, and Robert C. Hine, eds., *The Reform of the Common Agricultural Policy* (Basingstoke: Macmillan, 1998).

86. "Franco-German fractures."

87. "Frankreich muss mehr in EU-Kasse einzahlen," *Süddeutsche Zeitung,* September 17, 1998, p. B1.

88. Klaus Hänsch, "Zwei Konzepte für ein Europa?" *Frankfurter Allgemeine Zeitung,* April 24, 1998, p. 11; Gerald Braunberger, "In der Wagenburg," *Frankfurter Allgemeine Zeitung,* April 22, 1998, p. 17. See also the warnings in the whole issue of *Internationale Politik* devoted to "Deutschland-Frankreich: Tandem auf Schlingerkurs," September 1998; Jacqueline Hénard, "Schlechte Aussichten," *Die Zeit,* July 8, 1999, p. 8; Helmut Schmidt, "Patrioten setzen auf Europa," *Die Zeit,* August 12, 1999, p. 8; the conference report "Franco-German Relations and European Integration: A Trans-Atlantic Dialogue" (Washington: American Institute for Contemporary German Studies, September 16, 1999); and Dominique Moïsi, "Gute Nachbarn," *Die Zeit,* December 9, 1999.

89. "Franco-German fractures."

90. For one consideration of this issue, see Timothy Garton Ash, "Is Britain European?" *International Affairs,* vol. 77, no. 1 (January 2001), pp. 1–13.

91. Timothy Garton Ash, "Europe's Endangered Liberal Order," *Foreign Affairs,* vol. 77, no. 2 (March/April 1998), pp. 51–65; and Mitsuko Uchida, "Chalk and Cheese," *Prospect,* February 1998, pp. 124–28.

92. Eberhard Wisdorff, "Bonn fordert strikte Anwendung der Subsidiarität/ Kohl und die Kompetenzen der EU," *Handelsblatt*, May 6, 1998, p. 2; "Freier Markt für Europas Patienten," *Süddeutsche Zeitung*, April 29, 1998, p. 1.

93. For Austria's complaints about a double standard in the EU's punishment of small countries and indulgence of large countries and in its toleration of the far right presence in Berlusconi's government, see "Hämischer Blick von Wien nach Rom," *Neue Zürcher Zeitung*, January 10, 2002. See also Ulrich Ladurner, "Berlusconi ohne Maske," *Die Zeit*, January 10, 2002, p. 1; and Michael Merlingen, Cas Mudde, and Ulrich Sedelmeier, "The Right and the Righteous? European Norms, Domestic Politics and the Sanctions against Austria," *Journal of Common Market Studies*, vol. 39, no. 1 (2001), pp. 59–77.

94. For one expression of the lingering sensitivities of small countries at being ordered about by their bigger allies, see "Absage an selbst ernanntes 'EU-Direktorium,'" *Neue Zürcher Zeitung*, November 30, 2001.

95. The key texts are available in the documentation sections of *Transatlantic Internationale Politik*, vol. 1, no. 4 (Winter 2000), pp. 117–34; vol. 2, no. 1 (Spring 2001), pp. 150–54; vol. 2, no. 2 (Summer 2001), pp. 167–70; and vol. 2, no. 3 (Fall 2001), pp. 121–45.

96. The English translation of the Social Democratic resolution is available at (http://spd.de/). See also "Radikale Schritte," *Der Spiegel*, April 30, 2001, p. 17; "Neues Bekenntnis Schröders zu Europa," *Neue Zürcher Zeitung*, May 7, 2001; and Schröder's statement, "Bürger und Parlamente umfassend einbeziehen," June 22, 2001 (www.bundesregierung.de/dokumente/artikel/ ix_44711_5945.htm).

97. For examination of the issue of an EU constitution, see Ingolf Pernice, "The Nice Summit and a European Constitution," *Transatlantic Internationale Politik*, vol. 1, no. 4 (Winter 2000), pp. 17–24; and Weiler, *The Constitution of Europe.*

98. For the European Council's mandate to the convention, see the documentation section in *Transatlantic Internationale Politik,* vol. 3, no. 1 (Spring 2002).

99. Nikolaïdis gave this analysis in a panel on "The Federal Vision: Legitimacy and Levels of Governance in the U.S. and the EU" at the ESCA conference, Madison, Wis., May 31–June 2, 2001.

Chapter Nine

1. "Eine neue Form der Selbstverteidigung," *Die Zeit*, October 18, pp. 3ff.

2. Christopher Swann, "Minds concentrated on the problem," *Financial Times*, "World Economy" section, November 30, 2001, p. V.

3. Christopher Bennett, "Aiding America," *NATO Review*, vol . 49 (Winter 2001/2002), pp. 6–7; NATO Press Release (2002)003, January 16, 2002.

4. Paul Kennedy, "The eagle has landed," *Financial Times*, February 2, 2002, p. 1; International Institute for Strategic Studies, *The Military Balance, 2001–2002* (Oxford University Press, October 2001); "Misdirected Defense Dollars," *New York Times*, January 16, 2002.

5. Clark S. Judge, "Hegemony of the Heart," *Hoover Institution Policy Review* (December 2001) (www.policyreview.org/DEC01/judge.html).

6. William Safire, "That Dog Won't Bark," *New York Times*, January 24, 2001.

7. "What September 11th Really Wrought," *Economist*, January 12, 2002, pp. 23–25.

8. Stanley Sloan, "Is NATO Relevant?" *Transatlantic Internationale Politik*, vol. 3, no. 1 (Spring 2002); Stanley Sloan, *NATO, the European Union and the Atlantic Community: The Transatlantic Bargain Reconsidered* (Lanham, Md.: Rowman and Littlefield, 2002).

9. Constanze Stelzenmüller and Michael Thumann, "Kein Feind, kein Ehr,'" *Die Zeit*, January 10, 2001, p. 3.

10. Francois Heisbourg, "Europe and the Transformation of the World Order," *Survival*, vol. 43, no. 4 (Winter 2001), pp. 143–48.

11. Fischer made this a major point in his presentation before the Bundestag vote on Germany's first foreign combat mission since World War II. Approval was overwhelming, with 505 in favor, 11 against, and 12 abstentions. See "Bundestag stimmt Bundeswehr-Missionzu," *Frankfurter Allgemeine Zeitung*, June 12, 1999, p. 1.

12. Speech at the 16th International NATO Workshop, Vienna, June 21, 1999 (www.nato.int/). Significantly, Solana had also been an opponent of America's Vietnam war and even of his native Spain's entry into NATO in the 1980s.

13. For example, the editor of *Liberation*, Jacques Almaric, wrote on June 23, 1999, "This sick Serbia and its demons must be Europeanized, just as Kosovo must be Europeanized, in order for all its inhabitants to overcome their hatreds and turn their attention to matters other than vengeance." On the same day the Danish daily *Aktuelt* wrote, "There are some virtues that must be defended with weapons. One of them is the right of a group of people to defend itself against violence of Kosovo proportions. That was the basic reason we established NATO. After the Berlin Wall's fall, it [is now becoming] a real pan-European security organization." Reported in Radio Free Europe's *Western Press Review*, June 23, 1999 (www.rferl.org/nca/features/).

14. In Joseph Nye's application of the categories of American security interest as defined by William Perry and Ashton Carter, Kosovo was initially only on the "C list" of "contingencies that indirectly affect U.S. security but do not directly threaten U.S. interests." Once Milosevic responded to NATO airstrikes by the wholesale expulsion of Kosovo Albanians, the conflict rose

in importance to Washington, but only to the "B list" of threats to U.S. interests but not to U.S. survival. Joseph Nye, "Redefining the National Interest," *Foreign Affairs*, vol. 78, no. 4 (July/August 1999), pp. 22–35; William Perry and Ashton Carter, *Preventive Defense* (Brookings, 1999).

15. This sentiment did surface, despite NATO's success, and it would have been far stronger had NATO been humiliated in Kosovo. In summer 1999 columnist Bill Thompson said flatly in the *Fort Worth Star-Telegram*, "American intrusion in the Balkans can never succeed because it is exactly that—an intrusion into a situation that is none of America's business." Quoted by Don Hill, *Western Press Review*, August 5, 1999 (www.rferl.org/nca/features/).

16. For the evaluation by Wesley K. Clark, supreme allied commander, Europe, of how close NATO was to failing by the last week in May, see Michael Ignatieff, "The Virtual Commander," *New Yorker*, August 2, 1999, pp. 30–36; and Wesley K. Clark, *Waging Modern War* (New York: Public Affairs, 2001). Josef Joffe sums up the dilemmas of twenty-first-century high-tech warfare as "no casualties on our side," "no casualties on their side," and "do it fast—before public opinion collapses" ("Three Unwritten Rules of the Serbian War," *New York Times*, July 25, 1999). More acerbically, John Steinbruner concluded that "in effect, the air operation accepted civilian casualties to prevent military ones and did so at an implicit rate of 1,000 to one or even more. That is not a practice that could ever be resumed in Kosovo or defended in any other instance." See Steinbruner, "The Consequences of Kosovo," *Politik und Gesellschaft*, no. 3 (1999), pp. 263ff.

17. Interview, 1999.

18. The phenomenon is explored in detail in David C. Gompert, Richard L. Kugler, and Martin C. Libicki, *Mind the Gap* (Washington: National Defense University Press, 1999). See also "Schwindende Bedeutung reiner Territorialverteidigung," *Neue Zürcher Zeitung*, June 17, 1999; William Drozdiak, "War Showed U.S.-Allied Inequality Arms Gap May Alter Roles of NATO States," *Washington Post*, June 28, 1999, p. A1; "Frankreichs Kosten im Kosovo-Krieg," *Neue Zürcher Zeitung*, July 3, 1999; and Hans Rühle, "Kosovo und Europas Verteidigungsillusionen: Wachsende Kluft zwischen Rhetorik und Praxis," *Neue Zürcher Zeitung*, August 2, 1999.

19. "'Es gab nie ein Alternative,'" *Der Spiegel*, June 21,1999, pp. 34ff.

20. See, for example, the running coverage in *Der Spiegel*, as well as articles such as Bernd Ulrich, "Amerikas Krieg, Europas Frieden," *Tagesspiegel*, June 5, 1999; and Manfred Bissinger, "Schröder im Glück," *Die Woche*, June 11, 1999, p. 1.

21. For one refutation of this view as "grotesque," see Stefan Cornelius, "Der gute und der böse Polizist," *Süddeutsche Zeitung*, June 12, 1999, p. 4. German defense minister Rudolf Scharping emphatically rejects this view as well, arguing, "We do not have too much America in NATO, but too little

Europe" ("Ran an Milosevics Vermögen," *Die Woche*, June 11, 1999, pp. 6ff.). For basic documents and commentary on the Kosovo crisis and war, see the University of Cambridge series *International Documents and Analyses*, vols. 1 and 2, *The Crisis in Kosovo 1989–1999* and *The Kosovo Conflict* (Linton, U.K.: Book Systems Plus, 1999). For a nuanced essay on Balkan animosities, see William W. Hagen, "The Balkans' Lethal Nationalisms," *Foreign Affairs*, vol. 78, no. 4 (July/August 1999), pp. 52–64.

22. See, for example, William Pfaff, "While Europe Dithers, NATO Advances Eastward," *International Herald Tribune*, June 24, 1999; and Peter Rodman (Nixon Center), "Reality Check: Success Has Its Costs," and Alan Rousso (Carnegie Endowment's Moscow Center), "Peace in Yugoslavia: Who Gains?" available in David Johnson Lists #3362, June 26, 1999, and #3364, June 27, 1999, respectively (davidjohnson@erols.com). Rodman states, "Where the Administration sees [in Kosovo] vindication for the Atlantic Alliance, for U.S. leadership, and for universal values, the rest of the world now sees America's dominance as one of the world's biggest problems. The Europeans are only accelerating the construction of their autonomous institutions in foreign and security policy, vowing never again to be so tied to the Americans."

23. For Solana's own description of the aims of European foreign policy, see his speech given in Copenhagen, "The Development of a Common Foreign and Security Policy and the Role of the High Representative," February 11, 2000. See also the companion speech by Christopher Patten in Berlin, "The Future of the European Security and Defense Policy and the Role of the European Commission," February 16, 2000. Both speeches are available on the EU's website (http://europa.eu.int).

24 . Telephone interview, June 18, 1999.

25. Among EU members, France, Portugal, and Spain will have gone to a career army by 2003. That leaves Denmark, Germany, Greece, Italy, and Sweden with conscription. So far, any notion of professional armed forces has been anathema in the linchpin country of Germany; the draft has been too valuable as an educator, socializing West German youth in the 1960s and 1970s and east German youth in the 1990s away from authoritarianism and toward egalitarian democracy.

26. François Heisbourg, "L'Europe de la defense dans l'Alliance atlantique," *Politique Etrangere*, vol. 2 (Summer 1999).

27. Others did their sums slightly differently. Peter Rodman calculated that Western Europe's "combined defense budgets add up to two-thirds of the Pentagon's [but] yield less than a quarter of America's deployable fighting forces." Rodman, "Fallout from Kosovo," *Foreign Affairs*, vol. 78, no. 4 (July/August 1999), pp. 45–51.

28. See "'Europa braucht einen militärischen Führungsstab,'" *Frankfurter Allgemeine Zeitung*, June 18, 1999.

29. For one of the clearest statements of this view, see UN secretary-general Kofi Annan's acceptance speech on receiving the Nobel Peace Prize on December 11, 2001, available on the *New York Times* website at (www. nytimes.com). For a brief comparison of this shift with revisions of international law to combat piracy and the slave trade in the Enlightenment era, see Shlomo Avineri, "Israelis and Palestinians on the Morning After," *Transatlantic Internationale Politik*, vol. 2, no. 4, pp. 41-46.

30. Interview, June 1999.

31. For an exploration of the U.S.-European issues that must be solved in setting up the EU rapid reaction force and pursuing the Common European Security and Defense Policy, see Robert Hunter, *The European Security and Defense Policy: NATO's Companion—or Competitor? An American Perspective*, DRR-2622-ESDI (Washington: RAND, 2002).

32. For a summary of the dilemmas in forming a common European defense community prior to the Kosovo war, see Kori Schake, Amaya Bloch-Laine, and Charles Grant, "Building a European Defence Capability," *Survival*, vol. 41, no. 1 (Spring 1999), pp. 20–40.

33. Karl Feldmeyer, "Eine neue Ratlosigkeit," and "Scharping stärkt Krisenkräfte für das Kosovo," *Frankfurter Allgemeine Zeitung*, June 25, 1999, and July 1, 1999.

34. Interview, December 2001.

35. Elke Bohl, "Zurück zum Ius commune," *Frankfurter Allgemeine Zeitung*, December 28, 2001, p. 13.

36. James Blitz, "Italy falls into line with EU plans for common arrest," *Financial Times*, December 12, 2001, p. 1; "Curbing Crime—and Sovereignty," *Economist*, December 15, 2001, p. 28; James Blitz, "Europe's broker," *Financial Times*, January 18, 2002, p. 10.

37. Interview, December 2001.

38. Christian-Peter Hanelt and Felix Neugart, "Euro-Med Partnership,"*Transatlantic Internationale Politik*, vol. 2, no. 4 (2001), pp. 79–82.

39. For one expression of a chronic American aversion to any meddling by the EU in Israeli issues, see William Safire, "Sharon in Moscow," *New York Times*, September 6, 2001, carried in David Johnson List #5428, September 6, 2001.

40. Shlomo Shpiro, "German-Israeli Strategic Partnership," *Transatlantic Internationale Politik*, vol. 1, no. 4 (Winter 2000), pp. 81–85; Lily Gardner Feldman, *The Special Relationship between West Germany and Israel* (Boston: George Allen & Unwin, 1986).

41. Roy H. Ginsberg, *The European Union in International Politics* (Lanham, Md.: Rowman and Littlefield, 2001).

42. Ahto Lobjakas, "Russia: Analysts Ponder Integration into Euro-Atlantic Community," Radio Free Europe/Radio Liberty report carried in David Johnson's CDI Russia Weekly #189, January 18, 2002. See also Dmitri Trenin,

The End of Eurasia: Russia on the Border between Geopolitics and Globalization (Washington: Carnegie Endowment, 2002).

43. David C. Gompert, "The EU on the World Stage," *Transatlantic Internationale Politik*, vol. 3, no. 2 (Summer 2002).

44. Richard Wolffe, "US ready to abide by WTO tax-break ruling," *Financial Times*, January 26, 2002, p. 4; Jagdish Bhagwati, "Trade: the unwinnable war," *Financial Times*, January 29, 2002, p. 13.

45. See George A. Bermann, "Transatlantic Regulatory Cooperation," paper presented at the biennial European Community Studies Association conference, Madison, Wis., May 31–June 2, 2001.

46. Heisbourg, "Europe and the Transformation of the World Order," p. 145.

47. Gompert, "The EU on the World Stage."

48. For the evolution of the Enlightenment notion that peace is achievable, see Michael Howard, *The Invention of Peace* (Yale University Press, 2001). For the virtues of a "civilian," as distinct from a military, power, see Hanns Maull, "Germany and Japan: The New Civilian Powers," *Foreign Affairs*, vol. 69, no. 5 (1990/91).

49. Robert Cooper, *The Post-Modern State and the World Order* (London: Demos, 1996), p. 8. Jessica T. Mathews draws the same contrast to reach the related conclusion that power is now seeping away from states to nongovernmental organizations. She notes, "The absolutes of the Westphalian system—territorially fixed states where everything of value lies within some state's borders; a single, secular authority governing each territory and representing it outside its borders; and no authority above states—are all dissolving." Matthews, "Power Shift," *Foreign Affairs*, vol. 76, no. 1 (January/February 1997), p. 50.

50. For much gloomier interpretations of present-day Europe, see Mark Mazower, *The Dark Continent: Europe's Twentieth Century* (Harmondsworth: Penguin, 1998); Vladimir Tismaneanu, *Fantasies of Salvation: Democracy, Nationalism, and Myth in Post-Communist Europe* (Princeton University Press, 1998); and Christian Graf von Krockow, *Der deutsche Niedergang* (Stuttgart: Deutsche Verlags-Anstalt, 1998).

51. Cooper, *The Post-Modern State*, p. 33.

52. Helmut Schmidt, "Einer fur alle," *Die Zeit*, November 15, 2001, pp. 23ff.

53. See Brannon P. Denning and Jack H. McCall, "States' Rights and Foreign Policy," *Foreign Affairs*, vol. 79, no. 1 (January/February 2000), pp. 9–15.

54. This missive was received by Hubertus von Morr, German consul in Texas in the mid-1980s.

55. Jessica T. Mathews, "Strained Partners," *Foreign Policy*, no. 127 (November/December 2001), pp. 48–53.

56. Ibid.

57. Karsten D. Voigt, "The Labor Pains of a New Atlanticism," *Transatlantic Internationale Politik*, vol. 1, no. 1 (Spring 2000), pp. 3–10.

Chapter Ten

1. Peter Norman and Ralph Atkins, "Schröder proposes alliance to cut German joblessness," and "Germany's modernizer," *Financial Times*, May 11, 1998, pp. 1 and 14.

2. On lobbying by the estimated 13,000 "interest representatives" already in place in Brussels, see Helen Wallace and William Wallace, *Policy-Making in the European Union* (Oxford University Press, 1996); Sonia Mazey and Jeremy Richardson, eds., *Lobbying in the European Community* (Oxford University Press, 1993); Helen Wallace and Alasdair Young, eds., *Participation and Policy-Making in the European Union* (Oxford: Clarendon, 1997); Justin Greenwood and Mark Aspinwall, eds., *Collective Action in the European Union: Interests and the New Politics of Associability* (London: Routledge, 1998); Justin Greenwood, *Representing Interests in the European Union* (Basingstoke: Macmillan, 1997); Claus Schnabel and Rüdiger Tiedemann, "Brüsseler Spitzen—gefragt wie nie," *Frankfurter Allgemeine Zeitung*, February 11, 1995, p. 13; Lionel Barber, "Lobbyists in search of a fast Ecu," *Financial Times*, January 27, 1997, p. 8; R. Pedler and M. C. P. M. van Schendelen, eds., *Lobbying the European Union* (Aldershot: Dartmouth, 1994); H. Randall, ed., *Business Guide to Lobbying in the EU* (London: Cartermill, 1996); and "The Brussels Lobbyist and the Struggle for Ear-Time," *Economist*, August 15, 1998, p. 25.

3. European Commission, "Agenda 2000: Überblick über die Legislativvorschläge der Europäischen Kommission," March 19, 1998.

4. Martin Wolf, "Union that defies modern taboos," *Financial Times*, "The Birth of the Euro" special section, April 30, 1998, p. 3.

Suggestions for Further Reading

Books

Acheson, Dean. *Present at the Creation*. Reprint, W. W. Norton, 1987.

Ackrill, Robert. *The Common Agricultural Policy*. Sheffield: Sheffield Academic Press, 2000.

Anderson, Benedict. *Imagined Communities*. London: Verso, 1991.

Arbatov, Alexei G., Karl Kaider, and Robert Legvold. *Russia and the West: The 21st Century Security Environment*. Armonk, N.Y.: M. E. Sharpe, 1999.

Åslund, Anders. *Building Capitalism: The Transformation of the Former Soviet Bloc*. Oxford University Press, 2001.

———. *How Russia Became a Market Economy*. Brookings, 1995.

Åslund, Anders, and Georges de Menil, eds. *Economic Reform in Ukraine: The Unfinished Agenda*. Armonk: N.Y.: M. E. Sharpe, 2000.

Bail, Christoper, Wolfgang H. Reinicke, and Reinhardt Rummel, eds. *EU-US Relations: Balancing the Partnership*. Baden-Baden: Nomos, 1997.

Baldwin, Richard E. *Towards an Integrated Europe*. London: Center for Economic Policy Research, 1994.

Bark, Dennis L., ed. *Reflections on Europe*. Stanford, Calif.: Hoover Institution Press, 1997.

Begg, Iain, and Nigel Grimwade. *Paying for Europe*. Sheffield: Sheffield Academic Press, 1998.

Ben-Sasson, H. H., ed. *A History of the Jewish People*. English trans. Harvard University Press, 1976.

Bertram, Christoph. *Europe in the Balance*. Washington: Carnegie Endowment for International Peace, 1995.

Bettzuege, Reinhard, ed. *Aussenpolitik der Bundesrepublik Deutschland. Dokumente von 1949 bis 1994.* Bonn: German Foreign Ministry, 1995.

Bideleux, Robert, and Ian Jeffries. *A History of Eastern Europe: Crisis and Change.* London: Routledge, 1998.

Bingen, Dieter. *Die Polenpolitik der Bonner Republik von Adenauer bis Kohl 1949–1991.* Baden-Baden: Nomos, 1998.

Black, Stanley W., ed. *Europe's Economy Looks East: Implications for Germany and the European Union.* Cambridge University Press, 1997.

Brown, J. F., and others, eds. *Western Approaches to Eastern Europe.* New York: Council on Foreign Relations, 1992.

Brown, Michael, and others, eds. *Nationalism and Ethnic Conflict.* MIT Press, 1997.

Brzezinski, Mark. *The Struggle for Constitutionalism in Poland.* St. Martin's, 1997.

Brzezinski, Zbigniew. *The Grand Chessboard.* Basic Books, 1997.

Buchan, David. *Europe: The Strange Superpower.* Aldershot: Dartmouth, 1993.

Bukkvoll, Tor. *Ukraine and European Security.* London: Pinter for Royal Institute of International Affairs, 1997.

Bulmer, Simon, and William Paterson. *The Federal Republic of Germany and the European Community.* London: Allen and Unwin, 1987.

Bunce, Valerie. *Subversive Institutions: The Design and the Destruction of Socialism and the State.* Cambridge University Press, 1999.

Bundesinstitut für ostwissenschaftliche und internationale Studien. *Aufbruch im Osten Europas. Jahrbuch 1992/93.* Munich: Carl Hanser, 1993.

Calleo, David P. *Beyond American Hegemony.* Basic Books, 1987.

———. *Rethinking Europe's Future.* Princeton University Press, 2001.

Calleo, David P., and Eric R. Staal, eds. *Europe's Franco-German Engine.* Brookings, 1998.

Centre d'Information et de Recherche sur l'Allemagne Contemporaine (Paris), Deutsche Gesellschaft für Auswärtige Politik, and others. *Handeln für Europa. Deutsch-französische Zusammenarbeit in einer veränderten Welt.* Opladen: Leske + Budrich, 1995.

Christiansen, Thomas, and Emil Kirchner, eds. *Europe in Change: Committee Governance in the European Union.* Manchester University Press, 2000.

Chryssochoou, Dimitris N., *Democracy in the European Union.* London: I. B. Tauris, 2000.

Clark, Bruce. *An Empire's New Clothes.* London: Vintage, 1995.

Clark, Wesley K. *Waging Modern War.* New York: Public Affairs, 2001.

Clough, Patricia. *Helmut Kohl.* Munich: Deutscher Taschenbuch Verlag, 1998.

Colchester, Nicholas, and David Buchan. *Europower.* Times Books, 1990.

Connolly, Bernard. *The Rotten Heart of Europe.* London: Faber and Faber, 1995.

Cooper, Andrew, ed. *Niche Diplomacy: Middle Powers after the Cold War.* Basingstoke: Macmillan, 1997.

Cooper, Robert. *The Post-Modern State and the World Order.* London: Demos, 1996.

Cornish, Paul. *Partnership in Crisis: The US, Europe and the Fall and Rise of NATO.* London: Pinter for Royal Institute of International Affairs, 1997.

Coulson, Andrew, ed. *Local Government in Eastern Europe.* London: Edward Elgar, 1995.

Cowles, Maria Green, James Caporaso, and Thomas Risse, eds. *Transforming Europe.* Cornell University Press, 2001.

Cox, Michael, Adrian Guelke, and Fiona Stephen, eds. *A Farewell to Arms?* Manchester University Press, 2000.

Crampton, R. J. *Eastern Europe in the Twentieth Century.* London: Routledge, 1994.

Crouch, Colin, ed. *After the Euro.* Oxford University Press, 2000.

Dahl, Robert. *Democracy and Its Critics.* Yale University Press, 1989.

———. *On Democracy.* Yale University Press, 1999.

Dawisha, Karen, and Bruce Parrott, eds. *The Consolidation of Democracy in East-Central Europe.* Cambridge University Press, 1997.

———. *Democratic Changes and Authoritarian Reactions in Russia, Ukraine, Belarus, and Moldova.* Cambridge University Press, 1997.

Deutsche Bundesbank. *The Monetary Policy of the Bundesbank.* Frankfurt: Deutsche Bundesbank, March 1994.

Diamond, Larry, and Marc F. Plattner, eds. *Capitalism, Socialism, and Democracy Revisited.* Johns Hopkins University Press, 1993.

Dinan, Desmond, ed. *Encyclopedia of the European Union.* Boulder, Colo.: Lynne Rienner, 2000.

Domanski, Henryk. *On the Verge of Convergence.* Budapest: Central European University Press, 2000.

Doyle, Michael. *Ways of War and Peace.* W. W. Norton, 1997.

Dreher, Klaus. *Helmut Kohl.* Stuttgart: Deutsche Verlags-Anstalt, 1998.

Dunay, Pal, and others., eds. *New Forms of Security.* Aldershot: Dartmouth, 1995.

Dyson, Kenneth, ed. *The European State in the Euro-Zone.* Oxford University Press, 2001.

———. *The Politics of the Euro-Zone.* Oxford University Press, 2000.

Eberwein, Wolf-Dieter, and Karl Kaiser, eds. *Germany's New Foreign Policy.* Houndmills: Palgrave, 2001.

Eichengreen, Barry. *European Monetary Union: Theory, Practice, and Analysis.* MIT Press, 1997.

———, ed. *Transatlantic Economic Relations in the Post-Cold War Era.* New York: Council on Foreign Relations, 1998.

Emerson, Michael. *Redrawing the Map of Europe*. Basingstoke: Macmillan, 1998.

European Commission. *Agenda 2000: For a Stronger and Wider Union*. Brussels: European Commission, 1997.

Falk, Richard, and Tamas Szentes, eds. *A New Europe in the Changing Global System*. United Nations University Press, 1997.

Feldman, Lily Gardner, ed. *Cooperation or Competition? American, European Union, and German Politics in the Balkans*. Washington: American Institute for Contemporary German Studies, 2001.

Freudenstein, Roland, ed. *VII. Deutsch-Polnisches Forum: Deutschland und Polen im veränderten Europa*. Bonn: Europa Union Verlag for the German Society for Foreign Policy, June 1993.

Friend, Julius. *The Linchpin: French-German Relations, 1950–1990*. New York: Praeger, 1991.

Fukuyama, Francis. *The End of History and the Last Man*. Free Press, 1992.

———. *Trust*. Free Press, 1995.

Fullbrook, Mary, ed. *National Histories and European History*. UCL Press (University College, London), 1993.

Gärtner, Heinz, Adrian Hyde-Price, and Erich Reiter, eds. *Europe's New Security Challenges*. Boulder, Colo.: Lynne Rienner, 2001.

Garnett, Sherman. *Keystone in the Arch*. Washington: Carnegie Endowment for International Peace, 1996.

Garton Ash, Timothy. *History of the Present*. New York: Penguin, 1999.

Gellner, Ernest. *Conditions of Liberty: Civil Society and Its Rivals*. New York: Penguin, 1994.

———. *Nationalism*. NYU Press, 1997.

Genscher, Hans-Dietrich. *Erinnerungen*. Berlin: Siedler, 1995.

Gill, Graeme, *The Dynamics of Democratization*. St. Martin's, 2000.

Ginsberg, Roy. *The European Union in World Politics: Baptism of Fire*. Lanham, Md.: Rowman and Littlefield, 2001.

Goldgeier, James. *Not Whether but When: The U.S. Decision to Enlarge NATO*. Brookings, 1999.

Gompert, David C., Richard L. Kugler, and Martin C. Libicki. *Mind the Gap*. National Defense University, 1999.

Gompert, David C., and F. Stephen Larrabee, eds. *America and Europe: A Partnership for a New Era*. Cambridge University Press, 1997.

Goodby, James E. *Europe Undivided: The New Logic of Peace in U.S.-Russian Relations*. Washington: U.S. Institute of Peace Press, 1998.

Gordon, Philip. *NATO's Transformation*. Lanham, Md.: Rowman and Littlefield, 1997.

Grabbe, Heather, and Kirsty Hughes. *Enlarging the EU Eastwards: Prospects and Challenges*. London: Pinter for Royal Institute of International Affairs, 1998.

Granville, Brigitte, and Peter Oppenheimer, eds. *Russia's Post-Communist Economy.* Oxford University Press, 2001.

De Grauwe, Paul. *The Economics of Monetary Integration.* Oxford University Press, 1997.

Greenwood, Justin. *Representing Interests in the European Union.* Basingstoke: Macmillan, 1997.

Greenwood, Justin, and Mark Aspenwill, eds. *Collective Action in the European Union.* London: Routledge, 1998.

Haass, Richard N. *The Reluctant Sheriff: The United States after the Cold War.* New York: Council on Foreign Relations, 1997.

Hardt, John P., and others, eds. *Parliamentary Responsibility for Economic Transition in Central and Eastern Europe.* Government Printing Office for Congressional Research Service, rev. ed., 1996.

Hausner, Jerzy, and Grzegorz Mosur, eds. *Transformation Processes in Eastern Europe: Western Perspectives and the Polish Experience.* Krakow: Polish Academy of Sciences and Friedrich Ebert Stiftung, 1993.

Hayes-Renshaw, Fiona, and Helen Wallace. *The Council of Ministers.* St. Martin's, 1997.

Henning, C. Randall, and Pier Carlo Padoan, *Transatlantic Perspectives on the Euro.* Brookings, 2000.

Heuser, Beatrice. *Transatlantic Relations.* London: Pinter for Royal Institute of International Affairs, 1995.

Hill, Christopher, ed. *National Foreign Policies and European Political Cooperation.* London: Allen and Unwin, 1983.

Hoffman, Eva. *Shtetl.* Boston: Houghton Mifflin, 1999.

Holbrooke, Richard. *To End a War.* Random House, 1998.

Howard, A. E. Dick, ed. *Constitution Making in Eastern Europe.* Washington: Woodrow Wilson Center Press, 1993.

Howard, Michael. *The Invention of Peace.* Yale University Press, 2001.

Hrbek, Rudolf, and others, eds. *Die Europäische Union als Prozess.* Bonn: Europa Union Verlag, 1998.

Hunter, Robert. *The European Security and Defense Policy: NATO's Companion—or Competitor? An American Perspective.* DRR-2622-ESDI. Washington: RAND, 2002.

Huntington, Samuel. *The Third Wave.* University of Oklahoma Press, 1991.

Hutchings, Robert L. *American Diplomacy and the End of the Cold War.* Washington: Woodrow Wilson Center Press, 1997.

Ignatieff, Michael. *Blood and Belonging.* London: BBC Books, 1994.

———. *Virtual War: Kosovo and Beyond.* Henry Holt, 2000.

Ingersent, Ken A., and A. J. Rayner, *Agricultural Policy in Western Europe and the United States.* Cheltenham: Edward Elgar, 1999.

Ingersent, Ken A., A. J. Rayner, and Robert C. Hine, eds. *The Reform of the Common Agricultural Policy.* Basingstoke: Macmillan, 1998.

Johnson, Simon, and others. *Starting Over in Eastern Europe: Entrepreneurship and Economic Renewal.* Harvard Business School Press, 1995.

Jopp, Mathias, Andreas Maurer, and Otto Schmuck, eds. *Die Europäische Union nach Amsterdam.* Bonn: Europa Union Verlag, 1998.

Judt, Tony. *A Grand Illusion? An Essay on Europe.* Hill and Wang, 1996.

Karp, Regina Cowen, ed. *Central and Eastern Europe.* Oxford University Press for SIPRI, 1994.

Kennedy, Ellen. *The Bundesbank: Germany's Central Bank in the International Monetary System.* New York: Council on Foreign Relations Press, 1991.

Keohane, Robert O., and Stanley Hoffmann. *The New European Community.* Boulder, Colo.: Westview, 1991.

Kohl, Helmut, with Kai Diekmann and Ralf Georg Reuth. *Ich wollte Deutschlands Einheit.* Berlin: Propyläen, 1996.

Kolboom, Ingo, and Ernst Weisenfeld, eds. *Frankreich in Europa.* Bonn: Europa Union Verlag for the German Society for Foreign Policy, 1993.

Kolodko, Grzegorz. *From Shock to Therapy.* Oxford University Press, 1999.

Kornai, Janos. *The Road to a Free Economy.* W. W. Norton, 1991.

Küsters, Hanns Jürgen, and Daniel Hofmann, eds. *Deutsche Einheit: Sonderedition aus den Akten des Bundeskanzleramtes 1989/90. Dokumente zur Deutschlandpolitik.* Munich: R. Oldenbourg, 1998.

Kuzio, Taras. *Ukraine under Kuchma: Political Reform, Economic Transformation and Security Policy in Independent Ukraine.* Basingstoke: Macmillan, 1997.

Larres, Klaus, and Torsten Oppelland. *Deutschland und die USA im 20. Jahrhundert: Geschichte der politischen Beziehungen.* Darmstadt: Wissenschaftliche Buchgesellschaft, 1997.

Larrabee, F. Stephen. *East European Security after the Cold War.* Santa Monica, Calif.: RAND, 1993.

Läufer, Thomas, ed. *EG-Polen-Ungarn: Die Vertragstexte von Maastricht und die Europa-Abkommen.* Bonn: Europa Union Verlag, 1993.

Leonard, Dick. *Guide to the European Union.* London: Economist, 1994, 1998.

Lieven, Anatol. *Chechnya: Tombstone of Russian Power.* Yale University Press, 1998.

Lieven, Dominic. *Empire.* Yale University Press, 2000.

Linz, Juan J., and Alfred Stepan. *Problems of Democratic Transition and Consolidation: Southern Europe, South America, and Post-Communist Europe.* Johns Hopkins University Press, 1996.

Lippert, Barbara, and Peter Becker, eds. *Towards EU-Membership.* Bonn: Europa Union Verlag, 1998.

Ludwig, Michael. *Polen und die deutsche Frage.* Bonn: Europa Union Verlag for the German Society for Foreign Policy, December 1990.

Lundestad, Geir. *"Empire by Integration": The United States and European Integration, 1945–1997.* Oxford University Press.

Malcolm, Noel. *Kosovo: A Short History.* Basingstoke: Macmillan, 1998.

Mandelbaum, Michael. *The Dawn of Peace in Europe.* New York: Twentieth Century Fund, 1996.

Marsh, David. *Germany and Europe: The Crisis of Unity.* London: William Heinemann, 1994.

Masson, Paul R., Thomas H. Krueger, and Bart Turtelboom, eds. *EMU and the International Monetary System.* Washington: International Monetary Fund, 1997.

Mayhew, Alan. *Recreating Europe: The European Union's Policy toward Central and Eastern Europe.* Cambridge University Press, 1998.

Mazey, Sonia, and Jeremy Richardson, eds. *Lobbying in the European Community.* Oxford University Press, 1993.

McAuley, Mary. *Russia's Politics of Uncertainty.* Cambridge University Press, 1997.

McCarthy, Patrick, ed. *France-Germany 1983–1993.* St. Martin's, 1993.

McFaul, Michael. *Russia's Unfinished Revolution.* Cornell University Press, 2001.

McGuire, Steven. *Airbus Industrie: Conflict and Cooperation in US-EC Trade Relations.* Basingstoke: Macmillan, 1997.

McNamara, Kathleen R. *The Currency of Ideas: Monetary Politics in the European Union.* Cornell University Press, 1998.

Miall, Hugh. *Shaping the New Europe.* London: Pinter for Royal Institute of International Affairs, 1994.

Michalski, Anna, and Helen Wallace. *The European Community: The Challenge of Enlargement.* London: Royal Institute of International Affairs, 1992.

Michta, Andrew A. *The Soldier-Citizen.* St. Martin's, 1997.

Milward, Alan S. *The European Rescue of the Nation-State.* London: Routledge, 2d ed., 2000.

Moravcsik, Andrew. *The Choice for Europe.* Cornell University Press, 1998.

———, ed. *Centralization or Fragmentation?* New York: Council on Foreign Relations, 1998.

Moser, Peter, Gerald Schneider, and Gebhard Kirchgässner, eds. *Decision Rules in the European Union.* Houndmills: Macmillan, 2000.

Müllerson, Rein. *International Law, Rights and Politics.* London: Routledge, 1994.

Muravchik, Joshua. *Exporting Democracy.* Washington: American Enterprise Institute, 1991.

Nelson, Joan M., ed. *A Precarious Balance: Democracy and Economic Reforms in Eastern Europe*, vol. 1. San Francisco: Institute for Contemporary Studies and others, 1994.

Neunreither, Karlheinz, and Antje Wiener, eds. *European Integration after Amsterdam.* Oxford University Press, 2000.

Newhouse, John. *Europe Adrift.* Pantheon, 1997.

Niblett, Robin, and William Wallace, eds. *Rethinking European Order.* Houndmills: Palgrave, 2001.

Nicolaïdis, Kalypso, and Robert Howse, eds. *The Federal Vision: Legitimacy and Levels of Governance in the US and EU.* Oxford University Press, 2001.

Nye, Joseph S., Jr. *The Paradox of American Power.* Oxford University Press, 2002.

O'Donnell, Guillermo, Philippe C. Schmitter, and Laurence Whitehead. *Transitions from Authoritarian Rule.* Johns Hopkins University Press, 1986.

O'Donnell, R., ed. *Europe: The Irish Experience.* Dublin: Institute for European Affairs, 2000.

van Oudenaren, John. *Unifying Europe.* Lanham, Md.: Rowman and Littlefield, 2000.

Di Palma, Giuseppe. *To Craft Democracies.* University of California Press, 1990.

Pedler, R., and M. C. P. M. van Schendelen, eds. *Lobbying the European Union.* Aldershot: Dartmouth, 1994.

Peterson, John, and Helene Sjursen, eds. *A Common Foreign Policy for Europe?* London: Routledge, 1998.

Piening, Christopher. *Global Europe: The European Union in World Affairs.* Boulder, Colo.: Lynne Rienner, 1997.

Pinder, John. *The European Community and Eastern Europe.* New York: Council on Foreign Relations for the Royal Institute of International Affairs, 1991.

———. *The European Union: A Very Short Introduction.* Oxford University Press, 2001.

Polish Academy of Sciences. *Political Consciousness and Civic Education during the Transformation of the System.* Warsaw, 1994.

Polonsky, Antony, ed. *POLIN: Studies in Polish Jewry,* vol. 13. London/ Portland: Littman Library of Jewish Civilization, 2000. Focuses on the Holocaust and its aftermath.

Pond, Elizabeth. *Beyond the Wall: Germany's Road to Unification.* Brookings, 1993.

Poznanski, Kazimierz Z. *Poland's Protracted Transition: Institutional Change and Economic Growth 1970–1994.* Cambridge University Press, 1996.

Pridham, Geoffrey, and Tatu Vanhanen, eds. *Democratization in Eastern Europe.* London: Routledge, 1994.

Prizel, Ilya. *National Identity and Foreign Policy: Nationalism and Leadership in Poland, Russia and Ukraine.* Cambridge University Press, 1998.

Przeworski, Adam. *Democracy and the Market: Political and Economic Reforms in Eastern Europe and Latin America.* Cambridge University Press, 1991.

———. *Sustainable Democracy.* Cambridge University Press, 1995.

Putnam, Robert D. *Bowling Alone: The Collapse and Revival of American Community.* Simon and Schuster, 2000.

Randall, H., ed. *Business Guide to Lobbying in the EU.* London: Cartermill, 1996.

Regelsberger, Elfriede, and others, eds. *Foreign Policy of the European Union: From EPC to CFSP and Beyond.* Boulder, Colo.: Lynne Rienner, 1997.

Rohde, David. *Endgame: The Betrayal and Fall of Srebrenica.* Farrar Straus and Giroux, 1997.

Rouget, Werner. *Schwierige Nachbarschaft am Rhein.* Bonn: Bouvier, 1998.

Rueschemeyer, Dietrich, Marilyn Rueschemeyer, and Bjorn Wittrock, eds. *Participation and Democracy East and West: Comparison and Interpretations.* Armonk: M. E. Sharpe, 1998.

Sbragia, Alberta M., ed. *Euro-Politics.* Brookings, 1992.

Schmitter, Philippe C., *How to Democratize the European Union . . . and Why Bother?* Lanham, Md.: Rowman and Littlefield, 2000.

Schoenbaum, David, and Elizabeth Pond. *The German Question and Other German Questions.* London/New York: Macmillan/St. Martin's, 1996.

Schönfelder, Wilhelm, and Elke Thiel. *Ein Markt—eine Währung.* Baden-Baden: Nomos, 1996.

Schöpflin, George. *Politics in Eastern Europe 1945–1992.* Oxford: Blackwell, 1993.

Schumpeter, Joseph A. *Capitalism, Socialism, and Democracy.* 1942; reprint, London: Allen and Unwin, 1976.

Serfaty, Simon. *Taking Europe Seriously.* St. Martin's, 1992.

———. *Memories of Europe's Future: Farewell to Yesteryear.* Washington: Center for Strategic and International Studies, 1999.

Shaw, Josephine. *The Law of the European Union.* Basingstoke: Macmillan, 1996.

Shore, Cris. *Building Europe.* London: Routledge, 2000.

Siedenberg, Axel, and Lutz Hoffman, eds. *Ukraine at the Crossroads: Economic Reforms in International Perspective.* Heidelberg: Springer, 1998.

Siedentop, Larry. *Democracy in Europe.* London: Penguin, 2000.

Silber, Laura, and Allan Little. *Yugoslavia: Death of a Nation.* New York: TV Books/Penguin, 1995, 1996.

Simon, Jeffrey. *Central European Civil-Military Relations and NATO Expansion.* McNair Paper 39. Washington: National Defense University, April 1995.

Sloan, Stanley. *NATO, the European Union and the Atlantic Community: The Transatlantic Bargain Reconsidered.* Lanham, Md.: Rowman and Littlefield, 2002.

Smith, Bruce L. R., and Gennady M. Danilenko, eds. *Law and Democracy in the New Russia.* Brookings, 1993.

deSoto, Hernando. *The Mystery of Capital: Why Capitalism Triumphs in the West and Fails Everywhere Else.* London: Bantam, 2000.

Stent, Angela E. *Russia and Germany Reborn: Unification, the Soviet Collapse, and the New Europe.* Princeton University Press, 1999.

Taylor, Paul. *The European Union in the 1990s.* Oxford University Press, 1996.

Thomas, William I., and Florian Znaniecki. *The Polish Peasant in Europe and America*, ed. Eli Zaretsky. 1918; University of Illinois Press, 1996.

Thurow, Lester. *Head to Head.* New York: Warner Books, 1992.

Tismaneanu, Vladimir. *Fantasies of Salvation.* Princeton University Press, 1998.

Trenin, Dmitri. *The End of Eurasia.* Washington: Carnegie Endowment for International Peace, 2002.

Turner, Adair. *Just Capital: The Liberal Ecomomy.* Basingstoke: Macmillan, 2001.

Ullman, Richard H. *Securing Europe.* Princeton University Press, 1991.

Varese, Federico. *The Russian Mafia.* Oxford University Press, 2001.

Wallace, Helen, and William Wallace. *Policy-Making in the European Union,* 3d ed. Oxford University Press, 1996.

Wallace, Helen, and Alasdair Young. *Participation and Policy-Making in the European Union.* Oxford: Clarendon, 1997.

Wallace, William. *Regional Integration: The West European Experience.* Brookings, 1994.

Walzer, Michael, ed. *Toward a Global Civil Society.* Providence: Berghahn for the Friedrich-Ebert-Stiftung, 1995.

Weidenfeld, Werner, ed. *Europa-Handbuch.* Gütersloh: Bertelsmann Foundation, 1999.

Weidenfeld, Werner, and Wolfgang Wessels, eds. *Jahrbuch der Europäischen Integration 1997–98.* Bonn: Institut für Europäische Politik, 1998.

Weiler, J. H. H. *The Constitution of Europe.* Cambridge University Press, 1999.

White, Stephen, Alex Pravda, and Zvi Gitelman, eds. *Developments in Russian Politics 5.* Duke University Press, 2001.

Wilson, Andrew. *Ukrainian Nationalism in the 1990s.* Cambridge University Press, 1996.

Woodward, Susan L. *Balkan Tragedy: Chaos and Dissolution after the Cold War.* Brookings, 1995.

World Bank. *Transition, the First Ten Years.* Washington, 2002.

Yost, David. *NATO Transformed: The Alliance's New Roles in International Security.* Washington: U.S. Institute of Peace Press, 1999.

Young, Alasdair R., and Helen Wallace. *Regulatory Politics in the Enlarging European Union.* Manchester University Press, 2000.

Young, Thomas-Durell, ed. *Command in NATO after the Cold War: Alliance, National, and Multinational Considerations.* Carlisle Barracks, Pa.: U.S. Army War College, 1997.

Zelikow, Philip, and Condoleezza Rice. *Germany Unified and Europe Transformed*. Harvard University Press, 1997.

Zimmermann, Warren. *Origins of a Catastrophe*. Times Books, 1996.

Articles and Papers

For the purposes of this book, the *Financial Times*, with its superb coverage of European issues, served as the newspaper of record. Except for some special sections, articles from dailies and weeklies cited in footnotes are too numerous to list here.

Allen, David. "Institutional tensions in the CFSP/CESDP: Brusselsisation and Transgovernmentalism." Paper presented at the biennial meeting of the European Community Studies Association (hereafter ECSA), Madison, Wis., May 31–June 2, 2001.

Andreani, Gilles, Christoph Bertram, and Charles Grant. "Europe's Military Revolution." London: Center for European Reform, 2001.

Andrews, David M. "History as Destiny: The Committee of Governors and the Origins of EMU." Paper presented at the annual meeting of the American Political Science Association, September 2–5, 1999.

Andrews, John. "The European Union: Family frictions." Survey. *Economist*, October 22, 1994.

Audretsch, David B., and others. "The New Economy in Germany and the United States: Policy Challenges and Solutions." New Economy Study. Washington: American Institute for Contemporary German Studies, January 2002.

Bennett, Christopher. "Aiding America." *NATO Review*, vol. 49 (Winter 2001/2002), pp. 6ff.

Bermann, George A. "Transatlantic Regulatory Cooperation." Paper presented at ECSA, Madison, Wis., May 31–June 2, 2001.

Bieber, Roland. "Zur Kompetenzabgrenzung der Europäischen Union." *Integration*, vol. 24, no. 3 (July 2001), pp. 308–13.

Biukovic, Ljiljana. "Extending the Reach of EU Law to Non-Member States." Paper presented at ECSA, Madison, Wis., May 31–June 2, 2001.

Börzel, Tanja. "Pace-Setting, Foot-Dragging, and Fence-Sitting: Member State Responses to Europeanization." Paper presented at ECSA, Madison, Wis., May 31–June 2, 2001.

Broder, Henryk. "Unser Kampf." *Der Spiegel*, April 29, 1991, pp. 255–67.

Brusis, Martin. "Between Eligibility Requirements, Competitive Politics and National Traditions: Recreating Regions in the Accession Countries of Central and Eastern Europe." Paper presented at ECSA, Madison, Wis., May 31–June 2, 2001.

Bulmer, Simon. "Policy Transfer in the European Union: An Institutionalist Perspective," paper at ECSA, Madison, Wis., May 31–June 2, 2001.

Chalmers, Malcolm. "The Atlantic Burden-Sharing Debate—Widening or Fragmenting?" *International Affairs*, vol. 77, no. 3 (July 2001), pp. 569–85.

Christian Democratic Union/Christian Social Union Bundestag Caucus. "Reflections on European Policy." September 1, 1994. The "Lamers paper."

Collingnon, Stefan, and Susanne Mundschenk. "Die internationale Bedeutung der Währungsunion." *Integration*, vol. 21, no. 2 (April 1998), pp. 77–85.

Croft, Stuart, Jolyon Howorth, Terry Terriff, and Mark Webber. "NATO's Triple Challenge." *International Affairs*, vol. 76, no. 3 (July 2000), pp. 495–518.

Danderstädt, Michael. "EU-Osterweiterung: Wirkungen, Erwartungen und Interessen in den Beitrittsländern." *Integration*, vol. 21, no. 3 (July 1998).

Dornbusch, Rudi. "Euro Fantasies." *Foreign Affairs*, vol. 75, no. 5 (September/October 1996), pp. 110–24.

Economist. "From here to EMU." October 23, 1993, pp. 29ff.

Feldstein, Martin. "EMU and International Conflict." *Foreign Affairs*, vol. 76, no. 6 (November/December 1997), pp. 60–73.

Freudenstein, Roland. "Poland, Germany and the EU." *International Affairs*, vol. 74, no. 1 (January 1998), pp. 41–54.

Gaddy, Clifford G., and Barry W. Ickes. "Beyond a Bailout: Time to Face Reality about Russia's 'Virtual Economy.'" Brookings, 1998 (www.brookings.edu/fp/w-papers/gaddy/gaddick1.htm).

Garton Ash, Timothy. "Europe's Endangered Liberal Order." *Foreign Affairs*, vol. 77, no. 2 (March/April 1998), pp. 51–65.

———. "Is Britain European?" *International Affairs*, vol. 77, no. 1 (January 2001), pp. 1–13.

Goldgeier, James. "NATO Enlargement: Anatomy of a Decision." *Washington Quarterly*, vol. 21, no. 1 (Winter 1998), pp. 85–102.

Glenn, John K. "European Enlargement and the Transformation of the Nation-State." Paper presented at ECSA, Madison, Wis., May 31–June 2, 2001.

Gompert, David C., François Heisbourg, and Alexei G. Arbatov. "The Day After: An Assessment." *Survival*, vol. 43, no. 4 (Winter 2001–02), pp. 137–154.

Gomulka, Stanislaw. "Economic and Political Constraints during Transition." *Europe-Asia Studies*, vol. 46, no. 1 (1994), pp. 83–106.

Gordon, Philip H. "The Transatlantic Allies and the Changing Middle East." Adelphi Paper 322. London: International Institute for Strategic Studies, 1998.

———. "Europe's Uncommon Foreign Policy." *International Security*, vol. 23, no. 2 (Winter 1997–98), pp. 74–100.

———. "NATO after 11 September." *Survival*, vol. 43, no. 4 (Winter 2001–02), pp. 89–106.

Grabbe, Heather. "How Does Europeanization Affect CEE Governance? Conditionality, Diffusion and Diversity." *Journal of European Public Policy*, vol. 8, no. 6 (2001), pp. 1013–31.

———. "The Sharp Edges of Europe: Extending Schengen Eastwards." *International Affairs*, vol. 76, no. 3 (July 2000), pp. 519–36.

Grant, Charles, and others. "Europe after September 11." London: Center for European Reform, 2001.

———. "EU 2010: An Optimistic Vision of the Future." London: Center for European Reform, 2001.

Grieshofer, Ulrike. "Mediating International Conflicts: Can the European Union Do It Effectively?" Thesis, Stanford Law School, May 2001.

de Haan, Jakob. "Independence and Democratic Accountability of the ECB." Paper presented at ECSA, Madison, Wis., May 31–June 2, 2001.

de Haan, Jakob, and Sylvester C. W. Eijffinger. "The Democratic Accountability of the European Central Bank: A Comment on Two Fairy-Tales." *Journal of Common Market Studies*, vol. 38, no. 3 (September 2000), pp. 393–407.

Hardt, John. "Putin's Economic Strategy and U.S. Interests." Report for Congress RL31023. Congressional Research Service, June 19, 2001.

Henning, C. Randall. Statements before the Senate Committee on the Budget, "American Interests and Europe's Monetary Union," October 21, 1997; and before the House Subcommittee on Domestic and International Monetary Policy, April 18, 1998.

Hoffmann, Stanley. "Goodbye to a United Europe?" *New York Review of Books*, May 27, 1993, pp. 27ff.

Holtrup, Petra. "Transatlantic Climate Change." *Transatlantic Internationale Politik*, vol. 2, no. 3 (Fall 2001), pp. 15–20.

Hosli, Madeleine O. "Negotiating the European Economic and Monetary Union." Paper presented at ECSA, Madison, Wis., May 31–June 2, 2001.

Jacobs, Francis B. "Institutional Dynamics after Nice: Views from the European Parliament." Paper presented at ECSA, Madison, Wis., May 31–June 2, 2001.

Jacquet, Pierre. "EMU: A Worthwhile Gamble." *International Affairs*, vol. 74, no. 1 (January 1998), pp. 55–71.

Jensen, Donald N. "How Russia Is Ruled in 1998." Radio Free Europe/Radio Liberty (RFE/RL) special report, August 1998 (www.rferl.org/nca/special/ruwhorules/index.html).

Journal of Democracy, July 1992. Special issue on Schumpeter.

Kohl, Helmut. Major excerpts from speeches between 1982 and 1994 in Reinhard Bettzüge, ed. *Aussenpoltik der Bundesrepublik Deutschland. Dokumente von 1949 bis 1994*. Bonn: Verlag Wissenschaft und Politik for German Foreign Ministry, 1995. Government declarations thereafter as distributed by the German Information and Press Service.

Krupnick, Charles. "NATO, the European Union, and Changing Concepts of Security in Central and Eastern Europe." Paper presented at ECSA, Madison, Wis., May 31–June 2, 2001.

Kupchan, Charles A. "Reviving the West." *Foreign Affairs*, vol. 75, no. 3 (May/June 1996), pp. 92–104.

Lehmann, Wilhelm. "Institutional Dynamics after the Nice Summit." Paper presented at ECSA, Madison, Wis., May 31–June 2, 2001.

Light, Margot, Stephen White, and John Löwenhardt. "A Wider Europe: The View from Moscow and Kyiv." *International Affairs*, vol. 76, no. 1 (January 2000), pp. 77–88.

Lindner, Rainer. "Die Ukraine zwischen Transformation und Selbstblockade." Ebenhausen: Stiftung Wissenschaft und Politik, March 1998.

Lippert, Barbara, Gaby Umbach, and Wolfgang Wessels. "Europeanization of CDD Executives: EU Membership Negotiations as a Shaping Power." *Journal of European Public Policy*, vol. 8, no. 6, 2001, pp. 980–1012.

Ludlow, Peter. "Beyond Maastricht: Recasting the European Political and Economic System." Working Document 79. Brussels: Center for European Policy Studies, July 1993.

Marples, David. "Belarus: An Analysis of the Lukashenka Regime." *Harriman Review* (Spring 1997), pp. 24ff.

"Marshall Plan and Its Legacy." Special section. *Foreign Affairs*, vol. 76, no. 3 (May/June 1997), pp. 157–221.

Mathews, Jessica. "Power Shift." *Foreign Affairs*, vol. 76, no. 1 (January/February 1997), pp. 50–66.

Matser, Willem. "Towards a New Strategic Partnership." *NATO Review*, vol. 49 (Winter 2001/2002), pp. 19–21.

Mearsheimer, John J. "Back to the Future: Instability in Europe after the Cold War." *International Security*, vol. 15, no. 1 (Summer 1990), pp. 5–56.

———. "The False Promise of International Institutions." Working Paper 10. John M. Olin Institute for Strategic Studies, Harvard University, November 1994.

Merlingen, Michael, Cas Mudde, and Ulrich Sedelmeier. "The Right and the Righteous? European Norms, Domestic Politics and the Sanctions against Austria." *Journal of Common Market Studies*, vol. 39, no. 1 (March 2001), pp. 59–77.

Meyer, Dirk. "The Provisions of the Charitable Welfare System and the Challenge of the Free Market." *German Studies Review*, vol. 20, no. 3 (October 1997), pp. 371–98.

Miller, Steven E. "The End of Unilateralism or Unilateralism Redux?" *Washington Quarterly*, vol. 25, no. 1 (Winter 2002), pp. 15–29.

Müller-Brandeck-Bocquet, Gisela. "Frankreichs Europapolitik unter Chirac und Jospin." *Integration*, vol. 24, no. 3 (July 2001), pp. 258–73.

Neville-Jones, Pauline. "Dayton, IFOR and the Future of Bosnia." Paper presented at the annual conference of the International Institute for Strategic Studies, Dresden, September 1–4, 1996.

Nye, Joseph. "The US and Europe: Continental Drift?" *International Affairs*, vol. 76, no. 1 (January 2000), pp. 51–59.

Olszanski, Tadeus Andrzej. "Ukraine and Russia: Mutual Relations and the Conditions That Determine Them." Warsaw: Center for Eastern Studies, November 2001.

Orenstein, Mitchell. "Vaclav Klaus: Revolutionary and Parliamentarian." *East European Constitutional Review* (Winter 1998), pp. 46–55.

Padoa-Schioppa, Tommaso. "The Euro and Politics." *Transatlantic Internationale Politik*, vol. 1, no. 4 (Winter 2000), pp. 11–16.

Pernice, Ingolf. "The Nice Summit and a European Constitution." *Transatlantic Internationale Politik*, vol. 1, no. 4 (Winter 2000), pp. 17–24.

Peterson, John. "The US and EU in the Balkans." Paper presented at ECSA, Madison, Wis., May 31–June 2, 2001.

Philippart, Eric. "U.S.-EU Relations and Transatlantic Governance." Paper presented at ECSA, Madison, Wis., May 31–June 2, 2001.

Pitschas, Rainer. "Interkulturelles Sicherheitsmanagement—Polizeikooperation im Raum der Freiheit, der Sicherheit und des Rechts." *Integration*, vol. 24, no. 3 (July 2001), pp. 289–302.

Pollack, Mark A., and Gregory C. Shaffer. "The Challenge of Reconciling Regulatory Differences." Paper presented at ECSA, Madison, Wis., May 31–June 2, 2001.

Putnam, Robert D. "Bowling Alone." *Journal of Democracy* (January 1995), pp. 65–78.

Ruggiero, Cristina M. "The European Court of Justice and the German Constitutional Court: Is There More Than One Legal 'Master' of European Integration? The Case of the EU Banana Regulations." Paper presented at ECSA, Madison, Wis., May 31–June 2, 2001.

Schönfelder, Wilhelm, and Elke Thiel. "Stabilitätspakt und Euro-X-Gremium—Die stabilitätspolitische Untermauerung der WWU." *Integration*, vol. 21, no. 2 (April 1998), pp. 69–76.

Schwartz, Herman. "Eastern Europe's Constitutional Courts." *Journal of Democracy*, vol. 9, no. 4 (October 1998), pp. 100–14.

Sedelmeier, Ulrich. "Sectoral Dynamics of the EU's Accession Requirements." Paper presented at ECSA, Madison, Wis., May 31–June 2, 2001.

Sherr, James. "Russia, Geopolitics and Crime." Conflict Studies Research Center (CSRC), Royal Military Academy Sandhurst, February 1995 (gopher://marvin.nc3a.nato.int/00/secdef/csrc/csrc2.1%09%09%2B).

———. "Russian Great Power Ideology: Sources and Implications." CSRC, Royal Military Academy Sandhurst, July 1996 (gopher://marvin.nc3a.nato.int/00/secdef/csrc/f54.txt%09%09%2B).

———. "Russia and Ukraine: Towards Compromise or Convergence?" CSRC, Royal Military Academy Sandhurst, August 1997 (gopher:// marvin.nc3a.nato.int/00/secdef/csrc/f60all.txt%09%09%2B).

Thiel, Elke. "German Politics with Respect to the European Economic and Monetary Union." Paper presented at the American Institute for Contemporary German Studies, Washington, May 18, 1995.

———. "Wirtschaften unter Euro-Bedingungen." Berlin: Stiftung Wissenschaft und Politik, October 2001.

Tolz, Vera. "What Is Russia? Post-Communist Debates on Nation-Building." Paper presented at the annual conference of the British Association for the Advancement of Slavic Studies, Cambridge, April 5, 1998.

Umbach, Frank. "The Role and Influence of the Military Establishment in Russia's Foreign and Security Policies in the Yeltsin Era." *Journal of Slavic Military Studies*, vol. 9, no. 3 (September 1996), pp. 467–500.

U.S. Senate Budget Committee. Hearing on "Europe's Monetary Union and Its Potential Impact on the United States Economy." October 21, 1997. Including statement by Deputy Secretary of the Treasury Lawrence H. Summers.

Thygesen, Niels. "Why Economic and Monetary Union Is an Important Objective for Europe." *SAIS Review*, vol. 14, no. 1 (Winter–Spring 1994), pp. 17–34.

Vachudova, Milada Anna. "The Leverage of International Institutions on Democratizing States: Eastern Europe and the European Union." Working Paper RSC 2001/33. European University Institute.

Wagner, Helmut. "Perspectives on European Monetary Union." Research Report 7. Washington: American Institute for Contemporary German Studies, 1998.

Wallace, William. "From the Atlantic to the Bug, from the Arctic to the Tigris? The Transformation of the EU and NATO." *International Affairs*, vol. 76, no. 3 (July 2000), pp. 475–93.

Walt, Stephen M. "International Relations: One World, Many Theories." *Foreign Policy*, vol. 110 (Spring 1998), pp. 29–46.

Waltz, Kenneth N. "The Emerging Structure of International Politics." *International Security*, vol. 18, no. 2 (Fall 1993), pp. 44–79.

Winiecki, Jan. "The Polish Generic Private Sector in Transition: Developments and Characteristics." *Europe-Asia Studies*, vol. 54, no. 1 (January 2002), pp. 5–29.

Wintz, Mark. "Lessons for the CFSP: Explaining Multinational Security Policy Change in the Former Yugoslavia." Paper presented at ECSA, Madison, Wis., May 31–June 2, 2001.

Zubek, Radoslaw. "A Core in Check: The Transformation of the Polish Core Executive." *Journal of European Public Policy*, vol. 8, no. 6 (2001), pp. 911–32.

Interviewees *(Partial List)*

d'Aboville, Benoit
French ambassador to Poland
Adam, Rudolf
European correspondent; later deputy director, Bundesnachrichtendienst intelligence agency
Aden, Hans
First secretary, Swedish Embassy, Kyiv
Appatov, Semyon
Chair, Department of International Relations, Odessa University
Apostolov, Nikolay
Bulgarian ambassador to Germany
Arnot, Alexander
German ambassador to Ukraine
Asher, Jim
Agricultural consultant, Kyiv
Åslund, Anders
Senior associate, Carnegie Endowment for International Peace
Bagger, Hartmut
Lt. Gen., general inspector of the German armed forces (equivalent of the U.S. chairman of the Joint Chiefs of Staff)
Bahr, Jerzy
Polish ambassador to Ukraine
Balcerowicz, Leszek
Polish finance minister and vice prime minister, member of parliament
Bandler, Donald
U.S. diplomat in Paris and Bonn; later senior director for European Affairs, U.S. National Security Council

Barnett, R. A.
British deputy head of mission to Poland
Bartoszewski, Wladyslaw
Polish foreign minister
Bergsdorf, Wolfgang
Minister-director, German Interior Ministry
Bertram, Christoph
Director, German Institute for International and Security Affairs
Biedenkopf, Kurt
Minister-president of Saxony
Bielecki, Jan Krzysztof
Polish prime minister, member of parliament, and leader of the Liberal Democratic party in the early 1990s
Bindenagel, J. D.
Chargé, U.S. Embassy to Germany
Bingen, Dieter
Director, German Polish Institute, Darmstadt
Black, David
U.S. Agency for International Development, Kyiv
Blakely, Pollard
Agricultural attaché, British Embassy, Kyiv
Blankert, Jan Willem
European Union Delegation, Warsaw
Boden, Johan
General director, South Foods, Kakhovka (Ukraine)
Bogdan, Angela
First secretary and consul, Canadian Embassy, Warsaw
Bohlen, Avis
U.S. ambassador to Bulgaria
Boshkov, Alexander
Bulgarian deputy prime minister
Bressand, Albert
Director, Promethée, Paris
Broomfield, Nigel
British ambassador to Germany
Broukhovetsky, Viatcheslav
President, Kyiv Mohyla Academy
Brümmer, Claus
Coordinator for German Business Counsel, Kreditanstalt für Wiederaufbau, Kyiv
Brzezinski, Ian
Security adviser in parliamentary Council of Advisers, Ukraine; later adviser to U.S. Senator William V. Roth and to Senate Foreign Relations Committee

Brzezinski, Zbigniew
   Former U.S. national security adviser
Burns, Nicholas
   Senior director for Russia, Ukraine and Eurasia Affairs, U.S. National
   Security Council, 1990–95; State Department spokesperson 1995–97
Buteiko, Anton Denisovich
   Ukrainian first deputy foreign minister
Bylynskyj, Markian
   Director of Field Operations, Pylyp Orlyk Institute for Democracy, Kyiv
Byrt, Andrzej
   Polish ambassador to Germany; later Polish deputy foreign minister
Cameron, Fraser
   Adviser, Directorate General I.A, European Commission; later head of the
   political section, European Commission Delegation, Washington
Campbell, Robert
   Economics professor, University of Indiana and Kyiv Mohyla Academy
Charlton, Allan
   British deputy head of mission to Germany
Chornovil, Viacheslav
   Ukrainian member of parliament
Chrobog, Jürgen
   German ambassador to the United States; later state secretary, German
   Foreign Ministry
Cieslik, Miroslaw
   Chargé, Polish Embassy, Kyiv
Cimoszewicz, Wlodzimierz
   Polish prime minister
de Clercq, Willi
   Member of European Parliament
Constantinescu, Emil
   Romanian president
Cooper, Robert
   Counselor, British Embassy, Germany
Czaplinski, Kazimierz
   History professor, Wroclaw University; chairman of Club of Catholic In-
   tellectuals in the 1970s
Czyzewski, Adam B.
   Economist, World Bank Representation
Dabrowski, Marek
   Economist, World Bank
Davis, Jim
   Agricultural and opera consultant, Kyiv
Dijckmeester, Alexander
   EU ambassador to Poland

Dimitrov, Konstantin
  Bulgarian deputy foreign minister
Domanski, Henryk
  Sociologist, Polish Academy of Sciences
Dubovka, Nina
  Head of the regional teachers' trade union, Odessa
Dulnev, Lev
  Deputy general director, Windenergo Ltd., Kyiv
Earle, Hobart
  Conductor of the Odessa Philharmonic
Ebel, Robert E.
  Director, Energy and National Security, Center for Strategic and International Studies
Elbe, Frank
  Director, office of German foreign minister Hans-Dietrich Genscher; later German ambassador to Poland
Eppinger, Monica
  Diplomat, U.S. Embassy, Kyiv
Falenski, Hans-Joachim
  Head of staff, foreign policy section, Christian Democratic Union/Christian Social Union parliamentary group in the Bundestag
Fischer, Joschka
  Member of the Bundestag; later German foreign minister
Fishel, Gene
  Ukrainian Desk, Intelligence and Research, U.S. State Department
Flyaks, Alexander
  Vice president, Parus-Bearbrook supermarket, Dnipropetrovsk
Freeland, Halyna
  Director, External Relations, Ukrainian Legal Foundation
Frej, William
  Director, U.S. Agency for International Development, Warsaw
Freudenstein, Roland
  Director, Konrad Adenauer Foundation, Warsaw
Freytag, Dirk
  Chief of staff for Alexandre Lamfalussy, European Monetary Institute
Frick, Helmut
  Minister in the German Embassy, Warsaw
Fried, Daniel
  U.S. ambassador to Poland; later National Security Council
Frishberg, Alex
  Partner, Law Offices Frishberg & Partners, Kyiv
Fritsch, Conrad
  Project manager, Agricultural Land Share Project, RONCO Consulting Corporation, Kyiv

Garnett, Sherman
Senior associate, Carnegie Endowment for International Peace
Genscher, Hans-Dietrich
German foreign minister; member of the Bundestag; president, German Council on Foreign Relations
Geremek, Bronislaw
Polish foreign minister
Gibowski, Wolfgang
Deputy chief, Press and Information Section, German chancellery
Gomolka, Alfred
Member of European Parliament
Gruber, Josef
Director, Konrad Adenauer Foundation, Sofia
Guerot, Ulrike
Head of EU section, German Council on Foreign Relations
Gummich, Andreas
German Economic Advisory Group, Kyiv
Gurvits, Edward I.
Mayor of Odessa
Hajnicz, Artur
Polish Senate chancellery
Hardt, John
Senior specialist, post-Soviet economies, Congressional Research Service
Harrison, Alistair
Counselor, British Embassy to Poland
Hassner, Pierre
Professor, Fondation Nationale de Sciences Politiques, Paris
Hawrylyshyn, Bohdan
Chairman, International Centre for Advanced Studies, Kyiv
Henning, Randall
Associate, Institute for International Economics, Washington
Heyken, Eberhard
German ambassador to Ukraine
Holbrooke, Richard
U.S. ambassador to Germany, later troubleshooter in former Yugoslavia
Holzer, Jerzy
Institute of Political Studies, Warsaw
Hombach, Bodo
Special coordinator for the Southeast European Stability Pact
Horelick, Arnold
Fellow, RAND
Hoyer, Werner
Member of parliament and state minister in German Foreign Ministry

Hryshchenko, Kostyantyn
  Ukrainian deputy foreign minister
Hume, Ian
  World Bank representative, Warsaw
Hunter, Robert
  U.S. ambassador to NATO
Ischinger, Wolfgang
  State secretary, German Foreign Ministry; later German ambassador to the United States
Jankowski, Maciej
  President, Solidarity trade union, Mazowsze region
Jaresko, Natalie
  Head of Economics Section, U.S. Embassy, Kyiv; later executive vice president, Western NIS Enterprise Fund
Jaruzelski, Wojciech
  Last president of the Polish People's Republic
Jarzembo, Georg
  Member of European Parliament
Kaiser, Karl
  Director of studies, German Council on Foreign Relations
Kaminski, Antoni
  Professor, Warsaw Institute of International Relations
Kapeliushniy, L. V.
  Editor in chief, *Slovo*, Odessa
Kapitanova, Ginka
  Executive director, Foundation for Local Government Reform, Sofia
Karkoszka, Andrzej
  Polish deputy defense minister
Kaufmann, Daniel
  World Bank resident representative, Kyiv
Kavalski, Jan
  World Bank resident representative, Warsaw
Kharchenko, Ihor
  Head of Planning Staff, Ukrainian Foreign Ministry; later ambassador to the United Nations and ambassador to Romania
Khmara, Stepan
  Ukrainian member of parliament
Kimmett, Robert
  U.S. ambassador to Germany
Kinach, Jaroslav B.
  Resident representative, European Bank for Reconstruction and Development, Kyiv
Kiselyov, Stanislav
  Founder, Radio Glas, Odessa

Klaiber, Klaus Peter
Deputy secretary-general, NATO; later EU representative in Afghanistan
Klaer, Karl-Heinz
Secretary of state, plenipotentiary for Federal and European Affairs, state government, Rhineland-Palatinate
Knotter, Paul
World Bank resident representative, Warsaw
Kölsch, Eberhard
European correspondent; later deputy head of mission at German Embassy in Washington
Kohl, Helmut
German chancellor
Kolodko, Grzegorz
Polish finance minister and vice prime minister
Konoplyov, Sergey
Program officer, Eurasia Foundation, Kyiv; later director, Ukrainian National Security Project, Harvard
Kopets', Anatoliy
Deputy chief of city administration, Lviv
Koralewicz, Jadwiga
Rektor, Collegium Civitas, Warsaw
Kornblum, John
U.S. ambassador to Germany
Kosminski, Jerzy
Polish ambassador to the United States
Kostenko, Yuriy
Ukrainian ambassador to Germany
Kostenko, Yuriy
Ukrainian environment minister
Kostov, Ivan
Bulgarian prime minister
Kostrzewa, Wojciech
President, BRE bank, Warsaw
Krawchenko, Bohdan
Director, Institute of Public Administration and Local Government, Kyiv
Kryshtalowych, Helen
Squires and Dempsey, Kyiv
Krzeminski, Adam
Commentator, *Polityka*, Warsaw
Kuchma, Leonid
President of Poland
Kushnariov, Yevhen P.
Chief of staff to Ukrainian president Leonid Kuchma
Kwasniewski, Alexander
President of Poland

von Kyaw, Dietrich
German chancellor's permanent representative to COREPER
Lambsdorff, Otto Graf
Member of the Bundestag
Lamers, Karl
European spokesperson for the Christian Democratic Union/Christian Social Union parliamentary group in the Bundestag
Lamfalussy, Alexandre
Director, European Monetary Institute
Landau, Jean-Pierre
Former undersecretary for foreign affairs, French Ministry for the Economy
Lavrynovych, Oleksandr
Member of Ukrainian parliament
Leinen, Jo
Member of European Parliament
Lenain, Patrick
IMF senior resident representative, Kyiv
Lendvai, Paul
Intendant (managing director), Austrian Broadcasting
Lippert, Barbara
Deputy director, Institute for European Policy, Berlin
Luczywo, Helen
Editor in chief, *Gazeta Wyborcza*, Warsaw
Lyschynski, Roman
Counselor in Canadian Embassy, Kyiv; later head of the NATO office, Kyiv
Mallaby, Christopher
British ambassador to Germany
Marchuk, Yevhen
Ukrainian prime minister; then member of parliament
Matussek, Thomas
Counselor, German Embassy, Washington
Mertes, Michael
Director-general, Social and Political Analysis and Cultural Affairs in Helmut Kohl's chancellery
Metzger, Peter
German ambassador to Bulgaria
Meyer-Landrut, Andreas
Chief of the German president's office; later Daimler-Benz representative in Moscow
Miller, Bowman
Director, Office of Analysis for Europe and Canada, Bureau of Intelligence and Research, U.S. State Department
Miller, William
U.S. ambassador to Ukraine

Millotat, Christian
Brig. Gen., deputy chief of staff, Eurocorps
Minchev, Emil
Counselor, Bulgarian Embassy to Germany
Minchev, Ognyan
Executive director, Institute for Regional and International Studies, Sofia
Moïsi, Dominique
Deputy director, French Institute for International Relations
Möllers, Felicitas
German Economic Advisory Group, Kyiv
Moore, Lou
Agricultural adviser, U.S. Agency for International Development, Poznan
Moroz, Oleksandr
Member and former speaker of Supreme Rada, Kyiv
Müller, Wolfgang
Ukrainian section, German Ministry of the Economy
von Münchow-Pohl, Bernd
Head of Ukrainian section, German Foreign Ministry
Murphy, Richard
Senior associate, Center for Strategic and International Studies, Washington
Nanivskaya, Vera
World Bank Mission, Kyiv: 1996
Naumann, Klaus
Maj. Gen., general inspector of the German armed forces (equivalent of U.S. chairman of the Joint Chiefs of Staff); later chairman, NATO Military Committee
Nemtsov, Boris
Member of the Russian Duma
Nowina-Konopka, Piotr
Member of Democratic Union, Sejm; later rector, College of Europe, Warsaw
Nyberg, Jan
Counselor, Swedish Embassy to Poland
Nyberg, Rene
Deputy director general, Finnish Ministry of Foreign Affairs
Olechowski, Andrzej
Head of Citizen's Platform party, Warsaw
Onyszkiewicz, Janusz
Polish defense minister
Papadiuk, Roman
First U.S. ambassador to independent Ukraine
Parmentier, Guillaume
Adviser, French Defense Ministry; later director, French Center on the United States (CFE), French Institute for International Relations

Parrish, C. A. M.
Capt., defense attaché, British Embassy, Kyiv
Parvanov, Georgi
Chairman of the Supreme Council, Bulgarian Socialist Party
Pauls, Christian
Political director, German Foreign Ministry
Philipov, Vladimir
Foreign policy adviser to the Bulgarian president
Pieronek, Tadeusz
Bishop, spokesperson for the Polish Episcopate
Pifer, Steven
U.S. ambassador to Ukraine
Pikhovshek, Vyacheslav
Director, Ukrainian Center for Independent Political Research
Pleuger, Gunter
State secretary, German Foreign Ministry
von Ploetz, Hans-Friedrich
State secretary, German Foreign Ministry
Poettering, Hans-Gert
Member of European Parliament
Polt, Michael
U.S. deputy chief of mission to Germany
Ponomarenko, Anatoliy
Ukrainian ambassador to Germany
Poptodorova, Elena
Euroleft M.P., Bulgaria
Rau, Karin
Representative of German business in Kyiv
Redman, Charles
U.S. ambassador to Germany
Reilly, Tim
External affairs director, JKX Oil and Gas, Kyiv
Rejt, Jerzy
Chair, Union of Ukrainians in Poland
Regulski, Jerzy
Founder of the Warsaw Foundation for Local Democracy
Reiter, Janusz
Polish ambassador to Germany; later director, Center for International Relations, Warsaw
Rewald, Roman
Lawyer, Weil, Gotshal, and Manges, Warsaw
Rey, Nicholas
U.S. ambassador to Poland
Rodlauer, Markus K.
IMF resident representative, Warsaw

Ruban, Volodymyr
Editor, *Den'*; later, editor, *Vseukrainskie Vedemosti*, Kyiv
Rubin, Eric
Chief of the political section, U.S. Embassy, Kyiv; later assistant press
secretary for Foreign Affairs, U.S. National Security Council
Rühe, Volker
German defense minister and Bundestag member
Rühl, Lothar
State secretary in German Defense Ministry; later columnist for *Die Welt*
Rychard, Andrzej
Professor of Sociology, Polish Academy of Sciences
Rzepka, Anna
Director, local self-government Sejmik, Kielce, Poland
Rzhimeshevsky, Konstantyn
Director of Foreign Economic Relations, Odessa
Saryusz-Wolski, Jacek
Polish undersecretary of state for European Integration and Foreign As-
sistance, Council of Ministers; later vice rector, College of Europe, Warsaw
Scharioth, Klaus
Political director-general, German Foreign Ministry
Schäuble, Wolfgang
Majority parliamentary leader in Bundestag until September 1998
Scharping, Rudolf
Bundestag deputy; later German defense minister
Schönfelder, Wilhelm
German chancellor's permanent representative to COREPER
Seiters, Rudolf
Deputy, Bundestag, Christian Democratic Union/Christian Social Union
leader
Shcherban, Vladimir P.
Member of Ukrainian parliament
Shcherbak, Yuriy
Ukrainian ambassador to the United States
Shea, Jamie
NATO spokesperson
Shpek, Roman
Ukrainian National Agency for Reconstruction and Development
Simons, Thomas
U.S. ambassador to Poland
Siwiec, Marek
State secretary in Polish president's office
Sliwinski, Krzysztof
Ambassador to the Jewish Diaspora (outside Israel), Polish Foreign
Ministry

Sloan, Stanley
NATO specialist, Congressional Research Service
Smeshko, Ihor
Maj. Gen., military attaché in Ukrainian Embassy to the United States; later director of Strategic Planning and Analysis in the President's Office, Kyiv
Solana, Javier
NATO secretary-general; later EU high representative for foreign policy
Stark, Jürgen
State secretary, German Finance Ministry; later vice president, Bundesbank
Staudacher, Wilhelm
Chief of staff to German president Roman Herzog
Stechel, Walter
Head of Ukrainian economy section, then Russian economy section, German Foreign Ministry
Steiner, Michael
National security adviser to Chancellor Gerhard Schröder, 1998–2001
Stoecker, Volkmar
Minister, German Embassy in Warsaw; then head of the U.S. section, German Foreign Ministry
Stolzman, Maria
Member of Polish parliament and director of the Water Supply Foundation
Stomma, Swiatoslaw
Warsaw
von Studnitz, Ernst-Jörg
Deputy head of West German representation office in East Germany; later German ambassador to Russia
Sturen, Carl
General director, South Foods, Kakhovka (Ukraine)
Stützle, Walther
Undersecretary, German Defense Ministry
Szlajfer, Henryk
Senior deputy director, Polish Institute of International Affairs
Szmajdzinski, Jerzy
Member of Parliament, Warsaw
Szczypiorski, Andrzej
Novelist
Tabachnyk, Dmytro
Chief of staff to Ukrainian president Leonid Kuchma; later member of Supreme Rada
Talbott, Strobe
Deputy secretary of state, U.S. Department of State
Tarasyuk, Borys
Ukrainian foreign minister

Teltschik, Horst
Foreign policy adviser to Chancellor Helmut Kohl; later member of BMW board

Teriokhin, Serhii
Member of Ukranian parliament

Tietmeyer, Hans
President, Bundesbank

Tindemanns, Leo
Member of European Parliament

Tomala, Mieczyslaw
Professor, Polish Institute of International Affairs

Towpik, Andrzej
Undersecretary of state, Polish Foreign Ministry

Tsok, Nadiya
Adviser to member of Ukrainian parliament Ivan Zayets

Vasileev, Ilian
Director, Bulgarian Agency for Foreign Investments

Veldkamp, Caspar
Dutch diplomat, Warsaw

Verheugen, Günter
Foreign policy coordinator of the German Social Democratic parliamentary caucus; later EU commissioner for enlargement

Vershbow, Alexander
Senior director for European Affairs, U.S. National Security Council; later U.S. ambassador to NATO and then ambassador to Russia

Vogel, Wolfdietrich
Minister, German Embassy to Poland

van Walsum, A. Peter
Dutch ambassador to Germany

Walter, Norbert
Chief economist, Deutsche Bank

Washchuk, Roman
Counselor, Canadian Embassy, Kyiv

Wasylyk, Myron
Adviser to the chairman, State Property Fund of Ukraine

Weise, Hans Heinrich
Planning Staff, German Defense Ministry

Weisser, Ulrich
Chief, Planning Staff, German Defense Ministry

Welteke, Ernst
President, Hessen Central Bank; later president, Bundesbank

Whitehead, Cynthia
Environmental consultant, Brussels

Winiecki, Jan
President, Adam Smith Research Center, Warsaw

Wolff-Paweska, Anna
Director, Western Institute, Poznan
Wolthers, Pieter Jan
Counselor, Dutch Embassy, Warsaw
Wroblewski, Andrzej Krzysztof
Deputy editor, *Polityka*, Warsaw
Wziezinski, Wojciech
Rector, University of Wroclaw
Yavlinsky, Grigory
Member of the Duma
Zayets, Ivan
Member of Ukrainian parliament
Zhelyazkov, Zachary
Executive director, Bulgarian Privatization Agency
Zhelyazkova, Antonina
Chair, International Center for Minority Studies and Intercultural Relations, Sofia
Zoellick, Robert
Undersecretary of state, U.S. Department of State; later U.S. trade representative

Index

Adenauer, Konrad, 24, 25–27
Afghanistan war. *See* September *11* terrorism
Agricultural policy: Delors Package, 30–31; ECC provisions, 24; EU policies, 47, 49, 50, 86, 182–83
Albright, Madeleine, 63
Amsterdam Treaty, 100, 181
Andreatta, Beniamino, 103, 104
Anti-Ballistic Missile Treaty, 7, 196, 224–25
Arnold, Agnieszka, 124
Arthuis, Jean, 99
Åslund, Anders, 153, 154
Austria: EC/EU membership, 2, 85; EFTA membership, 25; and federalization proposal, 189; Freedom Party issue, 184–85; Partnership for Peace exercises, 75
Automobile industry, 168

Baker, James, 57
Balcerowicz, Leszek, 106–07, 116
Balkan conflicts: Baltic country participation, 71; Clinton and Bush policies compared, 7; Kosovo's lessons, 198–211; Maastricht conference negotia-
tions, 40; as NATO justification, 53–54; NATO role in Bosnia, 55–60, 73; trends away from, 133
Baltbat and Baltnet forces, 71
Banca d'Italia, 103
Banque de France, 42, 80
Bartoszewski, Wladyslaw, 10, 121
Beedham, Brian, 95
Belarus, 139, 152
Belgium: economic performance, 102, 163; Eurocorps participation, 34; Schengen Agreement, 29; Treaty of Rome, 23, 24
Berlin: airlift, 21–22; and French-German relationship, 25–26
Berlusconi, Silvio, 212, 214
Bertram, Christoph, 206, 214–15
Biedenkopf, Kurt, 31, 91
Biological Weapons Control Treaty, 7, 196–97, 225
Bitterlich, Joachim, 87
Blair, Tony: EU policies, 99–100, 183; federalized Europe proposals, 187; on Kosovo war, 200; and Sept. *11* terrorism, 193, 211–12, 215
Bolkestein, Frits, 169